PREDICTION AND PREVENTION OF READING FAILURE

PREDICTION AND PREVENTION OF READING FAILURE

Edited by Nathlie A. Badian

York Press, Inc.
Baltimore, Maryland

This book was manufactured in the United States of America.

Typography by Type Shoppe II Productions Ltd.

Printing and binding by Data Reproductions Corporation

Cover design by Joseph Dieter, Jr.

Library of Congress Cataloging-in Publication Data

Prediction and prevention of reading failure / edited by Nathlie A. Badian.
        p. cm.
   Includes bibliographical references and index.
   ISBN 0-912752-57-2
      1. Reading (Early childhood)--Ability testing. I. Badian, Nathlie A.

LB1139.R4 P74 2000
372.43--dc21   00-043525

Contents

Foreword   vii

Introduction   ix

1. Screening for Early Reading Failure   1
   Valerie Muter

2. Do Preschool Orthographic Skills Contribute to Prediction of Reading?   31
   Nathlie A. Badian

3. Systemic Screening and Intervention of Reading Difficulty   57
   Angela J. Fawcett and Roderick I. Nicolson

4. Application of Frith's Developmental Phase Model to the Process of Identifying At-Risk Beginning Readers   87
   Diane J. Sawyer, Jwa K. Kim, and Sally Lipa-Wade

5. Prevention and Prediction of Reading Problems   105
   Bente E. Hagtvet

6. From Identification to Intervention: Improving Kindergarten Screening for Risk of Reading Failure   133
   Jane M. Flynn

7. Preschool Phonological Awareness and Success in Reading   153
   Carol A. Christensen

8. Questioning the Role of Syllables and Rimes in Early Phonological Awareness   179
   Myra Gipstein, Susan A. Brady, and Anne Fowler

9. A Case for Early Onset-Rime Sensitivity Training in At-Risk Preschool and Kindergarten Children   217
   Judith A. Bowey

10. What Do You Get if You Add /mmm/ to Ice? Training Phoneme Awareness in Kindergarten: An Intervention Study with Children of Dyslexic Parents   247
    Dorthe Klint Petersen

11. Phonemes and Rhyme in the Development of Reading and Metaphonology: The Dundee Longitudinal Study   275
    Lynne G. Duncan and Philip H. K. Seymour

Index   299

Foreword

In November 1997, The Orton Dyslexia Society (now The International Dyslexia Association) convened a symposium in San Francisco on the early recognition of possible reading failure. The reports presented there were published in a book entitled *Preschool Prevention of Reading Failure*, which we edited and which was published by York Press.

Since that time there has been a wealth of research concerned with the early identification of children likely to have difficulty in learning to read.

As a follow-up to the previous volume, Nathlie Badian, long recognized for her work in this field, has assembled eleven chapters for a book written by outstanding investigators in the United States, England, Scotland, Scandinavia, and Australia. Each chapter includes an extensive list of references. Taken together they provide a rich resource for future investigators.

Many of the reports detail programs for the discovery of possible precursors of reading disability before regular reading instruction has begun. Even though there may be differences in the neurological, intellectual, and language make-up of children with such problems, most can be taught to read by appropriate methods. Proper testing can not only identify problems, but can serve as a guide for innovative teaching.

Early intervention can do much to reduce the impact of the specific language disability named "dyslexia."

Mary W. Masland
Richard L. Masland, M.D.

Introduction

NATHLIE A. BADIAN

It is generally acknowledged that phonological awareness, and awareness of phonemes, in particular, is a crucial factor in reading success and, not unexpectedly, several chapters of this book focus on the development of phonological awareness or sensitivity in young children and its predictive effect on later reading and spelling. The general consensus among the authors contributing to the volume is that awareness of rhyme develops very early, followed by awareness of syllables, word onset and rime, and, eventually, phonemes. The authors also tend to agree that awareness of phonemes develops largely as a result of reading instruction.

Because of the developmental progression of phonological awareness, the age at which a specific phonological measure is administered will tend to determine its power to predict later reading. For example, rhyme may be a sensitive predictor of reading in very young children, but by the time a child has entered kindergarten at age 5, it is unlikely to be predictive. Conversely, phonemic awareness at 4 years of age may not be an effective predictor of reading, although at age 5 or 6 years, it may predict very well. Thus, the age or stage of development at which it is appropriate to administer a specific phonological measure as a predictor of reading is a matter of crucial importance.

Although phonological awareness or sensitivity is the main focus of many of the chapters in this volume and one or more tests of phonological awareness are included in predictive batteries described by several more authors, other predictive measures discussed include letter knowledge, verbal memory, tests of general language, such as syntax and semantics, orthographic processing, and fine motor skills. The accuracy of teacher judgement of early risk status is also discussed. In some chapters well-designed intervention studies are described and the intervention studies of other researchers are reviewed.

Several authors confirm that preschool and kindergarten letter knowledge is one of the best predictors of reading. In some studies children named the letters; in others they gave the sounds associated with the letter forms. As with phonological awareness, stage of development may be a factor in the predictive power of letter knowledge. For preschool or beginning kindergarten children, naming letters is generally an effective predictor of reading. By late kindergarten, letter sounds may be more effective. The interaction between phonological awareness and letter knowledge in reading acquisition is stressed by some authors.

Variables which may affect the success of phonological training programs also tend to include age and type of phonological task. For example, studies in this volume demonstrate that phonemic awareness training for preschool children generally has disappointing results. Such training is more likely to have a beneficial effect on reading if provided to kindergarten children, and especially if it includes letter-sound recognition. Preschool training in rhyming reported in this volume also had no effects on later reading. As recommended by at least one author, training based on word onset and rime may be more effective for preschoolers. The type of phonological training that will be most helpful for preschool children is an area requiring further research, however.

The chapters in this book were written by well-known researchers from around the world who present the reader with a stimulating cross-cultural perspective on the prediction and prevention of reading failure. Countries represented are Australia, Denmark, England, Norway, Scotland, and the United States. In writing the chapters, the authors follow a variety of formats. The main focus of some chapters is the author's own research, while other authors present more general overviews of research on the topic. A brief summary of each chapter follows.

Drawing on her own research and that of her colleagues in England, Valerie Muter stresses, in Chapter 1, that letter knowledge at school entry is the best single predictor of later word recognition and spelling. There is an additional significant contribution from the product of letter knowledge and phonological awareness. Preschool phonological measures at 4 years of age did not predict reading at 9 years. At 5 and 6 years of age, however, phoneme awareness predicted reading, though rhyming did not. Muter hypothesizes that phonological skills are less stable in young children and, therefore, less predictive of reading. She suggests that it may be more appropriate to delay screening for children at risk for reading failure until the end of the preschool period. Muter also describes an early diagnostic instrument for children aged 4 to 7 years which she and her colleagues have developed. Letter knowledge and phoneme deletion have proved to be the best predictive subtests of this battery.

In Chapter 2, I report on a cohort of children followed from before kindergarten entry to late grade 7. Preschool measures that accounted for the most variance in predicting reading and spelling through grade 7 were letter naming and sentence memory, but an orthographic task (visual matching of letters and letter sequences) also contributed significant independent variance. The same three measures also predicted, with a high degree of accuracy, which individual children would be persistent poor readers both in the original cohort and in a second validating cohort. A preschool phonological task (syllable segmentation) was a relatively weak predictor of reading and spelling, as was rapid automatized naming of pictured objects. Findings suggest that early orthographic processing, defined as establishing accurate visual representations of letters and words in memory, contributes to prediction of reading and should not be neglected in predictive research.

In Chapter 3, Angela Fawcett and Roderick Nicolson describe their Dyslexia Early Screening Test (DEST) developed in England and report on studies adopting the support techniques related to the screening test. The DEST is designed for children aged 4.5 to 6.5 years and is based on the authors' own research with dyslexic children. The authors stress that the two key requirements of any screening tests are the percentage of at-risk children who are identified by the test as valid positives and the percentage of not at-risk children who are misclassified as at risk (false positives). The DEST includes phonological measures (discrimination, rhyming, alliteration), digit and letter naming, and tests of verbal memory, fine motor skills, cerebellar function, and temporal order. It is normed on approximately 1000 children. In a longitudinal cohort tested at age 5, the subtest most highly correlated with reading at 8 years of age was digit naming. Depending on the cutoff score, DEST identified 75% to 90% of later poor readers, with a false positive rate of 7% to 12%. A computer-based reading intervention program (RITA) is described and compared with traditional small-group reading support and with a control condition. Both interventions were effective, compared with controls, but RITA had greater impact on spelling than on reading.

In Chapter 4, Diane Sawyer, Jwa Kim, and Sally Lipa-Wade discuss their research in which a battery of tests based on Frith's Developmental Phase Model was administered to children in late kindergarten. Measures included letter names and sounds and several phonological tasks. Phoneme segmentation was not included, on the grounds that it is a later developing skill supported by first grade reading instruction. The single best predictor of achievement through grade 2 and of grade 3 spelling was letter sounds. The authors hypothesize that letter naming may be less predictive of reading by late kindergarten, than when assessed earlier. Rhyming tasks were not useful predictors. Poor performance on the screening battery effectively identified children whose later word reading and spelling were poor.

Bente Hagtvet describes a Norwegian longitudinal study in Chapter 5 in which children were followed from age 4 to 9 years of age. They were assessed annually with oral language measures, including phonemic awareness at age 6 years. Hagtvet points out the neglect of relevant syntactical and semantic measures in the prediction of reading. Oral language comprehension and expression at age 4 predicted reading (sentence reading, text comprehension) at age 9 at approximately the same level as phonemic awareness at age 6. An interesting finding was that there was a combined effect of pre-reading emotional symptoms and language on later reading ability. Seriously impaired readers exhibited both oral language weakness and an increased tendency to engage in off-task behavior before they started school. The author suggests that prevention of reading problems should focus not only on language stimulation, but also on supporting the emotional system of the child.

In Chapter 6, Jane Flynn discusses the kindergarten screening test she has developed (Literacy Screening Battery: LSB) and her Teacher Rating Scale (TRS). The LSB is a group-administered test and consists of seven subtests that cover phonological awareness, logographic/orthographic processing, semantics and syntax. A major aim of Flynn's research is to help kindergarten teachers improve their ability to predict which children are at risk for reading failure. The TRS failed to predict 36% of children who were poor readers later, compared with 20% missed by the LSB. Together, the two instruments missed only 12% of poor readers. Findings suggest that kindergarten teachers would benefit from training in differential diagnosis. Flynn also recommends multiple screenings (beginning of kindergarten, end of kindergarten, and beginning of grade 1) to increase the accuracy of identifying children at risk. However, adequate assessment of risk depends also on assessment of the quality of the subsequent reading instruction a child receives.

Carol Christensen of Australia reviews her own research and that of others in Chapter 7. Some of her conclusions are that preschool rhyme and alliteration are relatively poor predictors of reading and so also is the ability to segment words into onset and rime. However, awareness of word onset may be the key to development of phonemic awareness, which is more likely to emerge after a child has begun to learn to read. Christensen also found a significant effect of letter knowledge on reading and a significant interaction effect of letter knowledge and phonological awareness for all reading measures. Children will have an advantage in learning to read and spell if, as preschoolers, they learn to identify letters and to detect their sounds in words. Activities for enhancing preschool phonological awareness skills are provided in this chapter. Christensen also reports studies in which prereaders trained in phonological awareness are compared with untrained children. Training only in rhyming skills was not associated with better reading, but children trained in phonemic awareness performed better than untrained children in later reading.

In Chapter 8, Myra Gipstein, Susan Brady, and Anne Fowler report on a study of the sensitivity of preschoolers aged 4 and 5 years to three kinds of phonological stimuli: rhyme, syllable, and rime. Performance of the children on the rhyme condition was significantly better than on the syllable condition, which significantly surpassed rime. All children were tested in ability to read real and nonsense words. Children classified as readers were significantly higher on the phonological measures than nonreaders. The authors state that rhyme awareness may be a sensitive predictor in younger or at-risk groups of children. Ability to detect word onsets emerges later than sensitivity to rhymes or syllables. They suggest that syllable and phoneme segmentation are good predictors for kindergarten children because awareness of them is still developing at that time. The chapter also includes activities to help young children pay attention to the sound structure of words.

In Chapter 9, Judith Bowey of Australia summarizes the outcome of programs in which preschoolers have been trained in phonemic awareness and draws the conclusion that such training has generally had disappointing results for children at risk for reading difficulties, especially when the training has been implemented by regular teachers. Results have been more successful when such training has been provided to somewhat older kindergarten children and has included letter-sound recognition. Bowey makes a case for phonological sensitivity training to preschoolers at risk for later reading difficulties, with the training focusing on mastery at the onset-rime level and including letter instruction. Such programs are likely to succeed in orienting children to focus attention on the sound structure of language. Training should progress to phoneme sensitivity tasks only when the onset-rime tasks are thoroughly mastered. It should not be assumed that onset-rime sensitivity training will generalize to phonemes without explicit phoneme sensitivity training.

The Copenhagen Dyslexia Study is described by Dorthe Petersen of Denmark in Chapter 10. In this study, children of dyslexic and normal readers have been followed from before kindergarten entry until the beginning of grade 3. Annual tests included linguistic and phonological measures. The children of dyslexic and normal readers were each divided into two groups. One group from each set of children received phoneme awareness training for 17 weeks in kindergarten. For most of the children of dyslexic parents, the phonemic awareness training was a success. The small number of children who did not benefit from training differed from those who made gains only in pre-training pronunciation accuracy. Training effects were still apparent in grades 2 and 3. At the beginning of grade 2, significantly more of the untrained than trained children of dyslexic parents were possibly dyslexic. This study is important in demonstrating that phoneme awareness training of kindergarten children at high risk for dyslexia is likely to have long-term beneficial effects upon reading.

In Chapter 11, Lynne Duncan and Philip Seymour of Scotland discuss the Dundee Longitudinal Study. The children of this study were tested at 4 years of age and followed for 2 years. As part of the study, preschool letter-sound knowledge and phonological awareness (rhyme and alliteration) were compared as predictors of reading. After controlling for memory and vocabulary differences, letter-sound knowledge was the strongest predictor of reading. Preschool rhyme production was not a good predictor of reading progress. In fact, it had a higher correlation with later arithmetic, than with reading. In another part of the study, preschool children were provided with training in rhyming skills two or three times weekly for several months. Findings were that this training did not produce any beneficial effects on later reading development. The authors stress that attempts to identify children with poor phonological skills at the preschool level are problematic. The earliest point at which reading difficulty can be detected is during the first school year. Reading problems are manifested by a slowness in acquiring knowledge of the full set of letter-sounds and in developing explicit awareness of phonemes.

Contributors

Nathlie A. Badian, Ed.D.
Harvard Medical School
Boston, Massachusetts 02115
and
Holbrook Public Schools
Holbrook, Massachusetts
02343

Judith A. Bowey, Ph.D.
School of Psychology
University of Queensland
Brisbane, Queensland 4072
Australia

Susan A. Brady, Ph.D.
Psychology Department
University of Rhode Island
Kingston, Rhode Island
02881
and
Haskins Laboratories
270 Crown Street
New Haven, Connecticut
06510

Carol A. Christensen, Ph.D.
Graduate School of Education
University of Queensland
Queensland 1072
Australia

Lynne G. Duncan, Ph.D.
Department of Psychology
University of Dundee
Dundee DD1 4HN, Scotland
United Kingdom

Angela J. Fawcett, Ph.D.
Department of Psychology
University of Sheffield
Western Bank
Sheffield S10 2TP
United Kingdom

Jane M. Flynn, Ph.D.
LaCrosse Area Dyslexia
  Research Institute, Inc.
LaCrosse, Wisconsin 54602
and
Saint Mary's University of
  Minnesota
Winona, Minnesota

Anne Fowler, Ph.D.
Haskins Laboratories
270 Crown Street
New Haven, Connecticut
06510

Myra Gipstein, Ph.D.
Psychology Department
University of Rhode Island
Kingston, Rhode Island
02883

Bente E. Hagtvet, Ph.D.
Institute of Special Needs
  Education
University of Oslo, Boks 1104
Blindern
0347 Oslo
Norway

Jwa K. Kim, Ph.D.
Department of Psychology
Middle Tennessee State
 University
Murfreesboro, Tennessee
 37132

Sally Lipa-Wade, Ph.D.
State University of New York
Geneseo, New York
(Retired)

Valerie Muter, Ph.D.
Department of Psychology
University of York
York YO10 5DD
United Kingdom

Roderick I. Nicolson, Professor
Department of Psychology
University of Sheffield
Western Bank
Sheffield S10 2TP
United Kingdom

Dorthe Klint Petersen, Ph.D.
Center for Reading Research
Department of General and
 Applied Linguistics
University of Copenhagen
Njalsgade 86
DK-2300 Copenhagen S
Denmark

Diane J. Sawyer, Ph.D.
Department of
 Dyslexic Studies
Middle Tennessee State
 University
Murfreesboro, Tennessee
 37132

Philip H. K. Seymour, Professor
Department of Psychology
University of Dundee
Dundee DD1 4HN, Scotland
United Kingdom

Chapter • 1

Screening for Early Reading Failure

Valerie Muter

Recognizing reading failure at the earliest stages of schooling has become a serious focus of researchers, educators, and even politicians in the last ten years. It follows that the impetus to develop screening and associated early intervention instruments has constituted a significant step forward in the systematic early identification and management of children at risk of reading problems. Children's early success in learning to read appears to color their attitude toward reading later in life. Indeed, Cunningham and Stanovich (1997) claim that "rapid acquisition of reading abilities might well help the development of the lifetime habit of reading" (p. 934). In support of their argument, they report the findings of a study in which childrens' first grade reading skills were related to their reading comprehension and exposure to print as many as 10 years later; children who made a good start in reading in grade 1 read more and understood what they were reading far better in Grade 11 than those who were slow to start. Making a successful early start in reading clearly has a long-term sustaining effect, an observation that carries huge implications for the cultural, economic, and educational future of any society.

It is not difficult to enumerate the advantages to be reaped from early identification of reading failure. Children whose at-risk status has been recognized at ages 5 or 6 will have far less educational ground to make up than those children identified later in their schooling. Furthermore, from the evaluating psychologist's perspective, assessing a child of 5, 6, or 7 results in a test profile that is "purer" and, therefore, easier to interpret than one obtained from an older child whose pattern of scoring may have become distorted through experiential factors, for example, different teaching methods or compensatory strategies the child has developed. Most teachers acknowledge the greater ease of working with younger children who have not yet experienced excessive frustration and feelings of failure that can adversely affect their motivation and response to instruction. Also, teachers often find it easier to work with youngsters who have not established too many bad habits that must be unlearned before they can be replaced by new and more effective strategies. Additionally, there may be negative behavioral consequences of untreated persisting reading problems. Many failed readers who have effectively "given up" are significantly at risk of becoming increasingly disruptive or even disturbed. Indeed, recent research has demonstrated a substantial link between early reading failure and later social adjustment problems and delinquent behavior (see Maughan 1994 and 1995). Finally, and most powerful politically, is the economic advantage of early identification. Implementing a two to three times weekly teaching program over a one-year period for a 6-year old is clearly far cheaper than having to provide long-term daily help (or even special schooling) to a late-diagnosed 10-year old whose behavior is becoming increasingly anti-social.

COGNITIVE PREDICTORS OF EARLY READING SKILL IN THE NORMAL POPULATION—PHONOLOGICAL AWARENESS AND LETTER KNOWLEDGE

What we understand about identifying children at risk of reading failure largely stems from research that takes what might be termed a "predictor approach," both in normal and at-risk populations. Predictors are skills or abilities that have been demonstrated to contribute to reading development, and which are in themselves definable, measurable, and potentially modifiable through teaching. These established predictors then form the basis either for screening of preschool or grade 1 children, or more conservatively, for initial diagnostic assessments of young children whose histories suggest that they may be at risk (for example, other family members with literacy problems, early developmental delay or unevenness).

Within the normal population, the most extensively studied predictor of early reading skill over the last twenty years has been phonological awareness. Research into individual differences in children's sensitivity to speech sounds within words has resulted in the conclusion that these are strongly causally related to the normal acquisition of beginning reading skill. Phonological abilities can be measured in a variety of ways. Adams (1990) divides phonological tasks that successfully predict reading skill into four main types. First are syllable and phoneme segmentation tasks in which the child taps, counts out, or identifies syllables and/or phonemes within words, e.g., for the word "cat," the child taps three times to indicate the three phonemes within the word (Liberman et al. 1974). Second are phoneme manipulation tasks that require the child to delete, add, substitute, or transpose phonemes within words, e.g., in a consonant deletion task, "cat" without the "c" says "at" (Bruce 1964). Third come sound blending tasks in which the examiner provides the phonemes of a word and the child is asked to put them together, e.g., "c-a-t" blends to yield "cat" (Perfetti et al. 1987). Finally, there are rhyming tasks that include knowledge of nursery rhymes (MacLean, Bryant, and Bradley 1987), and identification of the "odd word out" (non-rhyming word) in a sequence of three or four words, as in the sound categorization task of Bradley and Bryant (1983) (e.g., the odd word out in the series "cat, pat, fan" is "fan"). Some phonological awareness tasks are clearly easier than others and may be demonstrated in children as young as 2 and 3 years (e.g., syllable blending, syllable segmentation, and some aspects of rhyming skill). Other skills do not emerge until later in development, and may depend on exposure to print and even explicit reading instruction (e.g., phoneme segmentation and manipulation tasks). This would seem to suggest that there is a two-way interactive process between phonological skills and learning to read. Indeed, there is clear evidence that reading plays a reciprocal role in promoting more advanced phonological awareness (Cataldo and Ellis 1988; Perfetti et al. 1987).

Although some phonological skills are available at a rudimentary level to children as young as 2 and 3 years of age, they are not necessarily stable abilities at that age. However, as demonstrated in a study of children from 2 to 5 years (Lonigan et al. 1998), phonological sensitivity becomes increasingly stable during the preschool years. In addition, a number of long-term longitudinal studies have shown that phonological processing abilities are remarkably stable during the primary school years (Wagner, Torgesen, and Rashotte 1994; Wagner et al. 1997; Muter and Snowling 1998). In other words, level of phonemic skill at an early age is significantly predictive of later phonemic ability. As Wagner and his associates conclude, phonological processing abilities should be viewed as stable and coherent individual difference variables akin to other cognitive abilities, as opposed to more transitory indices of reading-related knowledge that might vary from year to year. This observed stability is essential for any variable that might be included in an early screening battery to identify children who later have significant and, if untreated, persisting reading problems.

It is well accepted that phonological skills are causally related to the development of reading, but the nature of these skills and their precise bearing on reading requires elucidation, and, indeed, is an area of some controversy. How many sorts of phonological skills are there, and if there are different sorts, which ones play the most important role in the beginning stages of learning to read? Do different phonological skills influence reading at different stages of development? In general, early correlational/factor analytic studies of phonological awareness suggested that a single factor accounts for individual variance in phonological ability (Wagner and Torgesen 1987; Stanovich, Cunningham, and Cramer 1984). More recent studies have indicated that it may be possible to derive multiple, admittedly intercorrelated, factors within the phonological domain. Yopp (1988) uncovered two factors from a principal components analysis of ten phonological awareness tests given to 96 kindergarten children. The factors were highly correlated and appeared to reflect two levels of difficulty rather than two qualitatively different kinds of skill— simple phonemic awareness required only one cognitive operation (e.g., blending) while complex/compound phonemic awareness involved more than one cognitive operation (e.g., deletion) and placed a heavier burden on memory. Other studies have claimed to identify differing types of phonological ability. For instance, the longitudinal study by Wagner, Torgesen, and Rashotte (1994) uncovered two non-redundant factors in first and second grade readers, namely phonological "analysis" (breaking words down into sounds) and phonological "synthesis" (blending sounds).

Clearly, the usefulness of making distinctions between highly correlated phonological ability factors really depends on the nature of their predictive relationships with reading. If different factors differ in their predictive power, then it may be important to distinguish between them. If they do not, then it is simpler merely to consider differences in phonological skill as a unitary construct. Also, taking a developmental perspective, it is important to emphasize that although different phonological skills may be highly intercorrelated, this is not incompatible with a developmental model in which these skills develop at different times and have different causal relationships with reading ability that are dependent on the age of the child and the stage he or she has reached in the reading process.

   Relevant to my own research is the influential theoretical position held by Goswami and Bryant (1990) who maintain that
phonological skills relate to different levels of analysis for spoken
words, and that awareness of these levels develops at different
rates. They propose that tasks of rhyming skill tap the child's understanding of onset and rime units within words, the onset being
the consonant or consonant cluster that precedes the vowel, and
the rime being the vowel and succeeding consonants. Rhyming
tasks may be performed by children as young as 4- and 5-years old
and are highly predictive of later success in reading (Bradley and
Bryant 1983). Goswami and Bryant (1990) propose that the ability
to segment phonemes within words is a very different skill that
develops later, partly as a consequence of learning to read, and is
thought to be closely related to learning to spell.
   Charles Hulme, Margaret Snowling, Sara Taylor and I (Muter
et al. 1998) studied 38 normal children during their first two years
of learning to read. Principal components analysis of a battery of
phonological measures, initially administered when the children
were prereaders, identified two distinct and relatively independent
factors: rhyming (defined by measures of rhyme detection and
rhyme production) and segmentation (defined by measures of
phoneme identification, phoneme blending, and phoneme deletion). Segmentation was strongly correlated with attainment in
both reading and spelling at the end of the first year of learning to
read, while rhyming was not. By the end of the second year, however, rhyming had started to exert a predictive effect on spelling,
though not on reading. The relative salience of rhyming and segmentation skill to beginning literacy development has generated
heated debate in the scientific literature (see Bryant 1998; Hulme,
Muter, and Snowling 1998). Although Bryant (1998) maintains
strongly that there is an important predictive relationship between
rhyming and reading, other studies, like ours, have also suggested
that segmentation may be a more influential phonological skill in
the beginning stages of learning to read than rhyming (Duncan,
Seymour, and Hill 1997; Seymour and Duncan 1997; Wimmer,
Landerl, and Schneider 1994). The studies by Seymour and his colleagues have suggested that even when children start school with
well established rhyming skills, they are not disposed to use this
knowledge in their initial attempts at reading. In their studies, the
introduction of letters and the alphabetic principle (learning to
connect letters with their sounds) resulted in the children becoming more proficient in identifying smaller phonemic rather than
larger rime units within words. Wimmer, Landerl, and Schneider
(1994) found that rime awareness was only minimally predictive

of reading and spelling achievement at the end of grade 1 in German-speaking children, but that it gained substantially in predictive importance for reading and spelling achievement in grades 3 and 4. These findings, together with our own and those of Seymour and his colleagues, suggest that rhyming skills have relevance at a later stage in reading development, and that rhyming ability may have a particular bearing on children's ability to apply analogical strategies (Goswami 1990; Muter, Snowling, and Taylor 1994). Clearly, the resolution of this controversy is crucial not only from a theoretical standpoint, but also in respect to knowing which phonological skills to prioritize, both for the development of early screening instruments and in the teaching of reading to children in their early years at school.

A further predictor candidate that relates strongly to reading skill, and which may be an even more powerful determiner of beginning progress in learning to read than phonological segmentation ability, is the acquisition of letter knowledge. Early large scale studies found prereaders' letter knowledge to be a very good predictor of first-grade reading skills (Chall 1967; Bond and Dykstra 1967). More recently, Byrne et al. (1997) found that letter knowledge accounted for more variance in a decoding task within a teaching experiment with preschool and kindergarten children than did a measure of phonemic awareness. Preliminary analyses of an ongoing longitudinal study of nearly 100 normal children, conducted by myself, Margaret Snowling and Charles Hulme, have highlighted letter knowledge skill on entry to school as the best single predictor of word recognition one year later. It is clear that knowledge of letter names or sounds is an important prerequisite for children learning to read and spell in an alphabetic language such as English. There are a number of possible reasons for this. Most obviously, knowledge of letter sounds is necessary for children to understand that there is a systematic relationship between the spelling patterns of words and their pronunciations. Alternatively, it can be argued that from the very earliest stages of learning to read, young children are creating maps between the orthographic representations of words and their phonological forms (Ehri 1992; Rack et al. 1994). The creation of such maps, however, depends upon knowledge of the phonetic characteristics of the sounds for which letters stand.

Our recent longitudinal study (Muter et al. 1998) showed that letter skill predicted both reading and spelling during the first year at school. In fact, not only did segmentation and letter knowledge make separate and specific contributions to beginning literacy, but there was also an additional significant contribution from the product term "Letter Knowledge x Segmentation" which reflected the interaction of the two component skills. The product term exerted a small additional influence on reading, and a massive effect on spelling. We may relate this finding to the results of experimental and field training studies that have shown that in order to progress in reading, children need to forge meaningful connections between their developing phonological skills and their appreciation of print (Byrne and Fielding-Barnsley 1989; Bradley and Bryant 1985; Ball and Blachman 1988; Tunmer and Hoover 1992; Iverson and Tunmer 1993)—what Hatcher, Hulme and Ellis (1994) refer to as "phonological linkage." It is thus not simply having adequate phonological awareness and letter knowledge that permits good progress in learning to read, rather both these factors are important and they act in an interactive fashion.

Relatively few studies have reported on the influence of early language (especially phonological) skills on much later reading development. Those studies that have reported this influence show a strong relationship between phonological abilities at kindergarten and grade 1 and word level reading skill towards the end of primary school (Stuart 1990; Stuart and Masterson 1992; Schneider and Naslund 1993; Klicpera and Schabmann 1993; Wagner et al. 1997). In our own long-term longitudinal study of 34 children, we found that one of the best predictors of reading skill at age 9 was the phoneme deletion measure obtained at ages 5 and 6 years (Muter and Snowling 1998). Consistent with the results of our earlier longitudinal study (Muter et al. 1998), it was the segmentation (in this case, deletion) measure that was predictive of reading skill in the later primary years; rhyming scores obtained at ages 5 and 6 did not predict reading skill at age 9. Bearing in mind the observed stability and the established long-term predictive power of phonological skills, it is evident that they are prime candidates for inclusion in any early screening measure of reading achievement. On a cautionary note, we found that phonological measures taken at age 4 years did not predict reading skill at age 9. This suggests that it may be more appropriate to delay screening for children at risk for reading failure until the end of the preschool period.

COGNITIVE PREDICTORS OF EARLY READING SKILL IN THE NORMAL POPULATION—VERBAL MEMORY, NAMING AND SEMANTIC/SYNTACTIC SKILLS

The role of verbal short-term memory in early reading development has been nearly as controversial as that of the contribution made by specific phonological processes to reading. It is well documented in the scientific literature that short-term verbal memory is closely related to level of reading skill, whether the materials are digits and letters (Katz, Healy, and Shankweiler 1983), words (Brady, Shankweiler, and Mann 1983) or sentences (Mann, Liberman, and Shankweiler 1980). Whether verbal memory span is an important predictor of reading skill independent of children's phonological abilities is not entirely clear. Hansen and Bowey (1994) found in their correlational study of 7-year olds that both phonological analysis and verbal working memory accounted for unique variance in three reading measures. Similarly, preliminary results from our ongoing longitudinal study suggest that verbal short-term memory (for words) is a unique concurrent predictor, alongside phonological segmentation and letter knowledge, of word recognition after one year of formal schooling. However, other studies have suggested that short-term verbal memory does not significantly predict reading skills after controlling for phonological abilities (Rohl and Pratt 1995; Wagner, Torgesen, and Rashotte 1994).

Gathercole and Baddeley (1989) have conceptualized non-word repetition tasks as measures of phonological working memory that may relate to reading skill. Gathercole, Baddeley, and Willis (1991) failed to uncover a relationship between non-word repetition and reading ability in the first year at school, although the correlation between these skills was statistically significant by year two. Furthermore, Muter and Snowling (1998) found that in a discriminant function analysis for good versus poor reading accuracy skill at age 9, the best long-term predictor set consisted of the phoneme deletion and non-word repetition scores at ages 5 and 6, with a successful classification rate of 80%. However, Snowling, Chiat, and Hulme (1991) have suggested that non-word repetition should not be construed purely as a memory test but rather as a measure sensitive to the integrity of phonological representations. Wagner, Torgesen, and Rashotte (1994) would agree with this view; they propose that various phonological processing tasks, including those of short-term verbal or working memory, are tapping the quality of underlying phonological representation, and it is the quality of these representations that, in turn, affects children's ability to learn to read.

The speed and accuracy with which pictures, digits, and letters can be named is a well documented linguistic correlate of reading ability that is thought to reflect phonological memory or retrieval processes. Individual differences in what is referred to as rapid automatized naming have been shown to predict reading development in the first grade (Felton and Brown 1990) and in the third and fourth grades (Badian et al. 1990). Naming speed with digits and letters appears to be more predictive than with pictures, not a surprising finding given the more reading-related symbolic nature of the former stimuli. Whether a naming difficulty in a poor reader reflects a problem in the process by which representations are retrieved or whether the problem lies in the phonological representations themselves being indistinct or unrefined continues to be an area for debate. Most recently, Manis, Seidenberg, and Doi (1999) have proposed a model of reading development in which they suggest that naming tasks account for distinct variance in reading when compared to phoneme awareness because naming involves arbitrary associations between print and sound whereas phoneme awareness is more related to the learning of systematic spelling-sound correspondences. Learning arbitrary associations between sounds and letters probably plays a central role in the development of early reading skill, whereas knowledge of segmental phonology is relevant to both the earlier and later phases of learning to read.

Hulme and his colleagues have explored the relationship between short-term memory and phonological processing by examining speech rate; that is, the speed with which a specified word or words can be spoken (see Hulme and Roodenrys 1995 for a review). They present evidence from developmental studies that has demonstrated a close relationship between changes in speech rate and increases in memory span. With regard to reading, McDougall et al. (1994) studied the relationship between memory span, speech rate, and phonological awareness in good, average, and poor readers. They were able to demonstrate that differences in reading ability are associated with differences in the efficiency of the speech-based rehearsal component of short-term memory span as measured by a speech rate task. Children's scores on the test of speech rate made a significant contribution to reading skill independent of that made by two measures of phonological awareness. Furthermore, after accounting for speech rate, memory span made no contribution to reading skill. Conversely, however, speech rate did predict reading skill even after controlling for the effects of memory span. Margaret Snowling and I obtained similar results as to the relative salience of speech rate and memory span in 9-year-old normal readers (Muter and Snowling 1998). Hulme and his colleagues suggest that speech rate provides an index of the speed and efficiency with which phonological representations of words in long-term memory can be activated, and that this is a skill separate from the phonological processes tapped by measures of phonological awareness. Thus, in speech rate, we appear to have a quick and easy-to-implement technique that can complement and supplement the more extensively documented measures of phonological awareness and letter knowledge.

The foregoing discussion has highlighted the importance of measures of phonological processing ability and letter knowledge in the prediction of literacy success or failure. Increasing attention has been paid of late to other non-phonological language skills that might have a bearing on how easily children learn to read. Tunmer (1989) emphasized the importance of syntactic awareness as an independent contributor to early reading skill. In a longitudinal study, he administered tests of verbal ability, phonological awareness, syntactic awareness, and reading to 100 children at the end of first grade and again one year later. The results clearly demonstrated that both phonological and syntactic awareness influenced reading comprehension through phonological recoding (as measured by a non-word reading test). In addition, Tunmer and Chapman (1998) have suggested that young readers often combine incomplete phoneme-grapheme information with their knowledge of sentence constraints in order to identify unfamiliar words. This increases their word-specific knowledge (including irregular words) and their knowledge of grapheme-phoneme correspondences. The ability to use contextual information allows young readers to monitor their accuracy of word identification by providing them with immediate feedback when their attempted readings of unfamiliar words fail to conform to the surrounding grammatical context. They can then make the necessary adjustments to their subsequent attempts at reading the unfamiliar word up to the point where their response satisfies both the phoneme-grapheme relations within the word and its surrounding sentence constraints.

Further support for the combined phonology-context view of reading comes from our recent study (Muter and Snowling 1998) in which grammatical awareness was found to be an important concurrent predictor of reading accuracy at age 9 (alongside that of phonological segmentation ability). Indeed, it is important to note that grammatical awareness in this study was a predictor of reading accuracy in context, as measured by a prose reading test, but not of a pure measure of decoding skill, namely non-word reading. Thus, grammatical knowledge interacts with decoding ability to increase word identification skills. This may be particularly true of older children who have moved beyond single word decoding of simple text toward an increasing appreciation of the value of context and content cues contained in more complex reading materials. Of relevance to the age at which children might take advantage of contextual information is the finding from our ongoing longitudinal study that measures of syntactic or grammatic awareness failed to predict reading skill in the first year of learning to read. However, as Willows and Ryan (1986) have shown, children become increasingly sensitive to semantic and syntactic features in reading tasks from grades 1 through 3. Thus, syntactic and semantic abilities may gather in predictive importance later in elementary schooling when children read in context and when there is greater emphasis on comprehension skills. Indeed, children need to develop syntactic and semantic skills that are sufficiently refined to enable them to make sense of contextual cues as they proceed from early single word decoding to the mastery of more complex text. Consistent with this idea, Nation and Snowling (1998) found that the extent to which children can use a spoken sentence context to facilitate decoding depends on their verbal skills. They presented children with a printed word, either in isolation or following a spoken context. Not surprisingly, the children's reading accuracy increased when context was made available to them. However, what was of particular interest was that the children who benefited most were those with poor phonological skills but good verbal ability, while the children who benefited least were those with relatively weak verbal skills.

There are other ways in which syntactic awareness might influence reading development. For instance, the availability of context enables children to monitor their ongoing reading comprehension processes. Bowey (1986) found that performance on a syntactic awareness task was correlated with measures of reading comprehension and comprehension monitoring, even after controlling for the effects of general verbal ability. Also, children with good syntactic or grammatic awareness might try out different pronunciations of words in which a single letter sequence is associated with more than one pronunciation; in this way, children come to learn about complex relationships between orthographic patterns and pronunciations.

Although it has been consistently demonstrated that phonological awareness has both a powerful and long-term bearing on reading progress and outcome, the effects of other reading-related language measures may be either more transitory, or fail to exert an effect that is independent of other abilities. Wagner et al. (1997) found that individual differences in naming speed and vocabulary influenced subsequent individual differences in word-level reading initially, but that these influences faded with development. This finding for naming speed is consistent with the model proposed by Manis, Seidenberg, and Doi (1999) who suggest that naming speed is related to the learning of arbitrary sound-print connections that may, in turn, determine ease of letter knowledge acquisition in kindergarten through first grade. Additionally, in the Wagner et al. study, individual differences in phonological memory did not independently influence subsequent individual differences in word-level reading at any point during their 5-year longitudinal study. This was in contrast to the findings for phonological awareness; the influence of individual differences in this skill over subsequent reading ability extended at least to fourth grade. These findings on the stability and long-term predictive power of reading-related measures may well have a bearing on which tasks are to be selected for use in a screening instrument, the more stable, influential, and independent skills being the obvious measures of choice.

NON-COGNITIVE PREDICTORS OF EARLY READING SKILL

Thus far, I have addressed cognitive predictors of early reading success. However, there are non-cognitive determinants of children's early progress in reading which, although not directly relevant to a screening evaluation, nonetheless should be taken into account when appraising the needs of an individual child. It has been suggested that home environment may be a likely source of experiences that can enhance the development of both oral and written language skills.

It is well documented that young children's level of language proficiency and their reading skill are closely correlated with socioeconomic status (SES) of the parents, with middle-class children attaining higher levels of language and literacy than their lower-class or deprived peers (Feagans and Farran 1982; White 1982). Of particular relevance to predicting early reading success and failure from phonological measures is the relationship between socioeconomic status, reading progress, and phonological sensitivity. Raz and Bryant (1990) and Bowey (1995) have suggested that SES differences in word level reading in young children are mediated partly through pre-existing differences in phonological sensitivity. Raz and Bryant (1990) reported strong SES differences in reading performance even when IQ score effects were covaried. Furthermore, when phonological sensitivity scores were covaried, SES differences were no longer significant in the tests of reading accuracy. This suggests that SES differences in phonological sensitivity may mediate SES differences in word level reading achievement. Bowey

(1995) conducted a longitudinal study of 5-year olds differing in SES during their first year of learning to read. Marked differences on a wide variety of measures emerged when the children were grouped according to high or low SES. When general verbal ability effects were controlled, differences in phonological sensitivity and word level reading remained. Thus many children from lower socioeconomic groups may be arriving at school with underdeveloped phonological awareness that, of course, then put them at a serious disadvantage in acquiring early reading skills. A study by Chaney (1994) found that not only did SES differences mediate progress in learning to read through language skills, but also through print awareness. Children from middle-class homes had richer and more varied exposure to printed materials, which in turn had an influence on the children's print awareness as assessed by measures of alphabet and book concepts. These findings together point to the importance of early screening and intervention programs, especially in disadvantaged areas, that focus strongly on language activities that foster children's sensitivity to sound patterns in words and that link these to their experience with print in alphabet and story books.

A further relevant home-related factor in determining beginning reading may be that of early home literacy experiences, especially parent's reading to preschoolers. Scarborough and Dobrich (1994) reviewed 31 studies that looked at the impact of parents' reading to their preschoolers on the children's oral language and literacy development; 20 of these were correlational in methodology and 11 were intervention programs. Frequency of reading to preschoolers seemed to be the important factor. In general, the correlational studies showed that frequency of reading was associated with growth in lexical and semantic content of language and in developing literacy (but not in syntactic or phonological structures). In the intervention studies, more positive results emerged for oral language than for literacy outcome. However, although there appears to be a significant association between parent-preschool reading and language/literacy outcome, this is of modest proportions, with most correlations at or less than .28. A recent study by Senechal et al. (1998) contrasted frequency of storybook reading and frequency of parents teaching reading and writing of words with their impact on the children's oral and written language skills. The children, who were from middle-class schools, were studied while in kindergarten and grade 1. After controlling for parents' print exposure and the children's IQ, storybook exposure explained statistically significant unique variance in children's oral language skills, but not in their written language. In contrast, parent teaching of reading explained unique variance in the children's written language skills, but not in their oral language. The authors conclude that these findings are consistent with the hypothesis that storybook exposure may enhance children's oral language skills, whereas additional support in the form of reading instruction may be necessary to enhance written language skills.

PREDICTION IN CHILDREN AT RISK FOR DYSLEXIA

Another way of addressing the screening for early reading failure is to look at children who are at risk for, or who are known to have, dyslexia. Here we are investigating deficits in cognitive processes that are intrinsic to the child and that in turn lead to low levels of literacy. This approach is complementary to the extensive research described above that shows a strong and predictive relationship between phonological skills and learning to read in unselected populations. We have seen that current theories of early reading development propose that children set up direct mappings between printed words and representations of spoken words in the child's language systems (Ehri 1992; Rack et al. 1994). It follows from this that the status of children's underlying phonological representations determines the ease with which they learn to read. Since 1980, there have been many studies that point to language difficulties in the child with dyslexia, specifically at the level of phonology; thus, children with dyslexia typically perform poorly on a wide range of measures of phonological awareness, verbal short-term memory, rapid naming, speech perception, and verbal representation, tasks that essentially tap children's representation of, access to, and recall of phonological information (see Snowling 1995 for a review). Snowling argues that children with dyslexia often continue to read words using only partial cues and, therefore, make a large number of errors. They cannot abstract letter-sound correspondences from their experience with printed words and, therefore, fail to develop phonological or phonic reading strategies. One direct way of tapping level of phonic reading skill is to ask children to attempt to read nonsense words that cannot be recognized from previous experience nor accessed through semantic clues. Indeed, there is a great deal of evidence that dyslexic children's non-word reading skill is significantly worse than their other reading abilities (Rack, Snowling, and Olson 1992).

Dyslexia is a life-long difficulty, though its manifestation can change with maturation and experience. Cognitive and educational manifestations that are evident at one point in development may not be present at another. Individuals also respond to teaching that may resolve or at any rate ameliorate some deficits. Similarly, compensatory strategies may develop in the individual in response to teaching and experience. There is accumulating evidence that dyslexia is an inherited condition. Olson et al. (1997) have shown that there are strong genetic influences on both phonological and orthographic coding. However, the results of most large scale twin studies have tended to show that there is greater heritability of phonologically based reading skills (e.g., as measured by a non-word reading test) than of orthographic skills (e.g., selecting the correct spelling from phonologically viable pairs) (Olson et al. 1989). Most recently, Gayan and Olson (1999) have estimated the heritability of phonological awareness at .89, significantly higher than for other components of the reading process (.68 for word recognition, .77 for phonic decoding, and .76 for orthographic decoding).

Studies of children with known dyslexic problems have their limitations. Because it is well established that the relationship between phonological skills and reading is a reciprocal one, it follows that the observed phonological deficits in individuals with dyslexia could have been influenced by the reading impairment itself. To circumvent this problem, and to complement the retrospective studies, some researchers have concentrated on looking at young children who are highly at risk for developing dyslexia. It follows from the genetic research on dyslexia that this condition must show a tendency to run in families. One way of identifying children at risk for dyslexia before they have had the opportunity to learn to read is to select children from families where there is high incidence of dyslexia and to then contrast their performance on language tasks with children from families in whom there is no dyslexia.

Hollis Scarborough (1990, 1991) compared the performance of reading disabled children from dyslexic families on language, phonological, and preliteracy measures at several different ages, with that of normal reading children from non-dyslexic families, all of whom had been recruited for the study at age 2. The children in the reading disabled group were significantly poorer than those in the control group on tests of expressive syntax and sentence comprehension at 30 to 48 months, and on tests of phonological awareness, letter-sound knowledge, letter identification, and object naming at 60 months. Scarborough suggested that children with dyslexia have a broader language disorder that is not simply reflected in reading failure. This disorder is expressed as different observable weaknesses at different ages; first, syntax problems, then weaknesses in phonological awareness, naming and other preliteracy skills; and finally, difficulties with reading and spelling during the school years. The fact that different cognitive skills have differing predictive power according to the age at which they are assessed is an important consideration when devising predictor instruments; a series of tests relevant for 3-year olds may have a very different language content, beyond that of difficulty level, from that devised for 5-year olds.

More recent studies of children at risk for dyslexia have also highlighted differences between high risk and low risk children on phonological awareness tasks and letter knowledge/identification (Lefly and Pennington 1996; Byrne et al. 1997; Elbro, Borstrøm, and Petersen 1998). Gallagher, Frith, and Snowling (2000) looked at reading outcome at age six from language scores obtained at 45 months in a group of children at risk for reading difficulties. Half of such children were delayed in their early literacy development when compared with low risk children. Gallagher, Frith, and Snowling (2000) found that the strongest predictor was letter knowledge, a finding with a clinical sample that reinforces our observation from our ongoing longitudinal study that letter knowledge is the most powerful of the predictors of early literacy. Furthermore, the at-risk children with delayed literacy were subject to a mild delay in all aspects of spoken language, semantic and syntactic as well as phonological. The literacy delayed children in this study who were making the best progress were those with better vocabulary and expressive language skills. Thus, eventual success in overcoming early reading delay may depend not only on the status of the children's phonological deficit but also upon how successfully they can use syntactic and semantic skills to compensate for their likely decoding inadequacies. Studies of early reading skill and at-risk status need to address, not only the core cognitive deficiencies that give rise to the reading problem, but also the availability and integrity of complementary cognitive resources that the child is able to bring to the reading task by way of compensation.

SCREENING TESTS AND THEIR IMPLEMENTATION

Prediction studies such as those described above tell us a great deal about the knowledge and skills young children bring to bear on the task of learning to read. They might also, if generated from sufficiently large samples of children, provide norms for the purposes of screening young children, or against which individual "slow starter" youngsters might be compared. However, whether such studies can suggest a strategy for reliably identifying those specific children who go on to have severe and persisting reading problems that necessitate special intervention is a rather more complex issue. When considering individual children, it is not always possible to conclude with confidence that a child with a low score on a measure of phonological awareness will necessarily go on to have significant and persisting reading difficulties. In Bradley and Bryant's (1985) longitudinal study of early readers, only 30% of those children who initially produced good sound categorization scores went on to become exceptionally good readers. Of greater relevance to the early identification issue is the finding that just 28% of those who initially produced poor sound categorization scores became exceptionally poor readers. These authors suggest that a phonological awareness test on its own might not be a particularly effective way of predicting persisting reading problems. More recent studies that have used a number of independent predictors have reported higher sensitivity ratings of 48% (Schneider and Naslund 1993), 42% (Badian 1988) and 56% (Butler et al. 1985). An even higher sensitivity was achieved in a study by Badian (1994) in which she was able to predict the problems of 14 out of 15 poor readers. However, a high sensitivity such as this may be at the cost of a relatively high number of false alarms, depending on where the cut-off point for group inclusion is placed. So in the Badian (1994) study, 10 out of 24 children did not develop reading difficulties as predicted. At the extreme, adopting a large number of predictors in order to achieve higher prediction also has its disadvantages. Using a large number of independent predictors will provide an almost perfect or even a perfect prediction (Elbro, Borstrøm, and Petersen 1998). Beyond the practical limitations of time and cost, this is not in itself desirable theoretically or methodologically. Prediction is best when each measure is strongly correlated with the outcome measure of reading, but uncorrelated with the other measures (Tabachnick and Fidell 1989). Thus, the goal of any screening measure is to select the fewest independent measures necessary to provide a good prediction of reading outcome in which each measure predicts a substantial and independent segment of the variability in reading outcome.

A number of tests have employed phonological awareness measures as screening or diagnostic instruments. Diane Sawyer's Test of Awareness of Language Segments, TALS (1987) can be used as a screen for children at the kindergarten or grade 1 level, but also is recommended for use diagnostically and prescriptively for older children who are already exhibiting delay in learning to read. In this test, children are required to segment language, first from sentences-to-words, then words-to-syllables and finally from words-to-sounds. Torgesen and Bryant's Test of Phonological Awareness, TOPA, (1994) is a group administered test in which children use pictorial material to demonstrate their ability to identify initial sounds (kindergarten version) or end sounds (elementary version) within words. Predictive validation studies have shown that kindergartners' TALS or TOPA scores significantly predict reading skill through to third grade (Sawyer 1987; Torgersen and Bryant 1994). Wagner, Torgesen, and Rashotte (1999) have recently produced the Comprehensive Test of Phonological Processing (CTOPP) which includes a wide range of phonological awareness, phonological memory, and rapid naming tasks.

Bearing in mind Bradley and Bryant's (1985) caution against relying on a single measure to predict reading outcome reliably, Margaret Snowling, Charles Hulme, and I were eager to develop a multi-measure screening and early diagnostic instrument that would be simple and economical, and provide good prediction, while at the same time being in accord with recent research findings and with current theoretical perspectives on early reading development. We wanted to include phonological awareness tests that were representative of the skills young children bring to bear on their earliest reading experiences and that reflected our theoretical position on the relationship between phonological skill and reading. Since phonological skills are the most stable and robust of the available predictor skills, and in view of their ability to predict reading skill independently over long periods of time, we reasoned that these should be given selection priority over more transitory predictors like vocabulary or naming skill. We selected two measures we believed assessed children's ability to segment words into syllables or phonemes—a test of syllable and phoneme completion, and a test of beginning and end phoneme deletion. Although we firmly believe that the current evidence favors segmentation over rhyming as being the better predictor of beginning literacy, we did not want to exclude measures of onset-rime awareness completely. There is a well documented view that rhyming skill may have a bearing on later stages of learning to read, and in particular on children's ability to adopt analogical strategies. We have seen that there is increasingly strong evidence emerging as to the paramount importance of letter knowledge acquisition in early reading development. Thus, a test of letter knowledge as an indicator of the thoroughness and possibly ease with which the letter identities have been learned is an obligatory component of an early screening battery. Finally, we wished to include a measure of children's phonological memory processes either through the adoption of a span test, or as our more recent research suggests, more economically and powerfully, a test of speech rate.

The result was the *Phonological Abilities Test, PAT,* published by the Psychological Corporation UK (Muter, Hulme, and Snowling 1997). The *PAT* comprises four phonological awareness subtests (Rhyme Detection, Rhyme Production, Word Completion —Syllables and Phonemes, Beginning and End Phoneme Deletion), a Speech Rate test (timed repeating of the word "buttercup"), and a test of Letter Knowledge. The test was standardized on 826 children aged 4 to7 years, and norms provided in 6-month age bands between 5 and 7 years (and in a 12 month age band for the 4-year olds). When given in full, the *PAT* takes approximately 25 to 30 minutes to administer, with each subtest varying in administration time from around 3 minutes (Letter Knowledge and Speech Rate) to up to about 8 minutes (Beginning and End Phoneme Deletion). The individual subtests demonstrated good internal and test-retest reliability. Construct validation studies, using principal components analyses, indicated that the *PAT* is tapping separate and independent subskills within the phonological domain. Factor 1, on which the Word Completion and Phoneme Deletion subtests loaded highly, was interpreted as a Segmentation factor. Factor 2, on which only Speech Rate loaded highly was clearly measuring a different phonological skill, a finding consistent with the results of previous studies (McDougall et al. 1994; Muter and Snowling 1998). Factor 3, on which the Rhyme Detection and Production tests loaded highly, was interpreted as a Rhyming factor, sensitive to children's awareness of the onset-rime structure of words. Criterion-related validity studies have shown that the individual subtests correlate significantly with a concurrently administered standardized reading test (*British Abilities Scales Reading Test,* Elliott, Murray, and Pearson 1983). Multiple regression analyses have also demonstrated that the subtests are significant predictors of concurrent reading skill in the age range 5 to 7 years, with the best and most consistent predictor subtests being Phoneme Deletion and Letter Knowledge. The *PAT* given to 4-year olds showed poor criterion related validity, though of course few children in this age range had any measurable reading skill. Consistent with this are the findings from our earlier long-term longitudinal study (Muter and Snowling 1998) and our ongoing predictive validation study of the *PAT* which have suggested that phonological and related measures given to 4-year olds may not be good predictors of later reading skill. The *PAT*, like the *TALS*, may be used as a screening measure in the age range of 5 to 7 years (either when given in its entirety or using a subset of tests), or it may be administered to selected older children who are already experiencing reading problems and for whom a diagnostic and prescriptive phonological profile is required.

For older children for whom the *PAT* may be used diagnostically, reference is made not only to the norms (given in centiles), but also to the graphically represented *PAT* Profile. The following single case study illustrates how the *PAT* might be used diagnostically and as a prescription for teaching. Andrew, aged 7 years, 11 months, had a WISC III Verbal IQ of 101 (Wechsler 1992), and could thus be regarded as being of average ability. He scored at barely the 6 year level on a standardized test of single word reading (Wechsler Objective Reading Dimensions, WORD, Wechsler 1993), and he was unable to read any non-words from the Graded Nonword Reading Test (Snowling, Stothard, and McLean 1996). Andrew's scores on the Rhyme Detection, Rhyme Production, Beginning and End Phoneme Deletion and Letter Knowledge subtests were all at or under the 10th centile. He had no difficulty with Sentence or Phoneme Completion (50th centile) or with Speech Rate (75th centile). His *PAT* profile is shown in figure 1.

Although Andrew clearly has no problems with phonological short-term memory and his simple segmentation abilities are established, he is nonetheless experiencing great difficulty in many other aspects of phonological skill and in acquiring letter knowledge. His pattern of difficulty, taken together with his marked reading underachievement and his total lack of decoding ability, is clearly indicative of his having a specific literacy difficulty that has the hallmarks of dyslexia. He needs a systematic literacy training program that emphasizes phonological awareness and related skills. Of the phonological abilities in which Andrew is deficient, rhyming is the ability which appears earliest in the developmental progression of phonological skills. It is, therefore, recommended that he be trained in rhyming first. After that, Andrew needs to work on his phonological manipulation skills through exercises that teach him to add, delete, substitute, or transpose phonemes within words. Andrew also needs to be trained in his letter knowledge, with a teaching approach that emphasizes multisensory learning (feeling, writing, naming) of both letter names and sounds, and where there is the opportunity for a lot of practice and reinforcement. When Andrew is more phonologically aware, and when he knows all his letters, he should be exposed to "linkage" exercises that help him make important connections between his

⊚pat record form

Phonological Abilities Test		Year	Month	Day
Name ANDREW	Date Tested			
School	Date of Birth			
Examiner	Age	7	11	
Gender				

Test Scores		Raw Score	Centiles
Rhyme Detection	Number correct - (max 10)	4	<10
Rhyme Production	Number of words - day	1	
	Number of words - bell	1	
	Total:	2	10
Word Completion - Syllables and Phonemes	Number correct - syllables - (max 8)	8	50
	Number correct - phonemes - (max 8)	8	50
	Total: (max 16)	16	
Phoneme Deletion Beginning and End sounds	Number correct beginning sounds - (max 8)	0	<10
	Number correct end sounds - (max 8)	1	<10
	Total correct: (max 16)	1	
Speech Rate	A. Buttercup Time 1	1.7"	
	B. Buttercup Time 2	2.7"	
	C. Buttercup Time 3	3.7"	
	D. Mean Time ((A+B+C) / 3)		
	Words per second (10 / D)	1.43"	75
Letter Knowledge	Letters correctly identified - (max 26)	23	<10

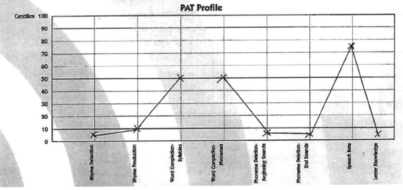

PAT Profile

Figure 1. *Phonological Abilities Test (PAT)* record form and *PAT* profile for Andrew.

improving speech sound sensitivity and his experience of print. After Andrew has worked through a program such as this, he should be ready to embark on a structured phonic-based program that teaches him about grapheme-to-phoneme consistencies and about sequential decoding skill.

THE WAY AHEAD

In achieving a better understanding of how phonological abilities influence reading skill, and in particular how phonological deficits might be avoided through pre-school intervention, we need to know more about the early sources of phonological awareness. Elbro (1996) and Elbro, Borstrøm, and Petersen (1998) have suggested that one possible precursor of phoneme awareness development is children's distinctness or "completeness" of phonological representation. This refers to the magnitude of the difference between a given representation and its neighbors. A phonological representation is highly distinct if many distinctive features serve to distinguish it from its neighbors. For instance, pronouncing the *e* in "boisterous" is a more distinct representation than omitting it, though both would be acceptable pronunciations. Elbro, Borstrøm, and Petersen attempted to measure young children's phonological distinctness by eliciting from them the most distinct pronunciation of a single word; the distinctness score was the percentage of selected vowels that were given a maximally distinct pronunciation. These authors found that the measure of distinctness made a significant and independent contribution to the prediction of poor phoneme awareness in grade 2 "at-risk" children with dyslexia who had been studied longitudinally since kindergarten. Elbro has proposed that children who become dyslexic have poorer access to the most distinct variants of spoken words than other children. An alternative predictor of later phoneme awareness considered by Elbro (1996) is the ease with which young children acquire knowledge of the segmental structure of words. Phonological representations that are initially holistic are gradually reorganized into increasingly smaller segments, ultimately segments of phoneme size (Fowler 1991). Thus awareness of segmental size, which is assumed to be driven by earlier vocabulary growth, is viewed as an important predictor of the ease with which children develop phonological processing skill (Walley 1993). Whether distinctness or segmental size of children's phonological representations proves the better predictor of later phoneme awareness is an issue for further contrastive research within a longitudinal framework.

An especially important future area for study is that of the acquisition of letter knowledge. There is emerging evidence that ease of acquiring letter identities is a very powerful predictor of beginning reading success. An important question is what are the determinants of the ease with which letter-sound connections are acquired? It is tempting to think that the relationships between phonemes and graphemes are learned in a rote, paired associate fashion. It is, therefore, assumed that given equal exposure, /w/-w and /t/-t are learned equally quickly. However, as Treiman, Weatherston, and Berch (1994) point out, it is easier for kindergartners to learn letter-sound correspondences when the sound of the letter is contained in its name (e.g., p, b, k) than when the letter name does not help to specify the sound (e.g., h, w). They also suggest that, not only do children bring their prior knowledge of letter names to their learning of alphabetic sound-to-letter relationships, but they also use their ability to segment letter names into their component phonemes. Thus, children's phonological awareness skills are intimately involved in their learning of phoneme-grapheme correspondences. The authors go on to suggest that more extensive teaching is needed for some phoneme-grapheme correspondences than for others. Thus, teachers may need to spend more time on the sounds of letters such as /y/ and /w/ than on the sounds of letters such as /b/ and /v/. However, the direction of influence between phonological segmentation and letter knowledge acquisition remains an area of dispute. While Treiman et al. and indeed others (Rack et al. 1994) have suggested that phonological awareness skills help to promote letter-sound knowledge acquisition, Barron (1991) and Johnston, Anderson, and Holligan (1996) have proposed that learning the alphabet may cause children to become explicitly aware of the phonological structure of words. Johnston, Anderson, and Holligan (1996) found that letter knowledge accounted for unique variance in phoneme awareness in four-year-old non-readers. Clearly, there is an interactive process between children's emerging letter-sound knowledge and their phonological awareness. The bi-directional nature of this relationship has been recently explored by Burgess and Lonigan (1998) in a one-year longitudinal study of children aged 4 to 5 years. Multiple regressions revealed that phonological sensitivity predicted growth in letter knowledge, and that letter knowledge predicted growth in phonological sensitivity after controlling for children's age and oral language skills. However, the size of letter knowledge's effect on phonological sensitivity was smaller than the effect of phonological sensitivity on growth in letter knowledge. The model of reading proposed by Manis, Seidenberg, and Doi (1999) would predict that letter or digit naming speed is likely to be another determiner, along with phonological awareness, of the ease with which letter identities are acquired.

It is anticipated that future screening instruments aimed at identifying early reading problems will need to address the following issues. First, the age at which children should be screened for reading difficulties is an important pedagogical concern. Phonological skills are less stable in young children, a factor that can impair their predictive relationship to later reading skill; consequently, it may be inadvisable to attempt large scale screening of preschool children, but instead to concentrate screening and early identification around the first year of formal schooling. Second, there is the need to adopt increasingly refined measures of phonological abilities that are sensitive to the core deficit in reading disorder. Part of this refinement process will stem from the determinance of the relative importance of some skills above others (for instance, rhyming versus segmentation, phonological distinctiveness versus segmental size) in predicting early literacy success. Third, we need to include measures that reflect the interaction of phonological awareness skills with other reading-related abilities, in particular letter knowledge acquisition—perhaps a measure that reflects "phonological linkage," the term adopted by Hatcher, Hulme, and Ellis (1994) to describe the magnitude of the connection between phonological skill and experience of print. Finally, it will be important to include other language-related tasks, such as verbal memory and semantic/syntactic tasks. This is partly because deficiencies in these skills may have an impact on subsequent reading development, but also because determining semantic/syntactic knowledge, for instance, may be predictive of the child's capacity to compensate for a core phonological weakness. An effective early screening instrument aims, not only to identify children at risk for reading failure, but also, through a study of the pattern of relative strength and weakness, to provide a prescription for the amelioration of the deficits and the simultaneous promotion of compensatory resources.

Our knowledge of the relationship between phonological abilities and early reading skill has flourished greatly over the last twenty years. This has resulted in the recent publication of a number of screening and early diagnostic reading instruments. With the expected increasing refinement of these over the next 20 years, one might envisage a time in the twenty-first century when early identification and intervention make illiteracy in adults and older children a rarity.

REFERENCES

Adams, M. J. 1990. *Beginning to Read: Learning and Thinking about Print.* Cambridge, MA: MIT Press.

Badian, N. A. 1988. Predicting dyslexia in a preschool population. In *Preschool Prevention of Reading Failure*, eds. R. L. Masland and M. W. Masland. Parkton, MD: York Press.

Badian, N. A. 1994. Preschool prediction: Orthographic and phonological skills, and reading. *Annals of Dyslexia* 44:3–25.

Badian, N. A., McAnulty, G. B., Duffy, F., and Als, H. 1990. Prediction of dyslexia in kindergarten boys. *Annals of Dyslexia* 40:152–69.

Ball, E. W., and Blachman, B. A. 1988. Phoneme segmentation training: Effect on reading readiness. *Annals of Dyslexia* 38:208–25.

Barron, R. 1991. Protoliteracy, literacy and the acquisition of phonological awareness. *Learning and Individual Differences* 3:243–55.

Bond, G. L., and Dykstra, R. 1967. The cooperative research program on first grade reading instruction. *Reading Research Quarterly* 2:5–142.

Bowey, J. 1986. Syntactic awareness in relation to reading skill and ongoing comprehension monitoring. *Journal of Experimental Child Psychology* 41:282–99.

Bowey, J. 1995. Socioeconomic status differences in preschool phonological sensitivity and first-grade reading achievement. *Journal of Educational Psychology* 87:476–87.

Brady, S., Shankweiler, D., and Mann, V. 1983. Speech perception and memory coding in relation to reading ability. *Journal of Experimental Psychology* 35:345–67.

Bradley, L., and Bryant, P. E. 1983. Categorizing sounds and learning to read: A causal connection. *Nature* 301:419–521.

Bradley, L., and Bryant, P. E. 1985. *Rhyme and Reason in Reading and Spelling.* I.A.R.L.D. Monograph No. 1. Ann Arbor: University of Michigan Press.

Bruce, L. J. 1964. The analysis of word sounds by young children. *British Journal of Educational Psychology* 34:158–74.

Bryant, P. E. 1998. Sensitivity to onset and rime does predict young children's reading: A comment on Muter, Hulme, Snowling and Taylor. *Journal of Experimental Child Psychology* 71:29–37.

Burgess, S. R., and Lonigan, C. J. 1998. Bidirectional relations of phonological sensitivity and prereading abilities: Evidence from a preschool sample. *Journal of Experimental Child Psychology* 70:117–41.

Butler, S. R., Marsh, H. W., Sheppard, M. J., and Sheppard, J. L. 1985. Seven year longitudinal study of the early prediction of reading achievement. *Journal of Educational Psychology* 77:349–61.

Byrne, B., and Fielding-Barnsley, R. 1989. Phonemic awareness and letter knowledge in the child's acquisition of the alphabetic principal. *Journal of Educational Psychology* 82:805–12.

Byrne, B., Fielding-Barnsley, R., Ashley, L., and Larsen, K. 1997. Assessing the child's and the environment's contribution to reading acquisition: What we know and what we don't know. In *Foundations of Dyslexia and Early Reading Acquisition*, ed. B. Blachman. Hillsdale, NJ: Erlbaum and Associates.

Cataldo, S., and Ellis, N. 1988. Interactions in the development of spelling, reading and phonological skills. *Journal of Research in Reading* 11:86–109.

Chall, J. 1967. *Learning to Read: The Great Debate.* New York: McGraw-Hill.

Chaney, C. 1994. Language development, metalinguistic awareness and emergent literacy skills of 3-year-old children in relation to social class. *Applied Psycholinguistics* 15:371–94.

Cunningham, A. E., and Stanovich, K. E. 1997. Early reading acquisition and its relation to reading experience and ability 10 years later. *Developmental Psychology* 33:934–35.

Duncan, L. G., Seymour, P. H. K., and Hill, S. 1997. How important are rhyme and analogy in beginning reading? *Cognition* 63:171–208.

Ehri, L. C. 1992. Reconceptualizing the development of sight word reading and its relationship to recoding. In *Reading Acquisition*, eds. P. B. Gough, L. C. Ehri and R. Treiman. Hillsdale, NJ: Erlbaum Associates.

Elbro, C. 1996. Early linguistic abilities and reading development: A review and a hypothesis. *Reading and Writing* 8:453–85.

Elbro, C., Borstrøm, I., and Petersen, D. 1998. Predicting dyslexia from kindergarten: The importance of distinctness of phonological representations of lexical items. *Reading Research Quarterly* 33:39–60.

Elliott, C. D., Murray, D. J., and Pearson, L. S. 1983. *British Abilities Scales.* Windsor, Berkshire, UK: NFER-Nelson Press.

Feagans, L., and Farran, D. C. 1982. *The Language of Children Reared in Poverty: Implications for Evaluation and Intervention.* New York: Academic Press.

Felton, R. H., and Brown, I. S. 1990. Phonological processes as predictors of specific reading skills in children at risk for reading failure. *Reading and Writing* 2:39–59.

Fowler, A. E. 1991. How early phonological development might set the stage for phoneme awareness. In *Phonological Processes in Literacy: A Tribute to Isabelle Y. Liberman*, eds. S. Brady and D. Shankweiler. Hillsdale NJ: Erlbaum Associates.

Gallagher, A., Frith, U., and Snowling, M. 2000. Precursors of literacy delay among children at risk of dyslexia. *Journal of Child Psychology and Psychiatry* 41:203–13.

Gathercole, S., and Baddeley, A. 1989. Development of vocabulary in children and short-term phonological memory. *Journal of Memory and Language* 28:200–13.

Gathercole, S., Baddeley, A., and Willis, C. 1991. Differentiating phonological memory and awareness of rhyme: Reading and vocabulary development in children. *British Journal of Psychology* 82:387–406.

Gayan, J., and Olson, R. 1999. Genetic and environmental influences on individual differences in IQ, phonological awareness, word recognition, phonemic awareness, word recognition, phonemic and orthographic decoding. Poster presented at the meeting of the Society for the Scientific Study of Reading, Montreal, Canada.

Goswami, U. 1990. A special link between rhyming skills and the use of orthographic analogies by beginning readers. *Journal of Child Psychology and Psychiatry* 31:301–11.

Goswami, U., and Bryant, P. E. 1990. *Phonological Skills and Learning to Read.* London: Erlbaum Associates.

Hansen, J., and Bowey, J. A. 1994. Phonological analysis skills, verbal working memory and reading ability in second grade children. *Child Development* 65:938–50.

Hatcher, P., Hulme, C., and Ellis, A. W. 1994. Ameliorating early reading failure by integrating the teaching of reading and phonological skills: The Phonological Linkage hypothesis. *Child Development* 65:41–57.

Hulme, C., and Roodenrys, S. 1995. Verbal working memory development and its disorders. *Journal of Child Psychology and Psychiatry* 36:373–98.

Hulme, C., Muter, V., and Snowling, M. 1998. Segmentation does predict early progress in learning to read better than rhyme: A reply to Bryant. *Journal of Experimental Child Psychology* 71:39–44.

Iverson, S., and Tunmer, W. E. 1993. Phonological processing and the reading recovery program. *Journal of Educational Psychology* 85:112–26.

Johnston, R., Anderson, M., and Holligan, C. 1996. Knowledge of the alphabet and explicit awareness of phonemes in pre-readers: The nature of the relationship. *Reading and Writing* 8:217–34.

Katz, R. B., Healy, A. F., and Shankweiler, D. 1983. Phonetic coding and order memory in relation to reading proficiency: A comparison of short-term memory for temporal and spatial order information. *Applied Psycholinguistics* 4: 229–50.

Klicpera, C., and Schabmann, A. 1993. Do German-speaking children have a chance to overcome reading and spelling difficulties? A longitudinal survey from second until eighth grade. *European Journal of Psychology of Education* 8:307–23.

Lefly, D. L., and Pennington, B. F. 1996. Spelling errors and reading fluency in compensated adult dyslexics. *Annals of Dyslexia* 41:143–62.

Liberman, I. Y., Shankweiler, D., Fischer, F. W., and Carter, B. 1974. Reading and the awareness of language segments. *Journal of Experimental Child Psychology* 18:201–12.

Lonigan, C. J., Burgess, S., Anthony, J. L., and Barker, T. A. 1998. Development of phonological sensitivity in 2- to 5- year old children. *Journal of Educational Psychology* 90:294–311.

McDougall, S., Hulme, C., Ellis, A. W., and Monk, A. 1994. Learning to read: the role of short-term memory and phonological skills. *Journal of Experimental Child Psychology* 58:112–33.

MacLean, M., Bryant, P. E., and Bradley, P. E. 1987. Rhymes, nursery rhymes and reading in early childhood. *Merrill-Palmer Quarterly* 33: 255–81.

Mann, V. A., Liberman, I. Y., and Shankweiler, D. 1980. Children's memory for sentences and word strings in relation to reading ability. *Memory and Cognition* 8:329–35.

Manis, F., Seidenberg, M., and Doi, L. 1999. See Dick RAN: Rapid naming and the longitudinal prediction of reading subskills in first and second graders. *Scientific Studies of Reading* 3:129–57.

Maughan, B. 1994. Behavioral development and reading disabilities. In *Reading Development and Dyslexia*, eds. C. Hulme and M. Snowling. London: Whurr.

Maughan, B. 1995. Long-term outcomes of developmental reading problems. *Journal of Child Psychology and Psychiatry* 36:357–71.

Muter, V., Hulme, C., and Snowling, M. 1997. *The Phonological Abilities Test, PAT*. London: The Psychological Corporation.

Muter, V., Hulme, C., Snowling, M., and Taylor, S. 1998. Segmentation, not rhyming predicts early progress in learning to read. *Journal of Experimental Child Psychology* 71:3–27.

Muter, V., and Snowling, M. 1998. Concurrent and longitudinal predictors of reading: The role of metalinguistic and short-term memory skills. *Reading Research Quarterly* 33:320–37.

Muter, V., Snowling, M., and Taylor, S. 1994. Orthographic analogies and phonological awareness: Their role and significance in early reading development. *Journal of Child Psychology and Psychiatry* 35:293–310.

Nation, K., and Snowling, M. 1998. Contextual facilitation of word recognition: Evidence from dyslexia and poor reading comprehension. *Child Development* 69:996–1011.

Olson, R., Wise, B., Connors, F., Rack, J., and Fulker, D. 1989. Specific deficits in component reading and spelling skills: Genetic and environmental influences. *Journal of Learning Disabilities* 22:339–49.

Olson, R., Wise, B., Johnson, M., and Ring, J. 1997. The etiology and remediation of phonologically based word recognition and spelling disabilities: Are phonological deficits the "hole" story? In *Foundations of
Reading Acquisition and Dyslexia*, ed. B. Blachman. Mahwah, NJ:
Lawrence Erlbaum Associates.

Perfetti, C., Beck, I., Bell, L., and Hughes, C. 1987. Phonemic knowledge
and learning to read are reciprocal: A longitudinal study of first grade
children. *Merrill-Palmer Quarterly* 33:283–319.

Rack, J. P., Hulme, C., Snowling, M., and Wightman, J. 1994. The role of
phonology in young children's learning of sight words: The direct
mapping hypothesis. *Journal of Experimental Child Psychology* 57:42–71.

Rack, J.R., Snowling, M., and Olson, R. 1992. The nonword reading deficit
in developmental dyslexia: A review. *Reading Research Quarterly*
27:29–53.

Raz, I.S., and Bryant, P.E. 1990. Social background, phonological awareness and children's reading. *British Journal of Developmental Psychology*
8:209–25.

Rohl, M., and Pratt, C. 1995. Phonological awareness, verbal working
memory and acquisition of literacy. *Reading and Writing* 7:327–60.

Sawyer, D. 1987 *Test of Awareness of Language Segments. TALS.* Austin,
Texas: PRO-ED.

Scarborough, H. 1990. Very early language deficits in dyslexic children.
Child Development 61:1728–43.

Scarborough, H. 1991. Antecedents to reading disability: Preschool language development and literacy experiences of children from dyslexic
families. *Reading and Writing* 3:219–33.

Scarborough, H., and Dobrich, W. 1994. On the efficacy of reading to
preschoolers. *Developmental Review* 14:245–302.

Schneider, W., and Naslund, J.C. 1993. The impact of metalinguistic competencies and memory capacity on reading and spelling in elementary
schools: Results of the Munich longitudinal study on the genesis of individual competencies (LOGIC). *European Journal of Psychology of
Education* 8:273–87.

Senechal, M. LeFevre, J., Thomas, E., and Daley, K. 1998. Differential effects of home literacy experiences on the development of oral and written language. *Reading Research Quarterly* 33:96–116.

Seymour, P.H.K., and Duncan, L. 1997. Small versus large unit theories of
reading acquisition. *Dyslexia* 3:125–34.

Snowling, M. 1995. Phonological processing and developmental dyslexia.
Journal of Research in Reading 18:132–38.

Snowling, M. Chiat, S., and Hulme, C. 1991. Words, nonwords and
phonological processes: Some comments on Gathercole, Ellis, Emslie
and Baddeley. *Applied Psycholinguistics* 12:369–73.

Snowling, M., Stothard, S., and McLean, J. 1996. *The Graded Nonword
Reading Test.* Bury St Edmunds, UK: Thames Valley Test Co.

Stanovich, K. E., Cunningham, A. E., and Cramer, B. B. 1984. Assessing
phonological processes in kindergarten children: Issues of task comparability. *Journal of Experimental Child Psychology* 38:175–90.

Stuart, M. 1990. Processing strategies in a phoneme deletion task.
Quarterly Journal of Experimental Psychology 42:305–27.

Stuart, M., and Masterson, J. 1992. Patterns of reading and spelling in 10-
year-old children related to pre-reading phonological abilities. *Journal
of Experimental Child Psychology* 54:168–87.

Tabachnick, B., and Fidell, L. 1989. *Using Multivariate Statistics.* New York: Harper Collins.

Torgesen, J., and Bryant, B. 1994. *Test of Phonological Awareness, TOPA.* Austin, Texas: PRO-ED.

Treiman, R., Weatherston, S., and Berch, D. 1994. The role of letter names in children's learning of phoneme-grapheme relationships. *Applied Psycholinguistics* 15:97–122.

Tunmer, W. E. 1989. The role of language-related factors in reading disability. In *Phonology and Reading Disability: Solving the Reading Puzzle,* IARLDM eds. D. Shankweiler and I. Y. Liberman. Ann Arbor: University of Michigan Press.

Tunmer, W. E., and Chapman, J. W. 1998. Language prediction skill, phonological recoding, and beginning reading. In *Reading and Spelling: Development and Disorders,* eds. C. Hulme and R. M. Joshi. Mahwah, NJ: Erlbaum and Associates.

Tunmer, W. E., and Hoover, W. A. 1992. Cognitive and linguistic factors in learning to read. In *Reading Acquisition,* eds. P. B. Gough, L. C. Ehri and R. Treiman. Hillsdale NJ: Erlbaum Associates.

Wagner, R. K., and Torgesen, J. K. 1987. The nature of phonological processing and its causal role in the acquisition of reading skills. *Psychological Bulletin* 101:192–212.

Wagner, R. K., Torgesen, J. K., and Rashotte, C. A. 1994. The development of reading- related phonological processing abilities: New evidence of bi-directional causality from a latent variable longitudinal study. *Developmental Psychology* 30:73–87.

Wagner, R. K., Torgesen, J. K., and Rashotte, C. 1999. *Comprehensive Test of Phonological Processing, CTOPP.* Austin, TX: PRO-ED.

Wagner, R. K., Torgesen, J. K., Rashotte, C. A., Hecht, S. A., Barker, T. A., Burgess, S. R., Donahue, J., and Garon, T. 1997. Changing relations between phonological processing abilities and word-level reading as children develop from beginning to skilled readers: A 5-year longitudinal study. *Developmental Psychology* 33:468–79.

Walley, A. C. 1993. The role of vocabulary development in children's spoken word recognition and segmentation ability. *Developmental Review* 13:286–350.

Wechsler, D. 1992. *Wechsler Intelligence Scale for Children* III. UK. London: The Psychological Corporation, Harcourt Brace.

Wechsler, D. 1993. *Wechsler Objective Reading Dimensions, WORD.* London: Psychological Corporation, Harcourt Brace.

White, K. R. 1982. The relation between socioeconomic status and academic achievement. *Psychological Bulletin* 91:461– 81.

Willows, D., and Ryan, E. 1986. The development of grammatical sensitivity and its relationship to early reading achievement. *Reading Research Quarterly* 21:253–66.

Wimmer, H., Landerl, K., and Schneider, W. 1994. The role of rhyme awareness in learning to read a regular orthography. *British Journal of Developmental Psychology* 112:469–84.

Yopp, H. 1988. The validity and reliability of phonemic awareness tests. *Reading Research Quarterly* 23:159–77.

Chapter • **2**

Do Preschool Orthographic Skills Contribute to Prediction of Reading?

Nathlie A. Badian

THE SEARCH FOR ACCURACY IN PRESCHOOL PREDICTION OF READING

In early prediction studies, a source of frustration has been the low success rate in identifying which individual children are likely to have a reading disability later (Badian 1988a; Scarborough 1998a). As has often been stressed, it is relatively easy to predict good reading, but whatever the predictive measures used, there is almost always a substantial proportion of children who appear at risk as preschoolers, but develop adequate reading skills (false positives), and other children who do not appear to be at risk but nevertheless turn out to be poor readers (false negatives). Two of the pioneers in early predictive research pointed out nearly 30 years ago that no predictive test battery is likely to identify every failing reader, and a predictive battery will also pick up as false positives children who succeed in later reading (Jansky and de Hirsch 1972). Recently, Scarborough (1998a) reviewed studies that attempted to predict the later reading skills of (mainly) kindergarten children. In her summary, Scarborough reported that, in the studies reviewed, 22% of children who developed reading disability were not initially classified as at risk, and 45% meeting risk criteria did not become disabled readers. This pattern of classification error was found to be quite similar across studies. In a recent study, not reviewed by Scarborough, all first grade poor readers were identified by a set of three kindergarten predictors, but 65% of the children low on the set of predictors were good readers at follow up (O'Connor and Jenkins 1999).

Unfortunately, many excellent predictive studies, often involving large numbers of children, provide us only with the tantalizing information that comes from correlation coefficients and regression analyses (e.g., Share et al. 1984; Vellutino and Scanlon 1987). Although correlation coefficients and regression analyses showing a strong relationship between preschool or kindergarten measures and later reading indicate that specific measures or sets of measures are useful predictors, they do not provide usable information for the practitioner, as they do not tell us how many good readers did well on a predictor and how many poor readers scored low on it.

Over a decade ago, Satz and Fletcher (1988) wrote that preschool screening had not improved significantly in the previous decade, with lack of predictive validity, in particular, cited as one of the most frequent problems. They pointed out that a typical correlation of .30 to .60 between a predictive test and the outcome variable is hardly impressive and stressed that such a correlation says virtually nothing about whether and how the predictor can be used clinically on an individual basis. Their recommendation that predictive outcome should be presented in a 2 x 2 array (Meehl and Rosen 1955), in which individual children are classified as valid or false, positives or negatives, has too often been ignored even in the following decade.

In order to use a 2 x 2 array, it is necessary to define risk and non-risk categories in reference to the pre-reading measures administered. At follow up, when the reading outcome measures are administered, poor reading must be precisely defined. After entering the numbers of individual children into each of the four categories in the array, the sensitivity, specificity, etc. of the predictors can be calculated. A retrospective method of obtaining data for the 2 x 2 array uses discriminant function analysis to determine the best set of predictors to separate good and poor readers (Badian 1994a, 1998a; Felton 1992; O'Connor and Jenkins 1999). Multiple regression analysis may indicate the set of variables that predicts reading most effectively.

In a series of predictive studies in which I followed several cohorts of children from preschool to grades 3, 6, or 8 (Badian 1982, 1986, 1988a, 1988b, 1990) the trend was toward over-identification of children as at risk for later reading problems. The percentages of poor readers who were misclassified as not at risk was more variable. As reported by Scarborough (1998a), such predictive misclassifications are typical of most studies. Thus, predicting which individual preschool children will be good or poor readers is a risky and often discouraging undertaking.

In attempts to improve individual prediction, I included personal and familial characteristics with the preschool measures (Badian 1986, 1988a, 1988b, 1990). In another approach toward improving accuracy of prediction, I added tests, believed to be closely related to reading, to the predictive battery, and eliminated others that showed little or no relationship to reading (Badian 1994a, 1998a). Added to the predictive battery were tests of serial naming speed (RAN Objects: Denckla and Rudel 1974), phonological awareness (syllable counting: adapted from Mann and Liberman 1984), and orthographic processing (visual matching). The orthographic processing task had been created for the battery a few years before, but after the follow-up studies reported earlier (Badian 1982, 1986, 1988a, 1988b, 1990).

SERIAL NAMING SPEED AS A PREDICTOR AND CORRELATE OF READING

Although serial naming speed has often been classified as a phonological measure, there is substantial evidence that it contributes to reading independently of phonological awareness (e.g., Bowers and Swanson 1991; Felton and Brown 1990; Manis, Seidenberg, and Doi 1999). The serial naming tests that researchers have found to have the most robust association with reading are tests of symbol naming speed (letters, numbers) (Badian et al. 1990; Bowers and Swanson 1991; Davis and Spring 1990; Felton 1992; Wolf 1991; Wolf, Bally, and Morris 1986). However, in a study of dyslexic children, chronological age controls and reading age controls, the only naming speed measure on which dyslexic children were significantly slower than younger reading-age controls was naming of pictured objects (Fawcett and Nicolson 1994).

There is less evidence for the role played by object naming speed in the prediction of reading. In general, in predictive studies of kindergarten children in which both symbol naming and object naming speed tests have been included, object naming speed has had lower correlations with reading in grades 1 to 4 than letter or number naming speed (Badian et al. 1990; Felton 1992; Wolf, Bally, and Morris 1986). Felton (1992) found that when IQ and age were partialled out, kindergarten object naming speed correlated insignificantly with composite reading vocabulary/reading comprehension at grade 3 level, in contrast to other naming speed tests. Wolf (1991) stresses that although symbol naming speed is strongly related to word recognition, object naming speed has a relatively strong relationship with reading comprehension.

Naming speed may have a stronger association with poor reading than with good reading, both concurrently and predictively (Badian 1993a; Felton and Brown 1990; McBride-Chang and Manis 1996; Meyer et al. 1998; Scarborough 1998b). In a one-year follow up of 81 kindergarten children at risk for reading disability, object naming speed was a significant predictor of word reading, even with IQ partialled out (Felton and Brown 1990). In a study of 170 children referred for an evaluation (mean age 7.9 years), the majority of whom were poor readers, object naming speed entered a regression first (23% of concurrent variance) for reading comprehension, ahead of IQ, phoneme awareness, other naming speed tests, and a measure of orthographic processing (Badian 1993a). Letter naming speed contributed most variance to word identification. Object and letter naming speed were among the strongest differentiators of good and poor readers. In a study of 55 children followed from grades 2 to 8, Scarborough (1998b) found that second grade object naming speed added significantly to prediction of eighth grade reading for disabled readers, but literacy scores were the best predictors of later reading for nondisabled readers. In a predictive study of both a random sample of 154 children and a sample of 64 very impaired readers, who were given a battery of tests at third grade level and followed up at grades 5 and 8, naming speed had predictive power only for poor readers (Meyer et al. 1998). The findings were interpreted as suggesting that impaired readers are qualitatively different from normal readers and that it is the automaticity of retrieval, not the knowledge of the names, that accounts for the predictive power of rapid naming.

In spite of the evidence that rapid naming of letters and numbers generally predicts reading, and word reading in particular, better than rapid naming of objects, it is not feasible to include tests of symbol naming speed in a battery for preschool children, as many of them cannot name letters or numbers, and not all of them can name colors accurately. For this reason, rapid naming of objects was the only naming speed test added to the test battery to improve prediction of reading.

PHONOLOGICAL AWARENESS AS A PREDICTOR OF READING

There is a voluminous amount of literature showing that phonological awareness, and especially awareness of phonemes, is a strong predictor of reading, and may have a causal relationship to reading (e.g., Elbro, Borstrøm, and Petersen 1998; Felton 1992; Jorm et al. 1986; Mann 1993; Muter 1994; Muter et al. 1997; Muter and Snowling 1998; O'Connor and Jenkins 1999; Share et al. 1984; Torgesen, Wagner, and Rashotte 1994; Torgesen et al. 1997; Vellutino and Scanlon 1987; Wagner and Torgesen 1987). Some of these studies also included tests of rapid naming.

Mann (1993) tested 100 kindergarten children and retested them one year later. The kindergarten measures included three tests of phoneme awareness. Scores on each test of phoneme awareness predicted 30% to 40% of variance in first grade reading. In another study, preschool children were tested on rhyming, phoneme segmentation, and letter naming and retested after one and two years of reading instruction (Muter 1994). After one year, both phoneme segmentation and letter naming made significant contributions to reading and spelling, but rhyming did not. After two years of reading instruction, phoneme segmentation and rhyming contributed to spelling, but not to reading. According to Muter's interpretation of this finding, once children have established the alphabetic principle, they use their increasing awareness of orthographic regularities to read words by visual-phonological connections. In another study, in which children were followed to age 9 years, phoneme deletion, nonword repetition, and letter knowledge at 5 and 6 predicted reading skills, but rhyming proved to be a poor predictor (Muter and Snowling 1998). Phoneme deletion at age 4 was also a poor predictor.

Elbro and his colleagues (1998), in a study of kindergarten children, half of whom were the children of dyslexic parents, gave a large battery of tests including several phonological measures, a picture naming speed test, and letter naming. The five strongest predictors of second grade reading difficulties were letter naming, initial phoneme deletion, phoneme identification, pronunciation accuracy, and distinctiveness of phonological representations. In a study in which a large battery that included several tests of phonological awareness and rapid naming was administered to 221 kindergarten children, the only measures that contributed to grade 3 reading were rapid naming of letters, general ability, and discrimination of initial consonants in words (Felton 1992). With general ability omitted, rapid naming of letters, discrimination of initial consonants, and auditory conceptualization predicted reading. In a recent study, three cohorts of children were tested in early and late kindergarten and in early first grade and reading was tested in late first grade (O'Connor and Jenkins 1999). Predictive measures included tests of phonological awareness, sound repetition, and rapid naming of letters. For cohorts 1 and 2 combined, rapid naming of letters had the highest kindergarten correlations with grade 1 word identification. Phoneme segmentation and rapid letter naming were the primary discriminators of reading disability. In a study of 200 children followed from second and third to fourth and fifth grade, rapid naming and phonological awareness were both strongly predictive of reading two years later (Torgesen et al. 1997). However, when prior levels of reading skill were included in the prediction, rapid naming no longer accounted for significant variance in later reading, although second and third grade phonological awareness did.

Although there is undisputed evidence that phoneme awareness is important in reading development in the early school years, its role and importance in later reading have been questioned (Scarborough et al. 1998). Scarborough and her colleagues presented data showing that mature readers may never have been aware of phonemes in words, and yet have reached high levels of reading achievement. Many predictive studies showing a relationship between phoneme awareness and later reading followed children to no later than about third grade or 9 years of age. An exception is Scarborough's (1998b) study, in which, in contrast to rapid naming, grade 2 phoneme deletion was only weakly related to eighth grade reading skill. In a study in which a cohort of children was followed to late sixth grade, first grade phoneme awareness had significant correlations with reading vocabulary and reading comprehension only from grades 1 to 3, although it continued to be related to spelling (Badian 1995).

As with tests of naming speed, there are limitations on the types of phonological measures that are appropriate for preschool children. Rhyme recognition is within the capabilities of preschool children, but Muter and her colleagues found that preschool ability to detect and produce rhymes was not predictive of later reading, although it did predict spelling (Muter 1994; Muter and Snowling 1998). Liberman et al. (1974) demonstrated that phonemic analysis was too difficult for preschool children. No preschool child, and only 17% of the kindergarten children they tested, was able to segment words by phonemes, though 46% of preschool children could segment by syllables. In a study of children followed from kindergarten to grade 1, kindergarten syllable counting had a significant correlation with first grade reading (Mann and Liberman 1984). However, in a later study of 221 children followed from kindergarten to grade 3, syllable counting was responsible for a nonsignificant amount of variance in reading, in contrast to phonological measures involving phonemes (Felton

1992). In their study of high-risk children, Felton and Brown (1990) found that syllable counting had a modest, but significant, correlation with word identification one year later, but with IQ partialled out, the correlation was no longer significant.

ORTHOGRAPHIC PROCESSING AS A PREDICTOR OF READING

An orthography refers to the system of marks that makes up a printed language, and orthographic processing or coding to the use of this system when processing written or oral language (Wagner and Barker 1994). In Adams' (1990) model of reading, the Orthographic Processor is the only processor that depends directly on print and, thus, reading is visually driven. When orthographic images are unstable, the establishment of reliable links to other processors (e.g., phonological) will be impeded (Adams and Bruck 1993).

Nearly ten years ago, Manis and his colleagues (1990) concluded that orthographic deficits may be an overlooked area of deficiency among dyslexic children. Yet, orthographic processing continues to be neglected in research, although interest appears to have increased in recent years (e.g., Berninger 1994, 1995). The neglect of orthographic processing is probably due to the strong evidence for the role of phonological awareness in reading skills. However, the difficulty in defining and measuring orthographic processing has probably contributed (Olson et al. 1994; Vellutino, Scanlon, and Tanzman 1994; Wagner and Barker 1994). A further factor contributing to the neglect may be confusion of orthographic processing with visual perception. Vellutino (1979) probably struck the death blow to visual perception as a predictor and correlate of reading, when he demonstrated that reading development depends primarily on linguistic factors.

If, as defined by Wagner and Barker (1994), an orthography is the system of marks that makes up a printed language, the stimuli for any measure of orthographic processing must be based on this system of marks, which includes letters, numerals, and punctuation marks. By contrast, the stimuli for tests of visual perception are generally nonalphabetic (e.g., geometric forms). Typical tests of orthographic processing involve homonyms: Which is a number: one, won? Which is the correctly spelled word: bote, boat? (See Olson et al. 1994). It is apparent that such tests cannot be attempted by children who have not yet learned to read and spell. These tests have been criticized by Vellutino, Scanlon, and Tanzman (1994) as evaluating word identification or spelling, rather than orthographic coding, as a basic cognitive ability that is common to both.

For all their limitations there is substantial evidence that performance on orthographic tests contributes to differences in reading ability, independently of phonemic awareness (Badian 1998b; Barker, Torgesen, and Wagner 1992; Bjaalid, Høien, and Lundberg 1996; Bråten et al. 1999; Cunningham and Stanovich 1998; Olson, Forsberg, and Wise 1994; Torgesen et al. 1997). As an example, in a series of hierarchical regression analyses Barker and his colleagues (1992) entered orthographic skills (two tests) into the analyses after age, IQ, and phonological ability (two tests). On each of five reading measures, administered to 87 third grade children, orthographic processing accounted for a significant independent proportion of the variance, though it played a stronger role in reading of text, than of isolated words. Other studies have demonstrated that dyslexic or reading disabled children do more poorly than normal readers on orthographic tasks (Badian 1998b; Hultquist 1997; Manis et al. 1990; Zecker 1991).

Stanovich (1992), quoting Ehri and Barron, stresses the importance of establishing accurate orthographic representations in memory. Ehri's research supports the view that in disabled readers there is an impairment in ability to store the visual representations of words in memory (e.g., Ehri and Saltmarsh 1995). Foorman (1994) states that insufficient attention to individual letters would seem to lead to incomplete or inaccurate "orthographic representations" and quotes Stanovich's (1992) proposal that overly global processing with insufficient attention to letters or groups of letters may underlie a deficit in forming orthographic representations. If orthographic imagery for single letters is unstable, the formation of automatic orthographic-phonological connections will be impeded (Badian 1997). The importance of establishing a strong network of orthographic-phonological connections has been stressed by several researchers (Adams and Bruck 1993; Berninger 1990; Bowers and Wolf 1993; Ehri 1992; Muter 1994).

The dilemma of how to measure orthographic processing skills is unresolved (Vellutino, Scanlon, and Tanzman1994; Wagner and Barker 1994). I (1993b, 1994b, 1996, 1997) argued that memory for the exact appearance and orientation of single letters and numerals (Jordan 1980) should be categorized as an orthographic test. This task does not require knowledge of word reading or spelling, although it is dependent on exposure to printed alphanumeric symbols. Strictly defined dyslexic children were significantly lower than non-dyslexic poor readers of much lower verbal IQ on this task (Badian 1994b, 1996, 1997). Although dyslexic children did not differ from reading-level (R-L) controls 2 years younger in the number of errors made, more than 2 times more dyslexic children than R-L controls had an orthographic deficit, based on age norms (Badian 1997). Their longer experience with print did not help dyslexic poor readers store reliable images of printed symbols. In a study of children diagnosed with reading problems at 6 to 8 years and followed up after a year or more of special help with reading, after IQ and age were accounted for, the best predictor of word identification was this simple orthographic measure (Badian 1993a). It surpassed phoneme awareness, naming speed, and confrontation naming.

Any task that is dependent on considerable experience with printed letters is not suitable for preschoolers. Yet, because of the evidence presented earlier that orthographic processing skills make an independent contribution to reading and that a deficit in orthographic processing may be an "overlooked" problem for dyslexic children (Manis et al. 1990), a predictive battery for prereaders should include an orthographic measure. The research batteries used to predict which prereaders are likely to develop a reading disability have seldom included a measure of early orthographic skills. An exception is an early predictive study (de Hirsch, Jansky, and Langford 1966; Jansky and de Hirsch 1972), which included Gates Matching Test. On this task the child has to find a match for a printed word. This matching task was one of the five variables that formed the final Predictive Index in the Jansky and deHirsch studies, and it entered the index in the third position.

The new test added to a preschool battery as a measure of incipient orthographic processing skills has letters and numerals, singly or in sequences of two to four, as its stimuli (Badian 1994a, 1998a). The child is asked to find a match for a target stimulus from four similar stimuli. This prereading test measures accuracy in observing, scanning, and processing "the system of marks that makes up a printed language," as orthography is defined by Wagner and Barker (1994).

FOLLOW-UP STUDIES OF THE REVISED PRESCHOOL TEST BATTERY

Preschool Measures

Preschool variables that will be included in the discussion of the follow ups at later grades are:

Preschool reading achievement (PRA). At the time the children were initially tested as preschoolers, parents were asked whether their child could read: Not at all, a few words, many words, books. Ratings were 1 (not at all) to 4 (books).

Socioeconomic status (SES). SES was determined from parental occupation, using a 5-point scale: 1 = professional; 2 = managerial, clerical, sales; 3 = skilled manual workers; 4 = unskilled manual workers; 5 = laborers.

Verbal IQ. Two subtests of the Wechsler Preschool and Primary Scale of Intelligence (WPPSI: Wechsler 1967), Information and Arithmetic, were converted into a short-form verbal IQ (VIQ), The validity coefficient of this short form is .83 (Sattler 1974, p.456). The norms in the WPPSI manual were used.

Language sample. the child tells a story about a picture. The story is scored by a language therapist on five attributes (vocabulary, syntax, prosody/fluency, articulation, mean length of utterance) using a 5-point scale for each attribute (0 = poor; 4 = superior).

Sentence memory. WPPSI Sentences (Wechsler 1967). The child repeats sentences after the examiner. Scoring was as indicated in the WPPSI manual.

Serial naming speed. RAN Objects (Denckla and Rudel 1974). The child names pictures of five common objects repeated in random order ten times in a 5 x 10 array. Scoring is based on the time taken.

Phonological awareness. Syllable counting (adapted from Mann and Liberman 1984). The child taps the number of syllables in ten words.

Orthographic processing. The child points to the one of four stimuli that matches the item on the extreme left of each row. The ten items are: u, d, j, bo, ((, 38, NAZ, 369, saw, drop. The response stimuli deviate from the target items mainly in sequencing or spatial orientation (e.g., droq, drop, borq, brop).

Untimed naming. The child names 13 upper case letters, shown one by one on cards, (Letter naming), and 8 common colors, demonstrated by crayons (Colors).

All test measures were converted to standard scores (M 100, SD 15), using the norms derived from the original group of 153 children given this battery as preschoolers. Verbal IQ was based on national norms, however.

Outcome Measures

In the spring of each year, the Stanford Achievement Test (SAT) (Psychological Corporation 1992) was administered to the children in their classrooms. The SAT subtests used in the follow-up studies were: Reading Vocabulary (Word Reading in grade 1), Reading Comprehension, Spelling, and Mathematics Computation (arithmetic). Individual achievement test scores were converted from national percentile ranks to standard scores (M 100, SD 15). Arithmetic was included to test the specificity of the predictors for reading/spelling.

Follow-up Study Including Orthographic Processing

The visual matching or orthographic task was administered to an earlier cohort of preschoolers, though not object naming-speed or the phonological task based on syllables (Badian 1995). With verbal IQ and age partialled out, orthographic matching had significant correlations with reading comprehension in grades 2 to 6, with spelling in grades 1 to 6, and with reading vocabulary in 3 of 4 years. Its highest partial correlation was with grade 6 reading comprehension ($r = .49$, $p < .001$). In this study, preschool untimed letter naming was a significant predictor of reading and spelling at every grade level. The continuing predictive power of the preschool orthographic task was in sharp contrast to that of first grade phonemic measures (phoneme deletion, phonological spelling), which had insignificant correlations with the two reading tests after grade 3.

Grade 1 Follow up Using the Revised Test Battery

The initial follow up of the revised preschool battery, which included the measures of orthographic processing, serial naming speed, and phonological awareness, took place after two years, when the children were in late first grade (Badian 1994a). In hierarchical regression analyses, in which each of the three added tests was entered in first, second, and third positions, all three accounted for a significant proportion of variance in word reading/ spelling and reading comprehension. When entered first, the orthographic task contributed the most variance to reading/spelling (32%) and naming speed to reading comprehension (19%). In further regression analyses, which included the other variables in the preschool battery, after preschool reading ability, verbal IQ, socioeconomic status (SES), and age were accounted for, the orthographic measure entered next for word reading/spelling (10% of variance), but sentence memory and letter naming contributed most to reading comprehension, with small, but significant amounts of variance added by naming speed and the orthographic task. The only variables on which each of three groups of readers differed significantly from one another when SES, preschool reading achievement, and verbal IQ were controlled, were the orthographic measure and letter naming (good > average > poor). The three variables shown by discriminant function analysis to separate poor readers from satisfactory readers most effectively were sentence memory, orthographic matching, and untimed color naming.

Because the predictive role played by orthographic matching in first grade word reading/spelling may be due to variations in print exposure in the preschool years, preschool readers were omitted in a comparison of the three groups of readers. Good readers (nonreaders as preschoolers) were significantly superior to average and poor readers on the orthographic task. With preschool letter naming ability controlled, orthographic matching continued to have significant correlations with reading measures. It was concluded that the ability to process printed alphanumeric symbols accurately facilitates reading acquisition, independently of experience with printed letters and numerals.

Follow up in Grade 2

I carried out a further follow up of the same cohort of children (Cohort 1) at the end of second grade and tested the validity of the findings by making a comparison with the following cohort of children (Cohort 2) in the same school district (Badian 1998a). After verbal IQ, preschool reading ability, SES, and age were partialled out, sentence memory accounted for the most variance in second grade reading vocabulary and reading comprehension for both cohorts, but letter naming, orthographic matching, and object naming speed accounted for significant variance in reading or spelling. The three variables selected by discriminant function analysis as the best discriminators of good and poor readers for both cohorts were the same as for Cohort 1 in first grade. Most poor readers in both cohorts were low on these three variables (85% to 90%), but of the children classified as at risk on the basis of the three variables, only 55% of Cohort 1 and 41% of Cohort 2 were poor readers in second grade. After following these preschool children to late second grade, I concluded that the phonological awareness task involving syllables was an ineffective predictor of reading and spelling.

Follow up of Cohort 1 to Seventh Grade

I have now followed Cohort 1 for 8 years: preschool to late seventh grade. Of the 118 children tested in first grade, 88 (39 boys, 49 girls) remained in seventh grade. All but two of the children continuing to seventh grade were white. Their mean age as preschoolers was 5.0 years (*SD* 0.3), and at the seventh grade follow up it was 13.0 years (range 12.6 to 13.6 years). Mean SES of the seventh grade group was 2.63 (*SD* 1.1) and mean preschool verbal IQ was 106.5 (*SD* 12.8).

The main aims of the seventh grade follow up were (1) to examine the predictive value over time of the three tests added to the preschool battery and (2) to predict individual persistent good and poor readers as accurately as possible.

As Cohort 1 has been followed for 8 years and given school achievement tests annually, hundreds of possible correlation coefficients can be generated. In order to show trends, the focus will be on three follow-up points in time: Grades 1, 4, and 7. The grade 1 results are based on the 98 children for whom at least 4 years of test scores were available from grades 1 to 6.

Simple correlation coefficients of the preschool variables with the achievement measures at grades 1, 4, and 7 are shown in table I.

Almost all preschool variables correlated significantly with the outcome measures, including arithmetic, at each grade level. For most predictors, the correlations were remarkably stable across the 6-year span from grades 1 to 7. The phonological task (syllable counting) correlated with reading vocabulary at approximately .4 at each grade level, which is the correlation Mann and Liberman (1984) found between kindergarten syllable counting and grade 1 word reading. Although the correlations of object naming speed with reading and spelling were very stable across the years, its correlations with arithmetic increased in the higher grades, with the result that by seventh grade object naming speed had the highest correlation with arithmetic of any variable. Verbal IQ tended to have higher correlations with reading and arithmetic at the two higher grades, while SES showed the reverse effect. With two exceptions (grade 1 language, grade 4 colors) all variables correlated significantly with arithmetic at each grade level, as well as with reading and spelling, indicating that no variable was a specific predictor of reading and spelling.

In stepwise regression analyses, in which only the preschool tests were included, the variables making the largest contributions to reading vocabulary at each grade level were letter naming and sentence memory, but the phonological measure contributed a

Table I. Correlations of Preschool Measures with School Achievement in Grades 1, 4, and 7.

| | School Achievement | | | | | | | | | | | |
| Grade Level Predictor | Reading Vocabulary | | | Reading Comprehension | | | Spelling | | | Arithmetic | | |
	1	4	7	1	4	7	1	4	7	1	4	7
PRA	.31**	.25*	.21*	.37	.27*	.27*	.29**	.35	.26*	.20*	.27**	.35
SES	-.40	-.33	-.26*	-.38	-.23*	-.23*	-.45	-.36	-.30**	-.22*	-.27**	-.32**
Verbal IQ	.47	.63	.57	.48	.65	.60	.46	.45	.46	.34	.56	.48
Sentences	.47	.63	.55	.50	.56	.50	.44	.38	.45	.25*	.41	.41
Language	.27**	.30**	.36	.30**	.26**	.34	.24*	.25**	.29**	.20ns	.23*	.32**
RAN Objects	.37	.34	.38	.45	.43	.39	.36	.37	.35	.34	.47	.50
Syllables	.40	.41	.36	.37	.38	.32**	.26**	.25*	.30**	.30**	.34	.35
Orthographic	.43	.41	.47	.44	.48	.49	.40	.40	.49	.41	.49	.49
Letter naming	.63	.56	.57	.59	.58	.55	.60	.51	.56	.41	.49	.42
Color naming	.25*	.40	.43	.34	.26**	.34**	.30**	.31**	.36	.25*	.18ns	.36

All variables are significant at $p < .001$, except where indicated: $*p < .05$, $**p < .01$, ns = nonsignificant.

PRA = preschool reading ability; SES = socioeconomic status.

small amount of significant variance at each grade level, the orthographic task at grade 1, and the language sample at grade 7. For reading comprehension, letter naming accounted for the greatest proportion of variance at each grade level, but sentence memory and the orthographic measure also added significant variance at each grade level, and object naming speed accounted for a significant proportion of variance at grades 1 and 4. Letter naming, sentence memory, and the orthographic task accounted for significant proportions of the variance in spelling at grades 1 and 7. At fourth grade level, the variables contributing to spelling were letter naming, object naming speed, and the orthographic task. For arithmetic, the orthographic measure entered the regression analysis first at grades 1 and 4, and object naming speed at grade 7. Letter naming contributed significantly at each grade level, in addition to naming speed and the orthographic task. Sentence memory accounted for significant variance only at grade 7 level. These results are given in table II.

Table II. Stepwise Regression Analyses: Preschool Tests Predicting School Achievement at Grades 1, 4, and 7.

	\multicolumn{8}{c}{School Achievement}							
	Reading Vocabulary		Reading Comprehension		Spelling		Arithmetic	
Grade	Predictor	R^2 added	Predictor	R^2 added	Predictor	R^2 added	Predictor	R^2 added
1							Ortho-graphic	.17***
	Letters	.39***	Letters	.35***	Letters	.36***	Letters	.07**
	Sentences	.08***	RAN Obj.	.12***	Sentences	.07***		
	Ortho-graphic	.04**	Sentences	.05*	Ortho-graphic	.03*	RAN Obj.	.04*
	Syllables	.02*	Ortho-graphic	.03*				
4							Ortho-graphic	.23***
	Sentences	.39***	Letters	.35***	Letters	.26***	Sentences	.11**
	Letters	.16***	Sentences	.15***	RAN Obj.	.08**		
	Syllables	.03*	Ortho-graphic	.07***	Ortho-graphic	.03*	Letters	.06**
			RAN Obj.	.02*			RAN Obj.	.04*
7	Letters	.33***	Letters	.30***	Letters	.33***	RAN Obj.	.25***
							Ortho-.graphic	.13***
	Sentences	.18***	Sentences	.16***	Sentences	.11***		
	Language	.03*	Ortho-graphic	.06**	Ortho-graphic	.05**	Letters	.05**
	Syllables	.03*					Sentences	.03*

*p < .05, **p < .01, ***p < .001

In further regression analyses, preschool age, verbal IQ, pre-school reading ability (PRA), and SES were entered first in that order. Mean achievement for grades 1 to 7 was also included in these analyses. For both reading measures, the three preschool variables that most consistently accounted for significant variance, after verbal IQ and the demographic measures were entered, were letter naming, sentence memory, and the orthographic test. However, naming speed also accounted for significant variance in reading comprehension (grade 1 and mean 1 to 7), and language for variance in both reading measures at grade 7 level and in the mean reading vocabulary. The phonological task contributed a small amount of variance in grade 7 reading vocabulary. Letter naming, sentence memory, and the orthographic task also contributed significantly to spelling (grades 1, 7, mean 1 to 7). At fourth grade level, naming speed, letter naming and the orthographic task added significant variance to spelling. After the four fixed variables, the only significant contributors to arithmetic were the orthographic task, naming speed, and letter naming, with naming speed entering first at grade 7 and for the mean score. The trend at all grade levels was for a negative relationship between age and school achievement, indicating that younger children tended to do better than older. After verbal IQ and age were entered, PRA accounted for a small proportion of variance in grade 1 reading, grade 4 spelling, and grade 7 reading comprehension, spelling, and arithmetic. Socio-economic status added significant variance in fourth position of entry to most aspects of achievement and at most grade levels. See tables III and IV for these regression analyses.

Discriminant Function Analyses to Determine the Best Predictors of Persistent Poor Reading

I defined persistent poor reading as mean scores (grades 1 to 6) more than one standard deviation below the mean of the group on at least two of the three reading/spelling subtests. Mean reading vocabulary, reading comprehension, and spelling scores were computed for each child for whom test scores were available for at least four of the years from grades 1 to 6 ($n = 98$). To reduce predictive error due to slow starters or late poor readers, a further criterion for persistent poor reading was low reading/spelling scores no later than grade 3, and also in grade 4 and later. Using these criteria, 14.3% (14/98) of Cohort 1 were poor readers. Although Cohort 1 was the focus of the follow-up study, I also studied the 91 children of Cohort 2, who had completed grade 5, to validate predictive findings from Cohort 1.

Table III. Regression Analyses: Preschool Variables Predicting Reading, with Demographic Variables and Verbal IQ Forced in First.

				Grade Level			
	1		4		7		Mean, Grades 1–7
	Predictor	R^2 added	Predictor	R^2 added	Predictor	R^2 added	Predictor	R^2 added
Outcome								
Reading								
Vocabulary	Age	−.01	Age	−.04*	Age	−.04	Age	−.02
	Verbal IQ	.21***	Verbal IQ	.36***	Verbal IQ	.29***	Verbal IQ	.38***
	PRA	.04*	PRA	.01	PRA	.01	PRA	.03*
	SES	−.07**	SES	−.03*	SES	−.04*	SES	−.03*
	Letters	.14***	Sentences	.09***	Letters	.09***	Sentences	.11***
	Sentences	.04**	Letters	.07***	Sentences	.08***	Letters	.06***
	Ortho-		Ortho-				Ortho-	
	graphic	.03**	graphic	.03*	Language	.03**	graphic	.04**
					Syllables	.02*	Language	.02*
Reading Comprehension								
	Age	−.01	Age	−.04**	Age	−.07*	Age	−.02
	Verbal IQ	.22***	Verbal IQ	.36***	Verbal IQ	.30***	Verbal IQ	.41***
	PRA	.07**	PRA	.01	PRA	.03*	PRA	.03*
	SES	−.05**	SES	−.04*	SES	−.02	SES	−.03*
							Ortho-	.10***
	Letters	.10***	Sentences	.09***	Letters	.08***	graphic	
	Sentences	.07***	Letters	.07***	Language	.05**	Sentences	.07***
			Ortho					
	RAN Obj.	.04**	graphic	.02*	Sentences	.03*	Letters	.05***
	Ortho-				Ortho-			
	graphic	.02*			graphic	.02*	RAN Obj.	.02*

*$p < .05$, **$p < .01$, ***$p < .001$

Mean grades 1–7 includes all 7 grades. PRA = preschool reading abilty; SES = socioeconomic status. The negative signs for Age and SES indicate that the relationship is in an inverse direction.

First, I examined the predictive power of the three most effective discriminators of good and poor readers in both cohorts at grade 2 level (sentence memory, orthographic processing, color naming). Using the score cutoffs established at that time (Badian 1998a), 20 of the 98 Cohort 1 children in the grade 6 follow up appeared at risk for poor reading. Thirteen of the 20 were persistent poor readers (65%), and 93% (13/14) of the persistent poor readers were valid positives (low on the predictors, low in reading). For Cohort 2, 11 of the 21 children (52%) classified as at risk by scores on the three preschool measures were persistent poor readers, and 85% (11/13) of the poor readers were valid positives. Predictive accuracy was 92% (Cohort 1) and 87% (Cohort 2).

Table IV.   Regression Analyses: Preschool Variables Predicting Spelling and Arithmetic, with Demographic Variables and Verbal IQ Forced in First.

| | Grade Level | | | | | | |
| | 1 | | 4 | | 7 | | Mean, Grades 1–7 | |
	Predictor	R^2 added	Predictor	R^2 added	Predictor	R^2 added	Predictor	R^2 added
Outcome								
Spelling								
	Age	−.01	Age	−.04	Age	−.04	Age	−.01
	Verbal IQ	.20***	Verbal IQ	.17***	Verbal IQ	.17***	Verbal IQ	.22***
	PRA	.03	PRA	.05*	PRA	.04*	PRA	.06**
	SES	−.11***	SES	−.04*	SES	−.05*	SES	−.06**
	Letters	.11***	Letters	.07**	Letters	.12***	Letters Ortho-graphic	.09***
	Sentences	.04*	RAN Obj.	.03*	Sentences	.06**	graphic	.04*
	Ortho-graphic	.02*	Ortho-graphic	.03*	Ortho-graphic	.04**	Sentences	.03*
Arithmetic								
	Age	.00	Age	−.04	Age	−.01	Age	.00
	Verbal IQ	.14***	Verbal IQ	.30***	Verbal IQ	.23***	Verbal IQ	.35***
	PRA	.01	PRA	.01	PRA	.06**	PRA	.04*
	SES	−.02	SES	−.02	SES	−.04*	SES	−.05**
	Ortho-graphic	.07**	Ortho-graphic	.09***	RAN Obj.	.07**	RAN Obj.	.09***
			RAN Obj.	.02	Ortho-graphic	.05**	Ortho-graphic	.06***
			Letters	.02*			Letters	.04**

*$p < .05$, **$p < .01$, ***$p < .001$

Mean grades 1–7 includes all 7 grades. PRA = preschool reading ability; SES = socioeconomic status. The negative signs for Age and SES indicate that the relationship is in an inverse direction.

I carried out further discriminant function analyses to determine which preschool variables would separate persistent good and poor readers most accurately. Sentence memory alone correctly classified 88% of Cohort 1. Adding letter naming increased accuracy to 95%, and orthographic processing to 97%. Only three children were incorrectly classified, and all were false negatives: that is, 3 of the 14 poor readers were incorrectly classified as not at risk. In a further follow up to grade 7, the same three variables gave almost identical results.

To validate this finding, I applied the same system of weighted scores generated by the computer in the discriminant function analysis to Cohort 2. The results for both cohorts are shown in table V. The percentage of children low on the three predictive tests who were poor readers was 1.00 for Cohort 1 (11/11) and .71 for Cohort 2 (10/14). The sensitivity, or percentage of poor readers who were identified by the predictors, was .79 (11/14) for

Table V. Accuracy in Classification of Persistent Good and Poor Readers in Cohorts 1 and 2 Based on Sentence Memory, Letter Naming, and Orthographic Processing.

| | Mean Reading (grades 1–6) | | | | | |
| | Cohort 1 | | | Cohort 2 | | |
Preschool predictors	Poor *n*	Good *n*	Total *N*	Poor *n*	Good *n*	Total *N*
Poor	11	0	11	10	4	14
Good	3	84	87	3	74	77
Total	14	84	98	13	78	91

	Cohort 1	Cohort 2
Misclassification rate:	3.1% (3/98)	7.7% (7/91)
False positive rate:	0.0% (0/11)	29.0% (4/14)
False negative rate:	21.0% (3/14)	23.0% (3/13)

Cohort 1 and .77 (10/13) for Cohort 2. The overall misclassification rates were 3.1% (3/98) for Cohort 1 and 7.7% (7/91) for Cohort 2, compared with 10.2% and 13.5% at the second grade follow up (Badian 1998a).

SUMMARY AND CONCLUDING REMARKS

A major aim of the study reported here was to see whether three tests added to a preschool battery would predict reading through late seventh grade level. Of particular interest was a measure of orthographic processing, because the role of orthographic processing in reading has been virtually ignored in preschool and kindergarten predictive batteries. I argued that the mounting evidence that orthographic problems contribute to the reading difficulties of some children suggests that early orthographic skills may add to the prediction of reading.

Although not as strong a predictor of reading as letter naming and sentence memory, with age, verbal IQ, preschool reading ability, and SES accounted for, the orthographic measure contributed a small, but significant proportion of the variance in reading and spelling at each grade level (1, 4, 7, mean 1 to 7), with only one exception. Orthographic processing was also one of the three variables that were the best discriminators of individual good and poor readers in grades 1 and 2 (Badian 1994a, 1998a), and of persistent good and poor readers (to grades 6 and 7). Preschool ability to observe similarities and differences in "the system of marks that makes up a printed language" (Wagner and Barker 1994) was a source of independent variance in reading. This finding is consistent with the literature which stresses that establishing accurate visual images or representations of letters and words in memory is an important factor in reading development (Ehri and Saltmarsh 1995; Foorman 1994; Stanovich 1992).

Because so few early predictive studies have included a measure of orthographic processing skills, there is little supporting evidence for the role of preschool orthographic measures in the prediction of reading. However, in a second grade follow up (Badian 1994a) and in the extended follow up reported here, the findings from the original cohort of children were applied to a second cohort from the same locality. The three best preschool discriminators (including orthographic processing) for Cohort 1 were nearly as effective in Cohort 2.

The phonological awareness measure included in this study involved syllables, because of the evidence that tasks involving phonemes are too difficult for preschool children. Although at the second grade follow up (Badian 1998a), I concluded that the syllable counting task was an ineffective predictor of reading, this task had significant correlations with reading and spelling in grades 1, 4; and 7, and added a small amount of significant variance to reading vocabulary in regression analyses. It can be concluded that preschool ability to segment syllables in words does add to prediction of reading vocabulary as much as eight years later, but that it is not a strong predictor. Determining which phonological tasks within the capabilities of preschoolers are the best predictors of reading requires further research.

Like the orthographic task, the phonological measure was overpowered by letter naming and sentence memory. Whether a specific variable contributes to prediction in multiple regression analyses depends in part on the power of the competing variables. Thus, a measure that is a fairly good predictor in one set of variables, may make no impact in another.

The third added measure, object naming speed, correlated significantly with the two reading measures and spelling at each grade level, with somewhat higher correlations with reading comprehension. It did not, however, add variance to reading vocabulary in any regression analysis, though it made some contributions to reading comprehension and spelling. Unexpectedly, object naming speed was a stronger predictor of arithmetic at grades 4 and 7 than of reading, accounting for 25% of the variance in seventh grade arithmetic. Skills involved in object naming speed may tap the demand for quick, automatic recall of stored numerical facts, which becomes greater in later arithmetic, or the relationship may lie in the need for speed and accuracy in scanning visual arrays.

In the study presented here, not only object naming speed, but all the preschool predictors, had significant correlations with arithmetic, as well as with reading and spelling. So none was specific to reading or spelling. Unfortunately few predictive studies have included outcome tests of arithmetic. Thus, it is not known whether the significant correlations of the predictors of this study with arithmetic are fairly universal or just a chance phenomenon. In one of the few studies to include arithmetic as an outcome measure, knowledge of letter names at ages 4, 5, and 6 was a significant predictor of arithmetic at 9, and so also was rhyme detection at ages 4 and 6, and phoneme deletion at age 5 (Muter and Snowling 1998). The nonspecificity of preschool predictors for reading should not come as a surprise, as many children with reading disability have a concomitant disability in arithmetic (Badian 1999). There is probably a common network of cognitive skills and learning mechanisms underlying both reading and arithmetic.

Another aim of this study was to predict, as accurately as possible, which individual children would be persistent poor readers from grades 1 to 6, and 1 to 7. The three preschool tests (sentence memory, orthographic processing, color naming) most effective in predicting second grade good and poor readers, also identified most persistent good and poor readers of both cohorts. However, many children showing a risk profile on the grade 2 criteria were persistent good readers (35%, 48%), although the percentages were lower than at second grade level. Greater accuracy for Cohort 1 was obtained through further discriminant analyses. The findings were then applied to Cohort 2. Sentence memory, letter naming, and the orthographic task classified 97% of Cohort 1 good and poor readers correctly and 92% of Cohort 2. For the combined cohorts, 84% of children with a risk profile on the three measures were persistent poor readers, and 78% of the poor readers were identified by the three measures.

The two preschool measures that added most to the prediction of reading at each grade level were letter naming and sentence memory. Both have a venerable history as predictors of reading and have frequently been among the small set of best predictors in preschool and kindergarten test batteries (e.g., Jansky and de Hirsch 1972; Share et al. 1984). This study also shows that, although not as strong a predictor of reading as letter naming and sentence memory, preschool orthographic ability contributes to prediction of reading and spelling. Like the other measures in the battery described here, orthographic ability also predicts arithmetic, and so can be considered useful as a generalized predictor of school achievement, but further validation of its usefulness is needed.

REFERENCES

Adams, M. J. 1990. *Beginning to Read: Thinking and Learning about Print.* Cambridge, MA: MIT Press.

Adams, M. J., and Bruck, M. 1993. Word recognition: The interface of educational policies and scientific research. *Reading and Writing: An Interdisciplinary Journal* 5:113–39.

Badian, N. A. 1982. The prediction of good and poor reading before kindergarten entry: A 4-year follow-up. *Journal of Special Education* 16:309–18.

Badian, N. A. 1986. Improving the prediction of reading for the individual child: A four-year follow-up. *Journal of Learning Disabilities* 19:262–69.

Badian, N. A. 1988a. Predicting dyslexia in a preschool population. In *Preschool Prevention of Reading Failure*, eds. R. L. and M. W. Masland. Parkton, MD: York Press.

Badian, N. A. 1988b. The prediction of good and poor reading before kindergarten entry: A nine-year follow-up. *Journal of Learning Disabilities* 21:98–103.

Badian, N. A. 1990. Background factors and preschool test scores as predictors of reading: A nine-year longitudinal study. *Reading and Writing: An Interdisciplinary Journal* 2:307–26.

Badian, N. A. 1993a. Predicting reading progress in children receiving special help. *Annals of Dyslexia* 43:90–109.

Badian, N. A. 1993b. Phonemic awareness, naming, visual symbol processing, and reading. *Reading and Writing: An Interdisciplinary Journal* 5:87–100.

Badian, N. A. 1994a. Preschool prediction: Orthographic and phonological skills, and reading. *Annals of Dyslexia* 44:3–25.

Badian, N. A. 1994b. Do dyslexic and other poor readers differ in reading-related cognitive skills? *Reading and Writing: An Interdisciplinary Journal* 6:45–63.

Badian, N. A. 1995. Predicting reading ability over the long term: The changing roles of letter-naming, phonological awareness, and orthographic processing. *Annals of Dyslexia* 45:79–96.

Badian, N. A. 1996. Dyslexia: A validation of the concept at two age levels. *Journal of Learning Disabilities* 29:102–12.

Badian, N. A. 1997. Dyslexia and the double deficit hypothesis. *Annals of Dyslexia* 47:69–87.

Badian, N. A. 1998a. A validation of the role of preschool phonological and orthographic skills in the prediction of reading. *Journal of Learning Disabilities* 31:472–81.

Badian, N. A. 1998b. The contributions of phonological and orthographic skills to reading. Poster session presented at the International Dyslexia Association conference, San Francisco, November.

Badian, N. A. 1999. Persistent arithmetic, reading, or arithmetic and reading disability. *Annals of Dyslexia* 49:45–70.

Badian, N. A., McAnulty, G. B., Duffy, F. H., and Als, H. 1990. Prediction of dyslexia in kindergarten boys. *Annals of Dyslexia* 40:152–69.

Barker, T. A., Torgesen, J. K., and Wagner, R. K. 1992. The role of ortho-
graphic processing skills on five different reading tasks. *Reading Research
Quarterly* 27:335–45.
Berninger, V. W. 1990. Multiple orthographic codes: Key to alternative in-
structional methodologies for developing orthographic-phonological
connections underlying word identification. *School Psychology Review*
19:518–33.
Berninger, V. W. (ed.) 1994. *The Varieties of Orthographic Knowledge, vol.1:
Theoretical and Developmental Issues.* Dordrecht, Netherlands: Kluwer.
Berninger, V. W. (ed.) 1995. *The Varieties of Orthographic Knowledge, vol.2:
Relationships to Phonology, Reading and Writing.* Dordrecht, Netherlands:
Kluwer.
Bjaalid, I. K., Høien, T., and Lundberg, I. 1996. The contribution of orthographic and phonological processes to word reading in young Norwe-
gian readers. *Reading and Writing: An Interdisciplinary Journal* 8:189–98.
Bowers, P. G., and Swanson, L. B. 1991. Naming speed deficits in reading
disability: Multiple measures of a singular process. *Journal of Experi-
mental Child Psychology* 51:195–219.
Bowers, P. G., and Wolf, M. 1993. Theoretical links among naming speed,
precise timing mechanisms and orthographic skill in dyslexia. *Reading
and Writing: An Interdisciplinary Journal* 5:69–85.
Bråten, I., Lie, A., Andreassen, R., and Olaussen, B. S. 1999. Leisure time
reading and orthographic processes in word recognition among
Norwegian third- and fourth-grade students. *Reading and Writing: An
Interdisciplinary Journal* 11:65–88.
Cunningham, A. E., and Stanovich, K. E. 1998. The impact of print expo-
sure on word recognition. In *Word Recognition in Beginning Literacy*, eds.
J. L. Metsala and L. C. Ehri. Mahwah, NJ: Erlbaum Associates.
Davis, J. M., and Spring, C. 1990. The Digit Naming Speed Test: Its power
and incremental validity in identifying children with specific reading
disabilities. *Psychology in the Schools* 27:15–22.
de Hirsch, K., Jansky, J., and Langford, W. 1966. *Predicting Reading Failure.*
New York: Harper and Row.
Denckla, M. B., and Rudel, R. 1974. Rapid "automatized" naming of pic-
tured objects, colors, letters and numbers in normal children. *Cortex*
10:186–202.
Ehri, L. C. 1992. Reconceptualizing the development of sight word reading and its relationship to recoding. In *Reading Acquisition*, eds. P. B.
Gough, L. C. Ehri, and R. Treiman. Hillsdale, NJ: Erlbaum Associates.
Ehri, L. C., and Saltmarsh, J. 1995. Beginning readers outperform older
disabled readers in learning to read words by sight. *Reading and Writing:
An Interdisciplinary Journal* 7:295–326.
Elbro, C., Borstrøm, I., and Petersen, D. K. 1998. Predicting dyslexia from
kindergarten: The importance of distinctiveness of phonological representations of lexical items. *Reading Research Quarterly* 33:36–60.
Fawcett, A. J., and Nicolson, R. I. 1994. Naming speed in children. *Journal
of Learning Disabilities* 27:641–46.
Felton, R. H. 1992. Early identification of children at risk for reading disabilities. *Topics in Early Childhood Special Education* 12:212–29.
Felton, R. H., and Brown, I. S. 1990. Phonological processes as predictors
of specific reading skills in children at risk for reading failure. *Reading
and Writing: An Interdisciplinary Journal* 2:39–59.

Foorman, B. P. 1994. Phonological and orthographic processing: Separate but equal? In *The Varieties of Orthographic Knowledge, vol.1*. Dordrecht, Netherlands: Kluwer.

Hultquist, A. M. 1997. Orthographic processing abilities of adolescents with dyslexia. *Annals of Dyslexia* 47:89–109.

Jansky, J., and de Hirsch, K. 1972. *Preventing Reading Failure*. New York: Harper and Row.

Jordan, B. T. 1980. *Jordan Left-Right Reversal Test*. Novato, CA: Academic Therapy Publications.

Jorm, A. F., Share, D. L., MacLean, R., and Matthews, R. 1986. Cognitive factors at school-entry predictive of specific reading retardation and general reading backwardness: A research note. *Journal of Child Psychology and Psychiatry* 27:45–54.

Liberman, I. Y., Shankweiler, D. Fischer, F. W., and Carter, B. 1974. Explicit syllable and phoneme segmentation in the young child. *Journal of Experimental Child Psychology* 18:201–12.

Manis, F. R., Seidenberg, M. S., and Doi, L. M. 1999. See Dick RAN: Rapid naming and the longitudinal prediction of reading subskills in first and second graders. *Scientific Studies of Reading* 3:129–57.

Manis, F. R., Szeszulski, P. A., Holt, L. K., and Graves, K. 1990. Variation in component word recognition and spelling skills among dyslexic children and normal readers. In *Reading and Its Development: Component Skills Approaches*, eds. T. H. Carr and B. A. Levy. San Diego: Academic Press.

Mann, V. A. 1993. Phoneme awareness and future reading ability. *Journal of Learning Disabilities* 26:259–69.

Mann, V. A., and Liberman, I. Y. 1984. Phonological awareness and verbal short-term memory. *Journal of Learning Disabilities* 17:592–99.

McBride-Chang, C., and Manis, F. R. 1996. Structural invariance in the associations of naming speed, phonological awareness and verbal reasoning in good and poor readers: A test of the double deficit hypothesis. *Reading and Writing: An Interdisciplinary Journal* 8:323–39.

Meehl, P. E., and Rosen, A. 1955. Antecedent probability and the efficiency of psychometric signs, patterns or cutting scores. *Psychological Bulletin* 52:194–216.

Meyer, M. S., Wood, F. B., Hart. L. A., and Felton, R. H. 1998. Selective predictive value of rapid automatized naming in poor readers. *Journal of Learning Disabilities* 31:106–17.

Muter, V. 1994. Influence of phonological awareness and letter knowledge on beginning reading and spelling development. In *Reading Development and Dyslexia*, eds. C. Hulme and M. Snowling. San Diego: Singular Publishing Group.

Muter, V., Hulme, C., Snowling, M., and Taylor, S. 1997. Segmentation, not rhyming, predicts early progress in learning to read. *Journal of Experimental Child Psychology* 65:370–96.

Muter, V., and Snowling, M. 1998. Concurrent and longitudinal predictors of reading: The role of metalinguistic and short-term memory skills. *Reading Research Quarterly* 33:320–37.

O'Connor, R. E., and Jenkins, J. R. 1999. Prediction of reading disabilities in kindergarten and first grade. *Scientific Studies of Reading* 3:159–97.

Olson, R. K., Forsberg, H., and Wise, B. 1994. Genes, environment, and the development of orthographic skills. In *The Varieties of Orthographic Knowledge vol.1*, ed. V. W. Berninger. Dordrecht, Netherlands: Kluwer.

Olson, R., Forsberg, H., Wise, B., and Rack, J. 1994. Measurement of word recognition, orthographic, and phonological skills. In *Frames of Reference for the Assessment of Learning Disabilities*, ed. G. R. Lyon. Baltimore, MD: Brookes.

Sattler, J. M. 1974. *An Assessment of Children's Intelligence.* Philadelphia: Saunders.

Satz, P., and Fletcher, J. M. 1988. Early identification of learning disabled children: An old problem revisited. *Journal of Consulting and Clinical Psychology* 56:824–29.

Scarborough, H. S. 1998a. Early identification of children at risk for reading disabilities: Phonological awareness and some other promising predictors. In *Specific Reading Disability: A View of the Spectrum*, eds. B. K. Shapiro, P. J. Accardo, and A. J. Capute, Timonium, MD: York Press.

Scarborough, H. S. 1998b. Predicting the future achievement of second graders with reading disabilities: Contributions of phonemic awareness, verbal memory, rapid naming, and IQ. *Annals of Dyslexia* 48:115–36.

Scarborough, H. S., Ehri, L. C., Olson, R. K., and Fowler, A. E. 1998. The fate of phonemic awareness beyond the elementary school years. *Scientific Studies of Reading* 2:115–42.

Share, D. L., Jorm, A. F., Maclean, R., and Matthews, R. 1984. Sources of individual differences in reading acquisition. *Journal of Educational Psychology* 76:1309–24.

Stanovich, K. E. 1992. Speculations on the causes and consequences of individual differences in early reading acquisition. In *Reading Acquisition*, eds. P. B. Gough, L. C. Ehri, and R. Treiman. Hillsdale, NJ: Erlbaum Associates.

Torgesen, J. K., Wagner, R. K., and Rashotte, C. A. 1994. Longitudinal studies of phonological processing and reading. *Journal of Learning Disabilities* 27:276–86.

Torgesen, J. K., Wagner, R. K., Rashotte, C. A., Burgess, S., and Hecht, S. 1997. Contributions of phonological awareness and rapid automatic naming ability to the growth of word-reading skills in second-to-fifth-grade children. *Scientific Studies of Reading* 1:161–85.

Vellutino, F. R. 1979. *Dyslexia: Theory and Research.* Cambridge, MA: MIT Press.

Vellutino, F. R., and Scanlon, D. M. 1987. Phonological coding, phonological awareness, and reading ability: Evidence from a longitudinal and experimental study. *Merrill-Palmer Quarterly* 33:321–63.

Vellutino, F. R., Scanlon, D. M., and Tanzman, M. S. 1994. Components of reading ability: Issues and problems in operationalizing word identification, phonological coding, and orthographic coding. In *Frames of References for the Assessment of Learning Disabilities*, ed. G. R. Lyon. Baltimore, MD: Brookes.

Wagner, R. K., and Barker, T. A. 1994. The development of orthographic processing ability. In *The Varieties of Orthographic Knowledge, vol.1*, ed. V. W. Berninger. Dordrecht, Netherlands: Kluwer.

Wagner, R. K., and Torgesen, J. K. 1987. The nature of phonological processing and its causal role in the acquisition of reading skills. *Psychological Bulletin* 101:192–212.

Wechsler, D. 1967. *Preschool and Primary Scale of Intelligence.* New York: Psychological Corporation.

Wolf, M. 1991. Naming speed and reading: The contributions of the cognitive neurosciences. *Reading Research Quarterly* 26:123–41.

Wolf, M., Bally, H., and Morris, R. 1986. Automaticity and retrieval processes, and reading: A longitudinal study in average and impaired readers. *Child Development* 57:988–1000.

Zecker, S. G. 1991. The orthographic code: Developmental trends in reading-disabled and normally achieving children. *Annals of Dyslexia* 41:178–92.

Chapter • **3**

Systematic Screening and Intervention for Reading Difficulty

Angela J. Fawcett and Roderick I. Nicolson

BACKGROUND: "SPECIAL EDUCATIONAL NEEDS" PROVISION IN THE UNITED KINGDOM

There is widespread concern over the literacy standards of children in Britain and North America, especially for those with special educational needs (SEN)[1]. Research suggests that the earlier such children can be identified, the more effective (and cost-effective) intervention will be, provided that the intervention is tailored to the child's abilities and skills. The problem confronting education providers is that, at least until recently, there was no systematic approach from early screening to proactive support. We have developed systematic procedures for identifying children at risk for reading difficulty, together with systematic teaching strategies to overcome reading difficulty. In this chapter, we describe the situation in Britain regarding the statutory requirements for assessment and support, and then outline the approach we have taken to achieve an effective and cost-effective screening→ assessment→support system. We describe the Dyslexia Early Screening Test (Nicolson and Fawcett 1996), and then studies adopting the screening/support technique, based on teaching in

---

[1]SEN is a UK term referring to "a learning difficulty which calls for special educational provision." It is somewhat broader than the US term "learning disabilities" in that it also includes children with visual, auditory, or motor disabilities.

small groups over a ten-week period. Finally the potential of this approach for pre-school children will be considered.

For many years it has been the dream of applied dyslexia researchers to develop a screening test that is able to identify children at risk for dyslexia before they fail to learn to read, that is, at 6 years or earlier. There is no doubt that, if feasible, such a screening procedure would be of immense help, in that a substantial body of evidence indicates that if children who are at risk of reading difficulty are given early support in pre-reading and reading-related skills such as phonological awareness, they can learn to read reasonably normally, though for dyslexic children continuing support is advisable (Bradley 1988; Lundberg, Frost, and Petersen 1988; Olson, Wise, and Rack 1989; Strag 1972). Yet, despite the clear value of early screening for dyslexia and despite excellent research in the area (see, for example, Scarborough 1991; Badian 1994; Pickering and Nicolson 1993) until recently there has been no acceptance of the viability of early screening. It is not possible within the constraints of this chapter to include a full review of the area, which is covered in detail in other chapters of this book (for reviews of the history see Horn and Packard 1985; Satz and Fletcher 1988; Badian et al.1990; and Jansky et al.1989). Here, an outline of the current situation in the United Kingdom must suffice.

In Britain, there has been a great deal of pressure on the government to implement change, leading to a system whereby children with SEN, who have different learning needs, can be identified and supported early. Children in the UK start school in the term in which their 5th birthday falls, and possibly as a "rising 5" enter the reception class at age 4.5 years. Starting in the year 2000, plans are afoot not only to introduce formal schooling from the age of 4.0, but also to formalize the nursery school curriculum to emphasize early literacy skills. Currently, the teaching of letter sounds begins in the first week of school, and by the second term it is expected that children will have an understanding of simple CVC words. All children would be expected to have their first reading book by the end of the first year, and many children will have "taken off" with their reading. Formal reading instruction is therefore in place in the UK considerably sooner than in the US, where it typically starts with 6-year olds in grade 1. Consequently, the UK regime provides good opportunities to identify problems in the first year of school (see Fawcett, Singleton, and Peer 1998 for a review of the area).

An important step forward in UK education has been provided by the UK Education Act (1993) and the subsequent Code of Practice on the Identification and Assessment of Special Educational Needs (Department for Education 1994), which clearly placed dyslexia on the mainstream school agenda. The Code of Practice provides a significant clarification in terms of identifying and supporting children with special educational needs of all types. The Code of Practice defines special educational needs as "a learning difficulty which calls for special educational provision" (2.1) and suggests (2.2) that around 20% of children will have special educational needs at some time, but the vast majority of these can be met by appropriate support within the child's school (plus outside help where necessary). This 20% will include children with a range of special educational needs, including those with generally low intelligence and those with physical and sensory disabilities, as well as those with specific learning difficulties (including dyslexia).

Although allowing considerable flexibility in its implementation, the Code advocates a five stage approach to identifying and supporting children with special educational needs. Initially it is the class teacher's responsibility to notice children with special needs and adapt the curriculum accordingly (Stage 1). If these support plans do not lead to progress, the school's SEN coordinator works with the class teacher (and, in secondary schools, with subject teachers) in drawing up an individual education plan (IEP) for the child specifying learning targets, teaching methods, resources, and then monitoring progress (Stage 2). At Stage 3 of the Code of Practice, external agencies are involved in the process. If the child continues to have very marked special educational needs, statutory assessment is considered (Stage 4). The assessment may then lead to a statement (Stage 5) that details the educational arrangements to be made and ensures ongoing support and monitoring. It is expected that around 2% will still be having problems despite the support offered in stages 1 to 3. Given that it is generally accepted that around 4% of the school population will be dyslexic (Badian 1984), and approximately 6% mildly/moderately dyslexic, it is clear that the implementation of the Code of Practice intends that only the most severe special educational needs require an assessment for a "statutory statement of special educational needs."

One of the key changes in the Code of Practice was that, for the first time in the UK, teachers were routinely required to identify children with difficulties and respond to their needs, thus avoiding the need for later statutory provision. In theory, this is a liberating development, facilitating immediate extra support for children who need it, and incurring the costs and delays inherent in the formal diagnosis by appropriately qualified educational psychologists only for the much smaller percentage of children who really need specialized support. In practice, however, many teachers were worried by the requirements of the Code of Practice. They were aware that they lacked the necessary expertise to identify children with dyslexia or other special educational needs. In addition, they did not have the resources to provide appropriate support for these children while teaching a class of thirty or more reception children.

EARLY SCREENING FOR DYSLEXIA

The 1994 Code of Practice was a breakthrough for the UK dyslexia community, not only in that dyslexia was explicitly included as a special educational need, but also because the stages in the Code represented strong advice given by ourselves and by Dr. Harry Chasty of the Dyslexia Institute among others as to how an effective assessment and support system could be instituted. Figure 1 shows in schematic form the relationship between an early suggestion of ours and the ensuing Code.

It may be seen that the first stage is labeled as screening. It is important to distinguish between screening—generally a quick, low cost, mass usage test administered by trained, but not specialized, personnel—and diagnosis, which is an intensive, individual test administered by a specialist. In the UK, diagnosis of dyslexia typically involves a full IQ test—the WISC-III (Wechsler 1991) or BAS II (Elliott 1996), an educational history, plus standardized tests of single word reading, comprehension, including speed and accuracy, and spelling. A test of free writing is frequently included, and more rarely, a personality test. A diagnosis of this type takes around 3 to 4 hours to complete. By contrast, a screening test should take no more than 30 minutes per child, and should be administered by a teacher or SEN co-ordinator or equivalent.

Requirements of a screening test

As with any psychometric test, screening tests should satisfy the three classic criteria of objectivity, reliability, and validity. However, because of the particular requirements of screening, there is a trade-off between the three classic criteria and the three constraints of quick administration, administration by non-specialists, and the need for a quantitative at-risk score. Two key aspects for any screening test are the "hit" rate (the percentage of really at-risk children who are screened as at risk) and the "false positive" rate (the percentage of really not at-risk children who are screened as at risk). An ideal screening instrument would have 100% hit rate and 0% false positive rate, but a more realistic target

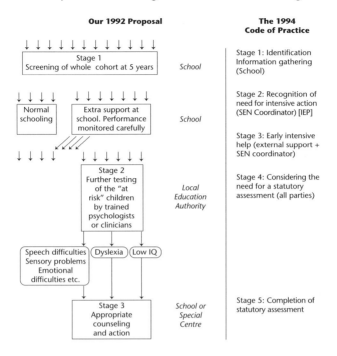

Figure 1.   Objective: systematic screening, assessment, and support

would be more like 85% hits and only 20% false positives[2]. Furthermore, given the intended use of screening tests as the first stage in the support process, the most useful screening tests are designed to quantify strengths as well as weaknesses.

It is much easier to predict which children are going to have strengths in literacy rather than those who are at risk. An excellent example of this derives from the meticulous approach of Badian (1994), which represents the insights resulting from her 15-year research program aimed at progressive refinement of her screening battery (see Badian 1982; 1986 for earlier work). This battery involved extensive specialized testing, and included three main categories of test: language, pre-academic, and visual motor. However, when the test was being developed, the seminal role of phonological skill had not yet been recognized. Subsequently, in order to improve the prediction of children with difficulties, Badian (1994)

---

[2]It should be noted that there is a trade-off between hits and false positives. Given any quantitative at-risk measure, one can increase the proportion of hits by relaxing the at-risk cutoff, but this will generally increase the proportion of false positives. Given that the likely distribution of at-risk scores for the population of schoolchildren is likely to be close to the normal distribution, relaxing the criterion too far will lead to a catastrophic increase in the proportion of false positives.

augmented her standard battery with tests of phonological awareness, naming speed, and orthographic processing. The addition of
the three new tests increased the success rate of the battery, accounting for 41% of the variance in reading/spelling at age 7. This
battery was good at identifying those children who were successful,
with an overall hit rate of 91%, but unfortunately, even with the
addition of the new tests, only 58% of the at-risk children did in
fact have reading difficulties at age 7. This is a problem common to
most screening tests, which can more easily identify children with
strengths, rather than pinpointing children with weaknesses.

It would appear, therefore, that even tests involving extensive
specialized testing (and therefore not ideal for large-scale screening)
are only moderately successful in identifying those children likely to
suffer from literacy difficulties. It is this rather disappointing cost effectiveness that dissuaded US education authorities from implementing large-scale screening procedures. Given the UK Code of Practice,
this was not an option open to UK educators—schools are required
(by whatever means) to identify children at risk of reading failure as
early as possible. In response to this problem a number of tests have
been developed in the UK (CoPS [Singleton 1995]; the Dyslexia Early
Screening Test [DEST] [Nicolson and Fawcett 1996]; Phonological
Assessment Battery [PhAB] [Frederickson, Frith, and Reason 1997];
and the Phonological Abilities Test [Muter, Hulme and Snowling
1996]). The DEST, which is described more fully in the following section, is the broadest conceptually of the above tests. It is a 30 minute
nationally normed test intended for use by teachers who are screening[3] children from 4.5 to 6.5 years, and that comprises a battery of
sub-tests selected to indicate likely reading failure.[4] The DEST leads to

---

[3]A conventional use of the term *screening* is to indicate "population screening," in which a short test is administered to all members of the population. In the
absence of a suitable alternative, we use *screening* here in a broader sense, to indicate relatively quick testing of some subset of the target population (such as those
children whose performance gives some cause for concern).

[4]The DEST comprises 11 sub-tests in five areas (literacy skills, phonological
awareness, verbal memory, motor skill and balance, and auditory processing). The
sub-tests are as follows. *Digit names* test knowledge of digits 1–9, *Letter names* tests
knowledge of 9 letters. *Rhyme* tests both for understanding of rhyme and of first letter
sounds; *Rapid naming* involves the time taken to speak the names of pictures on a
page full of common objects; *Discrimination* is the score on saying whether word pairs
such as "fuse" and "views" are identical. *Digit span* tests verbal memory for sequences
of digits. *Beads* is the number of beads threaded in 30 seconds; *Postural stability* reflects the degree of movement when pushed gently in the back; *Shape copying* tests
the accuracy of copying simple geometrical shapes. *Sound order* tests the ability to determine which of two sounds played shortly after each other was first. Scores on individual DEST sub-tests are -- (strong risk) for centiles 1 to 10, as in - (at risk) for centiles
11–25, o (average band) for centiles 26 to 75, as in + (above average) for centiles 76 to
90, and as in ++ (well above average) for centiles 91 to 100. The overall DEST score is
essentially the average of the scores on the individual sub-tests.

an at-risk index, together with a profile of strengths and weaknesses indicative of the appropriate types of support.

THE DYSLEXIA EARLY SCREENING TEST
(NICOLSON AND FAWCETT 1996)

Research Basis for the DEST

The key problem with any early screening test for literacy risk is that it is necessary to predict which children are likely to have problems with reading and literacy before they have been taught. Consequently, traditional methods for diagnosing dyslexia in terms of discrepancy between actual reading performance and that predicted on the basis of the child's intelligence cannot be applied. It is necessary, therefore, to develop a theoretical and pragmatic understanding of the likely precursors of the reading difficulties.

It is well established that lack of phonological awareness is one of the key precursors of reading difficulties (e.g., Bradley and Bryant 1983). However, it is also established that phonological awareness can be greatly improved by direct instruction, and consequently it is possible that if one relied only on phonological tests, some children would perform adequately but still have difficulties learning to read (they would therefore be missed in the screening) and some children would have poor phonological awareness through lack of experience, and so would turn out to be false positives. In developing the DEST, we considered it most appropriate to introduce a battery of tests, covering a range of skills, including skills not directly taught to pre-school children. In selecting the tests we relied heavily on skills known to be impaired in fully diagnosed (older) dyslexic children.

Recently, a wealth of evidence has been amassed about difficulties in a wide range of skills in dyslexia. This evidence is presented in detail in our edited book (Fawcett and Nicolson 1994, see the chapters by Rack, Stein, and Lovegrove). However, these investigations typically examined single skills with a small group of dyslexics and controls, and failed to indicate the relative severity of the deficits. In order to investigate this issue, therefore, a battery of tests was developed in our lab of every skill conceivable (over 50 tests for each child) including reading, spelling, phonological skill, motor skill, memory, speed of processing, and balance. Moreover, in order to check the effects of age, 8-, 12-, and 16-year-old matched dyslexic and control children were tested. The children with dyslexia performed significantly worse than the same-age controls on most tasks, and significantly worse even than their reading age controls on phoneme segmentation, picture naming speed, word flash (speeded reading), bead threading, blindfold balance, and dual task balance. Furthermore, 90% of the children with dyslexia showed marked impairments (performance at least one standard deviation below that of the controls) on at least two out of three tasks (dual task balance, segmentation, and picture naming speed) chosen to span the range of skills (see Nicolson and Fawcett 1994 for full details). Given that many of these skills are not directly taught at school, there seemed good reason to expect that many of them would also be useful predictors of dyslexia at age 5, and so they formed the basis of the battery of tests used in the prototype versions of the DEST.

Naturally the emphasis in designing the DEST was on the inclusion of tests on which there is a consensus in the research community. Our primitive skills testing confirmed the presence of severe phonological difficulties in the dyslexic panels, in line with a wealth of evidence of the importance of phonological skill in early reading (see Fowler 1991 for a review of the area, and Bradley and Bryant 1983; Hatcher, Hulme, and Ellis 1994; Rack 1985). Nevertheless, we were eager to augment our primitive skills tests with recent theoretical developments in dyslexia. Therefore tests of phonological skill, memory, knowledge, and motor skill were augmented by two further types of tests; tests of cerebellar function and tests of temporal order. Tests of cerebellar function were derived from research in our lab, based on the hypothesis that mild cerebellar dysfunction may underlie many dyslexic deficits (Fawcett, Nicolson, and Dean 1996; Nicolson and Fawcett 1999). Tests of temporal order (Tallal, Miller, and Fitch 1993), were based on the proposal that difficulties in rapid temporal processing of auditory information may underlie the phonological difficulties shown by dyslexic children.

DEST Sub-tests, Scoring and Interpretation

The above analysis led to the construction of the Dyslexia Early Screening Test that was designed to identify children at risk of failure and to produce a profile of performance which provides pointers to remedial intervention. The intention was that the tests adopted would cover a sufficiently wide range of skills in which our team and other researchers had found impairment, to give positive indicators of difficulty. Naturally, the tests selected (see table I) were based on those with the greatest severity and highest incidence in the general population of children with dyslexia (Nicolson and Fawcett 1994). We chose to augment tests of

Table I. Sub-tests in the Dyslexia Early Screening Test

	Test	Description
Test 1	Rapid Naming	Time taken to name 40 simple outline pictures. This is a version of the 'Rapid Automatized Naming' procedure (Denckla and Rudel, 1976)
Test 2	Beads	Number of beads threaded in 30 seconds
Test 3	Phonological Discrimination	Ability to detect subtle differences in spoken words (such as *fin vs thin*). Early versions of this test were based on those developed by Bishop (1985).
Test 4	Postural Stability	How much the child wobbles when pushed gently in the back with a calibrated testing device. Standard test of cerebellar function (balance). Evidence for cerebellar abnormality in dyslexia was established in Fawcett, Nicolson, and Dean (1996).
Test 5	Rhyme detection/ alliteration.	Ability to decide whether or not two spoken words rhyme, and to identify the first sound in a word. Both standard tests of phonological awareness. This test is a simplified form of that developed by Bradley and Bryant (1983).
Test 6	Digit Span	The ability to recall a series of digits in the order spoken. A test of working memory. A standard component of many IQ tests, for example the WISC (Wechsler 1991).
Test 7	Digits	Ability to name individual digits. A straightforward test of knowledge.
Test 8	Letters	Ability to name individual letters
Test 9	Sound order	Ability to decide which of two sounds was presented first, as the time between onset of the two is steadily decreased. Paula Tallal first suggested that language disordered children might have difficulties in deciding tone order in Tallal (1984).
Test 10	Shape copying	Ability to copy a series of shapes. Badian (1994).

phonological skill with tests of clumsiness, on the basis of research in our lab (Fawcett, Nicolson, and Dean 1996), as outlined above. The choice of tests has also been tuned to the requirements of the Code of Practice, (3.60-3.63). A key requirement is that "there is clear, recorded evidence of clumsiness, significant difficulties of sequencing or visual perception; deficiencies in working memory; or significant delays in language functioning" (3:61iii)—the statutory requirements for the initial stages in statementing.

It should also be noted that, its name notwithstanding, the DEST was also designed to screen for learning difficulties of all types, including language delay and general intellectual impairment, as well as specific learning difficulties, in particular dyslexia.

Norm collection

Over 100 schools nation-wide piloted the prototype DEST, evaluating the tests for ease of administration, and returning their data and comments to us. On the basis of these comments, modifications were made to the instructions, and tests of muscle-tone and processing speed were omitted from the final version. These two tests were omitted because they proved particularly difficult for teachers to administer, and required complex equipment. Each sub-test was designed to be fun, to take no more than a couple of minutes to administer, and to include a practice to ensure the child understood what was required. Phonological skills included phonological discrimination (after Bishop 1985), rhyming (a simplified version of Bradley and Bryant 1978, 1985), and alliteration. Speed tests included rapid automatized naming (Denckla and Rudel 1976); the motor skill tasks were bead threading and copying; and the test of cerebellar function (Fawcett, Nicolson, and Dean 1996) was postural stability (the degree of imbalance caused by a gentle push in the back). The knowledge tests were digit and letter naming. In addition, the test was augmented with a simplified version of the Tallal sound order test (Tallal, Miller, and Fitch 1993), adapted by us for use with younger children to be based on judging the order of a mouse squeak and a duck quack. Each sub-test may provide an independent positive indicator of dyslexia, but it is recommended that the profile as a whole be used to indicate whether or not a child is at risk of failure.

The scoring procedure allows the tester to identify each child at risk, without further reference to psychological expertise. It follows the simple but clear positive indicator system introduced by Miles in the Bangor Dyslexia Test (1982). Age-based norms were determined such that on each sub-test a child is scored either "– –", "–", "0", "+" or, "++." The individual scores for each sub-test may then be combined to derive an at-risk quotient (ARQ) for each child. An ARQ of 0.9 or greater is strong evidence of a child's being at risk, and an ARQ of 0.6 or greater is mild evidence of risk. At-risk children may then be referred to educational psychologists for full psychometric assessment of their needs. A skyline or profile chart may also be completed from the DEST which allows the pattern of the positive indicators of difficulty to be highlighted. This leads to suggestions for remediation, forming an Individual Education Plan (IEP), as specified in the Code of Practice. At-risk areas such as rhyming suggest possible remediation work, while digit span weakness suggests possible memory difficulties, and discrimination weakness may suggest hearing problems. Other areas of weakness, such as cerebellar impairments are less directly related to school work but may be useful for diagnosis rather than remediation.

An example of the DEST in use is presented in figure 2. This is based on a child aged 5:6 whose parents were concerned for his progress following a head injury that led to language delay and lethargy for a period. The Rapid Naming time was 66 seconds, which was looked up in the table of norms for 5:6 leading to an index of 0 (normal band). By contrast, the phonological discrimination score was only 5, which is no better than chance, leading to an index of double minus. The DEST results confirm the need for concern, with three tests scoring double minus, and five tests scoring minus, leading to an at-risk quotient of 1.1, which indicates strong risk. The profile indicates that support is needed in language and motor skills, and the particularly poor scores on discrimination and sound order suggest the need for further assessment of hearing.

The value of the approach was assessed by asking the teachers involved to comment on how well the children picked out as

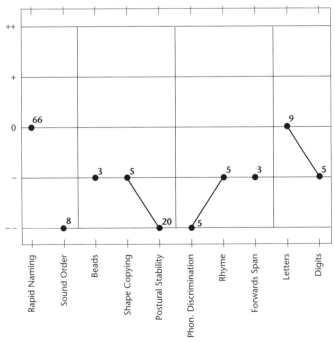

Figure 2.   Case Study of the DEST from *Annals of Dyslexia* 1998 based on Fawcett, Singleton, and Peer with permission of the International Dyslexia Association, July 24, 2000

at risk corresponded to their own prior judgements. Nineteen schools, who contributed data to the norms, completed and returned an informal questionnaire. Interestingly, all those participating considered that the approach was potentially valuable, and many commented that for some children, the DEST confirmed and strengthened the teacher's judgements, and, for other children, it alerted the teachers to problems that they had not noticed. On a scale of 1 to 4, where 1 = not useful and 4 = extremely useful, the DEST was allocated a mean score of 3.33. Eighty five percent of the teachers sampled in this questionnaire also found the test useful in revealing areas of difficulty for their children generally, as well as more profound problems for children with special educational needs. The + and ++ categories allow testers to identify areas of strength as well as weakness, which proved particularly useful in schools where the caliber of the intake is generally low, allowing those children with strengths to receive appropriate support to achieve their potential. Furthermore, the tests appeared to be well-judged for the children participating, in that the teachers' feedback indicated that few children suffered anxiety in doing the tests, most children had no difficulty completing the tests in one session, and both children and teachers enjoyed taking part. Feedback from the many schools participating in norm collection suggests that over 90% would like to see the DEST introduced as routinely as the current eye-test. The DEST was published in spring 1996, and has been normed on around 1000 children.[5] Norms for the DEST have been calculated for children at six monthly intervals, because pre-reading skills develop so rapidly at this stage. This means that the comparison groups for the norms are based

---

[5]The same approach is applicable to older children and to adults, and the Dyslexia Screening Test (DST, 6:6–16:5, Fawcett and Nicolson 1996) uses a set of 11 sub-tests covering a range of skills and knowledge (Rapid Naming, Beads, One minute reading test, Postural Stability, Phonemic Segmentation, Two minute spelling test, Backwards Digit Span, Nonsense passage reading, One minute writing, Verbal Fluency and Semantic Fluency). Originally, the DEST was designed for children up to the age of seven, but the pilot data suggested that by this age tests of literacy are necessary to differentiate children with problems, and therefore the DST was modified to make it appropriate for this age range. A novel feature of many of the tests included in the DST is that they emphasis fluency as well as accuracy, designed to identify the type of child whose performance is laborious but reasonably accurate. One minute reading, One minute writing, Two Minute spelling are all time limited, and the Nonsense passage reading is scored for speed as well as accuracy. The DST (UK versions) was published in spring 1996, and has been normed on 800 children plus 60 children with dyslexia. Around 5,000 copies of the DST and DEST are in use in schools throughout the UK and in other English-speaking areas of the world. The Dyslexia Adult Screening Test (DAST, Fawcett and Nicolson 1998) has also been published, including a four minute test of non-verbal reasoning, with two versions of the test normed for students and for the general population, 1200 in all.

on around 250 children in each age range, drawn from a variety of backgrounds.

THE VALIDATION STUDY

Having collected the norms for the DEST, the major requirement outstanding was to undertake a longitudinal predictive study where the progress of the 5-year-old cohort was followed through to the age of 7, in order to identify which of those identified as at risk at five years do indeed turn out to have significant reading difficulties. In March 1997, 97 children (mean age 7:9) who had been tested on the DEST in October 1994 (mean age 5:4), were retested on WORD (Psychological Corporation 1993) Reading and Spelling.[6] The group was unselected, comprising all those screened in Sheffield who remained in their original school. A scatterplot of DEST (1994) and WORD reading scores (1997) is presented in figure 3. The figure takes some understanding! The children are ranked in terms of reading age (RA) discrepancy, and this forms the smoothly increasing line moving from bottom left to top right of the figure. Also shown

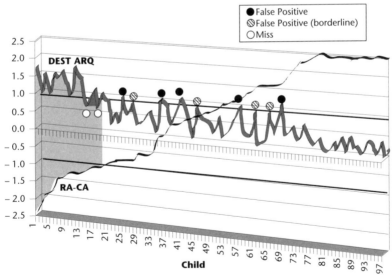

Figure 3.   DEST Validation study from *Annals of Dyslexia* 1998 based on Fawcett, Singleton, and Peer with permission of the International Dyslexia Association, July 24, 2000.

[6]This cohort of children was selected for ease of access for us, forming the complete cohort of children tested by the team in two schools in the Sheffield region.

is the DEST "at-risk quotient" (ARQ), and this forms the jagged line between 1.60 and 0 in the top half of the figure. Child 1 has an ARQ of 1.60—strongly at risk—and an RA discrepancy of –2.5 years (i.e., is 2.5 years behind in reading). Child 1 is therefore a hit for the DEST. We have defined an RA discrepancy of 1 year or more to indicate reading failure, and it may be seen that the children ranked 1 to 20 meet this criterion. When screening the children at age 5, our criterion for those who showed strong risk of dyslexia or other learning difficulties was a score of 1.0 or greater on the DEST. Looking at the outcomes for this group of children, it may be seen that this criterion was successful in identifying children who would later show problems, with the hit rate of 15/20 children (75%). Of the remaining 77 children, only 5 had a DEST ARQ of 1.0 or more, leading to a false positive rate of 5/77 (7%).

Interestingly, however, it is clearly possible to improve our hit rate by making slight retrospective modifications to our criteria. Thus, taking a DEST cut-off of 0.9, a hit rate of 18/20 (90%) is obtained, whereas the false positive rate increases to 8/77 (12%). In our view, it is preferable to have a cut-off score that identifies the majority of children at risk at the expense of being slightly over inclusive. Some structured early support would be beneficial to most children, even if it later transpired that they were not strongly at risk of failure. This led us to suggest that a category of mild risk should be introduced for those children with at-risk scores of 0.6 to 0.8. These results suggest that the predictive validity of the DEST is excellent, and can be increased by introducing a category of mild risk.[7]

Correlational analyses and other statistical analyses were also carried out on the data, which showed significant differences be-

---

[7]We consider that the false positive rate would have been even lower were it not for an ethical dilemma. From an experimental viewpoint, it would be ideal if schools were not made aware of any potential difficulties, so that none of the children identified as at risk on the DEST were supported in school. However, if a child is identified as being at risk at five years, we considered it unethical not to provide the support needed to help the child to learn to read normally. Consequently, feedback was given to all the schools involved in norm collection, and with tests expressly designed for teacher interpretation, it is clear from the profiles which children have problems, and in which areas. In fact, remedial training had been provided by a member of the Sheffield team for four out of the eight children who later fell into the false positive group in the validation study. Interestingly enough, these children clearly fulfilled the criteria for reading deficit, at the start of the training study, around 6 months before the re-test (see Maclagan 1999, for further details). Following systematic intervention over an 8 week period, these children had caught up with their peers sufficiently to drop out of the reading deficit group. This pilot work suggested that short-term intervention can be successful with young children at risk of reading failure, and fed into the next phase of the research, supporting children found to be at risk.

tween the children in the at-risk group, and the no-risk group on all subtests of the DEST. Digit names, rhyming, digit span, and rapid naming time were the most highly correlated with reading ability at age 8 ($r = 0.701$, 0.615, 0.520, and -0.443 respectively), with the ARQ (at-risk quotient) correlating at -0.64. However, the ARQ correlated most highly overall with reading deficit at 8, with a correlation of 0.675. This suggests that the combined ARQ score on the DEST at age 5 is more useful than the individual subtests in terms of identifying those children who will show reading difficulty at age 8.

Using the DEST for Support

Screening children to identify their risk levels should lead naturally to remediation targeted to their areas of weakness. However, even with the appropriate screening tools available to measure progress, the difficulty confronting designers of reading intervention schemes for children with special needs is that of devising a scheme that is both effective and cost effective. For an approach to be effective, it appears to need to be systematic, comprehensive—covering all aspects of the early reading processes—and individual, requiring extended support from a highly trained professional. These are inevitably costly, and though arguably cost effective when one considers the subsequent costs of not providing early support, they may be too costly to justify in a climate of economic stringency.

In two recent controlled studies (Nicolson et al. 1999; Fawcett et al. 1999), we evaluated the effectiveness and cost effectiveness of an early intervention approach designed to be viable in a realistic funding climate. In study A (Nicolson et al. 1999), four infant schools with different demographic characteristics were selected, and classes were screened to identify those children most at risk of reading failure. These children were given support in groups of four, twice weekly over 10 weeks, with the interventions taking place within the normal teaching day. The support program was based on the techniques advocated in Reason and Boote (1994), an individually adaptive, curriculum-based approach with the emphasis being on word building and phonics skills in the broad reading context. Control groups, matched for reading and age with the experimental groups, but with no explicit intervention, were used to allow comparative progress to be assessed.

In each of the four schools, a complete class of children was screened for performance on the Wechsler Objective Reading Dimension (WORD) Reading and Spelling tests, and the 16 lowest ranked children formed the experimental group. If necessary, a further class of children was also screened, and the lowest performing 16 children from the two classes were used. Control groups were obtained from schools in the same area with a similar cross-section of children. The control groups and experimental groups were matched for age and for reading performance. Further pre-tests were also administered, specifically the Dyslexia Early Screening Test (Nicolson and Fawcett 1996) and the British Picture Vocabulary Scale (BPVS) (Dunn et al. 1982), plus a curriculum based assessment.

In study B, a similar approach was used, with the same design, the same teachers, and the same program of support, but here a computer-based intervention was evaluated. Classroom technology can improve the cost effectiveness of reading support, but for optimal learning one must design the classroom environment so that computer, teacher, and learner work together to provide scientifically designed, motivating learning. In the approach adopted in study B, the computer acts as a Reader's Interactive Teaching Assistant (RITA), performing time-consuming chores (selecting problems, presenting learning experiences and materials, giving feedback, storing records, analyzing progress), thereby freeing the teacher to concentrate on high quality individual support. In this second study, teachers used RITA as part of their intervention, thereby permitting direct comparison with the teaching system alone and with standard classroom approaches to literacy development. On the basis of the surprising finding that 25% to 75% of the teachers' time was spent on preparing lessons and on recording progress, the RITA architecture has been re-designed to provide automatic facilities for storing and maintaining individual progress records, together with facilities to support the prior preparation of multi-activity lessons. A further planned feature, based on surveys of teacher requirements, is an "advice" facility, in which sample lessons for Reading Recovery (Clay 1993), Interactive Assessment and Teaching, and Orton-Gillingham are made available to indicate the commonalities and differences between the approaches.

For both studies, performance of the groups on reading-related standardized tests was measured both before and after the 10-week training period. The critical variable was the amount of improvement for the experimental groups and the control groups from pre-test to post-test. The differential improvement of the experimental group would give an indication of the effectiveness of the intervention. The interventions proved both effective—with a significant improvement in reading standard score—and cost ef-

fective, with the mean "effect size" for the intervention comparable to those reported for Reading Recovery (Clay 1993), yet with
only 10% of the costs.

It may be seen from figure 4 that both the traditional (study
A) and the computer-based interventions (study B) led to significant improvements in literacy standard scores.[8] A standard score
of 100 for a child indicates average performance for a child of that
age. It should be stressed that standard scores automatically take
age into effect, and so a stationary standard score value indicates
that a child is maintaining normal progress. It may be seen that,
overall, the trained groups were accelerated over the period of
training, whereas the control groups made little or no progress.

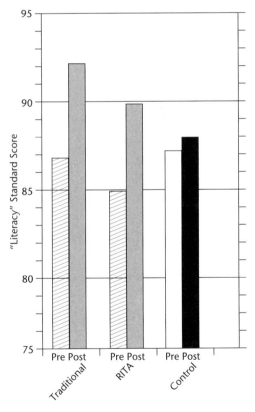

Figure 4. Effects of the interventions on the Composite Literacy
Standard Scores

[8]Literacy standard scores are an average of the reading and spelling standard
score. The published WORD reading scales provide only a coarse conversion of raw
scores to centiles and reading ages. Linear interpolation was used where appropriate to give a more sensitive conversion.

In intervention studies of this type, it is normal to convert the improvement to an effect size that gives an index of the improvement relative to the original performance mean and variation of the class (Cohen 1977). The effect size is calculated as the amount of improvement divided by the standard deviation of the original performance of the class(es). Effect sizes for the two studies are presented in table II, which indicates that, while both study A and study B were successful, the RITA program had greater impact on spelling than reading.[9]

In order to consider cost effectiveness, it is necessary to derive a quantitative measure of the gains and the costs. As noted above, children were trained in groups of four, for two half-hour sessions per week, over 10 weeks. Each group therefore received 10 hours of support, that is, 2.5 hours dedicated teacher time per child. The initial curriculum-based assessment took an average of 30 minutes per child. The DEST assessment took 30 minutes per child. The WORD and BPVS assessments were for formal evaluation purposes and would not be part of the normal support program, so need not be considered as part of the normal support costs. Consequently for the traditional study, the time per child was roughly 3.5 hours. The question of non-teaching preparation time is an important one. Our estimate is that with both traditional and computer-based teaching there was roughly equal preparation time, leading to a total estimate of 6 hours per child. A simple analysis of cost effectiveness is to calculate "added value effect size per 100 teacher hours," i.e., to divide the effect size by the teacher input needed to achieve it. This leads to figures of 11.6 (infant) and 9.7 (junior) for RITA compared with 12.0 and 5.5 respectively for the traditional intervention.

Table II.   Effect sizes for the improvements in the four studies.

Effect sizes are calculated by dividing the amount of improvement from pre-test to post-test for each group by the standard deviation of the cohort of all the classes in the pre-test. The "added value" effect size of an intervention is calculated by subtracting the control effect size from that of the intervention.

	Reading	Spelling	Literacy	Literacy Added Value
Traditional Intervention	0.94	0.95	0.95	0.72
RITA Intervention	0.30	0.98	0.92	0.69
Control	0.19	0.26	0.23	—

[9]One key factor here was the poor initial attainment of the infant school children in reading. Consequently a good deal of time had to be spent on letter recognition and production. For routine learning of letters it is preferable to have a linked vision and production approach, where the child looks at and then attempts to produce each letter.

These results compare favorably with comparable UK studies (e.g., Sylva, Hurry, and Plewis 1995; Hatcher, Hulme, and Ellis 1994) for both effectiveness and cost effectiveness. In the Sylva, Hurry, and Plewis study, two intervention techniques were evaluated, Reading Recovery and phonological training, again using at-risk six-year-old children. Reading Recovery proved very effective ("added value" effect size between schools for the Reading Recovery group on word reading was 0.70, and after one further year 0.41), whereas the phonological intervention was less effective (corresponding "added value" effect sizes 0.11 and 0.27). The Reading Recovery intervention involved, on average, 77 half hour daily individual lessons over 21 weeks, as opposed to 40 individual 10 minute sessions over 7 months for the phonological training. We calculate (excluding training and preparation time) cost effectiveness for these two interventions to be 1.8 and 1.1 for Reading Recovery (post-intervention and one year delay) and 1.1 and 2.7 for phonological intervention. It may be seen from these figures that our short-term interventions provide outstanding cost effectiveness, coupled with entirely satisfactory effectiveness.

DEST and Reading Progress

It has long been claimed by reading specialists that highly trained support teachers are needed to provide the necessary assistance for at least some children (e.g., Clay 1993; Sylva, Hurry, and Plewis 1995), with particular concern being expressed for dyslexic children (e.g., Snowling et al. 1996). It is therefore particularly interesting to consider those children who were not accelerated by the training, and in fact made little or no obvious progress despite the 10-week intervention. In both studies, there was a significant number of such children.

We shall discuss study A first. The intervention groups of 62 children were split into three categories, based on the outcome of their training: a group of 16 problem readers (defined as having a post-intervention reading age deficit of at least 6 months, and improvement over training of less than 6 months); an intermediate group of 27; and a group of 19 recovered readers (defined as no longer having a reading age deficit). It turned out that of all the pre-tests administered, the DEST score gave both the best hit rate (88%) for the problem readers and also the best discrimination (88% vs 28%) between problem readers and recovered readers.[10]

---

[10]It should, of course, be noted that the entire trained group were initially relatively poor readers (the bottom half of the class) and so the reasonably high incidence of at-risk scores even in the recovered readers is as expected.

Of the individual DEST sub-tests, letter names and beads had the highest at-risk rates for the problem readers but they also have high rates for the recovered readers. Rhyme, letter names, postural stability, and rapid naming had good predictive discrimination between problem readers and recovered readers, as did the BPVS. Of the 16 problem readers, 14 (88%) had a DEST score of 0.6 or worse, and 7 (44%) had a DEST score of 0.9 or worse.

Similar results were established in study B, and it was even found that if the intervention children were divided into high-risk and not at-risk groups on the basis of their initial DEST scores, then the high-risk groups made significantly less progress over the course of the intervention. In short, it would appear that around 30% of the intervention group (around 10% of the total cohort) may make relatively slight benefits from the small group intervention, whether traditional or computer based. For these children, a longer intervention may be necessary. The likelihood of being a problem reader was greater for older children (confirming that the sooner the support is provided the better) and for children with high scores on the Dyslexia Early Screening Test. This illustrates the screening→support approach in action.

In summary, a screening→assessment→support system would be of immense value to all those involved in education and learning difficulties. The Dyslexia Early Screening Test is a theoretically based, empirically validated, set of sub-tests that takes about 30 minutes to administer by a teacher or Special Educational Needs co-ordinator, and can be used from 4.5 years upward. It provides a quantitative at-risk index, together with an informative profile of skills. It fits naturally within the existing UK Code of Practice framework, providing valuable information for all concerned. The tests lead naturally to early support, on the "stitch in time" principle, forming the basis of an Individual Education Plan for each child. Early results for the DEST are very promising, and the tests are appropriate for use in the U.S. and other English-speaking countries.

PRE-SCHOOL SCREENING AND SUPPORT

The Pre-school Early Screening Test as a Stitch in Time

The research outlined above was innovative not only in introducing the screening and support very early in infant school, but also in undertaking detailed analyses of the cost effectiveness of the intervention (based on sound teaching practice) both for children who benefited from the intervention and those who appeared to make little progress. Results suggest that it is possible, given early screening and support, to provide an intervention that is not only effective in helping most of the poorest readers accelerate toward their peers, but is also cost effective, producing comparable effect sizes to Reading Recovery with only 10% of the resources (Nicolson et al. 1999). Given the success of the early school screening described above and given the current emphasis in the UK on baseline assessment and support at 4 years, it is natural to consider whether a similar approach might be viable at 4 years.

One promising approach is that adopted by Hannon, Nutbrown, and their colleagues, in which poor home environment was identified as a major source of difficulty in early literacy development (Nutbrown and Hannon 1997); consequently in the REAL (Raising Early Achievement in Literacy, Nutbrown 1997) project, they developed and are currently evaluating the effectiveness of a home-based system for helping parents help their children with literacy skills. Also of particular note here is their introduction of a unique assessment of early literacy, the Early Literacy Development Profile, that provides a much broader assessment of literacy than traditional skills-based assessments.

Other researchers come to early literacy support through an interest in special groups of children. Identification of the precursors of dyslexia and other reading difficulties before children start school is currently a popular research topic internationally. Three different approaches have been adopted: longitudinal studies from birth (e.g., Lyytinen 1997), studies of the development of children with a family history of dyslexia (e.g., Scarborough 1991; Locke et al. 1997) and studies of nursery age children (Muter et al. 1997; Gallagher, Frith, and Snowling 1999). In this chapter we have space only to outline some work with which we have been associated (Fawcett and Nicolson 1999) following on from an innovative community-based approach in Middleton, County Durham.

The Middleton in Teesdale Nursery/Infant Screening and Support System

One outstanding UK example of an integrated broad-based nursery screening assessment with consequent support is the Middleton Skills Screening Tests (MiST) and Middleton Rescue Package (MiRP), developed in nursery/infant school by an experienced teacher. Children are screened using the MiST at the age of four, and the results are then used to determine an individually appropriate rescue package, MiRP, which is used over the following three years. Evaluations of combined MiST and MiRP in the school suggest that the combination of nursery screening plus intervention is proving particularly successful. This rescue package takes place within a whole school policy of intervention using multisensory remediation. The MiRP adopts a skills development approach aimed at improving children's performance on a broad range of over one hundred skills, including language, motor, math, science, and IT skills. The screening and rescue package has proved fully effective, with 100% of the first cohort of children to use the system classed as readers by the time they moved up to junior school at age seven, by contrast with an expected incidence of around 20% who would normally show some reading deficit. Further small groups have also been assessed on MiST in neighboring areas, where the intervention package is not available, and their progress monitored similarly.

The MiST and the MiRP represent an unusually far-sighted and dedicated collaboration between nursery and primary school teachers. However, the resources and integration required make it unlikely that as currently constituted the support package would be suitable for widespread adoption. The opportunity that the MiST/MiRP package represents is that it can form the basis for a cost-effectiveness analysis that allows development of an approach that confers the majority of the benefits of the package at much reduced teaching cost, in much the same way that Reading Recovery provided the starting point for our work on the teaching of reading in infant school. Tracing the source of the problems further back into early childhood, it seemed possible to us that some of the tests we had already developed for the DEST could be modified for younger children. Indeed, some of the DEST tests had elements in common with the MiST, and therefore these two tests could be amalgamated to produce a new test that could be administered to nursery school children on a cost-effective routine basis.

Research to Develop the Pre-school Early Screening Test (PEST).

The primary objective of this current research was to develop and disseminate a three-stage, generalizable, screening-and-intervention package for four-year-old children that is both effective and cost effective, that is valuable even for children with learning disabilities, and that leads seamlessly into the system of screening and support we have recently developed for infant school children.

The research follows cohorts of children from the age of 4:0 to 5:8 years. The four groups of children assessed comprise the MiST/MiRP group, all of whom have ongoing support throughout the entire period; a control group, who are assessed at each stage but not given any specific intervention; a group of Sheffield nursery school children who are given a three-stage screening and intervention package (based in part on analyses of existing data on the MiST/MiRP approach); and a fourth group of special children taken from referrals within the Sheffield region for specific difficulties.

Data are currently available for the targeted intervention with the first cohort of 20 children from a nursery school in Sheffield, which includes a significant proportion of socially disadvantaged children. Most of the children took part in the intervention, with children with mild problems participating for two sessions weekly, and children with more severe problems three times weekly over a 10-week period. Those children found to have continued difficulties following this intervention were then given carefully designed individual support. Following a preliminary evaluation of a battery of tests derived from the MIST, and the DEST, plus other theoretically driven tests, the prototype PEST outlined in table III was derived. A program of intervention was delivered addressing key aspects of language and motor skill development. Following this intervention, the children were given a post-test on the prototype PEST, to assess progress on skills that had been judged to be important at this stage in development. None of these skills has been taught in the format in which it was

Table III.   The Prototype PEST

Test 1.	Dexterity	Bead threading (1 minute)
		Cutting out
Test 2.	Motor Development	Balance both feet
		Catching
		Jumping on both feet
Test 3.	Digit span	from DEST 6
Test 4.	Phonological discrimination	From DEST 3
Test 5.	Copying	Copying writing and simple shapes
Test 6.	Sequences	Copy sequence of bricks
		Memory for sequence of bricks
Test 7.	Sentence Repetition	Following instructions (motor sequence)
		Word Repetition (Speed and accuracy)
Test 8.	Rapid Naming	shortened form of DEST 1
Test 9.	Rhyming	simplified version of DEST 5
Test 10.	Visual memory	Matching shapes from memory
Test 11.	Sound Order	shortened form of DEST 11

pre- or post-tested, so we were looking for evidence of generalization from similar skills. Further evaluation will be undertaken on the prototype PEST tests over the course of the study, to establish which are the most predictive of difficulties for children of this age group and slightly younger.

The children selected for intervention had a range of problems, many of them age related. Some of the children were not yet prepared to follow instructions, or they could be somewhat shy which made them uncooperative. The intervention was designed to cover motor and language skills. All children had at least one language intervention, and one motor skill intervention per week, and the most severely affected had two language intervention sessions, and one motor skill intervention. Intervention took place three times weekly, in groups of two, for around 15 minutes, the upper limit of concentration for this age group. In each session, three skills were presented to maintain variety and interest, and maximize learning. The researcher/nursery nurse adapted the program to the needs of the children, spending a longer time on games that the children clearly enjoyed. At each stage, care was taken to provide the right mixture of familiarity and challenge, so that children were exposed to new skills. Motor skills included balancing on a wobble board while catching beanbags, or playing the game "Simon says." This is a game in which children must follow only instructions prefixed by "Simon says" and ignore all other instructions. Children were encouraged to pit themselves against a stop-watch, not only to emphasize the need to work quickly, but also to build up the amount of time they spent on task. Skills trained by both types of intervention explicitly included a range of concentration and listening skills. Interestingly enough, with the rhyming tasks, for example, it became clear that the standard nursery curriculum exposes a child to a range of experiences, which they are free to choose or not, depending on their readiness. Our aim was to introduce a more explicit teaching element, and to encourage all children to take part, while maintaining the element of fun, which is crucial for success at any age. Above all, we sought to provide instant reinforcement and feedback.

The preliminary results of the intervention were most pleasing. Notably, the pre-test, which had initially taken 2.5 hours per child, had been cut to 30 minutes for the post-test. This was partly attributable to the omission of the short-form BAS (Elliott 1996) and the BPVS, which shortened the test by about 45 minutes. Nevertheless, the greater compliance of the children was also a significant factor in the length of the testing sessions. Analysis of their performance suggested that they had learned to listen, to do what the researcher/nursery nurse asked, and to seek appropriate feedback on their performance. In other words, they were learning how to learn! These impressions were borne out by the results of the tests, which showed significant improvements in bead threading, digit span, digit naming, copying a sequence of movements, fine and gross motor skills, rhyming, sequencing, and sentence repetition. Further analysis is now underway for the second intervention for those children who needed further support following the initial intervention. However, naturally enough, there is considerable development between the ages of 4.0 and 4.3, and further data from a control group is now needed to establish the significance of these improvements. Nevertheless, bearing in mind that many children are still unable to cope with rhyming tasks on school entry, this progress seems to be impressive.

SUMMARY AND CONCLUSIONS

It has long been the aim of dyslexia researchers to identify the precursors of dyslexia and provide some proactive help before children fail, breaking into the cycle of deprivation that characterizes dyslexia. We have provided a range of tools toward this endeavor.

Consideration of figure 1 suggests that we have successfully fulfilled the majority of our objectives in terms of a systematic screening→assessment→support system to identify children at risk of failure. We constructed the DEST for children aged 4.5 to 6.5, based on a broad theoretical research base, and normed the test on 1000 children in the UK. We have successfully validated the DEST, which shows good predictive validity, correctly classifying 90% of children as at risk or not at risk. We have now introduced a category of mild risk which improves prediction further, covering the misses from our original categorization, and thereby identifying 100% of the at-risk children. The DEST has become a Psychological Corporation UK best-seller, and is increasingly used in schools throughout the UK, with further versions under development world-wide. More recently we have made significant progress toward designing and implementing the support that should follow from a screening index of at risk. We have evaluated a series of effective and cost effective approaches to remediation, using both traditional and computer based approaches, within short-term interventions. The DEST provides a valid index of children whose impaired pre-reading skills make them at risk for failure. The intervention packages, both traditional and computerized, provide an effective and cost effective mechanism for scaffolding learning, facilitating improvements in the developmental trajectory of these children. Those children whose learning is most resistant to improvement are highlighted by the DEST screening tests, providing teachers with a realistic assessment of those children who will need longer and more individual support. We hope that this approach toward support will become increasingly influential. Meanwhile, similar research is now in hand for younger nursery-school children, and preliminary results suggest that both the screening and the intervention are effective; the former in picking out those children at risk of failure, and the latter in providing support in their areas of weakness. The work we are undertaking builds on a long and fruitful history of screening and intervention over several decades, with pioneers such as Nathlie Badian providing some of the finest examples of best practice in the field.

ACKNOWLEDGEMENTS

The research on which this chapter was based was funded by grants HQ278/edu and HQ317/edu from the Nuffield Foundation and grant F/118/AF from the Leverhulme Trust. We gratefully acknowledge the co-operation of staff and children at Bluestone, Lydgate, and Norfolk infant schools in Sheffield and Starbeck, and Saltergate schools, Harrogate, together with Broomhall Nursery in Sheffield. We thank Dr. Rea Reason and Ray Lee for their roles in the research, and Dr. Susan Pickering for insights deriving from her Ph.D study. Finally, we acknowledge the invaluable contributions of the teacher/researchers on these projects, Helen Moss, Margaret Nicolson, and Michelle Tovey. Figures are reprinted with permission from the Annals of Dyslexia, 1998.

REFERENCES

Badian, N. A. 1982. The prediction of good and poor reading before kindergarten entry: A four year follow-up. *Journal of Special Education* 16:308–18.
Badian, N. A. 1984. Reading Disability in an epidemiological context: Incidence and environmental correlates. *Journal of Learning Disabilities* 17:129–36.
Badian, N. A. 1986. Improving the prediction of reading for the individual child: A four year follow up. *Journal of Learning Disabilities* 19:262–69.
Badian, N. A., McAnulty, G. B., Duffy, F. H., and Als, H. 1990. Prediction of dyslexia in kindergarten boys. *Annals of Dyslexia* 40:152–69.
Badian, N. A. 1994. Preschool prediction: Orthographic and phonological skills and reading. *Annals of Dyslexia* 44:3–25.

Bishop, D. 1985. Spelling ability in congenital dysarthria: Evidence against articulatory coding in translating between graphemes and phonemes. *Cognitive Neuropsychology* 2:229–51.

Bradley, L. 1988. Making connections in learning to read and to spell. *Applied Cognitive Psychology* 2:3–18.

Bradley, L., and Bryant, P. E. 1978. Difficulties in auditory organisation as a possible cause of reading backwardness. *Nature*, 271, 746–747.

Bradley, L., and Bryant, P. E. 1983. Categorising sounds and learning to read: A causal connection. *Nature* 301:419–21.

Bradley, L., and Bryant, P. E. 1985. *Rhyme and Reason in Reading and Spelling*. International Academy for research in learning disabilities series. Michigan: University of Michigan Press.

Clay, M. M. 1993. *An Observation Survey of Early Literacy Achievement*. Auckland, NZ: Heinemann.

Cohen, J. 1977. *Statistical Power Analyses for the Behavior Sciences*. New York: Academic Press.

Denkla, M. B., and Rudel, R. G. 1976. Rapid "Automatized" naming (R.A.N.). Dyslexia differentiated from other learning disabilities. *Neuropsychologia* 14:471–79.

DFEE 1994. Code of Practice on the identification and assessment of special educational needs. DFEE and Welsh Office, HMSO: London.

Dunn, L. I. M., Dunn, L. M., Whetton, C., and Pintillie, D. 1982. *The British Picture Vocabulary Scale*. Windsor: NFER-Nelson

Elliott, D. 1996. *British Ability Scales II*. Windsor, NFER-Nelson.

Fawcett, A. J,. and Nicolson, R. I. (eds) 1994. *Dyslexia in Children: Multidisciplinary Perspectives*. London: Harvester Wheatsheaf.

Fawcett, A. J., and Nicolson, R. I. 1996. *The Dyslexia Screening Test*. The Psychological Corporation, London.

Fawcett, A. J., and Nicolson, R. I. 1998. *The Dyslexia Adult Screening Test*. The Psychological Corporation, London.

Fawcett, A. J., Pickering, S., and Nicolson, R. I., 1993. Development of the DEST test for the early screening for dyslexia. In *Facets of Dyslexia and Its Remediation*, eds. S. F. Wright and R. Groner. Amsterdam: Elsevier Science Publishers B.V.

Fawcett, A. J., Nicolson, R. I., and Dean, P. 1996. Impaired performance of children with dyslexia on a range of cerebellar tasks. *Annals of Dyslexia* 46:259–83.

Fawcett, A. J., and Nicolson, R. I. 1999. Funded proposal to the Nuffield Foundation. Development and Evaluation of a Pre-School Screening and Rescue Package for Children with Special Needs.

Fawcett, A. J., Nicolson, R. I., Moss, H, Nicolson, M. K., and Reason, R. 1999. Effectiveness of Reading Intervention in Junior School. *British Journal of Educational Psychology*: Submitted.

Fawcett, A. J., Singleton, C. H., and Peer, L. 1998. Advances in early years screening for dyslexia in the UK. *Annals of Dyslexia* 48:57–88.

Fowler, A. E. 1991. How early phonological development might set the scene for phoneme awareness. In *Phonological Processes in Literacy*, eds. S. A. Brady and D. P. Shankweiler. Hillsdale, N.J.:Lawrence Erlbaum.

Frederickson, N., Frith, U., and Reason, R. 1997. *The Phonological Assessment Battery*. Windsor: NFER-Nelson.

Gallagher, A., Frith, U., and Snowling, M. 1999 in press. Language processing skills in pre-schoolers at risk of developmental dyslexia. *Journal of Child Psychology and Psychiatry*.

Hatcher, P., Hulme, C., and Ellis, A. W. 1994. Ameliorating early reading failure by integrating the teaching of reading and phonological skills. *Child Development* 65:41–57.

Horn, W. F., and Packard, T. 1985. Early identification of Learning Problems: A meta-analysis. *Journal of Educational Psychology* 77:597–607.

Jansky, J. J., Hoffman, M. J., Layton, J., and Sugar, F. 1989. Prediction: A six year follow up. *Annals of Dyslexia* 39:227–46.

Locke, J. L., Hodgson, J., Macaruso, P., Roberts, J., Lambrecht-Smith, S., and Guttentag, C. 1997. The development of developmental dyslexia. In *Dyslexia: Biology, Cognition and Intervention*, eds C. Hulme and M. Snowling, London: Whurr.

Lovegrove, W. 1994. Visual deficits in dyslexia: Evidence and implications. In *Dyslexia in Children: Multidisciplinary Perspectives*, eds. A. J. Fawcett and R. I. Nicolson. London: Harvester Wheatsheaf.

Lundberg, I., Frost, J., and Petersen, O. P. 1988. Long term effects of a preschool training program in phonological awareness. *Reading Research Quarterly* 28:263–84.

Lyytinen, H. 1997. In search of the precursors of dyslexia: A prospective study of children at risk for reading problems. In *Dyslexia: Biology, Cognition and Intervention*, eds. C. Hulme and M. Snowling. London: Whurr.

Maclagan, F. 1999. Screening and remediation for children with learning difficulties. Unpublished Ph.D. thesis, University of Sheffield.

Miles, T. R. 1982. *The Bangor Dyslexia Test*. Cambridge: Learning Development Aids.

Muter, V., Hulme, C., and Snowling, M. 1996. *Phonological Abilities Test*. London: The Psychological Corporation.

Muter, V., Hulme, C., Snowling, M., and Taylor, S. 1997. Segmentation, not rhyming, predicts early progress in learning to read. *Journal of Experimental Child Psychology* 65:370–96.

Nicolson, R. I., and Fawcett, A. J. 1994. Comparison of deficits in cognitive and motor skills among children with dyslexia. *Annals of Dyslexia* 44:3–26.

Nicolson, R. I., and Fawcett, A. J. 1996. *The Dyslexia Early Screening Test*. The Psychological Corporation, London.

Nicolson, R. I., Fawcett, A. J., Moss, H, Nicolson, M. K., and Reason, R. 1999. An early reading intervention study: Evaluation and implications. *British Journal of Educational Psychology* 69:47–62.

Nicolson, R. I., and Fawcett, A. J. 1999. Developmental dyslexia: The role of the cerebellum. *Dyslexia: An International Journal of Research and Practice* 5:155–77.

Nutbrown, C., and Hannon, P. 1997. *Preparing for Early Literacy Development with Parents: A Professional Development Manual*. NES Arnold / The REAL Project, Nottingham.

Nutbrown, C. 1997. *Recognising Early Literacy Development: Assessing Children's Achievements*. London: Paul Chapman Publishing Ltd.

Olson, R. K., Wise, B. W., and Rack, J. P. 1989. Dyslexia: Deficits, genetic aetiology and computer based remediation. *Irish Journal of Psychology* 10:594–608.

Psychological Corporation. 1993. *Wechsler Objective Reading Dimensions*. Sidcup, UK: The Psychological Corporation, Europe.

Rack, J. 1985. Orthographic and phonetic coding in normal and dyslexic readers. *British Journal of Psychology* 76:325–40.

Rack, J. 1994. Dyslexia: The phonological deficit hypothesis. In *Dyslexia in Children: Multidisciplinary Perspectives*, eds. A. J. Fawcett, and R. I. Nicolson, London: Harvester Wheatsheaf.

Reason, R., and Boote, R. 1994. *Helping Children with Reading and Spelling: A Special Needs Manual*. Routledge.

Satz, P., and Fletcher, J. M. 1988. Early identification of learning disabled children: An old problem revisited. *Journal of Consulting and Clinical Psychology* 56,6:824–29.

Scarborough, H. 1991. Antecedents to reading disability: Preschool language development and literacy experiences of children from dyslexic families. *Reading and Writing* 3:219–33.

Singleton, C. 1995. *Cognitive Profiling System*. Newark, UK: Chameleon Educational.

Snowling, M. J., Goulandris, N., and Defty, N. 1996. A longitudinal study of reading development in dyslexic children. *Journal of Educational Psychology* 88:653–69.

Stein J. F. 1994 A visual deficit in dyslexia. In *Dyslexia in Children: Multidisciplinary Perspectives*, eds. A. J. Fawcett. and R. I. Nicolson. London: Harvester Wheatsheaf.

Strag, G. 1972. Comparative behavioural ratings of parents with severe mentally retarded, special learning disability, and normal children. *Journal of Learning Disabilities* 5:52–56.

Sylva, K., Hurry, J., and Plewis, I. 1995. The effectiveness of Reading Recovery and phonological training for children with reading problems. London: Thomas Coram Research Unit. Full report for School Curriculum and Assessment Authority.

Tallal, P. 1984. Temporal or phonetic processing deficit in dyslexia? That is the question. *Applied Psycholinguistics* 5:167–69.

Tallal, P., Miller, S., and Fitch, R. H. 1993. Neurobiological basis of speech - A case for the pre-eminence of temporal processing. *Annals of the New York Academy of Sciences* 682:27–47.

Wechsler, D. 1991 *Wechsler Intelligence Scale for Children III* (WISC III). San Antonio, Texas: The Psychological Corporation.

Chapter • 4

Application of Frith's Developmental Phase Model to the Process of Identifying At-Risk Beginning Readers

Diane J. Sawyer, Jwa K. Kim,
and Sally Lipa-Wade

As a beginning teacher, I (Sawyer) was assigned to a class of the poorest readers in 5th grade. I spent the year asking, alternately, why some were still non-readers, and how they might have been helped earlier. A few years later, I read *Preventing Reading Failure* (de Hirsh, Jansky, and Langford 1966) and soon began my own explorations into understanding the reading process as well as untangling the plethora of predictors of reading failure (Sawyer 1988; 1992).

Over time, I came to the conclusion that an effective plan to prevent reading failure must be rooted in a theoretical framework that could both predict the course of normal reading acquisition and explain why normal progress for a particular child might be stalled. Only when students at risk of failure in reading and writing can be identified reliably and assisted effectively in starting up again, can prevention of reading failure become a dependable reality. Effective preventive instruction must target the particular stumbling blocks responsible for stalled development. In this context, an effective screening tool must not only predict who is likely to fail, it must also provide guidance in targeting intervention to address the array of stumbling blocks impeding different students within the at-risk group.

Uta Frith's phase theory of reading acquisition (1985) captured the diverse predictors of reading success that had been documented in a host of research studies over more than 30 years (Daneman 1991). Further, it organized these into a logical, hierarchical ordering of phases of reading development. Each phase described the types of skills to be acquired and consolidated into coordinated action. Each phase provided the platform upon which to build new skills associated with the next phase of development. Linnea Ehri (1994) provided an elaboration of the phases in Frith's model and helped to clarify the process of transition from one phase to the next.

Drawing on the work of these two outstanding researchers, the staff in the Tennessee Center for the Study and Treatment of

Child: _____
Age: _____ Grade: _____

Logographic Phase
___ can segment spoken sentences into words
___ can segment spoken words into syllables (*hel-i-cop-ter*)
___ understands concept of word and word boundaries in print
___ identifies most alphabet letters by name
___ can write alphabet letters
___ can recognize some familiar words
___ can recognize rhyming words

Early Alphabetic Phase
___ can identify initial sound in spoken words
___ can identify final sound in spoken words
___ can produce rhyming words
___ can say the sound associated with most consonants
___ can blend spoken sounds into a word
___ can segment spoken words of two or three phonemes (*s-o, t-a-p*)
___ can read and spell most initial and final consonants in one-syllable words

Late Alphabetic Phase
___ can segment spoken words of four or more phonemes (*d-e-s-k, b-l-a-s-t*)
___ can manipulate phonemes in words of 3 phonemes
___ can read and spell consonant blends correctly
___ can read and spell preconsonant nasals correctly (la*m*p, po*n*d)
___ has mastered reading and spelling short vowels in one-syllable words
___ can read pseudowords which are of comparable difficulty to real words read

Early Orthographic Phase
___ can distinguish between the short and long vowel sound in spoken words
___ is gaining automaticity of word recognition
___ has mastered reading and spelling long vowel—silent *e* pattern in one-syllable words
___ can delete one phoneme from a blend in spoken words
___ has mastered reading and spelling high frequency long vowel patterns in one-syllable words
___ has mastered reading and spelling r-controlled vowel patterns in one-syllable words
___ has mastered reading and spelling most common vowel digraphs in one-syllable words
___ spells most homophones correctly
___ reads simple two-syllable words

Late Orthographic Phase
___ is gaining automaticity in reading passages
___ spells plurals and inflectional endings correctly (e.g., men, ant/ent, all pronunciations of -ed)
___ understands syllable patterns
___ is learning prefixes, suffixes, and root words
___ is learning about stressed and unstressed syllables
___ is learning the conventions of combining syllables
___ is continuing to gain fluency in reading and writing

Key: + always does (mastered)   Completed by: _____
     +/– sometimes does (instructional)   Position: _____ Date: _____
     – never does

Figure 1.   Developmental Phases Checklist

Dyslexia created a checklist of competencies within each phase of the developmental hierarchy. This checklist is presented in figure 1.

The checklist is used to classify the competencies of students with very poor skills in reading and spelling whom we evaluate in this Center. We found the checklist was a valuable tool to target the appropriate entry point for remediation, as well as to identify specific skill gaps that probably accounted for the student's stalled or limited progress. Elements listed within a given phase are descriptive of the skills to be attained, but are not intended to suggest a specific sequence for instruction or acquisition.

Early in 1996, we hypothesized that a screen comprised of tasks that sample early developmental competencies, as outlined in the Center checklist, might be an effective tool for both identifying and targeting instruction across the range of at-risk beginning readers. The purpose of this study was to assess the power of selected benchmark competencies associated with the early phases of Frith's theoretical model, to identify those likely to experience continued delays or failure in reading and spelling.

METHOD

Participants

Participants were drawn from all seven kindergarten classes in one school in a small Tennessee city. The school serves a mixed socioeconomic population. A large proportion of families are college-educated homeowners; however, the school also serves children from blue-collar working families and several low-cost apartment complexes. Twenty percent of students in 1995-96 were eligible for free lunches (17%) or reduced fee lunches (3%).

In mid-April, kindergarten teachers were asked to consider every child in their classes and to designate each as being either in the top 50% of achievers or the lower 50%. Sixty-seven students were identified as being among the lower 50% of achievers.

A sentence dictation task was administered as a whole class activity in every classroom. This was scored according to the number of phonemic elements that were acceptably coded (following Clay 1979). The sentence, "I can see a mother kitty and her baby." contains a maximum of 28 codable elements. This counts *th* in "mother" as one element and *er* in "mother" and "her" as well as *ee* in "see" as two codable elements. In counting acceptable coding, however, *kn* for "can," *se* for "see," or *hr* for "her" would each receive credit for two acceptably coded elements. Scoring the dictated sentence in this way led to the identification of four additional students. Originally classified among the top achievers, they failed to meet the criterion (50% of sounds coded acceptably) established for success on the dictation task. A total of 71 students, 44 boys and 27 girls, were given the full screening test. Approximately 90% were Caucasian. African American, Hispanic, and Asian students made up the remaining 10%.

Data Collection

The screening battery was administered to each child over a three-week period spanning the end of April and beginning of May. One teacher in the school, with extensive kindergarten experience, administered all tasks to every child. Tasks included:

1. Sentence Segmenting: showing the number of words in a spoken sentence using colored blocks. Eleven sentences were presented, ranging in length from two to seven words.
2. Syllable Segmenting: showing the number of syllables in a spoken word using colored blocks. Eight words were presented, each containing two or three syllables.
3. Rhyme Production: producing a word that rhymes with one spoken by the examiner. Five stimulus words were presented.
4. Letter Name Recognition: naming a lower case letter when pointed to by the examiner. Eight letters were presented (*x, b, j, n, q, h, g,* and *w*).
5. Letter Sound Associations: giving the sound of a lower case letter pointed to by the examiner. Thirteen letters were tested (*b, c, s, m, f, t, g, h, j, k, l, p,* and *r*).
6. Sound Blending: blending separate sounds spoken by the examiner into a word. Eleven real words and three nonsense words were presented.
7. Logo Recognition: giving the exact name for the product (e.g., Kool-Aid) or vendor (e.g., McDonalds) when shown the word that had been cut out of a package label. Four common names from labels were presented.
8. Letter Rhyme Recognition: telling which of two pairs of letter names rhyme (e.g., Y/L or V/P). Six sets of rhyming/not rhyming pairs were presented.
9. Word Rhyme Recognition: telling if two words pronounced by the examiner do or do not rhyme. Five word pairs were presented.

The total items correct for each task were recorded.

In April of the following year, another sentence dictation task, as well as the Letter Name list of the Developmental Spelling Assessment Test (DSA; Ganske 1993), were administered to all first grade students. Words on this list are all one-syllable, short vowel words. Scores were collected for those students who had participated in the kindergarten screening the previous year. Scores (in normal curve equivalents) that these students obtained on the Word Analysis, reading Vocabulary, and Spelling subtests of the mandated state achievement tests were also collected at the end of each year. For students retained in a grade, we collected scores for only the tests administered following the first year in the grade. These subtest tasks varied in complexity from grade to grade but generally were as follows:

Word Analysis—Student selected a word within a group of four that had the same sound as the sound targeted in a word spoken by the examiner (e.g., "Find the word that has the same beginning sound as 'will'.").

Vocabulary (reading)—Student selected one word from four that means about the same as a printed target word (e.g., "Find the word that means about the same as _____ ").

Spelling—Student selected the one word in a list of four words or short phrases that is misspelled, or the one that is spelled correctly.

Attrition due to family moves and retentions in a grade yielded the following sample sizes: K = 71, Grade 1 = 55, Grade 2 = 44, Grade 3 = 26.

Data Analysis

To examine the underlying structure of the variables included in the screen, along with the kindergarten dictation task, correlational analyses and factor analyses were undertaken. To determine if there were differences in performance on the screen tasks as well as on the state achievement measures when those who were retained in kindergarten or grade 1 were compared to those who had not been retained, analyses of variance were undertaken. Similar analyses were conducted to compare achievement of students who scored below the 50% correct criterion on five or more of the screen tasks with students who met or exceeded the criterion score. Finally, stepwise regression analyses were conducted to identify the most powerful predictors of performance on the grade 1 measures of phonological recoding and on the norm-referenced state achievement tests, grades 1 through 3.

RESULTS AND DISCUSSION

Achievement on the sentence dictation task and each of the nine screening tasks is presented in table I. Among the students in this

Table I.   Means and Standard Deviations for Scores Obtained on the
           Kindergarten Screening Tasks

Task	Mean $n = 71$	SD	Range	% Met Criterion
Sentence Segmenting	6.13	3.4	0-11	42
Syllable Segmenting	3.6	2.8	0-8	63.4
Letter Rhyme Recognition	4.13	1.86	0-6	77.5
Word Rhyme Recognition	5.04	1.20	2-6	90.2
Rhyme Production	4.07	1.25	0-5	91.6
Letter Name Recognition	6.17	1.9	1-8	90.2
Letter/Sound Association	9.4	3.9	0-13	81.7
Sound Blending	6.19	5.26	0-14	50.7
Logo (Specific Word)	.83	1.08	0-4	25.4
Sentence Dictation	14.13	6.8	0-26	42

sample, there was wide variation in performance on each task.
Scores ranged from 0 to all correct for seven of the ten. Selection
of only those considered to be in the lower 50% of their classes did
not seriously restrict the variance within the group. On average,
performance met or exceeded the 50% correct criterion established
for acceptable performance, on seven of the ten tasks. Recognition
of the product name cut from a package or label proved to be difficult for most. Sound blending and syllable segmenting were challenging for many. Only half of the students met or surpassed the
criterion score for these tasks. In contrast, letter naming as well as
recognition and production of rhyming words were relatively easy
tasks for all.

The Relationship Among the Screen Tasks

A correlational analysis was undertaken to examine the degree of
association between and among tasks on the screen. The correlation matrix is presented in table II. Although only three correlations may be considered strong ($r = .50$ or above), several highly
significant correlations ($p < .01$) between tasks are apparent.
However, only the letter/sound task bears a significant relationship with every other variable.

In an attempt to discern the underlying structure of the
screen variables, a factor analysis was conducted. The promax rotation was selected because it assumes correlated underlying factors.
Results of this analysis are presented in table III.

The nine variables of the screen loaded on to three separate
factors. The kindergarten dictation task obtained a very low factor
loading on each. Low negative inter-factor correlations suggest
that factor I is essentially independent of all others. Factor II is

Table II.   Correlation Matrix for all Kindergarten Variables

Task	1	2	3	4	5	6	7	8	9	10
1. Sentence Segmenting		.38**	.17	.04	.15	−.034	.43**	.03	.30*	.28*
2. Syllable Segmenting			.27*	.19	.18	.20	.41**	−.004	.30*	.23
3. Letter Name				.34**	.21	.36**	.64***	.23	.23	.33**
4. Logos					.05	.19	.28*	.33**	.33**	.30*
5. Let Rhyme						.36**	.38**	.16	.26*	.23
6. Word Rhyme							.40***	.20	.15	.35**
7. Letter Sounds								.28*	.50***	.59***
8. Rhyme Production									.34**	.22
9. Sound Blend										.40***
10. Sentence Dictation										

$*p < .05; **p < .01; ***p < .001.$

Table III.   Factor Loadings of Kindergarten Screening Variables

Variables	Factor I	Factor II	Factor III	Percent of Variance Explained
Sentence Segmenting	.930			
Syllable Segmenting	.707			
Letter Sounds	.504			
Kindergarten Dictation	.32			
				.36
Logo		.827		
Rhyme Production		.801		
Sound Blending		.563		
Kindergarten Dictation		.31		
				.13
Rhyme Recognition				
Letters			.906	
Words			.757	
Letter Names			.425	
Kindergarten Dictation			.28	
				.11
				.60 Total
Inter-Factor Correlations				
Factor I		−.217	−.230	
Factor II			−.353	

marginally associated with factor III. The differentiation of variables across factors is globally suggestive of developmental linkages among tasks. Ability to perform recognition tasks (factor III) generally precedes ability to perform similar tasks requiring production (factor II). Analytic abilities (factor I) typically develop later. Within factor I, the internalization of letter/sound associations appears to link to the cognitive-analytic abilities sampled by segmentation of the speech stream into words and syllables. The ability to learn letter/sound correspondences requires that a child ignore meaning—the name given to the letter form—to learn a new and highly abstract non-name speech unit to label the same form.

Although phoneme segmentation is generally accepted as the essential precursor to establishing letter/sound correspondences, phoneme segmentation was not assessed in this study. This was a deliberate decision, made precisely because phoneme segmentation is a later developing skill whose emergence and refinement is supported through reading instruction experiences in grade 1. The ability to isolate elements of a thought unit, and to stand apart from the richer, integrated meaning—segmenting words in a sentence or syllables in a word—probably represents the foundational experiences out of which phoneme segmentation and letter/sound association learning emerges. Syllable segmenting is an early developing ability and has been shown to correlate with later reading achievement (see Wagner and Torgesen 1987 for an overview). I (Sawyer 1987) found that syllable segmenting, assessed at the beginning of kindergarten, accounted for 6% additional variance for end of grade 1 reading achievement, over and above that which was explained by a traditional readiness battery combined with a measure of oral vocabulary. The same contribution to the variance in reading at the end of grade 2 was noted for a measure of sentence segmenting taken at the end of kindergarten. Wentink (1997) demonstrated that Dutch poor readers with a second grade reading level improved their phonological decoding skills following an intensive intervention program that focused on word-internal syllabication skills. It is reasonable to assume that students who perform poorly on measures of sentence and syllable segmenting at the end of kindergarten are at risk of failure in reading at grade 1 and beyond.

Teacher Judgement in Identifying At-Risk Students

Teacher judgement is, perhaps, the most widely accepted and popularly valued predictor of future school success. Twenty children had been recommended for retention in either kindergarten (n = 9) or first grade (n = 11). The performance of the combined group of repeaters, on all variables in the screen and on all achievement variables for grade 1, was compared to those who had never been retained. Means and Standard Deviations are reported in table IV.

An analysis of variance procedure yielded no significant differences between the groups on any measure (p = .005 using the Bonferroni method). Teacher judgement of "at riskness" was not supported by differences in performance on the screening tasks or

Table IV. Means and Standard Deviations for Achievement on Kindergarten and Grade 1 Variables Among Retained and Non Retained Students

Variables	Retained		Not Retained	
	M	*SD*	*M*	*SD*
Students in Kindergarten[a]				
Sentence Dictation	13.25	7.35	14.51	6.59
Sentence Segmenting	5.40	3.80	6.42	3.19
Syllable Segmenting	3.75	2.80	3.56	2.80
Word Rhyme Recognition	5.0	1.34	5.06	1.15
Letter Name Rhyme Recognition	3.35	2.03	4.44	1.70
Rhyme Production	4.05	1.28	4.08	1.26
Letter Name	5.50	1.96	6.44	1.80
Letter Sound	8.90	4.54	9.58	3.66
Sound Blending	5.50	5.18	6.46	5.32
Logo	.70	1.08	.88	1.08
Students in Grade 1[b]				
Word Analysis	50.0	26.9	54.5	22.7
Vocabulary	52.8	19.9	52.7	23.5
DSA Spelling[c]	14.9	6.7	16.06	7.2
Dictation[c]	33.4	5.3	32.06	6.2

Note. [a]Retained N = 20; Not Retained N = 51. [b]Retained N = 18 for Word Analysis and Vocabulary; Not Retained N = 37. [c]Retained N = 10.

by measures of grade 1 achievement. This finding is consistent with that of earlier studies. For example, Kenny and Chekaluk (1993) noted that, over three years, accuracy of both test results and teacher judgement of student progress increased. Early on, teachers generally failed to identify the majority of disabled readers, probably due to the fact that indexes of reading ability are so limited. As these increase in number so, too, do opportunities to judge progress.

Assessing "At Riskness" Based on Student Performance on the Screen

To examine differences in performance on the screening tasks, in relation to subsequent school achievement, 15 students who had failed to achieve the 50% criterion on five or more of the screen tasks were now identified as the at-risk group. Their achievement on the various measures of word reading and spelling, grades 1 to 3, was compared to that of all others using the *t*-test procedure. Due to the small sample size at grade 3 (*n* = 4 and 22), and the large discrepancy between the two groups at every grade level, the homogeneity of variance test was performed prior to the *t*-test analysis. Achievement on measures of reading comprehension was excluded from this analysis because reading comprehension taps both decoding and language comprehension (Gough and Tunmer 1986; Hoover and Gough 1990). In the early stages of reading acquisition, poor decoding poses the greatest barrier to reading comprehension. Nevertheless, a related measure of comprehension was retained for this analysis. The reading vocabulary measures sample knowledge of word meaning. Thorndike (1973), in a very large, multinational study, found median correlations between vocabulary knowledge and reading comprehension to be in the range of .71 to .66 across ages 10 to18. In the present study, vocabulary is considered an indirect measure of reading comprehension. Results of the *t*-test procedure are presented in table V. A conservative level of significance, using the Bonferroni method, was selected to counter-balance the number of tests performed. The significance level was set at $p = .0125$ at grade 1, and $p = .017$ at grades 2 and 3.

Table V shows that poor overall performance on the screening tasks (less than 50% of the items correct on five or more tasks) does effectively identify students whose future achievement in word reading and spelling will be poor. The magnitude of difference between the performance of these students and others was greatest for measures of vocabulary and spelling across all grades. Group differences in the measures of word analysis, while

Table V. *t*-Test of Differences in Mean Achievement for Poorer vs. Better Performance on Screen Tasks

| | Students in Grade 1 | | | | |
| | Group I (N = 14–15) | | Group II (N = 41) | | t value |
	M	SD	M	SD	
Sentence Dictation	25.40	8.22	34.48	2.88	3.43*
Word Analysis	40.27	20.21	60.39	23.17	2.97**
Vocabulary	31.07	8.73	60.17	20.58	7.33**
Spelling (DSA)[a]	7.73	5.44	18.48	5.28	5.80**
	Students in Grade 2				
	Group I (N = 11)		Group II (N = 33)		t value
Word Analysis	47.55	29.44	63.18	19.29	2.04
Vocabulary	47.64	23.09	65.62	15.33	2.97*
Spelling	38.64	27.51	58.53	17.94	2.74*
	Students in Grade 3				
	Group I (N = 4)		Group II (N = 22)		t value
Word Analysis	35.00	9.42	75.86	20.20	3.92**
Vocabulary	32.25	20.76	67.64	19.58	3.30**
Spelling	28.50	13.33	69.91	22.58	3.53**

*$p < .05$; **$p < .01$ (using the Bonferroni method)
[a]DSA = Developmental Spelling Assessment Test

substantial, consistently yielded a lesser level of statistical significance. Inspection of individual scores on the norm-referenced measures of word analysis and reading vocabulary permitted us to assess the incidence of truly poor readers in each group—students whose scores fell below one standard deviation below the mean (NCE < 29). At grade one, 7 of the 14 poorer performers on the screen (50%) obtained low scores for reading Vocabulary but only 2 of the 41 (5%) better performers obtained similarly low scores. With respect to Word Analysis, 5 of the 15 in the poorer performing group (33%) obtained low scores, although only 3 of the 41 better performers (7%) obtained similarly low scores. A much greater proportion of students identified as at risk, based on performance on the screen, demonstrated low achievement in reading and spelling on norm-referenced measures in later years as well. At grade 2, 2 of the 11 poorer performers scored below average in Vocabulary, 3 in Word Analysis, 4 in Spelling. This compared to 0, 1, and 2, respectively among the 33 better performers. Similarly, at grade 3, one of the poorer performers scored below average on Vocabulary and Word Analysis while 3 were low scorers on spelling. In contrast, only one student of the 22 better performers scored below average on Vocabulary; no students in this group scored below average on the other subtests.

Predicting Future Achievement in Reading and Spelling

In an attempt to identify the power of tasks in the screening process to predict subsequent achievement for the full sample, a series of stepwise regression analyses were conducted. Results are presented in table VI.

Among the students in this sample, eight of the ten variables included in the screening process appear as the first or second best predictor of achievement in word reading or spelling on norm-referenced measures at grades 1 to 3, as well as on two criterion-referenced measures of phonological recoding at grade 1. The single best predictor of all achievement variables of interest through grade 2 was performance on the letter sound task. It was also the best predictor of spelling performance at grade 3. This finding is consistent with that of Badian and colleagues (1990). In that longitudinal study, letter sound knowledge was the only traditional pre-reading task found to be a significant predictor of reading achievement at grade 4. It also distinguished the poorest (dyslexic) readers from all others.

Letter naming was selected for the regression equations only for the prediction of achievement in spelling at grade 3 (10% of

Table VI. Stepwise Regression Analyses Using Variables of the Kindergarten Screen to Predict Achievement in Grades 1–3

Dependent Variable	Predictor Variables [Regression Weights] (Semi-partial r^2)						% of Variance Accounted for
Students in First Grade							
	Intercept	Let Snd	Let Rhym	Syll Seg	Rhym Prod	Logo	
Sentence Dictation	[15.89]	[0.765] (.579)	[0.760] (.051)	[0.506] (.049)	[0.863] (.037)	[0.863] (.019)	73.3%
	Intercept	Let Snd	Logo	Blend			
DSA Spelling	[2.383]	[1.302] (.564)	[1.887] (.072)	[0.334] (.045)			68.1%
	Intercept	Let Snd	K Dict				
Word Analysis	[22.71]	[2.456] (.327)	[0.797] (.036)				36.3%
	Intercept	Let Snd	Logo	K Dict	Sent Seg		
Vocabulary	[15.822]	[1.490] (.357)	[7.381] (.115)	[0.858] (.052)	[1.07] (.021)		54.6%
Students in Second Grade							
	Intercept	Let Snd	K Dict				
Word Analysis	[27.792]	[2.251] (.204)	[2.902] (.054)				25.8%
	Intercept	Let Snd	Blend	Word Rhym			
Vocabulary	[26.445]	[1.169] (.222)	[1.043] (.066)	[3.572] (.044)			33.2%
	Intercept	Let Snd	Syll Seg				
Spelling	[24.142]	[2.418] (.265)	[1.919] (.043)				30.8%
Students in Third Grade							
	Intercept	Rhym Prod					
Word Analysis	[39.326]	[7.651] (.174)					17.4%
	Intercept	Rhym Prod	K Dict				
Vocabulary	[25.813]	[6.70] (.266)	[1.275] (.105)				37.1%
	Intercept	Let Snd	Let Name	Logo			
Spelling	[53.318]	[4.258] (.136)	[-6.175] (.101)	[9.318] (.089)			32.6%

Note. Let Snd = Letter Sounds Production; Let Rhym = Letters rhyme recognition; Syllable Seg = Syllable Segmenting; Rhym Prod = Rhyming Word Production; Logo = Logo Words Recognition; Blend = Sound Blending; K Dict = Kindergarten Sentence Dictation; Sent Seg = Sentence Segmenting; Word Rhym = Recognition of Words that Rhyme; Let Name = Letter Name Recognition.

variance explained). The essential failure of letter naming to predict later achievement in reading and spelling within this sample is not consistent with previous studies (e.g., Bond and Dykstra 1967; Chall 1967). Only seven children failed to achieve the 50% correct criterion for naming eight letters. The potential impact of this task might have been limited by the restricted range of the items. However, it may also be that the power of this predictor is greatly diminished by the end of kindergarten. Letter naming has been reported as a highly significant predictor of later achievement in different language cultures when assessed at the beginning of the first year of schooling (Elbro, Borstrøm, and Petersen 1998; Christensen 1997 among others).

Recognition of rhyming words only contributed to the prediction of vocabulary scores (4.4%) at grade 2. Rhyme production did not contribute meaningfully to the prediction equations until grade 3. It appeared as the best predictor of word analysis (17.4% of variance explained) and vocabulary (26.6% of variance explained) at grade 3. Difficulty with rhyming tasks has been proposed as one cause of disabilities in reading and spelling (Bradley 1988). It has been suggested that rhyming may provide the bridge to knowledge of rime, and then onsets, which may, in turn, set the stage for acquiring phonemes segmentation, letter/sound knowledge, and decoding skill (Adams 1990; Bradley and Bryant 1985). One would expect that rhyming would, therefore, be a good predictor of grade 1 reading. When compared to other pre-reading abilities, however, rhyming has not emerged as a significant, independent, or collaborative predictor of reading achievement in kindergarten or grade 1 (Stanovich, Cunningham, and Cramer 1984; Christensen 1997). Based on a meta-analysis of several studies that examined the role of phonological awareness in beginning reading, Wagner (1988) suggested that synthesis tasks, such as sound blending, are causally related to reading but that analysis tasks, such as rhyming, develop reciprocally with reading. Only six children failed to reach the criterion score for either recognition or production of rhyming words in this study. This is consistent with the ceiling effect for rhyming at the end of kindergarten reported by Stanovich and colleagues (1984). As for letter naming, it may be that the critical time to capture the predictive power of rhyming tasks is at the beginning of kindergarten. However, the fact that each of these variables did contribute 4% to 26% of variance on one or more norm-referenced achievement measures at grades 2 and 3 might also suggest that these tasks are early representations of later developing cognitive competencies that have an impact on achievement of more complex reading.

One variable, not assessed in this study, for which rhyming is likely "standing in," is explicit phoneme segmentation.

The logo name recognition task was difficult for most. Seventy-five percent failed to reach criterion. However, it appeared as the second best predictor of vocabulary achievement at grade 1. Logo recognition explained 11.5% of the variance over and above that which was explained by letter/sound knowledge. It also entered the prediction equation for spelling achievement at grade 3, after letter/sound knowledge and letter name knowledge, and explained an additional 8.9% of the variance. Logo recognition requires visual analysis and recognition of visual details not typically attended to when the word is embedded in the full label context. This is an ability whose development is likely supported by experiences in grade 1 and beyond, which promote recognition of undecodable and high frequency words. The logo task, as an index of "at riskness," will probably not be informative before grade 1.

Sound blending proved difficult for about 50% of the sample. The overall predictive power of sound blending in this study may have been attenuated by the sampling restrictions imposed. However, blending ability did make a meaningful contribution to the variance explained in spelling performance at grade 1 (4.5%), and in vocabulary achievement at grade 2 (6.6%), over and above letter sound knowledge. Blending ability has been identified as a strong predictor of reading achievement through grade 4 (Chall, Roswell, and Blumenthal 1963). Instruction in sound blending has been shown to have a facilitative effect on future reading performance (Hatcher, Hulme, and Ellis 1994; Perfetti et al. 1987; Snider 1997). In the present study, it was not apparent that kindergarten classroom instruction addressed sound blending in any systematic way. The pattern of performance in blending among students in this sample suggests that some students will abstract information spontaneously from experiences in their surroundings that eventually is organized into competencies sampled by measures of this pre-reading skill. However, it is reasonable to expect that explicit instruction in sound blending will be necessary for at least some of the students who fail to reach criterion on this task.

CONCLUSIONS

Within the limitations of small sample size, this study suggests that it may be possible to identify effectively kindergarten students at risk of failure in reading and spelling using tasks that sample the hierarchical phases of skill acquisition proposed by Frith and elaborated upon by Ehri. Although letter sound association was the strongest and most consistent predictor of subsequent achievement, seven of the ten variables in the screening process were computer selected to be entered second into various equations and each explained meaningful additional variance (3.6%–11.5%).

Factor analyses lend support to the assumption that different tasks on the screen are sampling different underlying constructs. When juxtaposed with skills associated with the logographic and early alphabetic phases in the checklist provided, the rationale for the premise that the consolidation of skills at an early phase provides the foundation for acquiring skills in a later phase (Frith 1985), appears to be supported.

Achievement patterns on the various screen tasks suggest that measures of some pre-reading abilities may be time sensitive. Locke and colleagues (1997) came to a similar conclusion in their longitudinal study of developmental dyslexia. Recognition and production of rhyming words, as well as letter name recognition, may be better predictors of subsequent reading and spelling achievement if measured at the beginning of the kindergarten year. Similarly, identification of logo-specific words will probably be most informative if assessed near the end of grade 1.

IMPLICATIONS

Further research to examine the effectiveness of an abbreviated form of the kindergarten screen employed in this study is suggested. Analysis of individual performance on the various tasks indicates that five tasks should remain in the battery. These are sentence segmenting, syllable segmenting, rhyme production, letter sound associations, and sound blending. Collectively, these tasks tap the constructs underlying all three factors identified in the present study and do range across the logographic and early alphabetic phases of skill development as proposed by Frith. Administration of a sentence dictation task to whole classes appears to be an efficient approach to selecting those who may be at risk of failure and should participate in individual testing using the screen tasks. Taken together, the dictation task and the five screen tasks have the potential to cast a sufficiently broad net to identify a large proportion of those who may be at risk of failure in reading before grade 1.

The life-long effects of low literacy skills have roots that sprout in kindergarten, before intensive, formal instruction in reading typically begins. Kindergarten screening that identifies a major proportion of students at risk of school failure, and that focuses on a program of interventions, would contribute much to reversing this course of events.

REFERENCES

Adams, M. J. 1990. *Beginning to Read.* Cambridge, MA: MIT Press.
Badian, N. A., McAnully, G. B., Duffy, F. H., and Als, H. 1990. Prediction of dyslexia in kindergarten boys. *Annals of Dyslexia* 40:152–79.
Bond, G. L., and Dykstra, R. 1967. The cooperative research program in first-grade reading instruction. *Reading Research Quarterly* 2:5–142.
Bradley, L. 1988. Rhyme recognition and reading and spelling. In *Preschool Prevention of Reading Failure*, eds. R. L. Masland and M. W. Masland. Parkton, MD: York Press.
Bradley, L., and Bryant, P. E. 985. *Rhyme and Reason in Reading and Spelling.* Ann Arbor: University of Michigan Press.
Chall, J. 1967. *Learning to Read: The Great Debate.* New York: McGraw-Hill.
Chall, J., Roswell, F., and Blumenthal, S. 1963. Auditory blending ability: A factor in success in beginning reading. *Reading Teacher* 17:113–18.
Christensen, C. A.1997. Onset, rhymes, and phonemes in learning to read. *Scientific Studies in Reading* 1 (4):341–58.
Clay, M.1979. *The Early Detection of Reading Difficulties: A Diagnostic Survey with Recovery Procedures.* New Zealand: Heinemann Press.
Daneman, M. 1991. Individual differences in reading skills. In *Handbook of Reading Research Vol. 2*, eds. R. Barr, M. Kamil, P. Mosenthal, and P. D. Pearson. New York: Longman Press.
de Hirsch, K., Jansky, J. J., and Langford, W. S. 1966. *Predicting Reading Failure.* New York: Harper & Row, Publishers.
Ehri, L. 1994. Development of the ability to read words: Update. In *Theoretical Models and Processes of Reading 4th ed.*, eds. R. Rudell, M. Ruddell, and H. Singer. Newark, DE: International Reading Association.
Elbro, C., Borstrøm, I., and Petersen, D. K. 1998. Predicting dyslexia from kindergarten: The importance of distinctions of phonological representations of lexical items. *Reading Research Quarterly* 33(1):36–60.
Frith, U. 1985. Beneath the surface of developmental dyslexia. In *Surface Dyslexia*, eds. K. Patterson, M. Coltheart, and J. Marshall. London: Lawrence Erlbaum Associates, Inc. Publishers.
Ganske, K. 1993. *Developmental Spelling Assessment.* Barboursville, VA: Author.
Gough, P. B., and Tunmer, W. E. 1986. Decoding reading and reading disability. *Remedial and Special Education* 7:6–10.
Hatcher, P., Hulme, C., and Ellis, A. W. 1994. Ameliorating reading failure by integrating the teaching of reading and phonological skills: The phonological linkage hypothesis. *Child Development* 65:41–57.
Hoover, W. A., and Gough, P. B. 1990. The simple view of reading. *Reading and Writing: An Interdisciplinary Journal* 2:127–60.
Kenny, D. T., and Chekaluk, E. 1993. Early reading performance: A comparison of teacher-based and test-based assessments. *Journal of Learning Disabilities* 26(4):227–36.

Locke, J. L., Hodgson, J., Macaruso, P., Roberts, J., Lambrecht-Smith, S., and Guttentag, C. 1997. The development of developmental dyslexia. In *Dyslexia: Biology, Cognition and Intervention*, eds. C. Hulme and M. Snowling. London: Whurr Publishers, Ltd.

Perfetti, C. A., Beck, I., Bell, L. C., and Hughes, C. 1987. Phonemic knowledge and learning to read are reciprocal: A longitudinal study of first grade children. *Merrill-Palmer Quarterly* 33:283–319.

Sawyer, D. J. 1987. *Test of Awareness of Language Segments Administration Manual*. Rockville, MD: Aspen Publishers, Inc.

Sawyer, D. J. 1988. Studies of the effects of teaching auditory segmenting skills within the reading program. In *Preschool Prevention of Reading Failure*, eds. R. L. Masland and M. W. Masland. Parkton, MD: York Press.

Sawyer, D. J. 1992. Language abilities, reading acquisition, and developmental dyslexia: A discussion of hypothetical and observed relationships. *Journal of Learning Disabilities* 25:81–144.

Snider, V. E. 1997. The relationship between phonemic awareness and later reading achievement. *Journal of Educational Research* 90:203–10.

Stanovich, K., Cunningham, A. E., and Cramer, B. 1984. Assessing phonological awareness in kindergarten children: Issues of task comparability. *Journal of Experimental Child Psychology* 38:175–90.

Thorndike, R. L. 1973. *Reading Comprehension Education in Fifteen Countries*. New York: Wiley Press.

Wagner, R. K. 1988. Causal relations between the development of phonological processing abilities and the acquisition of reading skills: A meta-analysis. *Merrill-Palmer Quarterly* 33:283–319.

Wagner, R. K., and Torgeson, J. K. 1987. The nature of phonological processing and its causal role in the acquisition of reading skills. *Phonological Bulletin* 101:192–212.

Wentink, H. 1997. From graphemes to syllables: The development of phonological decoding skills in poor and normal readers. Doctoral dissertation, Katholieke Universiteit Njmegen, Holland: author.

Chapter • 5

Prevention and Prediction of Reading Problems

Bente E. Hagtvet

The idea that reading problems may be prevented is an optimistic implication in a great number of experimental studies carried out in the field of reading research during the last two decades (e.g., Ball and Blackman 1991; Bradley and Bryant 1983; Hatcher, Hulme, and Ellis 1994; Lundberg, Frost, and Petersen 1988). It has also become a main educational aim (e.g., Snow, Burns, and Griffin 1998). In principle, reading problems may be prevented by two main strategies. One is to establish programs with a generally preventive effect in inclusive settings in preschools and early schooling. The other is early identification of children at risk of developing reading problems for the purpose of giving them prophylactic, early, and special individualized help. The two approaches are, of course, not mutually exclusive, and most developed countries typically make use of both, often within the same educational context. However, in inclusive settings in practice, reading problems are not prevented by intervention in preschool and school to the extent one might expect on the basis of recent research. The programs tend to be too general and theoretically vague, and individually oriented prophylactic special help is typically offered only in extreme cases where a broad register of learning disabilities is involved, making prevention difficult. Also, the early symptoms signaling that a child is at risk for developing a reading problem are not always obvious. Therefore, it may be difficult for parents, health nurses, and teachers to identify correctly the child who is at risk. If the one-to-one tutoring somehow stigmatizes the child negatively, early prevention may even be unjustified. Finally, we have limited knowledge about the conditions under which prevention in natural contexts works and about the forces that may act as barriers to successful prevention. This lack of precise knowledge about the variables that mediate prevention in natural contexts may be the very reason prevention appears to be more efficient in experimental than in natural settings.

This chapter focuses on the dynamics between the potentials and content of prevention as suggested in recent experimental and longitudinal research and the barriers to successful prevention as indicated by practice and sociological theory. First, the potentials of preventing reading problems are highlighted with reference to early language precursors identified in recent longitudinal research. Second, some common barriers to prevention are discussed, in particular emotions that affect literacy development negatively, and that may even be a consequence of a stigma caused by the prevention itself. A study of the oral and written language development of Norwegian children aged 4 to 9 years is at the center of attention (Hagtvet 1996). This study underscores the need to have an integrative view on language and emotional development in preventing reading problems.

THE IMPORTANCE OF PREVENTING READING PROBLEMS

The causes of reading problems may be associated with factors related to the individual as well as to the environment, e.g., quality of instruction. It is a prominent and puzzling feature of many reading problems, in particular the so-called "specific" problems (dyslexia), that an apparently minor and subtle impairment or deficiency, most often a weakness in manipulating language, may have devastating effects, not only on reading and writing skills, but also on life opportunities. Failing to learn to read and write properly implies not only poor education, less good jobs, and sometimes poverty, but also loss of dignity and self-respect. This is amply documented in research on the social and emotional consequences of having reading problems. In a review article on the relationships, Bryan and Bryan (1990) specify the consequences of reading impairment. Failures in the process of learning to read and write are typically associated with test anxiety and problems of controlled attention, behavior problems, tendency to give up when confronted with challenges, tendency to be ignored by teachers as well as by friends, etc. A main reason for preventing reading failures is, therefore, that the consequences of not preventing them may be dramatic.

A second reason for focusing on prevention is that training studies document that prevention works. Children who were trained to handle phonemes and phoneme-grapheme connections in pre-school and the first years in school were better readers after a few years in school than were groups of control children without phonemic awareness training (Ball and Blackman 1991; Bradley and Bryant 1983; Hatcher, Hulme, and Ellis 1994; Lundberg, Frost, and Petersen 1988). And in the Bornholm study, where the experimental group received only 15 minutes of daily play-oriented training in phonemic awareness, the children at risk of developing reading problems at school entry scored as well as did average readers in the control group at the end of grade 3 (Lundberg et al. 1991). This suggests that a focused training program in kindergarten may not only raise the average reading level, it may actually prevent reading problems from developing in children at risk for such problems.

A third reason for preventing reading problems is the observation that they tend to be more or less cemented after only a few years in school. Badian (1988) studied the stability in reading scores across a span of nine years. Children who were poor readers at the end of grade 3 were typically poor readers at the end of grade 8 as well, suggesting that kindergarten and the first years in school is a rather critical period for developing good reading skills. The adage, "once a poor reader, always a poor reader" thus is not an empty saying. It is a rather precise description of the typical developmental pathway to reading disabilities. If success in reading is achieved by means of remedial intervention starting after years of failing to learn, it is most typically by means of intensive expert remedial treatment in special and often expensive settings, for example, in special schools for children with dyslexia (e.g., Finucci, Gottfredson, and Childs 1985; Gaskins 1998).

In summary, the importance of preventing reading problems is underscored in three lines of research. Clinical data document difficult life situations in the aftermath of reading problems. Experimental data show that training studies that focus on phonemic awareness and phoneme-grapheme correspondences have a preventive effect. And developmental data document that special education after grade 3 is extremely challenging and often unsuccessful (but see Bruck 1985, 1987; Finucci, Gottfredson, and Childs 1985; Gaskins 1998).

EARLY PRECURSORS OF READING PROBLEMS

Recent research on reading disabilities strongly underscores their linguistic basis (e.g., Badian et al. 1990; Bradley and Bryant 1983; Catts 1991; Catts et al. 1999; Hagtvet 1996; Hoover and Gough

1990; Lundberg 1982; Olson 1994; Perfetti 1985; Scarborough 1990; Snowling 1987; Vellutino 1979; Wagner and Torgesen 1987). In Scarborough's (1989, 1990) longitudinal study of children from dyslexic families, children who later developed reading problems showed less well developed syntax and also produced more phonological errors in their spontaneous speech as early as age 30 months. At age 42 months, the dyslexic children were also impaired in receptive and expressive vocabulary and, at age five years, they typically obtained low scores on active vocabulary and phonemic awareness tasks and letter knowledge. The whole language system, in other words, appeared to be somehow delayed, and different components of language appeared to relate to later reading problems at different times during the preschool years.

Other studies validate and extend Scarborough's finding. Children at risk of developing written language problems have been found to be poor at rhyming at age three to four years (Bryant et al. 1989), and also at non-word repetition, and in receptive and expressive vocabulary and letter knowledge (Gallagher, Frith, and Snowling 1996). At ages five and six, problems in manipulating the phonemic structure of words have been observed frequently, including the ability to connect the semantic and phonological lexicon through rapid naming (Badian 1995; Bradley and Bryant 1983; Elbro, Borstrøm, and Petersen 1998; Lundberg, Olofsson, and Wall 1980). And low scores on tests of syntax and morphology at age six predicted the ability to spell words correctly at age 8 (Bryant, Nunes, and Bindman 1999). More recently, arguments in favor of a broader linguistic basis of reading problems have been presented increasingly often (e.g., Bishop 1997; Catts et al. 1999, cf., also Tunmer and Hoover 1992, and Vellutino 1979). These early precursors of reading problems strongly underscore the importance of language stimulation, with a particular focus on phonological awareness, in any program aimed at preventing reading problems.

In a Norwegian study including 70 randomly selected children who were followed longitudinally from age four to age nine, a broad set of oral language variables was identified as predictive of reading ability (Hagtvet 1996, 1997). The children were selected for participation by the Norwegian Bureau of Statistics, in connection with the standardization of the Norwegian version of the Reynell Developmental Language Scales (Hagtvet and Lillestølen 1985; Reynell 1977). Being a norm sample, only those children were included for participation who did not have a diagnosed language delay or a sensory handicap at the time of recruitment to the study. This means that any language weaknesses revealed in these children during the process of the study have to be described as subtle, because they could not be detected in everyday life situations, and no child got any sort of preventive programs beyond general stimulation in nursery school or kindergarten.

The aim of the study was to investigate the relationship between preschool oral language skills and early written language development for the purpose of developing an improved rationale for early help for children at risk of developing reading problems.[1] Among other things, we identified early precursors of reading problems, assessed the success with which poor readers could be predicted on the basis of their language skills in preschool, and scrutinized those cases that were not correctly identified in preschool, i.e., the false positives and the false negatives. Using these procedures, factors contributing to unsuccessful predictions were identified.

The children were assessed yearly by means of a rather large battery of tests, observations, and interviews. General as well as individual profiles of development were described. The predictive validity of the Reynell Scales was assessed by means of logistic and multiple regression analyses. The Reynell is a test of oral language comprehension and language expression loading strongly on syntactical and semantic skills. These are skills that recent research has less often focused on when correlates of reading problems have been discussed. This is because phonological variables have appeared of greater relevance to the core problem(s) involved (probably due to the attraction of phonological variables) (but, see, e.g., Vellutino 1979; Catts et al. 1999, and Shankweiler and Crain 1986). A main finding was that semantically loaded reading tasks at age 9 were positively related to the Reynell at age 4, although reading tasks that demanded accurate decoding, e.g., word reading, nonword reading, or sentence reading, were less strongly related. For example, while 13% of the variance in Text comprehension at age 9 was explained by the Reynell at age 4 (after controlling for nonverbal IQ), the Reynell predicted only 4% of the variance in Word reading. This is only to be expected, because the Reynell does not pretend to measure those aspects of language typically associated with decoding, e.g., phonemic awareness. Extremely poor functioning was, however, well predicted. The four poorest decoders at age 9, in fact, also scored extremely poorly on the Reynell at age 4.

In one part of the study, we looked at the predictive power of the Reynell scale at age 4 and Phonemic awareness (phoneme

---

[1]Norwegian children have by tradition started school at age seven, which also was the case for the children participating in the present study. School entrance age was, however, reduced to age six in 1997.

analysis and phoneme synthesis) at age 6 (i.e., before they were formally introduced to reading and writing). We assessed the stability of scores in children scoring below the 33rd percentile at measurement 1 (ages 4 or 6 respectively) and measurement 2 (age 9). The hit rate (i.e., stability in scores below 33rd percentile) when predicting Sentence reading and Text comprehension at age 9, on the basis of the Reynell at age 4, was 57% and 60% respectively (Hagtvet 1996, 1997). For Phonemic awareness at age 6, the hit rates were 58% and 48% respectively. These findings indicate that prediction of individual development on the basis of one variable is done with great uncertainty, even though the predictor is theoretically related to the outcome measure. We should remember that the lower 33rd percentile in a random sample of children judged as "normal" at age 4 includes a number of children who are only marginally delayed and that the hit rate was higher in the lower extreme end of the distribution.

The challenge of predicting individual development was likewise highlighted in a study by Bradley and Bryant (1985) that included 300 British children. One aim of their study was to assess how well reading at age 8 could be predicted on the basis of phonemic awareness, defined as sound categorization at age 5. As before, one would expect a strong relationship between phonemic awareness at age 5 and reading ability at age 8. Regression analyses confirmed this expectation. Sound categorization at age 5 accounted for a fair amount of variance in reading at age 8, even after age and linguistic-cognitive abilities had been controlled for. However, only 28% ($n = 7$) of the children who scored poorly on sound categorization, attained low scores on sentence reading at age 8. Similarly low percentages of valid positives were found as poor word readers and poor spellers at age 8. Prediction of reading and spelling development at the level of individual cases, therefore, appears very difficult, even when the predictor presumably is a variable that is the most potent predictor on the basis of available theory and empirical evidence. In a study by Badian (1986), the precision in predicting reading problems reached 93% when broad composite scores were applied as predictors, as opposed to 43% when a screening test cut off was used. From a theoretical, as well as statistical position, this is only to be expected, because reading is a complex process, and predictions are always made with greater probability if more relevant information enters into the model.

The finding in the Norwegian study that the Reynell produced about the same hit rates as did Phonemic awareness was a surprise because Reynell was measured two years earlier than Phonemic awareness, and stability in scores presumably is less over great lapses in time. Also, phoneme analysis and synthesis may be described as part of the reading process itself, and phonemic awareness has generally been considered the most powerful predictor of reading problems in a number of studies (e.g., Høien and Lundberg 1991; Liberman and Shankweiler 1985; Perfetti, 1985; Snowling 1987; Stanovich 1988; Wagner and Torgesen 1987). However, most of the prediction studies that have explored the relation between phonemic awareness and reading do not cover children younger than five years. This may have resulted in a neglect of the influence that age of assessment has on the manifested predictive power of a theoretical construct. Syntactical and semantic measures obtained at ages 3 and 4 may, for example, be better predictors of later reading abilities than those obtained at ages 5 and 6. Prediction studies have furthermore tended not to include a broad range of semantic and syntactic variables (see Bowey and Patel [1988] for a discussion of the neglect of relevant syntactical and semantic measures in recent prediction studies of reading, and also Catts et al. 1999). On these grounds it is, at best, difficult to assess the relative predictive power of various preschool linguistic measures on the basis of existing studies. Also, outcome measures vary between studies. The outcome measures in the present study, Sentence reading and Text comprehension, were semantically and syntactically loaded. When using Word reading as the outcome measure, Phonemic Awareness measured at age six was the variable with the strongest predictive power, both when predicting individual development by stability in scores and when using regression analysis. Therefore, rather than undermining the predictive power of phonemic awareness, the results underscore the importance of general language abilities in reading comprehension and the importance of phonemic awareness to word decoding. Both general language stimulation and phonological awareness training (via play) should therefore be included in a program aiming at preventing reading problems.

BARRIERS TO PREVENTION

Out of the 70 children, 12 children with great instability in scores between ages 4 and 9 were sampled. Six of these were false negatives (wrongly predicted as not at risk on the basis of preschool scores) and six were false positives (wrongly predicted as at risk on the basis of preschool scores). Case studies identified potential barriers to successful prediction in a number of domains, e.g., measurement errors, emotional status of the individual, reading instruction in school, friends' interest in reading, relationship to teacher, and reading experience (Hagtvet 1996). This broad range of influential individual and environmental variables emphasize the need to take many variables into account when predicting individual development (see below). These are presumably also variables that have to be taken into account when planning and implementing an intervention program with a preventive effect. Many of the variables that act as barriers to successful prediction may also act as important mediators of successful prevention.

On assessing the children at age 4, clinical impression indicated a big difference in socio-emotional functioning between the advanced language users and the less advanced. The less skilled language users tended to be more restless, impatient, and physically active during assessment than were the skilled language users. Children with good oral language skills, in contrast, appeared interested and showed concentration and persistence. In tracing the tendency to be involved in off-task behaviors, a group of 13 poor decoders at age 9 was studied retrospectively. They scored statistically higher than the children who became good decoders on various measures of restlessness at age 4 (Hagtvet 1996). The ability to focus on task and to sit still on the chair at age 4 was related, for example, to later written language abilities. It should be underscored that these poor readers were not at all behavior problems, rather there were minor signs of restlessness; e.g., they left their chairs impulsively significantly more often (1 to 3 times) at age 4 than did the comparison groups during an assessment that lasted about an hour.

LANGUAGE AND OFF-TASK BEHAVIORS

The relation between language and emotional development is an underdeveloped area of research. We also know little about how the two domains together affect the school beginner learning to read and write. Although it is more or less taken for granted that reading disorders commonly lead to emotional reactions like stress, anxiety, and poor self esteem (e.g., Bryan and Bryan 1990), the potential cause of such variables is far less systematically investigated. In one perspective, this weighting of importance is only natural, because the relation between emotions and written language problems cannot easily be studied until after the reading problems have entered the arena, i.e., after the child has failed to learn to read normally in school. However, language competence is by itself developed in an emotional space created by the child and his or her caretaker. Mothers' talk to children ("baby talk") is loaded with affect, typically conveying closeness and warmth (Ferguson 1956, 1977). Early mother-child communication is in fact to a large extent a matter of communicating feelings (e.g., Bateson 1975; Bloom 1977, 1990; Trevarthen 1993). The early interchange of emotions in gaze and vocal sounds (proto conversation) is based on a sensitivity of timing that is extremely emotional and constitutes the ground on which later verbal turn taking is built. And much verbal interaction has the aim of creating emotional reactions. This is the case with verbal humor, for example jokes in which the punch line often demands manipulation of the two meanings of homonyms. On this basis, the lack of continued interest in how language develops in emotional space after the first year in a child's life is noteworthy. This lack of interest in first (oral and written) language learning is in some contrast to second language learning, where the relation is strongly emphasized. In fact, second language learning appears inefficient when the language learning situation is detached from emotional involvement and social interaction. Dutch children do not, for example, appear to learn to speak German from watching television with only German speech (Snow et al. 1976) and immigrant children who do not take part in the social-emotional networks of the native speakers typically pick up the semantic, syntactic, and prosodic nuances of the second language only insufficiently (McLaughlin 1987). This point tends to be ignored in oral and written first language learning, and the reason may be that emotional involvement is then taken for granted (Wold 1993). However, when first language learning for some reason is delayed, the emotional involvement, if at all available, is presumably interfering with, rather than supporting, language development—as is also the case in second language learning.

The present longitudinal study included systematic assessments of off-task behaviors typically associated with stress and anxiety at ages 6 and 9. The subjects' level of off-task behavior was assessed by means of a checklist of different behavior indicators as presented in theory of test anxiety. The checklist was not based on one particular theory, but was strongly inspired by the work of Wine (1971, 1980). On a scale ranging from 0 to 5 the following behaviors were evaluated: "fidgets on chair," "twists hair," "plays" with hands," "frowns eyebrows," and "bites lips" (see Appendix 1 for the check-list). The assessment was carried out by the tester during and after each assessment on the basis of observations during assessment. The item scores were added to get a composite score reflecting a child's general level of off-task behavior. The off-task behaviors were assumed to interfere with the child's ability to focus attention on task (e.g., Eysenck 1992; Wine 1980). To use a child's overt behavior as an indicator of emotional arousal appears meaningful, because research indicates that anxious children tend to look away from a task in a very concrete sense (e.g., Nottelman and Hill 1977). On this basis, Wine (1980) argues that a general "task avoidant strategy" may be typical of anxious children—and in particular, young children. Wine relates this to Luria's developmental theory regarding the gradual internalization of behaviors (Wine 1980:357): "with increasing age, these avoidant behaviors may become covert and internalized." We do not, of course, on this basis know for sure whether the behaviors reflect anxiety or some other latent trait sharing the same symptom pattern, e.g., the problems of concentration or nonpersistence typically found in children diagnosed as ADHD. However, this is of little concern to the issue in question, as off-task behaviors, no matter what causes them, presumably reflect some inner tensions distracting the child from concentrating on the task and the verbal communication. Therefore, off-task behaviors were presumed to interfere negatively with language learning.

At age 9, poor readers—not unexpectedly—showed significantly more emotional reactions than did good readers. It was of greater surprise that this tendency was also revealed at age 6, i.e., before these children started school and formally learned to read and write. Figure 1 gives an overview and visual picture of these developmental patterns for poor ($n = 13$), average ($n = 38$) and early ($n = 19$) readers respectively.[2] "Early readers" are interesting in this developmental perspective, because this category includes children who "taught themselves to read" before they started school at age 7. This is presumably a group to whom reading came particularly easily, because Norwegian nursery schools and kindergartens, by tradition, do not stimulate written language, and even

---

[2]Definition of poor readers: Poor readers had a score less than the 25th percentile at the end of Grade 2 (at age 9) on two out of three reading tests loading high on decoding abilities:

    I. Non-word reading (Olofsson and Lundberg 1985), i.e., reading of a list of nine short words with no meaning. The child's final score was a measure of accuracy corrected for speed.

    II. Word reading (Olofsson and Lundberg 1985) involved reading of 13 meaningful words that were regularly and irregularly spelled. The child's score was again accuracy, corrected for speed.

    III. Sentence reading (Dugstad 1978) consisted of 24 short sentences with a simple content presented as cloze tasks. In the empty space at the end of each sentence, the child had to fill in one out of five words that were presented as a list underneath each sentence, e.g., "You have to come____ (school, some, soon, us, bed)."

parents at the time of assessment hesitated to teach their children letters and reading and spelling strategies.[3] To allow for a direct comparison of group trends, the average z-score for a selection of variables for each of the three groups is represented by a plot. The variables reflect the ability to comprehend and use language, metalinguistic tasks (i.e., the ability to manipulate linguistic segments [words, morphemes and phonemes]), cognitive measures, and measures of off-task behaviors/emotionality. By this procedure, one gets an impression of average scores achieved by each of the three groups for the selected measures at ages 4, 6, 8, and 9.

At the left end of the horizontal axis are measures from the assessment at age 4: Socio-economic background (V1) and the Reynell (V2). Then follows linguistic/cognitive variables at age six: Block design (WISC) (V3), Comprehension of complex syntax (V4), Vocabulary (WISC) (V5), Morpheme awareness (V6), Phoneme awareness (V7), Emotionality (V8). V9 refers to Word reading at age 8, and at the right end of the figure are the cognitive/linguistic variables assessed at age 9: Block design (WISC) (V10), Comprehension of complex syntax (V11), Vocabulary (V12), Morpheme awareness (V13), Emotionality (V14), Word reading, corrected for reading speed (V15), and Sentence reading, corrected for reading speed (V16).[4]

---

[3]By tradition, there is a strong tendency among Norwegian kindergarten teachers as well as parents not to stimulate written language formally or informally before age seven. Reading and writing should be taught by qualified primary school teachers, whereas kindergarten teachers should stimulate social, motor, creative, and oral language abilities (Nurss 1988a, 1988b). The 1997 reform is traditional in the sense that literacy stimulation in Grade 1 is play oriented, and the children are not expected to learn to read and spell before Grade 2. Rather, the reform emphasizes the importance of play, phonemic awareness training through the use of language games, and informal teaching of written symbols. The ideal is a balanced view focusing phonemic awareness as well as views presented in the "emergent literacy tradition" (e.g., Clay, 1975; Sulzby, 1986).

[4]Instruments:
(V1) Socio-economic background, classified along a five-point-scale used by the Norwegian Bureau of Statistics (Album 1988). Age 4.
(V2) Reynell Developmental Language Scales (total score) (Reynell, 1977): Comprehension and language production. Age 4.
(V3) Block Design (WISC-revised) (Wechsler 1974). Age 6.
(V4) Syntactic comprehension (Rommetveit and Rommetveit 1980). Age 6. This test consists of 31 items and measures the ability to comprehend complex syntactic structures, like the passive, and structures where linguistic components are nested into each other, e.g., "Point at the picture where the bear who is being hit by the lady who falls over," "Point at the picture where the ball which the cat is playing with, falls down from the table," etc. The child is shown a set of pictures (two to four) and provided with a test sentence. The task is to point at the picture that matches the sentence. A score of one was given for a correct answer, and a score of 0 for incorrect answers.
continued

Three main characteristics stand out as striking when observing figure 1. First, the relative achievement levels of the three groups are stable across time. The group of poor readers scores below the average readers, who again score below the early readers on almost every variable at every age level. Secondly, and as mentioned above, the only two variables on which the poor readers score higher than the comparison groups are on off-task behaviors—here labeled Emotionality—measured at ages 6 and 9 (variables 8 and 14). Thirdly, the developmental profile of the poor readers is a mirror image of the developmental profile of the early readers. The peaks and dips of the two groups are in most cases associated with the same variables indicating that the early readers have "strengths" where the poor readers have "weaknesses," a finding that corroborates Clark's study on early readers in Scotland (Clark 1976).

(V5)   Vocabulary (WISC-revised) (Wechsler 1974). Age 6.

(V6)   Morpheme awareness/Grammatic Closure (ITPA) (Kirk, McCarthy, and Kirk 1968). Age 6.

(V7)   Phoneme awareness (phoneme analysis and synthesis of three-letter words) (Olofsson and Lundberg 1983). Age 6. The test was administered individually and organized as a game in which the tester and the child took turns in guessing pictures of objects. Each object referred to a word consisting of three phonemes. In Phoneme synthesis, the tester had a set of pictures (10 items) that the child could not see. The child's task was to guess what picture the tester had in mind when he or she labeled the pictures by saying the phonemes in each word, e.g., "Guess what my picture is now /g/ /å/ /s/ (goose)? What do the sounds /g/ /å/ /s/ make?" i.e., the tester analyzed, the child synthesized. Inspired by the Vygotskyan (1962) notion of the zone of proximal development, the child was given a modified and easier version of the task if he or she failed on the first attempt. Help was now offered by segmenting the word into a syllable and a phoneme, e.g., "What does /gå/ /s/ amount to together?"

In Phoneme analysis, the child was shown a set of pictures (11 items) that the tester could not see. The child's task now was to label the pictures by saying the phonemes, e.g., "Guess what my picture is now: /b/ /i/ /l/ (car)," i.e., the child analyzed, the tester synthesized. The child was given two points for a perfect synthesis/analysis of three phonemes, one point for analyzing/synthesizing two segments correctly, and a zero score when no evidence of phoneme analysis/synthesis could be detected.

(V8)   Off-task-behavior (see Appendix 1). Age 6.

(V9)   Word reading (Dugstad 1978) Age 8. Five words are written in a column next to a picture. The child's task is to mark out the word that goes with the picture. Altogether there are 65 tasks, and the child is told to read as accurately and as fast he or she can.

(V10) Block Design. Age 9.

(V11) Comprehension of complex syntax. Age 9.

(V12) Vocabulary. Age 9.

(V13) Morpheme awareness/Grammatic closure. Age 9.

(V14) Off-task-behavior. Age 9.

(V15) Word reading (Olofsson and Lundberg 1985). Age 9.

(V16) Sentence reading (Dugstad 1978). Age 9.

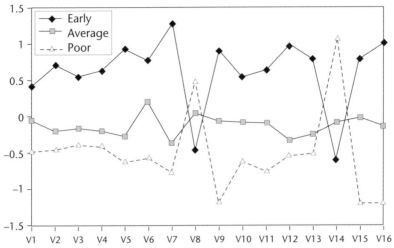

Figure 1. Development trends for poor, average and early readers. Average z-scores

The observation that the children at risk of developing a reading problem showed signs of stress and anxiety before they started school, indicates that a number of these children started school with a double vulnerability. In addition to being linguistically at risk, they were emotionally at risk. It is noteworthy that this is the case even at age 6, i.e., before the children experienced failures in learning to read and write in school. It is also noteworthy that this was observed in a group with no documented problems in oral language. This finding indicates that even a language problem which is so subtle that it may not be discovered in everyday life may be associated with feelings of worry, anxiety, and stress in the pre-school years. The early readers on the contrary showed an emotional strength, which in combination with their strong verbal abilities, in particular in manipulating linguistic segments and using and comprehending language in decontextualized ways, may act as an important resilience factor (Garmezy 1993). Being the poor readers' "weaknesses" and the early readers' "strengths," these oral language variables and off-task behaviors appear of particular relevance to written language mastery.

The same relation between language and emotion is observed in the bivariate correlations in table I, which portrays the pattern of bivariate correlations for Emotionality assessed at ages 6 and 9 and a selection of verbal and nonverbal variables at ages 4 through 9. Correlation coefficients in the upper square of the table portray verbal domains and those in the lower square refer to cognitive variables where the loading from the verbal domain is low.

Table I. Bivariate correlations between Emotionality and verbal- and nonverbal variables

	Emotionality 6	Emotionality 9
Emotionality, age 6	1.000	.347*
Emotionality, age 9	.347**	1.000
Socio-economic background, age 5	−.296*	−.183
Reynell, age 4	−.336**	−.431**
Comprehension of complex syntax, age 6	−.334**	−.321**
WISC Vocabulary, age 6	−.450**	−.312**
Morphemic awareness, age 6	−.467**	−.519**
Phonemic awareness, age 6	−.305*	−.364**
Comprehension of complex syntax, age 9	−.403**	−.503**
Vocabulary, WISC, age 9,	−.414**	−.419**
Morphemic awareness, age 9	−.460**	−.408**
Word reading, age 8	−.364**	−.498**
Sentence reading, age 8	−.343**	−.423**
Word reading, age 9	−.366**	−.350**
Sentence reading, age 9	−.370**	−.390**
Text reading, age 9	−.325**	−.464**
Block design, WISC, age 6	−.206	−.202
Visual memory, age 6	−.150	−.302*
Conservation, age 6	−.164	−.161
Block design, WISC, age 9	−.177	−.211
Visual memory, age 9	−.074	−.240*

$*p < .05; **p < .01$

Table I shows very different correlational patterns for the upper and lower squares. In the upper square, the correlation coefficients are moderate to high and in every case statistically significant. In the lower square, the coefficients are low and reach statistical significance only in a few cases at age 9. Hence, although coefficients between off-task-behavior/emotionality and linguistic variables are statistically significant, the coefficients for emotionality and nonverbal abilities in the lower squares generally are not.

This finding of a combined weakness in linguistic and emotional domains in the group of at-risk children, and vice versa in early readers, suggests a combined effect from language and emotions to reading ability.

INDIVIDUAL VARIATION

Correlations as well as average z-scores for groups refer to average development and functioning that may conceal individual variations within the group of poor readers. For this reason the individual developmental patterns of the 13 poor decoders identified at age 9 were scrutinized retrospectively (Hagtvet 1996). Three subgroups of poor decoders could be identified. Some group characteristics concerning Socio-economic background, Intelligence, Oral and Written language skills, and Off-task behavior are in general terms and relative to age mates (presented below). The groups' performance relative to age mates was stable across ages. The descriptions, therefore, regard performances across the developmental span of age 6 to age 9, unless otherwise stated:

Group A: $n = 5$ (4 boys and 1 girl)
Socio-economic background: middle class to upper middle class
    (age 4)
Oral language abilities: average
Intelligence: average to above average
Off-task-behavior: low to average
Reading problems: marginal, and with little struggle (ages 8 and 9)
Group B: $n = 2$ (1 boy and 1 girl)
Socio-economic background: middle class (age 4)
Oral language abilities: average
Intelligence: average to above average
Off-task-behavior: high
Reading problem: marginal, but with much struggle (ages eight
    and nine)
Group C: $n = 6$ (5 boys and 1 girl)
Socio-economic background: lower middle class. (age 4)
Intelligence: lower normal range
Oral language abilities: low
Off-task behavior: high
Reading problems: serious to moderate, with much struggle (ages 8
    and 9)

Subgroups A and B consist of children with only marginal reading problems. Also, other variables suggest strengths (e.g., socio-economic background, oral language skills, and intelligence). These children, therefore, had a greater compensatory potential than subgroup C. Yet, on the basis of observations made by Badian (1988) and Yule and Rutter (1976), for example, showing that reading abilities at age 9 to 10 correlate strongly with reading abilities at age 14, the children in Subgroups A and B are at risk of increased marginalization if not properly helped in school. This is particularly the case for subgroup B, who read with struggle and great dislike, as did also subgroup C. Judging from clinical experience, the lack of will and motivation to read is the greatest threat to progress in reading. Group C, in fact, included all the children with the most serious reading problems and was, for this reason alone, most seriously at risk of continued problems. Their oral language abilities were, in addition, consistently in the lower range—four of these children scored the poorest in the sample at age 4, and they were all easily distracted at both ages 6 and 9. The risk signs were thus not only obvious, once we went below the surface of daily life functioning, but also consistent.

Both figure 1 and table I, and also the clinical information as presented above, suggest a rather close relation between language development and development of emotional control and concentration, in particular, in connection with delays in language abilities, but also in children with a linguistic strength. This rather consistent relationship between language weaknesses and high scores on Off-task behavior suggests that emotions and language are more interdependent than the limited research interest in the area indicates. It also indicates that this relation should be given priority in future research and that off-task-behavior should be included in batteries of predictors of reading abilities.

Co-occurrence does not necessarily imply causal patterns. We do not know whether the primary cause of low functioning was to be found in a language weakness, or in the emotional system, or the child's temperament. In a developmental and educational perspective, the primary cause may also be of less importance than the mechanisms by which the two factors develop and interact. McGee and coworkers (1986) postulate a developmental pattern characterized by an interactive spiral in which language and emotions constitute cornerstones mutually reinforcing each other. They base their reasoning on a longitudinal study of reading disabilities and behavior problems in boys during the age period of 5 to 11 years. The reading disabled boys showed more behavior problems at school entry than did a control group of normally reading boys, and the problems increased along with increases in reading problems. The authors conclude that "behavior problems pre-date reading disability, while reading failure further exacerbates the existing problem behavior" (McGee et al. 1986:597).

The present study with its dual focus on language and behavior makes the "opposite" causal path just as plausible. The seriously poor readers showed signs of oral language weakness and an increased tendency to engage in off-task behaviors, relative to comparison groups of average and good readers, before they started school and failed in learning to read and spell. There was furthermore, as it also was in the New Zealand study (McGee et al. 1986), a tendency for increased off-task behaviors at age 9 (cf., figure 1). One probable hypothesis that should be tested in future research, is that a negatively working interactive spiral was initiated at a very early age, or as soon as a child started to feel insecure in linguistically demanding situations. Complementarily, we would presume positive interactive spirals—or resilience—for the child with an advanced command of language, even before he or she started school. This appears to have been the case for the "early readers"; their advanced language skills accelerated in both the oral and the written modality, as did also their self-confidence and ability to focus on task.

Data from the subjects' retelling and comprehension of verbal jokes may indirectly substantiate this argument. Verbal humor is presumably a realm that challenges a child's verbal and emotional capabilities simultaneously. This may explain why the group of poor readers did not want to tell jokes at age 6, were poor at telling jokes at age 9, and had problems in understanding verbal jokes both at ages 6 and 9 (Hagtvet 1998). Few experiences are so socially segregating as that of not understanding the humor of your own social group. Social verbal activities like joke telling make linguistic shortcomings public knowledge, and such activities may therefore act as mediators of the low self-concept which is often found in poor readers (e.g., Bryan and Bryan 1990). The causal path might, of course, work differently for different children, starting with socio-emotional restlessness in some children, and with language weaknesses in other children. The important point is that language and emotions/off-task-behavior are strongly related phenomena. This is emphasized in a study of early oral language development by Lois Bloom (1993).

THE INTERRELATION BETWEEN LANGUAGE AND
EMOTION DURING EARLY WORD LEARNING

Bloom's study of the first peak periods of word learning is a rare exception to the general neglect of "emotions and language" after the first year in a child's life. Bloom observed 14 mothers and children from New York City during play interactions. The study started when the children uttered their first word at around age 9 months and closed at around age 2 years when they started to connect words into simple syntactic structures. Bloom's aim was to document possible connections between the production of words during these play sessions and expression of negative, neutral, or positive affect.

The first words at around 9 to12 months were typically produced after a period of neutral affect. This is not an affect-less state, but a state of great attention and interest. Both positive and negative affects appeared to interfere negatively with language development. However, negative affects were more damaging than positive affects because words were very rarely expressed in negative affect. Furthermore, while the emotional state preceding the produced words was typically neutral, the words that were uttered were themselves often loaded with affect. They were words for persons, objects, and actions that presumably were causes of and consequences of the children's needs, e.g., "mamma," "block," and "no" when a child had problems in putting one block upon another block. The children, in other words, appeared to learn words for things that were emotionally important or actions that caused emotional reactions, suggesting that the energy behind the words was emotional. However, the process of producing the words was demanding on both concentration and energy, and Bloom argues that emotional arousal, which is also demanding on energy, interfered with the concentration needed to perform a challenging linguistic task. According to Bloom this explains why the uttering of words was typically preceded by neutral affect—emotions and language were competing for a limited reservoir of energy and attentional resources. After a word had been uttered, however, emotional reactions were regularly observed, e.g., in crying or laughing. Producing the word appeared to act as a catalyst for feelings, the very same effect that verbalizing may have in, for example, therapeutic sessions.

Great individual differences were observed. Early language learners spent more time in neutral affect. Amount of time spent in neutral affect at the time around 9 months to one year when the first word was produced, was in fact predictive of onset of two-word sentences around age 2. The more a child's behavior was characterized as "emotional" (positive or negative), the slower was the child's language development and vice versa.

This is an important finding. It suggests that producing words during peak learning periods is so attentionally demanding that it is interrupted by emotions of any kind—even positive emotions, such as strong joy and pleasure. It also has implications for the understanding of delayed language development, which is typically associated with strong and negative emotional reactions, and this again may interfere with language production. On this issue Bloom's study corroborates and extends observation in clinical settings, namely that emotions are not only initiators, but also inhibitors of language learning. It also illustrates how the negative (or positive) spiral suggested by McGee and coworkers may develop. However, the causal relationship between emotions and language is, on the basis of Bloom's findings, far from clear. Children may act affectively because they are unable to express themselves. They may also, for temperamental reasons, be geared toward emotional outbursts, which inhibits their language development. Different causal patterns may also be seen in different children. For written language learning, the relevance of Bloom's study is its focus on an active learning period as an emotionally vulnerable period and the documentation it offers of an interrelation between language and emotions that has been largely neglected in developmental studies. On this basis, and also on the basis of the positive correlation between off-task behaviors and language skills observed in the present study, even before school entry, the prevention of reading problems should not only focus on language stimulation, but also on supporting the emotional system of the child.

THE CHALLENGES OF PREDICTING READING PROBLEMS

One serious problem with prevention is that it is implicitly or explicitly associated with prediction, and prediction is an enigmatic phenomenon, in particular in connection with prediction of individual development, as discussed above. A prediction is a statement about a series of events before they occur, and prevention is the act(s) taken to avoid the events from occurring. Prevention and prediction are thus, in practical settings, two sides of the same coin, and the very reason for predicting is, in fact, very often to be able to act preventively, e.g., by changing the conditions that normally lead to the predicted result. Therefore, any educational intervention—preventive or remedial—involves a prediction of what will happen if the intervention does or does not take place. Prediction often has the humanistic aim of preventing dramatic and negative events from happening, whether these events be economic recessions, psychiatric illness, or learning disability. However, prediction has some, often unintended, side effects, which may act contrary to the desired sequence of events. There are two main problems associated with these acts in the service of the good. One is that predictions may be wrong. The other is that predictions may by themselves influence the course of events and thereby contribute to the falsification of the prediction itself.

While the oracle at Delphi based her predictions and advice on intuition, the theoretical models of scientific prediction were developed in the natural sciences where precise prediction is seen as the most stringent test of a scientific theory. Even the economist, Milton Friedman, would argue that the only test of a theory is predictive success (Hahn 1993). However, the "laws" of social science typically have a weak empirical and theoretical basis, for which reason predictions are typically formulated in probabilistic terms ("The probability for A, given B, equals r") (Popper 1968). However, predictions in (special) education often concern the development of individual cases, and as mentioned above, it has proved much more difficult to predict the development of the unique case than to predict the development of groups in probabilistic terms, in particular when the predictor is a narrowly defined variable.

At an individual level, the problems associated with prediction in psychological and educational interventions are of basically two kinds. One is the "error of neglect," i.e., of not identifying an at-risk child (a false negative). This neglect prevents a child from getting the intervention that might prevent the unwanted development to take place. The other is the "error of identification," i.e., of wrongly nominating an individual as at risk (a false positive). Identifying a case as "positive," be it done by means of an explicitly formulated diagnosis or not, includes an expectation of negative development.

An idea that is formulated in words, tends to change our perception and conception of the talked-about reality (Cassirer 1944; Whorf 1956). A diagnosis, for example, "at risk of developing a reading problem," may change the perception and decision making of the people to whom the "diagnosis" is made public and thereby stigmatize (Goffman 1963) the individual. The individual may as a consequence of the "stigma" be treated as different, and according to the law of "the self-fulfilling prophesy" (Rosenthal and Jacobson 1968) the child will become different. A stigmatization process may even be the consequence of not giving a diagnosis, as friends and family members, due to more incidental knowledge and observation, may create a diagnosis where none is officially stated. In an ongoing large-scale longitudinal study, including 140 children from families where one or both parents are dyslexic (Hagtvet et al. 1997), we interview the dyslexic parent about his or her school experiences. Many of these parents were never diagnosed, but were treated or were perceived as dumb rather than reading impaired. On the basis of their reports about the feelings of inferiority, loneliness, and alienation associated with remedial interventions, we have reasons to believe that much traditional special education has failed in improving reading skills due to the social psychological laws of stigmatization. This appears particularly probable in light of the above-mentioned relationship between negative affects and language learning. Whether the diagnosis was explicitly formulated as "dyslexic," or merely implied as "dumb," the prediction itself in quite a number of cases appeared to have influenced the development in undesired directions.

There is an, often unmentioned, inverse relationship between statistical predictions on the one hand and sociological and educational forces on the other. This regards both the false positives and the false negatives. Both the "law of self fulfilling prophesy" and the quality of the educational program will influence the realization or the falsification of the prediction. A destructive stigmatizing effect, in combination with a bad educational program, will contribute to the fulfillment of a prediction of negative development. Such "true positives" may be perceived by the statistician as successful prediction, by the educator as unsuccessful special education, and by the sociologist as the documentation of the effect of the "self-fulfilling-prophesy." If worse come to worst, a perfectly normal child, a so-called "late bloomer," where the child's only problem may be that he or she is "normal at the wrong moment" (Brügelmann 1998), may develop serious reading problems. The result is a high predictive validity, but this may be caused by a prematurely and wrongly formulated diagnosis that through a stigmatization process and the "law of self-fulfilling-prophesy" contributed to its own fulfillment. Complementarily, the false negatives (those who were expected to develop normally, but who did not) may be evidence of educational failures. They may, however, also be a sign of a wrong prediction model, e.g., due to incompetence on the part of the "expertise" surrounding the child. The court room could tell many stories of the frustrations associated with having a reading problem, but not having been diagnosed, and therefore not having received the kind of intervention that presumably would have made learning to read and write possible. Unsuccessful predictions may thus have many causes, and one often-ignored source is the power of the environment to break the prediction itself through competent (or incompetent) educational intervention.

PREVENTING READING PROBLEMS IN LIGHT OF THE CHALLENGES OF PREDICTION

I have discussed how language skills in preschool appear to be related to later written language skills and pointed at some precursors of reading skills. Although these have been documented to be predictive of reading problems in both longitudinal/developmental and experimental research, a case was made for the need to take a broader spectrum of variables than the linguistic ones into account when trying to prevent reading problems in natural contexts, in particular when focusing on individual cases. Language develops in close interaction with other individual and environmental variables, and these other variables may act as mediators as well as barriers to successful prevention. The child's emotional preparedness and ability to focus on task was highlighted as a particularly crucial, but often-neglected, mediating variable. Another "variable" is the prediction (i.e., the "at-risk stigma") itself. A main reason prevention in natural settings has not always had the intended success may very well be that the individual's emotional system and a stigmatizing effect of a diagnosis, e.g., "being at risk," was handled less professionally and with less concern than was the case for the "core problem." With prediction of individual development being challenging and the stigmatizing effect of a prediction "made public" being beyond control, a wise prevention strategy appears to be to stick to the present practice of reserving individually based programs of prevention in preschool for the more extreme cases. These are the cases where the advantages of early and individualized intervention are estimated to exceed the dangers of stigmatization considerably. However, even in these cases, extreme care should be taken to avoid the negative consequences of stigmatization.

In cases where at-risk signs are marginal, a generally oriented preventive program designed for inclusive settings, but implemented in a differentiated manner, appears to be the preferred alternative. On the basis of the research data cited in this chapter, such a program should be linguistic in focus, and with a particular emphasis on phonological awareness and on relating phonemes and phoneme patterns to graphemes and grapheme patterns (e.g., by means of pretend writing) (e.g., Snow, Burns, and Griffin 1998). With age appropriate, individualized, and balanced integration of other learning areas, with continuous attempts at creating success through positive learning experiences, and with individualized intervention initiated as soon as a child falls behind his or her age mates, optimal conditions for the prevention of reading problems should be established. In Scandinavia, experimental and quasi-experimental preschool training programs in natural settings focusing phonemic awareness training through play-oriented language games (Lundberg, Frost, and Petersen 1988) and different combinations of such games and grapheme-phoneme linkage (Hagtvet 1989; Lyster 1996) have shown optimistic results. Programs like Reading Recovery (Clay 1993) and Early Steps (Santa 1998), where failure in learning to read and spell is followed by early individualized instruction, have likewise demonstrated positive results. Yet, too many children are still struggling with reading, and unless we take advantage of the last decade's research on early precursors of reading difficulties in preventive educational programs that respect the enigmas of prediction, prevention of reading problems will continue to be an empty and misleading political slogan.

REFERENCES

Album, D. 1988. Kommentarer til standard for inndeling etter sosio økonomisk status. Rapport 88/18, Statistisk sentralbyrå. (Comments on Categorization of Socio-Economic Status. Report 88/18, Central Bureau of Statistics of Norway.)

Badian, N. A. 1986. Improving the prediction of reading for the individual child: A four-year follow-up. *Journal of Learning Disabilities* 19:262–69.

Badian, N. A.1988. The prediction of good and poor reading before kindergarten entry: A nine-year follow-up. *Journal of Learning Disabilities* 21(2):98–103.

Badian, N. A., McAnulty, G. B., Duffy, F. H., and Als, H. 1990. Prediction of dyslexia in kindergarten boys. *Annals of Dyslexia*, 40:152–67.

Badian, N. 1995. Predicting reading ability over the long term: The changing roles of letter naming, phonological awareness and orthographic processing. *Annals of Dyslexia* 45:79–96.

Ball, E. W., and Blackman, B. A. 1991. Does phoneme awareness training in kindergarten make a difference in early word recognition and developmental spelling? *Reading Research Quarterly* 26(1):49–66.

Bateson, M. C. 1975. Mother-infant exchanges: The epigenesis of conversational interaction. In Developmental Psycholinguistics and Communication Disorders, eds. D. Aaronson and R. Rieber. *Annals of the New York Academy of Sciences*, Vol. 263.

Bloom, K. 1977. Patterning of infant vocal behavior. *Journal of Experimental Child Psychology*, 23:367–77.

Bloom, K. 1990. Selectivity and early infant vocalization. In *The Development of Attention: Research and Theory*, ed. J. Enns. New York: Elsevier North-Holland.

Bloom, L. 1993. *The Transition from Infancy to Language.* Cambridge: Cambridge University Press.

Bishop, D. 1997. *Uncommon Understanding.* Hove, Sussex: Psychology Press.

Bowey, J. A,. and Patel, R. K. 1988. Metalinguistic ability and early reading achievement. *Applied Psycholinguistics*, 9:367–83.

Bradley, L., and Bryant, P.E. 1983. Categorizing sounds and learning to read - A causal connection. *Nature* 301(899):419–21.

Bradley, L., and Bryant, P. 1985. *Rhyme and Reason in Reading and Spelling.* Ann Arbor: University of Michigan Press.

Bruck, M. 1985. The adult functioning of children with specific learning disabilities: A follow-up study. In *Advances in Applied Developmental Psychology.* Vol.1, ed. I. E. Sigel. Norwood, NJ: Ablex Publishing Corporation.

Bruck, M. 1987. The adult outcomes of children with learning disabilities. *Annals of Dyslexia*, 37:252–63.

Brügelmann, H. 1998. From invention to convention. Children's different routes to literacy. In *Learning to Read: An Integrated View from Research and Practice*, ed. T. Nunes. London: Kluwer Academic Publishers.

Bryan, J. H., and Bryan, T. 1990. Social factors in learning disabilities: Attitudes and interactions. In *Perspectives on Dyslexia. Vol. 2*, ed. G. T. Pavlidis. London: Wiley.

Bryant, P. E., Bradley, L., Maclean, M., and Crossland, J. 1989. Nursery rhymes, phonological skills and reading. *Journal of Child Language*, 16:407–28.

Bryant, P., Nunes, T., and Bindman, M.1999. Morphemes and spelling. In *Learning to Read: An Integrated View from Research and Practice*, ed. T. Nunes. London: Kluwer Academic Publishers.

Cassirer, E. 1944. *An Essay on Man*. New Haven: Yale University Press.

Catts, H.1991. Early identification of dyslexia: Evidence of a follow-up study of speech-language impaired children. *Annals of Dyslexia*, 41:166–77.

Catts, H. W., Fey, M. E., Zhang, X., and Tomblin, J. B.1999. Language basis of reading and reading disabilities: Evidence from a longitudinal investigation. *Scientific Studies of Reading*, 3(4):331–61.

Clark, M. M. 1976. *Young Fluent Readers*. London: Heinemann.

Clay, M. M.1993. *Reading Recovery*. Postmouth, NH:: Heinemann.

Clay, M. M. 1975. *What did I Write? Beginning Writing Behavior*. Auckland, New Zealand: Heinemann.

Dugstad, B. S. 1978. Diagnostiske prøver for 2. og 3. skoleår. Ordop-pfatning og Leseforståelse. (Diagnostic tests for Grades 2 and 3. Word reading og reading comprehension.) Trondheim: Kontoret for peda-gogisk utviklingsarbeid, Skolesjefen, Trondheim.

Elbro, C., Borstrøm, I., and Petersen, D. K. 1998. Predicting dyslexia from kindergarten: The importance of distinctness of phonological represen-tations of lexical items. *Reading Research Quarterly* 33(1):36–60.

Eysenck, M. W. 1992. *Anxiety. The Cognitive Perspective*. Hillsdale, NJ: Lawrence Erlbaum.

Ferguson, C. 1956. Arabic baby talk. In *For Roman Jakobson*, ed. M. Halle. The Hague: Mouton.

Ferguson, C. 1977. Baby talk as a simplified register. In *Talking to Children*, ed. C. Snow and C. Ferguson. NY: Cambridge University Press.

Finucci, J. M., Gottfredson, L. S., and Childs, B. 1985. A follow-up study of dyslexic boys. *Annals of Dyslexia* 35:117–36.

Gallagher, A. M., Frith, U. and Snowling, M. J. 1996. Language processing skills in pre-schoolers at risk of developmental dyslexia. Manuscript.

Garmezy, N. 1993. Vulnerability and resilience. In *Studying Lives through Time*, eds. E. Funder, R. Parke , and C. Tomlinson-Keasey. Washington: American Psychological Association.

Gaskins, I. 1998. There's more to teaching at-risk and delayed readers than good reading instruction. *The Reading Teacher* 51(7):534–47.

Goffman, E. 1963. *Stigma: Notes on the Management of Spoiled Identity*. Englewood Cliffs, NJ: Prentice Hall.

Hagtvet, B. E. 1988. *Skriftspråkutvikling gjennom lek*. (Literacy Stimulation through Play). Oslo: Universitetsforlaget.

Hagtvet, B. E. 1989. Emergent literacy in Norwegian six-year-olds. From pretend writing to phonemic awareness and invented writing. In *Reading at the Crossroads*, ed. F. Biglmaier. Conference proceedings, the

6th European Conference on Reading. Berlin, July, 31.– August 3., 1989.

Hagtvet, B. E. 1996. Fra tale til skrift. Om prediksjon og utvikling av lese-ferdighet i fire- til åtteårsalderen. (*From Oral to Written Language. On the Prediction and Development of Reading Abilities during the Age Period Four through Eight*). Oslo: Cappelen.

Hagtvet, B. E. 1997. Phonological and linguistic-cognitive precursors of reading abilities. *Dyslexia* 3:163–77.

Hagtvet, B. E. 1998. Preschool oral language competence and literacy development. In *Problems and Interventions in Literacy Development*, ed. P. Reitsma and L. Verhoeven. Dordrecht: Kluwer Academic Publishers.

Hagtvet, B. E., and Lillestølen, R. 1985. *Reynells språktest*. Norsk håndbok. (Reynell Developmental Language Scales. Manual and Norwegian adaptation.) Oslo: Universitetsforlaget.

Hagtvet, B. E., Horn, E., LassenøL. M., Lauvås, K., Lyster, S. A. H., and Misund, S.1997. Developing literacy in families with histories of reading problems. *European Journal of Special Needs Education* 2:29–39.

Hahn, F. 1993. Predicting the economy. In *Predicting the Future*, ed. L. Howe and A. Wain. Cambridge: Cambridge University Press.

Hatcher, P. J., Hulme, C., and Ellis, W. 1994. Ameliorating early reading failure by integrating the teaching of reading and phonological skills: the phonological linkage hypothesis. *Child Development* 65:41–57.

Hoover, W. A. and Gough, B. P. 1990. The simple view of reading. *Reading and Writing: An Interdisciplinary Journal* 2:127–60.

Høien, T., and Lundberg, I. 1991 *Dysleksi*. Oslo: Gyldendal.

Kirk, S. J., McCarthy, J., and Kirk, W. D. 1968. *Illinois Test of Psycholinguistic Ability*. Urbana: University of Illinois Press.

Liberman, I. Y., and Shankweiler, D. 1985. Phonology and the problem of learning to read and write. *Remedial and Special Education* 6:8–17.

Lundberg, I. 1982. Linguistic awareness as related to dyslexia, In *Dyslexia, Neuronal, Cognitive & Linguistic Aspects*, ed. Y. Zotterman. NY: Pergamon Press.

Lundberg, I., Olofsson, Å., and Wall, S. 1980. Reading and spelling skills in the first school years predicted from phonemic awareness skills in kindergarten. *Scandinavian Journal of Psychology*, 21:159–73.

Lundberg, I., Frost, J., and Petersen, O.P. 1988. Long term effects of a preschool training program in phonological awareness. *Reading research quarterly* 28:263–84.

Lundberg, I., Frost, J., Pedersen, O..P., and Olofsson, Å. 1991. Long term effects of a preschool program for stimulating phonological awareness: The effect on low achieving children. Presented at the fourth European conference for research on learning and instruction, Turku, Finland, 24–26. August, 1991.

Lyster, S. A. H. 1996. Preventing reading and spelling failure. Unpublished doctoral dissertation, University of Oslo.

McGee, R, Williams, S., Share, D. L., Anderson, J., and Silva, P. A. 1986. The relationship between specific reading retardation, general reading backwardness, and behavioral problems in a large sample of Dunedin boys: A longitudinal study from five to eleven years. *Journal of Child Psychology and Psychiatry* 27(5):597–610.

McLaughlin, B. 1987. *Theories of Second-language Learning*. London: Edward Arnold.

Nottelmann, E. D., and Hill, K. T. 1977. Test anxiety and off-task behavior in evaluative situations. *Child Development* 48:225–31.
Nurss, J.1988. Development of written communication in Norwegian kindergarten children. *Scandinavian Journal of Educational Research* 32:33–48.
Nurss, J. 1989. Written language environments for young children: Comparison of Scandinavian, British, and American kindergartens. *International Journal of Early Childhood* 20(1):45–53.
Olofsson, Å., and Lundberg, I. 1983. Can phonemic awareness be trained in kindergarten? *Scandinavian Journal of Psychology* 24:35–44.
Olofsson, Å., and Lundberg, I. 1985. Evaluation of long term effects of phonemic awareness training in kindergarten. Illustrations of some methodological problems in evaluation research. *Scandinavian Journal of Psychology 26:21–34.*
Olson, R. K. 1994. Language deficits in "specific" reading disability. In *Handbook of Pyscholinguistics*, ed. M. Gernsbacher. New York, NY: Academic Press.
Perfetti, C. A. 1985. *Reading Ability.* New York: Oxford University Press.
Popper, K. 1968. *The Logic of Scientific Discovery.* London: Hutchinson.
Reynell, J. 1977. *Reynell Developmental Language Scales (revised).* Windsor: NFER.
Rommetveit, S., and Rommetveit, R. 1980. *Pek på.* (Point To: A Test of Sentence Comprehension). Oslo: Tiden.
Rosenthal, R., and Jacobson, L. 1968. *Pygmalion in the Classroom.* New York: Rinehart & Winston.
Santa, C. M. 1998. *Early Steps: Learning from a Reader.* Kalispell, MT:Scott.
Scarborough, H. 1989. Prediction of reading disability from familial and individual differences. *Journal of Educational Psychology* 81(1):101–8.
Scarborough, H. 1990. Very early language deficits in dyslexic children. *Child Development,* 61: 1728–41.
Shankweiler, D., and Crain, S. 1986. Language mechanisms and reading disorder: A modular approach. *Cognition* 24:139–68.
Snow, C. E., Arlman-Rupp, A., Hassing, Y., Jobse, J., Joosten, J., and Vorster, J. 1976. Mothers' speech in three social classes. *Journal of Psycholinguistic Research* 5:1–20.
Snow, C. E., Burns, M. S., and Griffin, P. 1998. *Preventing Reading Difficulties in Young Children. Report from the Committee on the Prevention of Reading Difficulties in Young Children.* National Research Council, USA.
Snowling, M. J. 1987. *Dyslexia.* Oxford: Basil Blackwell
Stanovich, K. E. 1988. Explaining the differences between the dyslexic and the garden-variety poor reader: The phonological-core variable-difference model. *Journal of Learning Disabilities* 21:560–612.
Sulzby, E. 1986. Writing and reading. Signs of oral and written language organization in the young child. In *Emergent literacy. Writing and Reading,* eds. W. H. Teale and E. Sulzby. Norwood, NJ: Ablex.
Trevarthen, C.1993. An infant's motives for speaking and thinking in the culture. In *The Dialogical Alternative,* ed. A. H. Wold. Oslo: Scandinavian University Press.
Tunmer, W. E., and Hoover, W. A. 1992. Cognitive and linguistic factors in learning to read, In *Reading Acquisition,* eds. P. B.Gough, L. C.Ehri, and R. Treiman. Hillsdale, NJ: Lawrence Erlbaum.

Vellutino, F. R. 1979: *Dyslexia: Theory and Research.* Cambridge, MA: MIT Press.
Vygotsky, L. 1962. *Thought and Language.* Cambridge, MA: MIT Press.
Wagner, R. K., and Torgesen, J. K. 1987. The nature of phonological processing and its causal role in the acquisition of reading skills. *Psychological Bulletin* 101:(2)192–212.
Wechsler, D. 1974. *Wechsler Intelligence Scale for Children - Revised.* New York: The Psychological Corporation.
Whorf, B. L. 1956. Science and linguistics. In *Language, Thought and Reality*, ed. J. Caroll. New York: Wiley.
Wine, J. D. 1971 Test anxiety and direction of attention. *Psychological Bulletin* 76(2):92–104.
Wine, J. D. 1980. Cognitive-attentional theory of test anxiety. In *Test Anxiety: Theory, Research, and Applications*, ed. I. G. Sarason. Hillsdale, N.J.: Lawrence Erlbaum.
Wold, A. H. 1993. Kommunikasjon i klasserommet og læring av andrespråk (Communication i the classroom and learning of second language.) *Norsk Pedagogisk Tidskrift* 1:17–31.
Yule, W., and Rutter, M. 1976. Epidemiology and social implications of specific reading retardation. In *The Neuropsychology of Learning Disorders*, eds. R. M. Knights and D. J. Bakker. Baltimore: University Park Press.

APPENDIX 1

OFF-TASK-BEHAVIOR—A CHECKLIST x)   **Score 0-5**

1. Frowning of eyebrows
2. Shakes head
3. Looks at tester for feedback
4. Looks at irrelevant items
5. Bites nails
6. Hands shake
7. Fidgets on chair
8. Twists hair
9. Plays with hands
10. Bites lips
11. Positive self oriented evaluation of competence
12. Negative self oriented evaluation of competence
13. Communication expressing somatic/physical problems
14. Long pause before response
15. Talks about irrelevant matters
16. Clears throat nervously

Total:

x) Inspired by Wine, 1971, 1980

Chapter • 6

From Identification to Intervention
Improving Kindergarten Screening for Risk of Reading Failure

Jane M. Flynn

Many studies document the efficacy of early intervention in prevention of school failure (Ball and Blachman 1991; Berrieta et al.1984; Byrne and Fielding-Barnsley 1991; Casto and Mastropieri 1986; Felton and Brown 1990; Hurford et al.1994; Lundberg, Frost, and Peterson 1988; Strag 1972). As early as 1972, Strag found that when students were diagnosed as reading disabled in grades 1 or 2, 82% were eventually able to achieve at grade level, although only 10% to 15% of students identified in grades 5 through 7 reached grade level functioning. More recently, phonological awareness programs in kindergarten and first grade have reduced reading failure in later grades (Ball and Blachman 1988, 1991; Felton and Brown 1990; Hurford et al.1994; Lundberg, Frost, and Peterson 1988). These studies have highlighted the importance of early identification of children at risk for school failure, leading to increased interest in preschool and kindergarten screening programs.

Despite the consensus regarding the value of early identification, however, experts disagree on how best to accomplish this goal. Some favor teacher rating scales, while others maintain that screening tests are more useful in early prediction. Adelman (1982) and Algozzine and Ysseldyke (1986) argued for the cost effectiveness and predictive validity of asking teachers who are already familiar with the children to predict those at risk for school failure. However, researchers generally have found that tests predict those at risk for reading failure better than teachers. Reported teacher prediction rates are disappointingly low, ranging from 15% to 41% correct identification of children at risk (Feshbach, Adelman, and Fuller 1974: Fletcher and Satz 1984; Flynn and Rahbar 1998a; LaTorre et al.1982: Stevenson et al.1976). In contrast, test identification rates of .71 and .80 were reported by Fletcher and Satz (1984) and Flynn and Rahbar (1998a) respectively.

These findings suggest that when detection of risk is important, screening tests are much better predictors than teacher ratings. Three questions arise from these data. First, why are teachers, who have spent most of a year interacting with their students, less able to predict risk than brief screening tests? Second, if tests are able to identify reasonable numbers of at-risk children, is it important to improve teacher prediction rates? Finally, if teacher prediction of risk is important, how can screening programs be improved to help teachers become better observers of their students and, ultimately, better able to intervene to reduce the incidence of reading failure?

A number of factors may contribute to the low teacher identification rate. One reason, reported by many of the kindergarten teachers in our screening program (Flynn and Rahbar 1998a), is that teachers are reluctant to predict failure in young children at a time of rapid and unpredictable growth spurts. Also, many teacher training programs lack adequate instruction in the theoretical and scientific underpinnings of reading development (Brady 1997), e.g., how speech maps to print (Moats 1994), therefore many teachers are unprepared to observe skill development in areas crucial to reading success. In addition, many screening programs test general developmental tasks rather than research-validated precursors critical to reading success, e.g., linguistic skills (Adams 1990; Brady 1997; Badian 1994; Blachman 1983; Stanovich and Siegel 1994; Wolf 1998). Such screening programs do not provide opportunities for teachers to observe their children engaged in reading-related tasks, which would lead to development of a conceptual framework for assessing risk. Nor do the results of general screening tests result in information that can be used to design specific interventions (Satz and Fletcher 1988; Majsterek and Ellenwood, 1995). Too often, these instruments are used to make inappropriate placement decisions, e.g., delayed school entrance, retention in grade, or transition programs (Gredler 1992).

We turn now to the second question. Because screening tests generally identify a reasonable number of children at risk, is it important to improve teacher prediction? We maintain that it is. Teachers who do not have a conceptual framework for observing reading-related risk signs may have lowered expectations for some children. They are likely to espouse discriminatory entrance age policies that are not supported by later outcomes (Gredler 1992; Flynn and Rahbar, 1993a, 1993b; Shepard and Smith 1986, 1989). For example, many kindergarten and primary teachers believe that younger children, boys in general, are more at risk for school failure. Therefore, many schools develop policies that adjust entrance ages upward, and parents of younger children (again, boys in particular) are often advised to give their children the "gift of time" by delaying school entrance for another year (Ames 1967). Younger children and boys are more likely to be retained in kindergarten (Gredler 1992; Shepard and Smith 1989).

The lack of educationally relevant screening tasks and follow-up information may contribute to the prevalence of the maturational view that readiness resides in the child and unfolds naturally with time. This view persists despite empirical and theoretical support for the interaction between school conditions and child-background characteristics in determining reading success or failure (Ausubel and Sullivan 1970; Bruner 1966; Gredler 1992; Johannson 1965; Vygotsky 1930-35/1978). Johansson (1965, p. 25) stated that ". . . if a child fails in one beginner's class it need not be on account of characteristics of the child; a child who's not ready for school in one class may well succeed in another, when the teacher applies different methods" (in Gredler 1992, p.17). By attributing the source of risk to something within the child and his or her background, teachers are ignoring the potentially powerful effect of early intervention in reducing or eliminating school failure.

Under-expectations for younger children and boys may occur also because of lack of information regarding later school achievement. It is true that younger children, and boys in general, often score lower on tests in kindergarten, first, and second grade (Flynn and Rahbar 1994; Shepard and Smith 1989; Davis, Trimble, and Vincent 1980). Research shows comparable achievement by third grade (Flynn and Rahbar 1994: Shaywitz et al.1990; Shepard and Smith 1989), but kindergarten teachers who lack long-term follow-up data on their students may remain skeptical of the research evidence.

Given the accumulating evidence for the social constructivist view that the child's development evolves as a result of the interaction between personal-familial characteristics and school experiences, improving teacher prediction and intervention skills is extremely important. Kindergarten teachers need to know how to observe developmental levels in research-validated precursors to reading achievement. They also need to know how to match children's profiles with research-validated interventions in order to intervene effectively. In this way screening becomes a mediating experience that leads to appropriate intervention rather than delayed school entrance or retention (Gredler 1992).

Having considered the question of whether improving teacher prediction is an important goal and responding in the affirmative, we turn now to the focus of this chapter: How to help kindergarten teachers improve their ability to predict risk of reading failure. When kindergarten teachers were asked to predict reading achievement on a five-point scale, we, like previous researchers, found a low teacher-identification rate (.30) of children who later failed (Flynn and Rahbar 1998a). We hypothesized that asking teachers to rate their children's current skill levels on precursors to reading would improve valid positive rates compared to our original rating scale which asked that they predict future reading success or failure. We also hypothesized that combining screening battery scores and teacher ratings on a skills-based instrument would improve overall prediction rates. Therefore, we developed a new rating scale that includes behavioral descriptions of emerging literacy skills. The Teacher Rating Scale (TRS) (Flynn 1997a) was designed to mirror the skills tested in our kindergarten screening test, the Literacy Screening Battery (LSB) (Flynn 1997b). We studied the utility of each instrument alone and in combination for predicting poor readers. Since the teacher prediction instrument was based on our screening instrument, the Literacy Screening Battery (LSB) is discussed first.

DEVELOPMENT OF THE LITERACY SCREENING BATTERY (LSB)

To meet the goal of early identification and effective intervention for children at risk for reading failure, we adopted three intermediate objectives: to develop a theory-based, psychometrically sound kindergarten literacy screening battery that could be administered to a group; to follow a large sample from kindergarten through fifth grade; and to determine whether the screening battery would add predictive utility over and above teacher ratings for identification of children at risk of reading failure.

To accomplish these goals we used Rumelhart's (1977) reading model to develop screening tasks. Rumelhart (1977) hypothesized that reading is an interactive process composed of lower-level phonological, logographic, and orthographic processes operating simultaneously and synergistically with higher-level semantic and syntactic processes. This view of reading has been supported by a number of sources influential in current reading theory (Adams 1990; Blachman 1983; LaBerge and Samuels 1974; Liberman and Shankweiler 1985; Stanovich 1986), by empirical and clinical studies of reading disabilities (Flynn and Boder 1991; Lyon 1985; Stanovich, Siegel, and Gottardo 1997), and by our research on neurophysiological characteristics of dyslexic subtypes (Flynn and Deering 1989; Flynn et al. 1992; Ramaden 1997).

To capture the changing relationship of reading processes to success from first through fifth grade, we specified developmental stages for acquisition of these processes. We postulated that early reading success depends on recognition of single words as logographs and on extraction of phonological principles. This Accuracy Stage of reading development corresponds to the Glued to Print Stage described by Chall (1983). By second or third grade normally developing readers have reached the Automaticity Stage (Chall's Ungluing From Print stage), characterized by instantaneous access to orthographic features. This, in turn, results in increased expressiveness and fluency as children are freed from the mechanics of word recognition. With the attainment of automaticity, the child's syntactic and semantic skills can be deployed more fully as the child enters the Focus on Meaning Stage in third grade and later.

We hypothesized that disruption in one or more of these processes results in failure at one of these three crucial stages for reading development. Difficulty in acquiring phonological, orthographic, or automaticity processes leads to early reading failure (first or second grade), although those children who have deficits in language comprehension but intact phonological/orthographic processing skills begin to fail at upper grades (third and up) when the demands of understanding text increase. This developmental sequence has been supported by empirical findings (Fletcher, Satz, and Scholes 1981; Jansky 1986; 1988; Satz et al. 1978; Shanahan 1984) and by theoretical writings (Chall 1983; Frith 1985).

After defining this developmental reading model, we developed screening tasks to measure precursors to phonological awareness, logographic/orthographic skills, semantics, and syntax. We were unable to identify a kindergarten-level precursor to automaticity that could be administered to a group. The Literacy Screening Battery (LSB) consists of seven subtests: Vocabulary, Syntax, Alphabet, Sounds, Phonemic Segmentation, Formcopy,

and Visual Discrimination. A description of each subtest and rationale for inclusion in the screening battery illustrates how the LSB
embodies our hypotheses of how and when reading develops.

Phonological Processes

To measure phonological awareness at the kindergarten level, we
constructed two subtests, Phonemic Segmentation and Sounds. The
Phonemic Segmentation subtest, a visual adaptation of the
Auditory Analysis Test (Rosner and Simon 1971), measures the ability to hold a sequence of sounds in working memory and to reconstruct an auditory gestalt. Children were asked to listen to a word,
silently reconstruct that word with a syllable or sound deleted, and
to circle the picture of the reconstructed word. Twenty-six stimuli
were used, ranging from syllable deletion ("Cowboy," take away
"boy" and circle the picture of what's left) to phoneme deletion
("feet," take away /f/, circle the picture of what's left). We also hypothesized that knowledge of sound-symbol relationships contributes to phonological processing skill. The Sounds subtest
required children to write the letters corresponding to ten sounds
dictated by the examiner. Phonological deficits, including difficulty
segmenting spoken language and identifying sounds or syllables,
have been cited as a major cause of reading disabilities (Adams
1990; Bradley and Bryant 1985; Ehri and Wilce 1985; Liberman and
Shankweiler 1985; Liberman et al. 1974; Wagner and Torgesen
1987). Phonological awareness tasks have proved to be sensitive
screening tasks at the kindergarten level (Badian 1994; Ball and
Blachman 1988, 1991; Majsterek and Ellenwood 1995).

Logographic/Orthographic Processes

In the Alphabet subtest, children were asked to write the 26 letters
of the alphabet dictated in random order. In addition, because our
early studies indicated that by the end of kindergarten, letter writing alone was too easy for discrimination of achievement groups,
children were asked to write as many words as they knew from
memory, with ten spaces provided for responses. The Visual
Discrimination subtest consisted of matching 15 sequences of geometric shapes, letters, numbers, or simple words. In the Formcopy
subtest, children were asked to copy 12 geometric shapes of increasing difficulty.

Although much of the current literature emphasizes linguistic skill as the major contributor to reading success and failure,

many kindergarten screening batteries have identified children with visual processing deficits who later failed in reading (Badian 1988; Jansky 1986, 1988; Jansky and de Hirsch 1972; Sears and Keogh 1993; Silver, Hagin, and Beecher 1978). Badian (1994) presented strong evidence for the predictiveness of visual discrimination/orthographic tasks in identifying those at risk for reading failure. Letter naming, writing letters and sounds to dictation, and alphabet recitation have consistently been among the most predictive screening measures in early identification studies (Badian 1986; Jansky and de Hirsch 1972; Jansky 1986; Satz et al.1978).

Semantic Processes

Knowledge of word meanings was represented in our battery by the Vocabulary subtest that consisted of 44 items, each with three pictorial choices. Items were chosen from our pilot studies and from reviews of existing tests of vocabulary and basic concepts (Bracken 1984; Boehm 1986; Dunn and Dunn 1981; Gardner 1985). Research support for testing receptive word knowledge as a predictor of reading achievement was provided by Shanahan (1984) who found that while early reading was predicted by sound-symbol skill, vocabulary diversity made a greater contribution to advanced reading status. Screening studies have also reported increasing correlation of kindergarten vocabulary scores with upper grade reading scores (Jansky 1986, 1988; Satz et al. 1978).

Syntactic Processes

The Syntax subtest consisted of 26 spoken sentences with four pictorial choices for each. Syntactical structures included noun and verb phrases, pronouns, indirect objects, negation, compound sentences, and embedded clauses. Fletcher, Satz, and Scholes (1981) found that kindergarten syntactical tasks contributed to reading achievement in upper grades, and measures of listening comprehension have consistently correlated with later reading achievement (Curtis 1980; Jansky 1986, 1988; Stanovich, Cunningham, and Freeman 1984).

The LSB met or exceeded recommended reliability and predictive validity standards for screening instruments (Brown 1983; Salvia and Ysseldyke 1991). Reliability studies revealed adequate internal consistency indices (> .80) for use of a Language Cluster score (Vocabulary + Syntax + Phonemic Segmentation), an Achievement Cluster score (Alphabet + Sounds), and the total score for screening decisions and for predictive follow-up studies. The LSB correctly predicted 73% to 81% of poor readers in three samples of children followed through third grade. In addition, five of the seven subtests met the .80 reliability criterion recommended by Brown (1983) and Salvia and Ysseldyke (1991) for instructional grouping decisions, the primary purpose of the LSB. Formcopy and Visual Discrimination did not meet the .80 criterion. Construct and criterion-related studies also supported the theoretical base of the LSB and its relationship to established, individually administered tests. For a complete discussion of the psychometric qualities of the LSB, see Flynn and Rahbar (1998b).

DEVELOPMENT OF THE TEACHER RATING SCALE

The Teacher Rating Scale (TRS) reflected the same precursors to reading represented in the LSB. First, we specified 10 skill categories: Letter Names, Sight Words, Visual Discrimination, Visual-Motor Skill, Letter Sounds, Rhyming, Decoding, Receptive Vocabulary, Oral Language, and Expressive Vocabulary. Next, we wrote behavioral descriptions for rating each characteristic on a scale of 1 to 10. For example, under "Letter Names," 1 was described as "recognizes less than 10 letters" and 10 as "recognizes and names all letters." Scores in each category were summed to produce a total reading prediction score with a minimum score of 10 and a maximum of 100. Table I depicts the relationship of the TRS categories to the companion LSB subtests and to the reading components identified by Rumelhart.

Table I. Relationship of Teacher Rating Scale and Literacy Screening Battery to Rumelhart's Reading Model

Rumelhart Reading Process	LSB Subtest	TRS Category
Phonological process	Phonemic Segmentation	Rhyming
	Sounds	Letter Sounds
		Decoding
Logographic process	Visual Discrimination	Visual Discrimination
	Formcopy	Visual Motor
Orthographic process	Alphabet	Letter Names
		Sight Words
Syntactic process	Syntax	Oral Language
		Expressive Vocabulary
Semantic process	Vocabulary	Receptive Vocabulary

Sample

Our sample consisted of all kindergarten children (*n* = 1,972) present the day of screening in 26 Midwestern school districts. This cohort was part of our five-year study of reading development in 5,317 children in 26 Minnesota and Wisconsin districts (Flynn and Rahbar 1993a, 1993b,1998a, 1998b). District K-12 enrollments for the first year of the study ranged from 418 to 7,455 students, with a median enrollment of 950. Both rural and small town communities, ranging from 500 to 50,000 inhabitants, were represented, with median incomes from $8,600 to $21,500 (1988 Chamber of Commerce data by community). Ethnic background of the communities served by these districts was primarily northern European, predominantly Norwegian, Irish, Polish, and German. Two districts reported minority populations of Hmong children.

Procedures and Materials

Kindergarten children in 221 classrooms were screened in March or April by the principal investigator and three research assistants. Because screening is not diagnosis, but rather a system for identifying children who need further assessment, the issue of personnel costs favors a group-administered screening test, few of which existed at the time this study was implemented. To ensure reliable and valid individual scores in a group setting, we devised developmentally appropriate screening procedures. Private "offices" in the form of tabletop carrels were used to reduce error variance associated with copying. Teachers and paraprofessionals assisted the screeners so that the adult-child ratio was no more than 1:6. Each subtest was contained in a separate booklet with no more than four items per page. Children were encouraged to mark an item only if they were sure of the answer to reduce error variance associated with guessing. The examiner moved to the next item after monitors signaled that all children had completed the current item. Because phonological deletion tasks were not a part of kindergarten curricula at that time, a training session using large pictures and a one-page pretest with feedback regarding correct responses was completed before administration of the Phonemic Segmentation subtest. The battery was administered on two separate days, with an activity break between each subtest. Each subtest required 10 to 20 minutes to complete. Total administration time, including breaks, averaged two hours. A very small number of children who became anxious or had difficulty staying with the tasks were taken to an alternative play setting and tested individually by the project screener.

Kindergarten teachers completed the Teacher Rating Scale for each of their students prior to the screening days. Some teachers elected to use the previous five-point prediction instrument, resulting in combined TRS and LSB data on 1,634 of the 1,972 children screened. It is important to note that district personnel were not informed of screening results to avoid biasing outcome. Our goal, at this point in our research program, was to identify valid precursors to reading achievement. Subsequent research was planned to investigate the interaction between risk profile and intervention programs, with inservice training to teachers on how to use the LSB to identify risk signs and match children with effective interventions.

COMPARISON OF THE TEACHER RATING SCALE AND THE LITERACY SCREENING BATTERY

Content and criterion-related validity studies used data from 1,634 kindergarten children for whom both TRS and LSB scores were available. First, we computed intercorrelations of TRS categories to determine whether the ratings contributed unique information suggestive of different skill domains. We expected relatively low correlations between items representing different domains, e.g., Receptive Vocabulary and Visual Motor Skills, however, all teacher ratings were moderately to highly correlated (.55 to .81, $p = .0001$), suggesting a "halo" effect rather than differential rating of specific precursors to reading. In contrast, the LSB intercorrelations were all in the low to moderate range (.16 to .51) with the exception of Alphabet and Sounds subtests, which correlated .67.

Next, correlations of TRS ratings with LSB subtest scores were computed to examine the degree of relationship between teacher ratings and subtest scores hypothesized to test common processes. Teacher Rating Scale early literacy ratings (Letter Names, Sight Words, Letter Sounds, and Decoding) correlated moderately to highly (.48 to .72) with LSB subtests Alphabet and Sounds, indicating that teachers' observations matched children's performance on these tasks fairly well. However, other TRS-LSB correlations were relatively low, ranging from .31 to .43. This suggested that teacher ratings of linguistic and visual processing skills for the most part were not highly related to children's performance on screening tasks measuring those skills.

We next used principal components analysis with varimax rotation to determine whether teacher ratings and LSB subtests clustered in theoretically meaningful ways. Previous principal components analysis of the LSB subtests suggested a three-factor solution consisting of language, orthographic/achievement, and visual processing factors, partially confirming our hypothesized model of reading development. This solution was stable across three different cohorts and two revisions of the LSB (Flynn and Rahbar 1998b). For the joint TRS-LSB analysis, we submitted scores from both instruments to principal components analysis with varimax rotation. In both a three-factor and four-factor solution, eight of the ten teacher ratings sorted in a largely uninterpretable factor, with some ratings contributing roughly equivalent loadings on two factors. The four-factor solution, reported in table II, accounted for a larger proportion of the variance explained and contained three interpretable factors: Factor II—an achievement factor consisting of four teacher statements plus LSB Alphabet; Factor III—LSB language subtests; and Factor IV—LSB Visual Processing subtests. Thus, it appears that, for the most part, teacher ratings reflected a more global and different view of children's pre-reading abilities compared to their performance on the LSB.

To investigate the predictive validity of the TRS separately and in conjunction with the LSB, we studied a subset of children for whom first and third grade reading achievement scores were available. These scores were provided by participating districts and because testing schedules varied, the follow-up sample for

Table II. Principal Components Analysis of LSB Subtests and TRS Statements—4 Factor Solution

Variable	Factors			
	I.	II.	III.	IV.
TRS Decoding Ability	.715	.501		
TRS Expressive Vocabulary	.879			
TRS Oral Language	.874			
TRS Receptive Vocabulary	.805			
TRS Rhyming Ability	.764			
TRS Sight Words	.598	.571		
TRS Visual Discrimination	.779			
TRS Visual Motor Skill	.613			
LSB Alphabet		.775		
TRS Letter Naming		.776		
TRS Letter Sounds	.555	.680		
LSB Sounds		.770		
LSB Phonemic Segmentation	.		.634	
LSB Syntax			.760	
LSB Vocabulary			.781	
LSB Visual Discrimination				.613
LSB Formcopy				.828

Note: 74% of variance accounted for. Factor loadings ≤.50 not reported.

predictive studies consisted of 210 children who had been tested in both first and third grade. This sample did not differ significantly from the screening cohort in distribution of age, socioeconomic status, place of residence, or sex.

Based on a 35% base rate of reading failure by third grade in our first cohort, we defined a score at or below the 35th percentile on the TRS as at risk for reading failure. Teacher ratings on the TRS resulted in a mean of 74 and a standard deviation of 19. Therefore, we used the raw score of 66 (corresponding to the 35th percentile) as the cut-off score for teacher prediction of children at risk. Risk status on the LSB was defined as a score at or below the 35th percentile on either the Language or Achievement Cluster.

Outcome measures provided by the participating districts consisted of identification for special reading services and reading percentile scores (composite or total reading percentile) on standardized tests, e.g., Iowa Test of Basic Skills (ITBS) (Hieronymus, Hoover, and Lindquist 1986), the Metropolitan Achievement Test (MAT6) (Prescott et al. 1985), or the Stanford Achievement Test (Gardner et al. 1982). Reading failure was defined as total reading percentile at or below the 40th percentile or enrollment in Title 1 or LD reading services in first, second, and/or third grade. The 40th percentile was chosen as the achievement test cutoff because most districts use this criterion for Title 1 eligibility. Although the 40th percentile is within the average range for reading achievement in the national norming samples for these tests, this cutoff identified only the lowest 23% of our follow-up sample.

After specifying predictive and outcome cutoff scores, we constructed 2 X 2 classification tables to examine the utility of the TRS and LSB in predicting children who failed in reading. Teachers correctly predicted 64% of poor readers and missed 36% of those who failed. Although the TRS represented a substantial improvement over our original teacher rating scale (30% correct identification of children who failed), identification rates were still substantially below that obtained by the group-administered LSB, which correctly predicted 80% of poor readers in this sample.

Despite the high identification rate of the LSB compared with most screening instruments (Gredler 1992; Keogh 1977; Mercer, Algozzine, and Triffiletti 1988) we were concerned that 20% of the poor readers were not identified by the test. We wondered whether a combination of the TRS and LSB cut scores might improve identification. Using a risk classification rule of either test (LSB) or teacher (TRS) cut score at or below the 35th percentile resulted in a positive identification rate of 88% of poor readers. However, the rate of over-identification also increased: Thirty-nine percent of the children predicted to fail by this criterion were good readers at the beginning of third grade. Predictive validity results for the TRS, the LSB, and the TRS-LSB are summarized in table III.

DISCUSSION

This study, using a skills-based rating instrument rather than teacher prediction of future achievement, resulted in a 34% improvement in teacher identification of children at risk. However, 36% of the children who later failed in reading were not identified by the Teacher Rating Scale. Overall, this study suggests that additional procedures are needed to help teachers identify and intervene early. First, kindergarten teachers would benefit from training in differential diagnosis and observation, particularly of precursors to literacy that are not part of a traditional kindergarten curriculum. We also believe that multiple screenings, including one at the beginning of kindergarten and another at the beginning of first grade, as well as the current end-of-kindergarten screening, would ensure more accurate identification of children at risk. Finally, studies of how child risk factors interact with different instructional environments could facilitate the ultimate goal of screening programs—to match child risk profiles with interventions proven effective in reducing reading failure.

The TRS and other rating scales that identify children's initial levels in reading precursors can serve as inservice tools to train teachers on observation of skills outside of traditional reading readiness areas. It would be important to provide this inservice training early in the kindergarten year. In our study, the rating scale was completed late in the year and teachers were not trained in differential diagnosis. The fact that their ratings on letter names and sounds generally matched screening results in these domains suggests that training on phonological, orthographic, and visual

Table III. Predictive Validity of the Teacher Rating Instrument (TRS), the Screening Test (LSB), and Teacher Rating and Screening Test Combined Criteria (TRS/LSB)

Variable	TRS	LSB	TRS/LSB
Valid positives	.64	.80	.88
Valid negatives	.86	.72	.57
False positives	.23	.31	.39
False negatives	.37	.20	.12

discrimination precursors would improve their ability to rate their children in these important emerging literacy skills.

We believe that screening children early in the kindergarten year would not only facilitate observation of important literacy precursors but also provide information for interventions during the kindergarten year. To achieve the goal of identifying children early in their kindergarten year, we recently developed the Early Literacy Screening Battery (ELSB), a downward extension of the LSB. The overlap of tasks and items between the ELSB and LSB holds promise for documenting the effects of instruction as well as for early identification. For example, in a pilot study of seven kindergarten classrooms screened in October ($n = 154$), there were no significant differences on ELSB subtests measuring vocabulary, syntax, alphabet recognition, sound recognition, or visual discrimination. However, at the end of the kindergarten year, the LSB results revealed significant differences between groups on vocabulary ($p = .0001$). Children in the classroom that focused on pre-academic skills with minimal attention to enriching oral language made on average only two points gain on the Vocabulary subtest, in contrast to gains of five to seven points for the other classrooms that were primarily literature-based.

Prediction of reading failure and effective intervention may also be enhanced if screening takes place at the beginning of first grade. Satz and Fletcher (1988) recommended re-screening to increase the confidence with which we identify children at risk. Equally important, re-screening will provide first grade teachers with instructionally relevant information. Multiple screenings are feasible if testing batteries are administered to groups in order to reduce time and personnel cost. Although classroom teachers can conduct their own screenings with the ELSB and LSB, it may be more valuable to allow teachers time to make observations of the children without the constraints of having to attend to the whole group as the main screener. In this way screening becomes an opportunity for teachers to make personal structured observations that can be used in planning interventions (Jansky 1988).

The potentially powerful interaction between child characteristics and instructional interventions must also be considered in assessment of risk. Although many studies have looked at child risk variables, few have studied the effects of instructional environments. Gates (1937) investigated the influence of instructional conditions on the reading success of children in first grade who had been tested previously to establish "mental ages" (Ames 1967). He found that a high quality of teacher instruction, a wide range of easy and interesting reading materials, and the use of diagnostic assessments were characteristic of the most successful classroom, in which 77% of the children with relatively low "mental ages" (4-5 to 5-11at the beginning of the year) were successful readers. This percentage of successful readers contrasted sharply with findings from another classroom, where only 15% with similar readiness levels met the criterion for reading success.

In another study of the interaction between first-grade readiness, Gesell developmental age scores, and instructional techniques, Zenka and Keatley (1985, in Gredler 1992) found that when the Writing to Read Program (Martin and Friedberg 1986) was added to the regular kindergarten curriculum, the incidence of "immature" children at the end of kindergarten was 29% less than in the non-enriched classrooms. It should be noted, however, that this study used a score at or above the 40th percentile on the Metropolitan Readiness Test as the criterion for readiness for first grade. Whether this criterion and intervention program fully captures the probability of children's success in reading is debatable.

Still fewer studies have investigated the effects of instructional programs on children with specific risk profiles, with the exception of the accumulating data concerning the effects of phonological awareness programs on children with deficits in processing speech sounds (Felton and Brown 1990; Hurford et al. 1994; Lundberg, Frost, and Peterson 1988; see, however, Olson and Wise 1997 and Torgesen 1997 for cautions regarding the transfer of phonological training to reading fluency). Our early kindergarten pilot study suggests that similar studies of vocabulary enrichment will yield important information for prevention of later reading failure. We know that the teacher whose children achieved the highest average gains in vocabulary (for both high and low scorers on the ESLB) used a literature-rich approach with deliberately planned redundancy in new concepts and vocabulary. Another teacher was especially effective in raising vocabulary scores of children who had been identified most at risk (lowest 33% at the beginning of the year). Further observation of and interviews with this teacher may yield specific techniques for intervention with low-scoring children. Given the demographics of this rural district where many children score low on the vocabulary and syntax subtests, these data suggest the importance of studying classroom-based interventions for reduction of reading failure in upper grades.

These studies highlight the importance of documenting teacher and instructional variables as well as child characteristics. Adequately assessing risk depends on assessment of the quality of the subsequent teaching instruction that a child will receive, one of the primary reasons early screening programs seldom identify more than 75% of the children who later fail (Gredler 1992; Jansky 1986, 1988; Keogh 1977). Matching children with specific risk profiles to instructional interventions proven to reduce the risk of failure would be a major improvement in the all-too-prevalent practice of screening children, deeming them not ready for reading instruction, and recommending delayed school entrance, transition room placement, or retention in kindergarten. By examining the patterns of improvements in children at risk who had been screened with instructionally relevant tasks at the beginning and end of kindergarten and given well-documented instructional programs, effective interventions could be identified. Teachers could make immediate use of screening information in matching child characteristics with instructional programs.

Our conclusion from these studies is that it is important to improve teacher prediction of children at risk of failure, not only to identify the greatest number of those at risk but also to provide inservice training for teachers on effective interventions. To move screening from identification to intervention, it is imperative that screening programs use theory-based, research-validated instruments that provide instructional guidance. These screenings should occur at crucial points in kindergarten and first grade in order to identify potential problems in acquisition of emerging literacy skills. Repeated screening should also provide information on the interaction between classroom instruction and child characteristics in preventing or lessening the impact of reading failure. It is our hope that kindergarten screenings will ultimately result in curriculum being adapted to meet the needs of the child, rather than the child being asked to wait until he or she is "ready" for the curriculum.

REFERENCES

Adams, M. 1990. *Beginning to Read: Thinking and Learning About Print.* Cambridge, MA: MIT Press.

Adelman, H. 1982. Identifying learning problems at an early age: A critical appraisal. *Journal of Clinical Child Psychology* 11:255–61.

Algozzine, B.,and Yssledyke, J. 1986. The future of the learning disabilities field: Screening and diagnosis. *Journal of Learning Disabilities* 19:394–38.

Ames, L. 1967. *Is Your Child In the Wrong Grade?* New York: Harper and Row.

Ausubel , D., and Sullivan, E. 1970. *Theory and Problems of Child Development.* New York: Grune and Stratton.

Badian, N. 1986. Improving the prediction of reading for the individual child: A four-year follow-up. *Journal of Learning Disabilities* 19:262–70.

Badian, N. 1988. The prediction of good and poor reading before kindergarten entry: A nine-year follow-up. *Journal of Learning Disabilities* 21(2):98–103.

Badian. 1994. Preschool prediction: Orthographic and phonological skills, and reading. *Annals of Dyslexia* 44:3–25.

Ball, E., and Blachman, B. 1988. Phoneme segmentation training: Effect on reading readiness. *Annals of Dyslexia* 38:208–25.

Ball, E., and Blachman, B. 1991. Does phoneme segmentation training in kindergarten make a difference in early word recognition and developmental spelling? *Reading Research Quarterly* 26:49–66.

Berrieta, C., Schweinhart, L., Barnett, W., Epstein, A., and Weikart, D. 1984. *Changed Lives: The Effects of the Perry Preschool Program on Youths through Age 19.* Ypsilanti, MI: High/Scope Educational Research Foundation.

Blachman, B. 1983. Are we assessing the linguistic factors critical in early reading? *Annals of Dyslexia* 33:91–109.

Boehm, A. 1986. *Boehm Test of Basic Concepts Pre-School Version.* San Antonio, TX: The Psychological Corporation.

Bracken, B. 1984. *Bracken Basic Concept Scale.* San Antonio, TX: The Psychological Corporation.

Bradley, L., and Bryant, P. 1985. *Rhyme and Reason in Reading and Spelling.* Ann Arbor, MI: The Psychological Corporation.

Brady, S. 1997. Informed Instruction for Reading Success: Foundations for Teacher Preparation. Position paper of The Orton Dyslexia Society. MD: Baltimore.

Brown, F. 1983. *Principles of Educational and Psychological Testing (3rd ed.).* New York: Holt, Rinehart, and Winston.

Bruner, J. 1966. *Toward a Theory of Instruction.* Cambridge, MA: Harvard University Press.

Byrne, B., and Fielding-Barnsley, R. 1991. Evaluation of a program to teach phonemic awareness to young children. *Journal of Educational Psychology* 83(4):451–55.

Casto, G., and Mastropieri, M. 1986. The efficacy of early intervention programs: A meta-analysis. *Exceptional Children* 52(5):417–25.

Chall, J. 1983. *Stages of Reading Development.* New York: McGraw-Hill.

Curtis, M. 1980. Development of components of reading skill. *Journal of Educational Psychology* 72:656–69.

Davis, B., Trimble, C., and Vincent, D. 1980. Does age of entrance affect school achievement? *Elementary School Journal* 80:133–43.

Dunn, L., and Dunn, L. 1981. *Peabody Picture Vocabulary Test Revised.* Circle Pines, MN: American Guidance Service.

Ehri, L, and Wilce, L. 1985. Movement into reading: Is the first stage of printed word learning visual or phonetic? *Reading Research Quarterly* 20:163–79.

Felton, R., and Brown, I. 1990. Phonological processes as predictors of specific reading skills in children at risk for reading failure. *Reading and Writing: An Interdisciplinary Journal* 2:39–59.

Feshbach, S., Adelman, H., and Fuller, W. 1974. Early identification of children with risk of reading failure. *Journal of Learning Disabilities* 7:639–44.

Fletcher, J., and Satz, P. 1984. Test-based versus teacher-based predictions of academic achievement: A three-year longitudinal follow-up. *Journal of Pediatric Psychology* 9(2): 193–201.

Fletcher, J., Satz, P., and Scholes, R. 1981. Developmental changes in the linguistic performance correlates of reading achievement: Differences in what predicts reading at different ages. *Brain and Language* 13:78–90.

Flynn, J. 1997a. *Teacher Rating Scale.* LaCrosse, WI: LaCrosse Area Dyslexia Research Institute, Inc.

Flynn. 1997b. *Literacy Screening Battery.* LaCrosse, WI: LaCrosse Area Dyslexia Research Institute, Inc.

Flynn, J., and Boder, E. 1991. Clinical and electrophysiological correlates of dysphonetic and dyseidetic dyslexia. In *Vision and Visual Dyslexia. Vol. 13,* ed. J. Stein. Basingstoke, England: MacMillan Press.

Flynn, J., and Deering, W. 1989. Subtypes of dyslexia: Investigation of Boder's system using quantitative neurophysiology. *Developmental Medicine and Child Neurology* 31:215–31.

Flynn, J., Deering, W., Goldstein, M., and Rahbar, M. 1992. Electrophysiological correlates of dyslexic subtypes. *Journal of Learning Disabilities* 25:133–41.

Flynn, J., and Rahbar, M. 1993a. The effect of age, sex, socioeconomic status, and kindergarten screening scores on reading achievement. *Proceedings of the 1993 American Statistical Association Conference* 785–90.

Flynn J., and Rahbar, M.1993b. Effects of age of school entrance and sex on achievement: Implications for pediatric counseling. *Developmental and Behavioral Pediatrics* 14(5):304–7.

Flynn, J., and Rahbar, M. 1994. Prevalence of reading failure in boys compared with girls. *Psychology in the Schools* 11:66–71.

Flynn, J., and Rahbar, M. 1998a. Improving teacher prediction of children at risk for reading failure. *Psychology in the Schools* 35(2):163–72.

Flynn, J., and Rahbar, M. 1998b. Kindergarten screening for risk of reading failure. *Journal of Psychoeducational Assessment* 16:15–35.

Frith, U. 1985. Beneath the surface of developmental dyslexia. In *Surface Dyslexia: Neuropsychological and Cognitive Studies of Phonological Reading.* eds. J. Marshall and M. Coltheart. London: Erlbaum.

Gardner, M. 1985. *Receptive One-Word Picture Vocabulary* Test. Novato: CA: Academic Therapy.

Gardner, E., Rudman, H., Karlsen, B., and Merwin, J. 1982. *Stanford Achievement Test.* San Antonio, TX: The Psychological Corporation.

Gates, A. 1937. The necessary mental age for beginning reading. *Elementary School Journal* 8:497–508.

Gredler, G. 1992. *School Readiness: Assessment and Educational Issues.* Brandon, Vermont: Clinical Psychology Publishing Company.

Hieronymus, A., Hoover, H., and Lindquist, E. 1986. *Iowa Tests of Basic Skills.* Chicago: Riverside.

Hurford, D., Johnston, M., Nepote, P. Hampton, S., Moore, S., Neal, J., Mueller, A., McGeorge, K., Huff, L., Awad, A., Tatro, C., Juliano, C., and Huffman, D. 1994. Early identification and remediation of phonological-processing deficits in first-grade children at risk for reading disabilities. *Journal of Learning Disabilities* 27(10):647–59.

Jansky, J. 1986. The case for prediction. Paper read at the 37th annual conference of The Orton Dyslexia Society, Philadelphia.

Jansky, J. 1988. Prediction: A six-year follow up. Paper read at the 39th annual conference of The Orton Dyslexia Society, Tampa.

Jansky, J., and de Hirsch, K. 1972. *Preventing Reading Failure: Prediction, Diagnosis, Intervention.* New York: Harper and Row.

Johansson, B. 1965. *Criteria for School Readiness.* Stockholm: Almquist and Wiksell.

Keogh, B.1977. Early ID: Selective perception or perceptive selection? *Academic Therapy* 12(3):268–73.

LaBerge, D., and Samuels, S. 1974. Toward a theory of automatic information processing in reading. *Cognitive Psychology* 6:293–323.

LaTorre, R., Hawkhead, F., Kawahira, R., and Bilow, L.1982. Kindergarten screening pilot project in Vancouver schools 1979-1980: A two-year following of the McCarthy Screening Test. *British Journal of Special Education* 6:23–41.

Liberman, I., Shankweiler, D., Fischer, F., and Carter, B.1974. Explicit syllable and phoneme segmentation in the young child. *Journal of Experimental Child Psychology* 18:201–12.

Liberman, I., and Shankweiler, D.1985. Phonology and problems of learning to read and write. *RASE: Remedial and Special Education* 6:8–17,

Lundberg, I., Frost, J., and Peterson, O. 1988. Effects of an extensive program for stimulating phonological awareness in preschool children. *Reading Research Quarterly* 23:263–84.

Lyon, G. R. 1985. Identification and remediation of learning disability subtypes: Preliminary findings. *Learning Disabilities Focus* 1:21–35.

Majsterek, D., and Ellenwood, A. 1995. Phonological awareness and beginning reading: Evaluation of a school-based screening procedure. *Journal of Learning Disabilities* 28:449–56.

Martin, J., and Friedberg, A. 1986. *Writing to Read.* New York: Warner.

Mercer, C., Algozinne, B., and Triffiletti, J. 1988. Early identification: An analysis of the research. *Learning Disability Quarterly* 11:176–88.

Moats, L. 1994. The missing foundation in teacher education: Knowledge of the structure of spoken and written language. *Annals of Dyslexia* 44:81–104.

Olson, R., and Wise, B. 1997. Problems in transfer from improved phonological skills to reading growth. Paper read at the 48th annual conference of The Orton Dyslexia Society, Minneapolis.

Prescott, G., Balow, I., Hogan, T., and Farr, R. 1985. *Metropolitan Achievement Tests: MAT6.* San Antonio, TX: The Psychological Corporation.

Ramaden, Z. 1997. Artificial intelligence: A data analysis system to subtype dyslexic children using electorencephalograms. Ph.D. dissertation. Marquette University, Milwaukee, WI.

Rosner, J., and Simon., D. 1971. The Auditory Analysis Test: An initial report. *Journal of Learning Disabilities* 4:384–92.

Rumelhart, D. 1977. Toward an interactive model of reading. In *Attention and Performance IV.* eds. S. Dornic and P. Rabbitt. Hillsdale, NJ: Erlbaum.

Salvia, J., and Ysseldyke, J. 1991. *Assessment: 5th Edition.* Boston: Houghton-Mifflin.

Satz, P., and Fletcher, J. 1988. Early identification of learning disabled children: An old problem revisited. *Journal of Consulting and Clinical Psychology* 56:824–29.

Satz, P., Taylor, G., Friel, J., and Fletcher, J. 1978. Some developmental and predictive precursors of reading disabilities: A six year follow-up. In *Dyslexia: An Appraisal of Current Knowledge.* eds. A. Benton and D. Pearl. New York: Oxford Press.

Sears, S., and Keogh, B. 1993. Predicting reading performance using the Slingerland procedures. *Annals of Dyslexia* 43:78–89.

Shanahan. 1984. Nature of the reading-writing relation: An exploratory multivariate analysis. *Journal of Educational Psychology* 76:466–77.

Shaywitz, S., Shaywitz, B., Fletcher, J., and Escobar, M. 1990. Prevalence of reading disability in boys and girls. *Journal of the American Medical Association* 264:998–1002.

Shepard, L., and Smith, M. 1986. Synthesis of research on school readiness and kindergarten retention. *Educational Leadership* 78–86.

Shepard, L., and Smith, M. 1989. *Flunking Grades: Research and Policies on Retention*. London: Falmer Press.

Silver, A., Hagin, R., and Beecher, R. 1978. Scanning, diagnosis, and intervention in the prevention of reading disabilities: I. SEARCH: The scanning measure. *Journal of Learning Disabilities* 11(7):439–49.

Stanovich, K. 1986. The Matthews effects in reading: Some consequences of individual differences in the acquisition of reading. *Reading Research Quarterly* 21:360–407.

Stanovich, K., Cunningham, A., and Freeman, D. 1984. Intelligence, cognitive skills, and early reading progress. *Reading Research Quarterly* 19:278–303.

Stanovich, K., and Siegel, L.1994. The phenotypic performance profile of reading-disabled children: A regression-based test of the phonological core variable-difference model. *Journal of Educational Psychology* 86:24–53.

Stanovich, K., Siegel, L., and Gottardo, A. 1997. Converging evidence for phonological and surface subtypes of reading disability. *Journal of Educational Psychology* 89(1):114–27.

Stevenson, H., Parker, T., Wilkinson, A. Hegion, A., and Fish, E. 1976. Predictive value of teachers' ratings of young children. *Journal of Educational Psychology* 68:506–17.

Strag, G.1972. Comparative behavioral ratings of parents with severely mentally retarded, special learning disability and normal children. *Journal of Learning Disabilities* 5:52–6.

Torgesen, J. 1997. Issues and conclusions about interventions: A research-based perspective. Paper read at the 48th annual conference of The Orton Dyslexia Society, Minneapolis.

Vygotsky, L. 1930-35/1978. *Mind in Society: The Development of Higher Psychological Processes*. Cambridge, MA: Harvard University Press.

Wagner, R., and Torgesen, J. 1987. The nature of phonological processing and its causal role in the acquisition of reading skills. *Psychological Bulletin* 101:192–212.

Wolf, M. 1998. What time may tell: Towards a reconceptualization of developmental dyslexia. The Norman Geschwind memorial lecture presented at the 49th annual International Dyslexia Association meeting, San Francisco.

Zenka, L., and Keatley, M. 1985. Progress toward excellence: Tulsa's kindergarten program. *ERS Spectrum* 3:3–8.

Chapter • 7

Preschool Phonological Awareness and Success in Reading

Carol A. Christensen

The last 20 years have been remarkably productive in terms of research on reading. With a consistency that is rarely found in educational research, the factors that can explain reading success and failure have become clearly documented. In one of the most comprehensive analyses of this research, Stanovich (1986) wrote, "Evidence is mounting that the primary specific mechanism that enables early reading success is phonological awareness: conscious access to the phonemic level of the speech stream and some ability to cognitively manipulate representations at this level" (p. 362). In the decade following Stanovich's paper, research has continued to be productive and to confirm the pivotal role phonological awareness plays in learning to read.

Historically, some general measures of cognitive capability such as general intelligence and language processing skills have had a significant positive relationship with reading. However, research has shown that phonological awareness is the most potent predictor of who will learn to read successfully and who is at risk of failure (Bradley and Bryant 1978; Share et al. 1984; Tunmer and Nesdale 1985). In fact, Muter et al. (1998) found that IQ does not have an independent relationship with reading other than its association with phonological awareness. In other words, the relationship between reading and IQ is fully accounted for by the relationship between phonological awareness and reading.

MEASURES OF PHONOLOGICAL AWARENESS

Phonological awareness refers to sensitivity to the phonetic structure of language. It is the understanding and awareness of speech sounds. It includes the ability to segment words into their constituent sound clusters (e.g., rhyme) and to identify individual phonemes. It also includes the ability to manipulate speech sounds (e.g., change tap into cap by substituting /k/ for /t/). Tasks requiring phonological awareness include recognition of rhyme and alliteration, blending of phonemes, phoneme substitution, and the appreciation of puns.

Early studies into the relationship between phonological awareness and reading demonstrated that measures of phonological awareness could distinguish between good and poor readers effectively (Bradley and Bryant 1978; Calfee, Lindamood, and Lindamood 1973). These studies indicated that competent readers performed better on measures of phonological awareness than poor readers. A diversity of tasks were used to assess phonological awareness including pig Latin games, rhyming, segmenting words into syllables and phonemes, and phoneme deletion and substitution tasks. The relationship was found to be consistent for children across grades. For example, Muter and Snowling (1998) found that phonological awareness had a significant positive correlation with reading when children were tested in preschool at age 4 years. The relationship was maintained when children were tested at ages 5, 6, and 9 years and later in grade 9. The relationship was maintained when children were tested at ages 5 and 6 years and later at age 9. For example, at 9, the correlation between a phoneme deletion task and age reading accuracy was .84.

Although the relationship between phonological awareness and reading was strong and consistent, correlation studies did not offer strong evidence of causation. There are a number of possible relationships that could result in a correlation. For example, reading may cause phonological awareness, or both phonological awareness and reading may be unrelated to each other directly, but are both caused by another, third, factor. A second set of studies sought to address some of these methodological problems. These studies measured children's phonological awareness before they began to learn to read. Children's reading was then assessed some time later and the relationship between their initial phonological skills and later reading skills measured. Once again, strong and consistent correlations were found between preschool children's levels of phonological knowledge and their subsequent development of reading. Thus, measures of phonological awareness in preliterate children significantly predicted later reading achievement (Blachman 1984; Bradley and Bryant 1983; Fox and Routh 1975; Share et al. 1984). For example, Vellutino and Scanlon (1987) initially tested children in kindergarten, most of whom were non-readers, on a range of measures of phonological awareness. They tested the same children again in oral reading at the end of grade 1. They found that measures of rhyme and phonemic segmentation significantly predicted reading ability. They tested rhyme by asking children to supply a rhyming word to match a pair of rhyming words they had been given. In a test they titled *sound-letter, consonants*, the researcher said a word and asked the children to say the initial letter. The *initial consonants substitution* measure presented children with a written word (e.g., *fit*) at the same time the researcher said the word. The children were then presented with four other words (e.g., *sit, pit, kit, bit*) and asked to identify each word.

Three tests measured children's letter knowledge. A *letter names* test asked children to name 20 letters presented to them in lower case and a *letter-sound, consonants* test asked children to supply the sound for 15 lower case letters. For a test they called *letter-sound, vowels*, children were asked to identify the five vowels when they were presented in lower case.

Vellutino and Scanlon found that each of these measures significantly predicted oral reading at the end of grade 1. However, the relationship between rhyme and reading seemed to be weaker than the relationship between reading and the other measures.

In another longitudinal study, Maclean, Bryant, and Bradley (1987) examined the relationship between rhyme, alliteration and early reading. They followed 66 children for 15 months. The children had a mean age of 3 years, 4 months at the beginning of the study. Initially they tested children's knowledge of nursery rhymes and gave the children three rhyme tasks. The first was *detection of rhyme* in which children were shown three pictures. Two of the pictures showed rhyming words and a third did not rhyme. Children named the objects, then indicated the one that did not rhyme. The *rhyme production* task asked the children to supply a word to rhyme with a word supplied by the researcher. Finally, in the *forced choice-rhyme* task, the researcher said two words and the child had to say the one that rhymed with, for example, *Joe*. There were two alliteration tasks. The *detection of alliteration* task was the same as the detection of rhyme task, but the children were asked to categorize words by their initial sound. The *alliteration production* task asked children to provide a word that started with the same sound as a word the researcher had just said (e.g., "tell a word that starts the same as *tap*"). Letter knowledge was tested by showing children a random series of plastic letters and asking them to produce either the letter sound or name.

They also gave children a *segmenting* task in which they gave the children a phrase and asked them to say a "little bit" of it. Children were prompted to produce words, syllables, and phonemes. However, very few children could complete this task successfully. It was considered too difficult for children of this age.

To examine the relationship between reading and phonological awareness, children were divided into those who had elementary reading skills and those who had not developed any skills at the end of the study. Maclean, Bryant, and Bradley found that children who developed early reading skills had more knowledge of nursery rhymes and had significantly higher rhyme and alliteration scores at the beginning of the study than children who did not. However, they did not show any difference in letter knowledge. Maclean, Bryant, and Bradley also found that knowledge of nursery rhymes was significantly related to subsequent development of rhyming skills. They suggest that knowledge of nursery rhymes leads to development of phonological awareness in general and rhyming in particular and that rhyme awareness subsequently facilitates the ability to read.

Tunmer, Herriman, and Nesdale (1988), examined the role of four forms of metalinguistic awareness in learning to read. They suggest that metalinguistic awareness "enables one to reflect on and manipulate the structural features of language" (p. 136). They looked at phonological awareness, word awareness, syntactic awareness, and pragmatic awareness. Word awareness is the ability to reflect on and manipulate words as sub-units of language. Syntactic awareness refers to the understanding of the mechanisms responsible for the structural arrangements of words. Pragmatic awareness is the "awareness of the relationships that obtain between a given sentence and the context in which it is embedded" (p. 136) so that language can be used for communicative purposes.

Tunmer, Herriman, and Nesdale tested 118 children at the beginning of schooling on three tests of metalinguistic awareness. They also tested the children's knowledge of letters and early reading abilities. They tested them at the end of the first year of schooling on three reading measures, including real word decoding, pseudoword decoding, and reading comprehension. The children were tested on the three reading measures again at the end of their second year of schooling. Letter knowledge was assessed by asking the children to give the name or sound of alphabetic letters written in upper and lower case. Phonological awareness was assessed by asking children to tap out the number of phonemes in non-words presented orally by the researcher. There were 20 items in all; 5 single-phoneme sounds (e.g., /o/, /a/), 10 two-phoneme syllables (e.g., *ez, da*), and 5 consonant vowel consonant (CVC) syllables (e.g., *baf, sug*).

Syntactic awareness was assessed by asking the children to correct a sentence of three or four words in length that contained word-order violations (e.g., *made biscuits Mum, dog the barked*). Pragmatic awareness was assessed by the children's ability to detect inter-sentence inconsistencies in prose presented orally. For example:

> Jenny has a very large window in her bedroom. One night when it was still very dark, Jenny looked out of the window. She could see the sun shining in the sky.

The correlations between preliterate kindergarten children's scores on the three metalinguistic measures and letter knowledge with their achievement in reading at the end of the first and second years of schooling are given in table I. The relationship between pragmatic awareness and the three reading measures was the smallest in magnitude and the relationship between letter knowledge and reading the largest.

Tunmer, Herriman, and Nesdale argue that their data suggest that phonological awareness in the form of phonemic segmentation skill and syntactic awareness develop during the preschool years and play a critical role in facilitating reading during the first two years of schooling. Pragmatic awareness also facilitates early reading, but is likely to be more critical later in children's development. Although children's knowledge of letter sounds and names was the strongest predictor of success in learning to read, the authors suggested that letter knowledge alone did not appear to be

Table I. Tunmer, Herriman, and Nesdale (1988) Correlations Between Measures of Metalinguistic Awareness in Kindergarten, and First and Second Grade Reading

	Word Reading	Pseudoword Reading		Comprehension	
	Grade	Grade		Grade	
	1	1	2	1	2
phonological awareness	.41**	.44**	.32**	.34**	.34**
syntactic awareness	.38**	.37**	.37**	.40**	.34**
pragmatic awareness	.23*	.24*	.41**	.29*	.27*
letter knowledge	.60**	.54**	.49**	.58**	.52**

*p < .01
**p < .001

sufficient to enhance reading. A minimal level of phonological awareness seemed to be necessary for children to learn to use their understanding of phoneme-grapheme correspondences to decode text.

Because of the plethora of tasks and measures used in research on phonological awareness, Stanovich, Cunningham, and Cramer (1984) compared the efficacy of ten phonological tasks in predicting reading achievement. Fifty-eight kindergartners were given the tasks. Reading achievement was tested one year later. The tasks included *rhyme supply* where the researcher gave children a word and they provided a rhyming word and *rhyme choice* where children were given a target word and three other words. They had to name the word that rhymed with the target word (e.g., *pet: barn, net, hand*). The *initial consonant same* task used the same format as rhyme choice, however children were asked to name a word that had the same initial consonant as the target word (e.g., *milk: sand, man, sheep*). The same procedure was used in the *final consonant same* task with children asked to supply a word that ended in the same sound (e.g., *meat: fin, coat, glass*). This task was also accompanied by a picture of the target word. *Strip initial consonant* required children to delete the initial phoneme from a word and say the embedded word (e.g., *pink: ink*). *Substitute initial consonant* required children to isolate the initial consonant and substitute a specified phoneme to produce a new word (e.g., *go: no*). In the *initial consonant different* task children had to listen to four words and choose the one that had the different initial sound (e.g., *bag, nine, beach, bike*). *Initial consonant not same* is similar to *initial consonant different* except that children need to identify the word that does not begin with the same sound as the target word (e.g., *mud: mice, dig, mouth*). *Final consonant different* required children to identify the final consonant that was different from the others in a list of four words (e.g., *rat, dime, boat, mitt*). *Supply initial consonant* presented children with a pair of words orally and asked them to identify the phoneme that was missing from the beginning of the second word (e.g., *cat -at*).

Stanovich, Cunningham, and Cramer found that phonological awareness measured in kindergarten effectively predicted reading ability one year later. All tasks had a significant correlation with reading except *rhyme choice, rhyme supply,* and *substitute initial consonant.* The magnitude of correlations is given in table II. Stanovich, Cunningham, and Cramer also found that, with the exception of *rhyme supply* and *substitute initial consonant,* all tasks significantly predicted who would become a skilled reader compared with a less skilled reader.

Table II. Stanovich, Cunningham, and Cramer (1984) Correlations Between Measures of Phonological Awareness in Kindergarten and First Grade Reading

Task	R
1. rhyme supply (pet: . . . .)	.11
2. rhyme choice (e.g. pet: barn, net, hand)	.30*
3. initial consonant same (e.g. milk: sand, man, sheep)	.39*
4. final consonant same (e.g. meat: fin, coat, glass)	.40*
5. strip initial consonant (e.g. pink: ink).	.42*
6. substitute initial consonant (e.g. go: no).	.09
7. initial consonant different (e.g. bag, nine, beach, bike).	.60*
8. initial consonant not same (e.g. mud: mice, dig, mouth).	.51*
9. final consonant different (e.g. rat, dime, boat, mitt).	.45*
10. Supplt initial consonant (e.g. cat -at)	.52*

*significant difference between good and poor readers.

The nature of the *substitute initial consonant* task essentially required the ability to rhyme. Therefore, it appears that measures that tapped initial phonemes rather than rhyme were effective in predicting reading, although rhyme did not appear to make a powerful contribution to later reading. The authors suggest that the rhyming tasks were relatively easy so that ceiling effects were obtained on the three tasks. Thus, the role of rhyming in facilitating early reading may not be evident from this study. Nevertheless, it does illustrate the pivotal role phonological awareness plays in learning to read.

I (Christensen 1997) examined the relationship between phonological awareness, letter knowledge, and reading of 630 preliterate children in their first week of schooling. I assessed children's ability to rhyme and identify initial consonants. Rhyme was measured by asking children to say a word that rhymes with a word said by the researcher. Three tasks measured children's knowledge of initial sounds. Children were asked to say a word given the initial consonant (e.g., /k/). Second, children were asked to identify the initial consonant in six CVC words given orally by the researcher (e.g., *mat*). Third, children were asked to identify the initial sound in words beginning with a consonant blend, i.e., CCVC (e.g., *train*). Children who could correctly identify initial phonemes in CVC words but could only identify the blend in CCVC words were considered to have sensitivity to onset. Children who could identify the phoneme in both tasks were considered to have phonemic awareness. Children's letter knowledge was assessed by asking them to give either the name or sound of upper and lower case letters.

At mid-year, I repeated the phonological awareness measures and assessed reading using the Clay Ready-to-Read-Words test. I assessed reading again at the end of the year using a decoding, and a sight word test, as well as, the Salford Sentence Reading Test.

On the phonological measures, children tended to score at or about either zero or 100 percent, suggesting that they either possessed the skill or did not. Consequently, correlation analyses seemed inappropriate. I conducted my analysis on the basis of six groups: children who demonstrated no phonological awareness (were not successful on any task), children who had rhyme only, children who had knowledge of onset only, children who were successful in onset and phoneme awareness, children who had rhyme and onset, and children who were successful on all tasks. Table III gives the mean score for each reading measure according to phonological group.

When the impact of children's phonological awareness before they learned to read on their subsequent reading achievement was examined, I found that there was no difference between children who had no phonological awareness and children who could rhyme in terms of their mid-year reading achievement. However, children who could rhyme at the beginning of the year performed significantly better on all end-of-year reading measures than children who could not. Children who had knowledge of either onset or phonemes performed better than children who could rhyme on the mid-year reading test. However, children who had some form of phonemic awareness generally performed better than children who only had knowledge of onset on the end-of-year reading measures. When children's phonological awareness at mid-year was examined, I found that children who had either rhyme awareness or awareness of onset did not perform any better than children who had no phonological awareness. Children with onset and rhyme awareness did better than children with no phonological awareness on The Salford Sentence Reading Test. However, children who had some kind of phonemic awareness did substantially

Table III. Mean Scores, Standard Deviations and Location of Significant Differences on Each Reading Test for Each Phonological Awareness Group Used by Christensen (1997).

Group	Clay		Decoding		Salford		Southgate	
	Mean	SD	Mean	SD	Mean	SD	Mean	SD
None	1.6	(2.5)	2.8	(2.8)	10.6	(9.7)	15.7	(6.1)
Rhyme Only	2.8	(3.2)	4.4*	(3.3)	16.5*	(13.8)	19.4*	(6.2)
Onset Only	5.4**	(3.9)	6.8*	(2.5)	22.6*	(11.0)	22.3*	(4.7)
Onset and Phoneme	5.3**	(4.7)	6.6**	(3.0)	26.0**	(18.5)	22.4*	(6.4)
Rhyme and Onset	5.3**	(4.1)	7.1**	(3.0)	25.7**	(17.5)	22.2*	(5.6)
Rhyme Onset and Phoneme	6.7**	(4.2)	7.3**	(2.5)	28.9**	(20.7)	24.1**	(4.4)

*significantly different from no awareness group

**significantly different from no awareness and rhyme only groups.

better on all three measures than children who did not. For example, children who had no phonological awareness at mid-year scored a mean of 3.7 (*SD* = 5.5) on the Salford, children with phonemic awareness scored a mean of 15.6 (*SD* = 18) and children with phonemic and rhyme awareness scored 20.7 (*SD* = 15.9).

I suggested that my data indicate that phonological awareness, particularly phonemic awareness that can develop before children learn to read, confers a considerable advantage on children in learning to read. This advantage increased throughout the first year of schooling. I also found that letter knowledge was consistently related to success in learning to read. Further, there was an interaction effect between letter knowledge and phonological awareness. Not only did letter knowledge and phonological awareness have independent positive relationships with learning to read, but their impact increased markedly when they coincided.

Thus, studies using a diversity of tasks and measures have consistently found a significant positive relationship between children's awareness of speech sounds and letters before they go to school or learn to read, and their subsequent success in learning to read. Some studies have found that the impact of preschool phonological awareness can extend for a considerable time into elementary school.

Muter and Snowling (1998) measured rhyme and phoneme awareness of 38 4-year-old pre-readers. They measured *rhyme detection* by asking children which of three words rhymed with a target word (e.g., *cat*: *fish*, *gun*, *hat*) and phoneme detection by asking children to remove the first phoneme from a single syllable word when given a pictorial representation (e.g., *bus _us*). They also assessed letter knowledge by asking children the names of the 26 letters written in lower case. Finally, they tested phonological working memory by asking children to repeat 40 non-words (e.g., *tull, ballop, thickery, perplisteronk*).

Muter et al. (1998) reported that phoneme detection and letter knowledge, but not rhyme, significantly predicted reading and spelling one year later when children were 5-years old. Two years after the initial measures were taken, when children were 6-years old, letter knowledge predicted reading achievement, and segmentation and letter knowledge predicted spelling. Muter and Snowling (1998) tested children 5 years later when they were 9 years. They found that non-word repetition and letter knowledge measured when children were 4-years old continued to be significantly related to children's reading accuracy scores. When children's phonological scores at 5 years were considered, all measures predicted reading accuracy, although the correlation between rhyme and reading was not as strong as the other measures. Phoneme detection, non-word repetition, and letter knowledge predicted non-word reading.

Stuart (1990) assessed the relationship between preschool phonological skills and long-term development in reading. He assessed reading and spelling of 9- and 10-year olds who six years earlier had been assessed for phonological awareness. There was a strong relationship between children's reading and spelling and their preschool phonological awareness. These studies provide convincing evidence that the potent influence of phonological skills on reading and spelling extends well past the preschool into the elementary years.

Does Phonological Awareness Play a Causal Role in Reading?

Although studies that found measures of phonological awareness predict success in learning to read support the notion that phonological awareness plays a causal role in learning to read, they were not conclusive. A third set of studies helped resolve the uncertainties of previous studies. These studies adopted an experimental design. Students in an experimental group were taught phonological skills while students in a control group were given another training program, which did not have a phonological component. Consistently, studies showed that students who received phonological training became better readers than students who were in the control group. In addition to clarifying the causal links between phonological awareness and reading these studies demonstrated the malleable nature of these skills and their potential to enhance children's reading in the long term.

It has been known for some time that instructional programs can have a significant impact on children's reading and spelling. In an early study, Chall (1967) conducted an analysis of the components of reading programs in terms of their ability to promote reading achievement. She found that children performed better in programs that focused on the relationships between sound and letters. Programs that had a strong phonetic component were more effective in facilitating children's learning to read.

One of the first training studies in phonological awareness for pre-readers was conducted by Lundberg, Frost, and Petersen (1988). They provided an instructional program to a group of 235 kindergartners and compared their performance to a control group. The training was provided before any formal reading instruction was begun. The phonological awareness training was provided daily for eight months by the children's regular teacher, who had undergone an extensive training program.

The phonological awareness program began with listening games that included nonverbal and verbal sounds. It then focused on rhymes including nursery rhymes, rhymed stories and rhyme production games. Next, games that focused on segmenting sentences into words were introduced. This was followed by clapping hands to mark syllables in words. Activities involving dancing, marching, and walking in pace with syllabic structure of words were introduced. This was followed by the introduction of phonemic awareness. At first, initial phonemes were segmented. When these had been mastered, phonemes within words were introduced. At the end of the training period, the experimental group performed significantly better than the control group on tests measuring rhyme, letter knowledge, word and phoneme segmentation, and synthesis. In grade one, the training group performed significantly better on tests of single-word reading and spelling.

Byrne and Fielding-Barnsley (1991) developed a program that focused on teaching children that different words can have the same sound. They focused on the notion of phoneme identity rather than phoneme manipulation, such as blending and segmentation. Using this approach, children learned to understand that a particular vocal gesture is repeated in different words. Byrne and Fielding-Barnsley used pictures of words that shared the same initial phoneme (e.g., *sun, sand, seal, sink*) and the same final phoneme (e.g., *bus, octopus, dress, hiss*). The program contained games, worksheets, and audiotapes that encouraged the understanding that words can share the same sounds. Activities were based on the classification of words that have shared sounds. For example, children would search posters or worksheets for objects beginning and ending in the same phoneme (e.g., things that begin or end with the sound /s/). Phoneme identity is measured in tasks that require word-to-word matching (e.g., "Does *sink* begin with the same sound as *sun*").

Byrne and Fielding-Barnsley provided the control group with the same duration of instruction. However, these students undertook tasks related to the classification of items based on formal or semantic criteria (e.g., *color, shape, animality, edibility*).

Sixty-four preschool children completed the phonemic awareness training. Sixty-four children started the semantic classification training but only 62 completed it. Children participated in the training for approximately 30 minutes per week for 12 weeks. Training was conducted on small groups of four to six children. Generous feedback on their performance was provided to all children.

At the end of the training period, the phonological training group showed substantial gains in phonemic awareness. In fact, all but three of the children scored at or near ceiling on the tests. In comparison, the control group made relatively small gains in phonemic awareness. Additionally, children in the experimental group had better awareness of phonemes that were not included in the training program. They also performed better than controls in word decoding.

Byrne and Fielding-Barnsley (1993, 1995) did follow-up testing after one, two, and three years. In the one-year follow up, they tested phonological awareness (phoneme identity and phoneme segmentation), real and pseudo-word identification, letter-sound knowledge, and real and pseudo-word spelling. They found that children who had participated in the phonological training group were significantly better at pseudo-word decoding, though not in real word identification or spelling.

The researchers reconstituted the analysis groups to include all children, regardless of training condition, who had passed the phonological tests, compared with all children who had failed. Sixty children from the experimental group and 16 children from the control group were in the phonological awareness group. Three from the experimental group and 40 from the control group formed the group that failed on the test. The phonological awareness group performed significantly better than the other group on all literacy measures, including decoding, word identification, and spelling. This indicated that phonological skills have a profound influence on later literacy development. A few children can develop these skills without systematic instruction; however, a systematic instructional program in preschool can have a profound impact on the development of phonological awareness and on children's subsequent competence in literacy.

After two years, the children in the experimental group continued to demonstrate superior performance. They had higher scores in non-word decoding. This advantage was sustained when the children were retested three years after the initial training. Additionally, the three-year follow up indicated that the children in the experimental group were superior in reading comprehension. Byrne and Fielding-Barnsley also note that a disproportionate number of children in the control group came to rely too heavily on sight word reading. It is quite remarkable that a program that provided approximately six hours of instruction in preschool continued to provide significant advantages to children up to three years later.

Layton et al. (1998) examined the effectiveness of a pre-school program aimed specifically at children whose development of phonological skills lagged behind those of other children. Initially, they provided general literacy experiences to a group of pre-schoolers. Then they selected 43 children who were generally developing normally but had poor rhyming skills. Half of these children were given training in phonological awareness and half were assigned to a control group. The phonological awareness group was given activities that encouraged the development of rhyming skills. Activities included learning and reciting new rhymes, generating rhymes, and identifying rhymes and non-rhymes. The control group was given categorization activities that had no emphasis on linguistic analysis. Children in the experimental group showed improved phonological skills compared with the control group. However, the researchers did not find significant differences between the groups in reading or spelling when they were tested during a one-year follow up. Children who did not participate in any training group because they had superior phonological skills at the commencement of the study did perform significantly better in both reading and spelling. The researchers suggested that poor implementation by the teachers may have contributed to the results. However, it is also feasible that training programs based on rhyme alone are not sufficient to improve reading and spelling skills.

Murray (1998) used an experimental design to examine the relative impact of phoneme identity compared with phoneme segmentation training on the early development of reading. He argued that children hear speech as a continuous stream. It is very difficult to hear individual phonemes from spoken language. For example, the word "train" is not perceived as /t/, /r/, /ei/, /n/. Rather it is heard as a continuous string, i.e., /chrein/. Therefore, segmentation of words into phonemes is an extremely difficult task and he suggests it is likely that it develops after children have begun to learn to read. On the other hand, phoneme identification is likely to be a prerequisite of reading. Byrne and Fielding-Barnsley's (1991) research suggests that training in phoneme identity tasks is more strongly related to reading than training in segmentation tasks. However, their results are not conclusive.

Murray tested the hypothesis by providing three types of experiences to children. One group was given phoneme identity training, one group was given phoneme manipulation skills, and a final control group was given general language experiences. He found that the phoneme manipulation group performed significantly better on blending and segmentation tasks. However, children in the phoneme identity training group performed significantly better in measures of phonetic cue reading and early decoding ability. This suggests that training in phoneme identity may facilitate young children's insight into the alphabetic principle and therefore, enhance their early reading skills. Murray suggests that his data indicate that phoneme identity knowledge and manipulation skills are two independent skills and that proficient decoding requires both. Thus, following instruction in phoneme identity, children should learn how to manipulate phonemes through blending and segmentation.

In an effort to examine the impact of adding a metacognitive component to phonological awareness training, Cunningham (1990) compared two phonemic awareness training programs and a control group. The first program she labelled *skill* and *drill*. The program consisted of a series of skills. Each unit introduced a skill in a story, the teacher modelled the skill, the children then practised the skill using games and worksheets. Skills focused on phonemic segmentation and blending. Initial sounds were segmented first, followed by final and then medial sounds. The skills were presented in a decontextualized format so that skills were not applied to reading activities.

The second experimental program was called *metalevel*. It taught similar skills, however, it explicitly linked teaching of the skills to reading activities. For example, children were told that when they came on a word "that they did not know, they could 'cut the word up' into its smallest pieces, think about what that word sounds like, and then think if they know any words that resemble that combination of sounds. . . . (Thus) the value and utility of this skill for future reading was explicitly emphasized by providing readers with an appreciation of task requirements and an awareness of the utility of their actions." (p. 435.)

Training for a control group consisted of children listening to a story and answering questions about the story.

Cunningham trained three groups of kindergartners and three groups of grade one children. Training was undertaken twice a week for 10 weeks. Each session was approximately 15 to 20 minutes long.

In both grades, both phonological awareness groups performed significantly better on a range of phonological measures than the control group. They also performed better in reading on the Metropolitan Achievement Test. There was no difference in reading scores for the two experimental groups for kindergartners. However, first graders in the metalevel group performed significantly better than the skill and drill group. Cunningham suggests that a program that explicitly emphasizes "interrelations between phonemic awareness and the process of reading, motivation to use phonemic awareness in decoding, and specific strategic behaviors to implement phonemic awareness" (p. 441) can be useful in enhancing reading by facilitation transfer and application of component skills in older children.

Not all programs have resulted in substantial gains in reading. In a smaller study, Byrne and Fielding-Barnsley (1995) asked teachers (rather than researchers) to provide the preschool phonological awareness program to children. They found that children in the experimental group developed greater phonological awareness than children in the control group when teachers rather than researchers delivered the program. However, the magnitude of effect was substantially less when teachers delivered the program.

Also pointing to the critical nature of teacher training, Schneider et al. (1997) examined the effectiveness of a phonological awareness program on 205 kindergarten children in Germany. The program was delivered by the regular class teacher. Class sessions were conducted for 15 to 20 minutes per day for approximately six months. Reading and spelling were then tested when the children were in grades one and two. The program followed the one developed by Lundberg, Frost, and Petersen (1988). It included listening games, identification of rhymes, segmentation of syllables, and synthesis and analysis of phonemes. Children's reading and spelling were tested in grades one and two. Schneider et al. found that children's phonological awareness improved significantly as a result of the training program. However, the improvement was not as dramatic as other studies have shown. They felt that this was in large part because of inconsistent implementation of the program by teachers. Children in classrooms where the program was consistently implemented showed significantly better achievement than control and inconsistently trained children in reading and spelling at the end of grade one. They also performed better in spelling at the end of grade two, but not in reading.

Schneider et al. repeated the experiment with more careful attention to teacher training and more stringent monitoring of the implementation of the program in classrooms. With more careful implementation, children in the training program showed substantial gains in reading and spelling at the end of grades one and two indicating that effects of phonological awareness training before children learn to read can have an enduring impact on their success in both reading and spelling.

Thus, the evidence is compelling that phonological awareness developed during the preschool years is inextricably linked to later development of high levels of competence in reading. However, a large range of skills and understandings has been used to measure and teach phonological awareness. It is not clear precisely what aspects of phonological awareness, what tasks or skills contribute to the development of good readers.

What Aspects of Phonological Awareness are Most Important in Reading?

Part of the difficulty is that phonological tasks vary on a number of dimensions. First, the linguistic unit may vary. For example, some tasks focus on rhymes, others on consonant blends and others on phonemes. These units also vary in their position in words. Tasks may focus on initial, medial, or final sounds. Linguistic units also vary in magnitude. Phonemes are the most basic unit, consisting of single speech sounds. Consonant blends consist of two or more phonemes. Rhymes consist of at least one consonant and one vowel.

Second, the nature of the task may vary. Many writers have identified the difference between analysis and synthesis of words or word segments. Analysis requires a student to segment words or syllables into their component parts. Synthesis requires students to combine isolated speech sounds to form words. Tasks also vary in the nature of analysis or synthesis to be performed. At an elementary level, children are simply asked to segment or synthesize the initial phoneme or consonant blend (e.g., say a word beginning with /s/ or say what sound *snake* begins with). Some tasks require matching (e.g., tell me a word that begins with the same sound as *sand*). At a more sophisticated level, students may be asked to analyze whole words, substitute phonemes (e.g. what does *sand* say if you change the /s/ to /h/?) or delete phonemes (e.g. what does *sand* say if you take away the /s/?). Some of these tasks require students to merely recognize a specified linguistic component, while others require students to generate a component for themselves. For example, asking if *"sand* begins the same as *sun"* requires the child to recognize the commonality between initial phonemes, while asking a child to say a word that begins with /s/ requires the child to generate a word that they have not been given. Finally, many tasks that have been used have a working memory component (e.g., which of these words starts with the same sound as *sand*: *fan, hat, sit, bad*?) while others do not (e.g., what does /sand/ begin with?).

To add to the complexity of the issues, linguistic and task components are not independent but rather, they intersect. Thus, a child could be asked to supply a word that has the same initial phoneme as *sand* or rhymes with *sand*.

It is clear that different tasks represent different levels of difficulty for children. For example, segmenting initial sounds has been consistently reported as easier than segmenting final sounds, and identification of medial vowels appears to be more difficult than final consonants (Lewkowicz 1980). Children generally learn to rhyme before they recognize phonemes and find tasks requiring rhyme easier to perform than tasks requiring phonemic awareness (Adams 1990; Layton et al. 1996; Maclean, Bryant, and Bradley 1987; Stanovich, Cunningham, and Cramer 1984).

A number of researchers have argued that some phonological awareness skills, particularly phonemic awareness, appear after children have learned to read and, therefore, are more likely a consequence rather than a cause of reading. Morais et al. (1979) found that Portuguese adults who had never learned to read were generally unable to delete or add a phoneme to the beginning of pseudowords. When adults were taught to read, they were able to accomplish tasks requiring phonemic manipulation quite easily. Support for the idea that phonemic awareness is acquired as a result of learning to read an alphabetically based language was provided by Read et al. (1986). They found that Chinese adults who had learned to read a logographic orthography demonstrated an inability to manipulate phonemes in a way similar to that of Portuguese non-readers.

Wimmer et al. (1991) found that very few children entering the first year of schooling demonstrated phonemic awareness as measured by a vowel substitution task. However, many children were competent at this task shortly after learning to read. Wimmer et al. argued that for most children the evidence supports the conclusion that development of the explicit ability to segment words into phonemes depends on the ability to read in an alphabetic code.

This does not necessarily mean that phonological awareness acquired before learning to read is not an important factor in facilitating reading ability. Some researchers have found that measures of phonological awareness load on a single factor suggesting that it is an unitary skill and that various tasks and measures tapped a single underlying construct (Stahl and Murray 1994; Valtin 1984). If phonological awareness were an unitary skill, evidence that phonological awareness emerges only after children have learned to read would indicate that it is an outcome rather than a cause of reading. However, a number of studies have suggested that phonological awareness does not comprise a single underlying entity. Rather it consists of a cluster of related skills, some of which may precede and facilitate learning to read and some of which are facilitated by learning to read (Perfetti et al. 1987).

Stanovich, Cunningham, and Cramer (1984) found that seven of the ten measures they used loaded on a single factor. However, these were all non-rhyming tasks. The three rhyming tasks they used did not contribute to the factor. Yopp (1988) extracted two factors. Tests measuring segmentation and blending of phonemes, sound isolation, and phoneme counting loaded on one factor. Tests of phoneme deletion and word-to-word matching loaded on another factor. As with Stanovich, Cunningham, and Cramer, measures of rhyming did not load highly on either factor. Yopp called the first factor *Simple Phonemic Awareness* and the second *Compound Phonemic Awareness*.

Muter et al. (1998) also found that their measures consisted of two independent factors. They identified one factor as rhyming, which included a rhyme detection and a rhyme production task. The other factor focused on segmentation, which included phoneme identification, phoneme deletion, and sound blending. Høien et al. (1995) identified three factors. The first was phonological segmentation, which consisted of a sound blending task, initial phoneme matching, and phoneme deletion. The second was a syllable task, which consisted of syllable counting, and the third was rhyme, which consisted of a rhyme recognition task. It appears that the phonological segmentation and rhyme factors paralleled Muter et al.'s rhyme and segmentation factors. Thus, researchers have consistently shown that rhyme and phonemic awareness appear to contribute to different aspects of phonological awareness.

If phonological awareness comprises a cluster of related skills, only some of which facilitate the acquisition of reading, it appears important to identify those precise facets of phonological processing that precede and enhance reading. Studies of the development of phonological awareness in young children have indicated that most skills seem to emerge from children's knowledge of onsets and rimes (MacKay 1972; Maclean, Bryant, and Bradley 1987; Treiman 1983; 1985). The onset is the consonant sound or sounds that precedes the vowel in a word. The rime comprises the vowel and any remaining consonants. (e.g. *cat*, /c/- /at/; /train/, /tr/- /ain/).

Treiman's suggestion that the onset-rime distinction is apparent in children's developing word analysis skills explains many of the findings related to very young children's phonological awareness. For example, a number of researchers have found that when analyzing monosyllabic words, many children make more errors on final consonants than initial ones (Fowler, Liberman, and Shankweiler 1977; Treiman and Baron 1981; Weber 1970). Additionally, children make more errors in reading vowels in words than in reading consonants (Shankweiler and Liberman 1972). They are also more likely to miss a vowel than consonants when asked to tap out the phonemes in a syllable. Treiman's (1985) explanation for this is that the vowel and final consonants of a syllable are not easily perceived as separate phonemes. Rather they are more easily recognized as a single perceptual unit - the rime. Initial consonants, on the other hand, are more easily segmented as the onset. Thus, where the onset is comprised of a consonant blend, children have difficulty in dissolving initial consonant clusters into individual phonemes. However, where the onset corresponds to a single phoneme, children can more easily segment phonemes (Kirtley et al. 1989).

THE DEVELOPMENT OF PHONOLOGICAL AWARENESS IN YOUNG CHILDREN

Based on the onset-rime analysis, it is possible to pose a developmental sequence for the emergence of phonological awareness. Phonological awareness commences with knowledge of rhymes that is derived from childhood experience with nursery rhymes and other language games (Bradley and Bryant 1985; Maclean et al. 1987). Knowledge of rime and then onset emerges from sensitivity to syllables and rhymes (Adams 1990). Awareness of onset may then be the key to development of phonemic awareness. Although knowledge of onset and rhyme is probably a prerequisite for learning to read, phonemic awareness is more likely to emerge after a child has commenced reading (Adams 1990; Bradley and Bryant 1985). Thus, Bryant, Bradley and Goswami (Bradley and Bryant 1985; Bryant et al. 1990; Goswami and Bryant 1990) have argued that rhyme is an essential prerequisite in learning to read. They suggest that children who can rhyme are sensitive to the rime segment of words and that this awareness facilitates children's ability to map sound and spelling at the level of the rime unit. This is the process that underpins learning to read. The development of phonemic awareness is thought to be more a consequence of reading than its cause.

I (Christensen 1997) found that most children appear to conform to this sequence in developing phonological awareness. Most children can rhyme before they demonstrate awareness of onset and show awareness of phonemes after they have begun to learn to read. However, I found a minority of students who did not conform to the expected developmental path. Eleven percent of students demonstrated awareness of phonemes before learning to read, and up to 19 percent showed awareness of onset or onset and phonemes before they developed rhyme awareness. Similarly, Muter and Snowling (1998) found a number of prereaders who were able to identify and manipulate phonemes.

I also found that the relationship between different phonological skills and reading changed over time and depended on the type of measure used to assess children's reading. However, children who had developed phonemic awareness generally showed superior performance in learning to read. In some cases, the difference was quite substantial. For example, children who had no phonemic awareness scored a mean of 10.6 on a sentence reading test and children who had rhyme scored 16.5. Children who had rhyme and phonemic awareness scored a mean of 28.9.

Consistent with a large number of studies that have shown that letter knowledge is one of the best predictors of reading (Adams 1990; Stevenson and Newman 1986; Tunmer, Herriman, and Nesdale 1988), I reported a significant effect for letter knowledge. In addition, I found significant interaction effects between letter knowledge and phonological awareness on all reading measures. The greater the child's level of phonological awareness, the greater the impact of letter knowledge in learning to read. For example, on the Clay Ready-to-Read-Words test for a child who had more phonological awareness, a unit increase in letter knowledge increased reading scores by more than double the increase for children with lower levels of phonological awareness. This trend was more pronounced in measures of reading taken after one year of schooling. For example, for children who had no phonological awareness before they began to learn to read, a unit increase in letter knowledge resulted in .66 of a unit increase in word recognition scores after one year of schooling. However, for children who had rhyme and phonemic awareness before they learned to read, a unit increase in letter knowledge resulted in a 1.95 increase in word recognition scores.

Similarly, Johnston, Anderson, and Holligan (1996) found that some preschoolers demonstrate phonemic awareness and that letter knowledge plays a key role in their development. They gave 51 four-year-old prereaders a battery of phonological tests that measured children's letter knowledge, rhyming skills, and explicit phonemic awareness. Some children could read common product names, but no child could read any words on the Clay Ready-to-Read-Words test or the British Ability Scales Word Reading test. Nineteen of the children were able to produce correct responses on a phoneme deletion task. Few children were able to segment entire words into phonemes. However, 25 children were able to segment some phonemes. Initial phonemes were easier to segment than medial or final phonemes. They found a significant association between children's knowledge of alphabetic letters and phonemic awareness indicating that letter knowledge played a role in facilitating development of phonemic awareness before children learned to read. The ability to recognize letters accounted for the unique variance in phoneme awareness and product name recognition over that accounted for by rhyme skills. However, rhyme did not account for any unique variance beyond that accounted for by letter knowledge.

Nation and Hulme (1997) traced the development of children's phonological, reading, and spelling skills from 5 to 9 years of age. They argued that phonemic segmentation skills were excellent predictors of children's development of reading and spelling. However, the ability to segment words into onset-rime was not. Rhyming and alliteration were statistically related to later reading and spelling ability, but, in comparison with phonemic awareness, they were relatively poor predictors. Similarly, Høien et al. (1995) found that although rhyme was statistically related to reading achievement, it was meager in comparison with the contribution of phonemic awareness.

Knowledge of letters and phonemic awareness also appear to be critically related to the development of reading disabilities. For example, O'Connor and Jenkins (1999) found that phonemic awareness and letter knowledge measured in kindergarten were the best predictors of reading disabilities one year later.

Thus, a wide range of evidence suggests that children will be most advantaged in learning to read and spell if, in preschool, they learn to identify letters and to detect their sounds in words. The advantages conferred by this knowledge are substantial and endure for many years. However, although ability to rhyme is not as strongly related to reading, it may nevertheless be a useful component of a phonological awareness program. Many researchers report that rhyme often develops before awareness of phonemes and that it is easier to master (Maclean, Bryant, and Bradley 1987). Layton et al. (1996) found that rhyme awareness was more likely within capabilities of preschool children and thus, they argued, a more valid indicator of their phonological awareness. But class routines and nursery rhymes may not be sufficient to develop rhyme awareness in a small number of children. Thus, it is possible that, although rhyme itself is not strongly related to later reading, it may facilitate the development of other phonological skills that are directly related to learning to read.

ACTIVITIES TO ENHANCE PRESCHOOL PHONOLOGICAL AWARENESS

This suggests that a range of preschool activities may promote children's later learning. These include learning nursery rhymes and rhyming games, identifying the sounds of alphabetic letters,

listening for sounds that occur at the beginning of words, and segmenting words into syllables and phonemes. Spector (1995) suggested seven facets to effective preschool programs to teach
phonological awareness:

1. *Engage children in activities that direct their attention to the sounds
   in words.* In particular they need to come to recognize that
   words share common sounds. For example, games and books
   that play with rhyme and alliteration are likely to focus attention on repetition of sounds across words. In keeping with
   Byrne and Fielding-Barnsley's (1991) work, activities that promote children's awareness of phoneme identities are likely to
   be particularly useful.
2. *Encourage children to segment and blend words.* The game "I spy"
   develops segmentation skills by teaching children to isolate
   initial phonemes. Elkonin (1973) taught children to segment
   words by using tokens to represent the phonemes in words. As
   the first phoneme is spoken in a word, the teacher places a
   token in a square drawn on a piece of paper. As the second
   sound is pronounced, a second token is placed in a square.
   This process is continued until the word is completed.
3. *Include training in letter-sound relationships.* Training programs
   that have been most successful in enhancing children's reading achievement have integrated segmentation and blending
   activities with instruction in letter-knowledge. Thus, Spector
   suggests that once a small number of letters have been mastered, letters can be substituted for Elkonin's tokens.
4. *Teach segmentation and blending as complementary skills.*
   Children can switch back and forth between segmenting and
   synthesizing words. For example, when using Elkonin's procedure, children can first segment a word into its component
   phonemes and then synthesize the letters to form the original
   word.
5. *Sequence activities systematically:* Begin with biphonemic words
   (e.g. *go, be*). Try breaking complex words in onsets and rimes.
   (e.g. *hit - /h/ /it/*). Practice words beginning with continuants
   (e.g. */m/; /s/*) before stop consonants (e.g. */b/; /g/*). Introduce
   words beginning with simple constants before consonant
   blends.
6. *Encourage transfer to novel tasks.* Children should practice segmentation and synthesis with words that have different sound
   structures. They should practice in a variety of contexts and
   explicit links should be made between segmentation and
   blending activities, and reading and writing.

7. *Teachers should have a clear understanding of the rationale for a phonological awareness program.* A clear understanding of the goals and purposes of the training program is essential for the teacher to be flexible and innovative in implementing the training program.

Most successful training programs focus on phoneme identity, and blending and segmenting phonemes. There are sound theoretical reasons why awareness of the smallest components of language—phonemes and letters—rather than larger units such as syllables, rimes, and consonant blends is central to learning to read and spell. Phonemes map directly on to graphemes when the child is learning to read. By establishing a firm understanding of phoneme-grapheme correspondences, children are able to decode a wider range of unfamiliar words. Automatic decoding is essential to high levels of text comprehension. Thus, by providing the essential prerequisite knowledge necessary for children to grasp phoneme-grapheme correspondences, preschool experiences may set in motion a sequence of learning that provides for strongly enhanced opportunities for students.

REFERENCES

Adams, M. J. 1990. *Beginning to Read.* Cambridge, MA: MIT Press

Blachman, B. 1984. Language analysis skills and early reading acquisition. In *Language Learning Disabilities in School-aged Children,* eds. G. Wallace and K. Butler. Baltimore, MD: Williams and Wilkins.

Bradley, L., and Bryant, P. E. 1983. Categorizing sounds and learning to read: A causal connection. *Nature* 30:419–21.

Bradley, L., and Bryant, P. E. 1985. *Rhyme and Reason in Reading and Spelling.* Ann Arbor: University of Michigan Press.

Bradley, L., and Bryant, P., E. 1978. Difficulties in auditory organisation as a possible cause of reading backwardness. *Nature* 27:746–47.

Bryant, P. E., Maclean, M., Bradley, L., and Crossland, J. 1990. Rhyme and alliteration, phoneme detection and learning to read. *Developmental Psychology* 26:429–38.

Byrne, B., and Fielding-Barnsley, R. 1991. Evaluation of a program to teach phonemic awareness to young children: A 2- and 3-year follow-up. *Journal of Educational Psychology* 87:488–503.

Byrne, B., and Fielding-Barnsley, R. 1993. Evaluation of a program to teach phonemic awareness to young children: A 1-year follow-up. *Journal of Educational Psychology* 85:104–111.

Byrne, B., and Fielding-Barnsley, R. 1995. Evaluation of a program to teach phonemic awareness to young children: A 2- and 3-year follow-up and a new preschool trial. *Journal of Educational Psychology* 87:488–503.

Calfee, R. G., Lindamood, P., and Lindamood, C. 1973. Acoustic phonetic skill and reading: Kindergarten through twelfth grade. *Journal of Educational Psychology* 64:293–98.

Chall, J. S. 1967. *Learning to Read: The Great Debate.* NY: McGraw-Hill.

Christensen, C. A. 1997. Onset, rhymes, and phonemes in learning to read. *Scientific Studies of Reading* 1:339–56.

Cunningham, A. E. 1990. Explicit versus implicit instruction in phonemic awareness. *Journal of Experimental Child Psychology* 50:429–44.

Elkonin, D. B. 1973. In *Comparative Reading: Crossnational Studies of Behaviour and Processes in Reading and Writing,* ed. J. Downing. NY: Macmillan.

Fowler, C. A., Liberman, I. Y., and Shankweiler, D. 1977. On interpreting the error pattern in beginning reading. *Language and Speech* 20:162–73.

Fox, B., and Routh, D. K. 1975. Analyzing spoken language into words, syllables, and phonemes: A developmental study. *Journal of Psycholinguistic Research* 4:331–42.

Goswami, U., and Bryant, P. E. 1990. *Phonological Skills and Learning to Read.* Hove: Erlbaum

Høien, T., Lundberg, I., Stanovich, K. E., and Bjaalid, I-K. 1995. Components of phonological awareness. *Reading and Writing* 7:171–88.

Johnston, R. S., Anderson, M., and Holligan, C. 1996. Knowledge of the alphabet and explicit awareness of phonemes in pre-readers: The nature of the relationship. *Reading and Writing: An Interdisciplinary Journal* 8:217–34.

Kirtley, C., Bryant, P., Maclean, M., and Bradley, L. 1989. Rhyme, rime and the onset of reading. *Journal of Experimental Child Psychology* 48:224–45.

Layton, L., Deeney, K., Tall, G, and Upton, G. 1996. Researching and promoting phonological awareness in the nursery class. *Journal of Research in Reading* 19:1–13.

Layton, L., Deeney, K., Upton, G., and Tall, G. 1998 A pre-school programme for children with poor phonological awareness: Effects on reading and spelling. *Journal of Research in Reading* 21: 36–52.

Lewkowicz, N. 1980. Phonemic awareness training: What to teach and how to teach it. *Journal of Educational Psychology.* 72:687–700.

Lundberg, L., Frost, J., and Petersen, O. P. 1988. Effects of an experimental programme for stimulating phonological awareness in pre-school children. *Reading Research Quarterly* 23:263–83.

Mackay, D. G. 1972. The structure of words and syllables: Evidence from errors in speech. *Cognitive Psychology* 3:210–27.

Maclean, M., Bryant, P., and Bradley, L. 1987. Rhymes, nursery rhymes, and reading in early childhood. *Merrill-Palmer Quarterly* 33:255–81.

Morais, P. Cary, L., Alegria, J., and Bertelson, P. 1979. Does awareness of speech as a sequence of phonemes arise spontaneously? *Cognition* 7:323–31.

Murray, B. A. 1998 Gaining alphabetic insight: Is phoneme manipulation skill or identity knowledge causal? *Journal of Educational Psychology* 90:461–75.

Muter, V., and Snowling, M. 1998. Concurrent and longitudinal predictors of reading: The role of metalinguistic and short-term memory skills. *Reading Research Quarterly* 33:320–337.

Muter, V., Hulme, C., Snowling, M., and Taylor, S. 1998. Segmentation, not rhyming, predicts early progress in learning to read. *Journal of Experimental Child Psychology* 71:3–27.

Nation, K., and Hulme, C. 1997. Phonemic segmentation, not onset-rime segmentation, predicts early reading and spelling skills. *Reading Research Quarterly* 32:154–67.

O'Connor, R. E., and Jenkins, J. R. 1999. Predicting reading disabilities in kindergarten and first grade. *Scientific Studies of Reading* 3:159–97.

Perfetti, C. A., Beck, I., Bell, L., and Hughes, C. 1987. Phonemic knowledge and learning to read are reciprocal: Evidence from first grade children. *Merrill-Palmer Quarterly* 33:283–319.

Read, C., Zhang, Y., Nie, H., and Ding, B. 1986. The ability to manipulate speech sounds depends on knowing alphabetic writing. *Cognition* 24:31–44.

Schneider, W., Kuspert, P., Roth, E., Vise, M., and Marx, H. 1997. Short- and long-term effects of training phonological awareness in kindergarten: Evidence from two German studies. *Journal of Experimental Child Psychology* 66:311–40.

Shankweiler, D., and Liberman, I. Y. 1972. Misreading: A search for causes. In *Language by Eye and by Ear*, eds. J. F. Kavanagh and I. G. Mattingly. Cambridge, MA: MIT Press.

Share, D. L., Jorm, A. E., Maclean, R., and Matthews, R. 1984. Sources of individual differences in reading acquisition. *Journal of Educational Psychology* 76:1309–24.

Spector, J. E. 1995. Phonemic awareness training: Application of principles of direct instruction. *Reading and Writing Quarterly: Overcoming Learning Difficulties* 11:37–51.

Stahl, S., and Murray, B. A. 1994. Defining phonological awareness and its relationship to early reading. *Journal of Educational Psychology* 86:221–34.

Stanovich, K. E. 1986. Matthew effects in reading: Some consequences of individual differences in the acquisition of literacy. *Reading Research Quarterly* 21:360–406.

Stanovich, K. E., Cunningham, A. E., and Cramer, B. B. 1984. Assessing phonological awareness in kindergarten children: Issues of task comparability. *Journal of Experimental Child Psychology* 38:175–90.

Stevenson, H. W., and Newman, R. S. 1986. Long-term prediction of achievement and attitudes in mathematics and reading. *Child Development* 57:646–59.

Stuart, M. 1990. Processing strategies in a phoneme deletion task. *Quarterly Journal of Experimental Psychology* 42:305–27.

Treiman, R. 1983. The structure of spoken syllables: Evidence from novel word games. *Cognition* 15:49–74.

Treiman, R. 1985. Onsets and rimes as units of spoken syllables: Evidence from children. *Journal of Experimental Child Psychology* 39:161–81.

Treiman, R., and Baron, J. 1981. Segmental analysis ability: Development and relation to reading ability. In G. E. Mackinnon and T. G. Waller, eds. *Reading Research: Advances in Theory and Practice*, Vol. 3. NY: Academic Press.

Tunmer, W. E., Herriman, M. L., and Nesdale, A. R. 1988. Metalinguistic abilities and beginning reading. *Reading Research Quarterly* 23:134–58.

Tunmer, W. E., and Nesdale, A. R. 1985. Phonemic segmentation skill and beginning reading. *Journal of Educational Psychology* 77:417–27.

Valtin, R. 1984. Awareness of features and functions of language. In *Language Awareness and Learning to Read*, eds. J. Dowling and R. Valtin. NY: Springer-Verlag.

Vellutino, F. R., and Scanlon, D. M. 1987. Phonological coding, phonological awareness, and reading ability: Evidence from a longitudinal and experimental study. *Merrill-Palmer Quarterly* 33:321–63.

Weber, R. M. 1970. A linguistic analysis of first-grade reading errors. *Reading Research Quarterly* 5:427–51.

Wimmer, H., Landerl, K., Linortner, R., and Hummer, P. 1991. The relationship of phonemic awareness to reading acquisition: More consequence than precondition but still important. *Cognition* 40:219–49.

Yopp, H. K. 1988. The validity and reliability of phonemic awareness tests. *Reading Research Quarterly* 23:159–77.

Chapter • 8

Questioning the Role of Syllables and Rimes in Early Phonological Awareness

Myra Gipstein, Susan A. Brady,
and Anne Fowler

It is now abundantly clear that skilled reading entails, among other things, explicit awareness of the phonemic structure of words (for reviews, see Adams 1990; Blachman 1997; Brady and Shankweiler 1991; Liberman, Shankweiler, and Liberman 1989; Wagner and Torgesen 1987). Awareness of phonemes as discrete entities is not typically achieved until school age and is often triggered by reading instruction itself. However, just as reading entails phoneme awareness, so phoneme awareness, in turn, may depend on a more general phonological sensitivity: a growing appreciation of the sound structure of language that develops throughout the preschool years, including the ability to isolate or identify words, syllables, and rhyming pairs (e.g., Liberman et al. 1974). Indeed, the extent to which general phonological awareness is attained is a strong predictor of how well a child will do at acquiring phoneme awareness and at learning to read. (See Bowey and Francis [1991] for an insightful summary and review of much of the relevant evidence.)

Although phonological sensitivity in the preschool years has been found to predict later phoneme awareness and reading performance (e.g., Chaney 1998; Snow, Burns, and Griffin 1998), our knowledge of the developmental progression from lack of awareness to full appreciation of the phonemic structure of words remains incomplete. To date, two fairly separate areas of research have explored sensitivity to phonological structure prior to school age. One, strongly influenced by linguistic theory and using experimental tasks, has focused on the awareness of the syllable and its internal onset/rime structure as the route to phoneme segmentation (e.g., Treiman and Zukowski 1991). The other, primarily based on observational data, has examined spontaneous rhyming and alliteration in early language play as the precursor to full linguistic awareness (e.g., Dowker 1989; Maclean, Bryant, and Bradley 1987).

Although there is little direct comparison of these two perspectives, we will argue that each makes fundamentally different claims about the sequence in which children become aware of phonological units within a word. In particular, we highlight the distinctions between the two views regarding whether the earliest awareness of the phonological structure of words usually occurs for syllables or for word rhymes. We believe that a better understanding of the typical progression of children's sensitivity to phonological units is critical both for appropriate assessment, and for the design of instructional activities that best meet the needs and abilities of preschool and kindergarten children.

Before describing the study itself, we review the results of prior studies of phonological awareness in young children, and examine the evidence for early sensitivity to rhymes and syllables. To refer to sublexical phonological units, we adopt terminology used by Shattuck-Hufnagel (1987) to describe the implicit lexical organization of both children and adults.[1] Following her framework, we will distinguish between two major hypotheses about phonological awareness development: 1) a *syllable-based* orientation that grants an important status to the syllable and to intrasyllabic units such as the onset and rime; and 2) a *word-based* orientation that focuses on sublexical units such as the word onset and the stressed vowel that are defined not in terms of the syllable but directly in terms of the word.

---

[1]Although Shattuck-Hufnagel's discussion concerns implicit organization as evident in linguistic behavior, and we are concerned with units on which children are able to focus attention in doing awareness tasks, it seems plausible that units that come to awareness are those that naturally exist in linguistic analyses.

BACKGROUND

Evidence for Syllable-Based Organization

Research on children's phonological awareness has long emphasized the developmental primacy of the syllable over the
phoneme, with numerous studies reporting that the ability to segment words into syllables is easier, and occurs earlier, than the
ability to segment words into phonemes (e.g., Content et al. 1986;
Fox and Routh 1975; Liberman 1973; Liberman et al. 1974;
Treiman and Baron 1981; Treiman and Zukowski 1991). For example, when Liberman et al. (1974) asked preschoolers, kindergartners, and first graders to tap out the number of syllables or
phonemes in words, the syllable task was performed more accurately than the phoneme task at each age level. Treiman and her
colleagues have replicated these earlier findings, and argue that
there is yet another level, *onset-rime*, intermediate between the syllable and the phoneme.[2] Treiman and Zukowski (1991) asked children whether two words presented to them had any sounds in
common. In one condition, the shared sounds constituted syllables (e.g., *ham*mer-*ham*mock; com*pete*-re*peat*); in a second, they
were onsets or rimes (e.g., *pl*ank-*pl*ea; sp*it*-w*it*); and in a third, they
were phonemes (e.g., *s*teak-*s*ponge; smo*ke*-ta*ke*). As was the case in
the Liberman et al. (1974) study, Treiman and Zukowski found
that the syllable task was easier than the phoneme task at each
grade level. Moreover, they found the onset-rime task to be easier
than the phoneme task and more difficult than the syllable task,
confirming their prediction of a developmental progression from
awareness of syllables, to onsets and rimes, to phonemes.

The idea that the awareness of phonemes should be the most
difficult sublexical level to isolate stems from speech perception
research demonstrating that phonemes are abstract and embedded
linguistic segments that overlap acoustically (and articulatorily)
with neighboring phonemes within a word, (Liberman et al. 1967)
making it impossible, for example, to produce stop consonants in
isolation. Extraction of phoneme segments in ordinary listening is
hypothesized to be an automatic function of the speech system,
occurring below conscious awareness (Liberman 1992). Whereas

---

[2]The onset is defined as the initial consonant or consonant cluster in each
syllable. An onset may consist of a single phoneme (e.g., *p*an) or a phoneme cluster
(e.g., *pl*an). The rime consists of the vowel(s) plus any remaining consonants
within a syllable. For example, the onset of "car" is "c" and its rime is "ar."
Similarly, the onset of "spa" is "sp" and its rime is "a." Every syllable has a rime,
but some have no onset (e.g., act, ear).

the parallel transmission of phonemes within the word may contribute to the difficulty of becoming explicitly aware of the individual segments, awareness of larger sublexical units is thought to be easier to attain (Gleitman and Rozin 1977; Liberman et al. 1977). As in the studies mentioned above, the syllable has often been proposed to be the likely "larger" unit in early phonological awareness. Note, for example, that unlike phonemes, syllables are clearly marked in the language; each is distinguished by a vocalic center with well-defined acoustic properties and can be produced in isolation.

Other kinds of evidence also suggest that syllable segmentation is easier (or more "natural") than phoneme segmentation. For example, although Portugese-speaking adults who have not been exposed to writing instruction have proven largely unable to perform oral phoneme segmentation tasks, they mastered syllable segmentation with relative ease (Morais et al. l986). Further evidence suggesting that syllables are more accessible than phonemes derives from historical research showing that writing systems in which the orthographic units represent syllable-level units have been independently created by a number of cultures, whereas the alphabetic writing system has evolved only once, and then, apparently, as much by accident as by insight (Gleitman and Rozin l977). Correspondingly, learning to read a syllabary is argued to be conceptually less difficult than acquiring the alphabetic writing system of English (DeFrancis 1991; Gleitman and Rozin l973).

Within linguistic theory itself, the syllable has often served as an important unit of analysis, motivated by the need to account for both phonotactic constraints (i.e., dictating possible phoneme sequences) and prosodic structure (e.g., Fudge 1969, 1987; Hooper 1972; Kahn 1976). Indeed, the role of the syllable has been a foundational assumption of a number of phonological theories whose focus has been the internal structure of the syllable (e.g., Clements and Keyser 1983; Fudge 1987; Selkirk 1982; Vennemann 1988). In these theories, which underlie Treiman and Zukowski's proposal for development of phonological awareness, it is generally agreed that the syllable is not a string of phonemes but has an internal hierarchical organization involving the onset (i.e., the pre-vocalic consonant[s]), the *vowel nucleus*, and the *coda*, (i.e., the final consonant[s]). The most prevalent hypothesis suggests that there is, in addition, an initial division into the onset and the rime (nucleus and coda), as in str-aight (e.g., Fudge 1987, 1989; Selkirk 1982).

This syllable-based, onset-rime hypothesis has obtained additional support from adult psycholinguistic data. For example, in both spontaneous and elicited speech errors, adults tend to exchange whole onsets (e.g., "throat cutting" → "coat thrutting" [from MacKay 1972]) far more often than parts of onsets or than other parts of the syllable (e.g., as in the hypothetical errors "croat thutting" or "thrut coating"). Similarly, in novel word games, adults were better able to follow rules involving onset and rimes (e.g., "kig" → "kaz ig"), than rules referring to subsets of these postulated units (e.g., "skig" → "saz kig")(Treiman 1983, 1986). It has been noted too that word games from a variety of cultures appear to adhere to the onset/rime, as in the case of Pig Latin (e.g., "Jane speaks" → "ane-Jay eaks-spay") (Fudge 1987). Likewise, errors in memory point to an onset-rime division within the syllable. For example, when adults were asked to repeat strings of nonsense syllables that exceeded their memory span, the errors produced in recall showed a preponderance of exchange errors involving whole onsets (Treiman and Danis 1988). (See Treiman [1989] for a complete review of the evidence that English syllables have an onset-rime structure.)

Still other evidence taken to support onset-rime organization stems from errors from young children learning to read and to write. Treiman (1993) notes that children are far more likely to read or write correctly the first letter of *pat* than the last letter of *tap*, presumably because the onset is more readily isolated than is a portion of the rime. Similarly, beginning writers frequently delete one of the phonemes when attempting to spell initial consonant clusters, apparently because of difficulty apprehending that clusters can be subdivided (Bruck and Treiman 1990; Shankweiler 1992; Treiman 1985). This interpretation is supported by other experimental demonstrations that young children are better able to recognize phonemes that comprise whole onsets than they are the same phoneme occurring as part of a cluster (Treiman 1985).

Evidence for Word-Level Organization

In contrast to the linguistically motivated focus on the syllable and its constituents, a quite separate area of research has examined linguistic sensitivity demonstrated in young children's spontaneous language play. This research suggests that "children first begin with an awareness of rhyme and alliteration and, through that awareness, gradually develop a more general phonological segmentation capacity" (Dowker 1989, p. 199). In contrast to the above noted experimental measures for comparing phoneme and syllable awareness, Dowker and others have relied primarily on observational measures to investigate early language play with particular focus on children's sensitivity to rhyme and alliteration.

Although the literature connecting language play with phoneme awareness is fairly small, a number of studies and much children's literature speak to an appreciation of alliteration (i.e., when initial onsets are repeated, as in *big brown bear*) and of rhyme (as in *silly willy*) in very young children.

In this paper, the word-level rhyme unit is defined as including the final stressed vowel and everything beyond, whether this consists of a portion of a syllable (e.g., *me-bee*) or more than a syllable (e.g., *mountain-fountain*) (Clements and Keyser 1983; Fudge 1987). Thus, the rhyme necessarily reflects word-level structure: only one rhyme exists per word and, as noted, this may occur within a syllable or may extend across a syllable boundary. Although rhymes restricted to the final or to the sole syllable (e.g., sal*oon*-bab*oon*, m*e*-b*ee*) meet criteria for rimes as traditionally defined, rhymes initiating in other, non-final syllables (e.g., *moun-tain-fountain*) are quite distinct. To reiterate, word-level rhyme incorporates the *only stressed vowel* in the word and *the remainder of the word*, however long, whereas syllable-based rimes are present in every syllable, regardless of stress. Here we distinguish word-level rhyme from the subsyllabic rime unit by the variation in spelling.

Observational studies suggest that rhyme and alliteration can emerge very early in childhood, with informal reports of spontaneous rhyming in children as young as, or even younger than, two years of age (Chukovsky 1968; Van Kleeck and Schuele 1987; see Bryant and Bradley 1985, for complete discussion). More formal studies of rhyming and alliteration are limited, but revealing (Bryant et al. 1989; Bryant et al. 1990; Chaney1992; Maclean, Bryant, and Bradley 1987). For example, in a longitudinal study examining sensitivity to phonological similarities, MacLean, Bryant, and Bradley (1987) report that some of the three-year olds they studied were able to detect rhyme and alliteration in oddity tasks in which they had to tell which one of three words did not belong, and that some were able to produce rhymes and alliterations when given a target word.

Perhaps the most extensive study of rhyme and alliteration was conducted by Dowker (1989), who examined the frequency of these phonological devices in original poems elicited from 133 children ranging in age from two to six years of age. When presented with two-line poems as models to emulate, 58% of her sample responded with at least one "poem," that is, a production with an "obvious rhythmical structure" (p. 185). The poets included 50% of the children under three and a half years of age and 67% of the children over that age. Several findings are of interest for the present purposes. First, rhyme was used much more frequently (in 42% of all poems) than was alliteration (in 26%), despite the fact that all children were presented with models of each type. Second, although there was a dramatic effect of age on productivity, the proportion of poems with rhyming devices did not vary over age. In sum, rhyming ability appears to develop very early, potentially before either alliteration or syllable segmentation skills.

Here we suggest that this rhyme research, albeit phenomenological, connects neatly with recent work on early phonological development. At one point, it was simply assumed that lexical items of children beyond the age of one or two years were represented in terms of the same phoneme and syllable categories as adult lexical entries; what differed with age was accessibility to conscious awareness. More recent research on children's early productions suggests that children start with only words and articulatory gestures (sometimes referred to as features or articulatory routines) and that they must go about constructing intermediate linguistic units such as the syllable and the phoneme (Studdert-Kennedy 1987). This shift in thinking suggests that changes in accessibility may depend on changes in lexical organization (for discussion see Fowler 1991; Treiman, Zukowski, and Richmond-Welty 1995; and Walley 1993).

Of particular relevance to our current concerns about the course of phonological awareness are studies of children's malapropisms (Aitchison and Straf 1981; Vihman 1981), defined in those studies to include incorrect variants of a target word, whether used consistently or not. Vihman's data, on children from one to five years of age, suggest that children, like adults, tend to preserve the correct number of syllables and the position and shape of the stressed syllable. However, whereas adults tend to preserve the initial consonant and vowel, even when not stressed, she reports that children were most likely to retain the stressed vowel and its surrounding consonants, next most likely to preserve word-final segments, and least likely to retain word-initial segments. This is largely in keeping with the findings from Aitchison and Straf (1981), who note that children tend to preserve the stressed vowel and word endings (e.g., *monuments* for *condiments*), whereas adult malapropisms tend to preserve word onset and the stressed vowel (e.g., *tumors* for *tubers*). Further, although adults generally maintain syllable structure, their malapropisms altered the number of syllables (e.g., *Bavarian* for *barium*) twice as often as those by the children (33% vs. 16%).

There are two lessons of relevance from these data: First, they suggest that not all segments, or syllables, in the word are equally

186 | Gipstein, Brady, and Fowler

salient. And second, they suggest that one cannot necessarily extrapolate from adult data what is most central for children. In particular, whereas much of the work on word-level structure in adults has focused on the unit of word-onset, this unit lacks support as being especially prominent for pre-school children. Rather, one would be encouraged to look to the stressed vowel, and its consonants. We find this very interesting in light of the anecdotal evidence pointing to the conspicuousness of rhyme, with its stressed vowel, for very young children.

Interestingly, even research on lexical organization in adults has begun to question the pre-eminence of syllable-level organization in English. Although our goal is not to test whether the syllable constitutes a 'real' psycholinguistic unit, we present these concerns because they add to our motivation to question the potential role of syllable structure in phonological awareness.

One line of evidence raising doubts about the status of the syllable in English is the frequent difficulty in defining where one syllable ends and another begins. For example, although one measure of syllable awareness in young children involves segmenting words into their component syllables, this task proves to be difficult in English for even the most literate and reflective adult speakers of English. For the word "butter," is it /bu-ter/, /but-er/, or /but-ter/? Although linguists have a notation to indicate this apparent "ambisyllabicity" (e.g., /bu[t]er/; Kahn 1976), the ambiguity apparently can detract from the status of the syllable itself. In French, a language with clear syllable boundaries, French speakers show evidence of syllable-level organization when asked to identify strings of phonemes (Mehler et al. 1981). Thus, when asked to detect the string /pa/, French students responded faster to "pa-lace" than to "pal-mier," consistent with the syllable boundaries. Analogously, subjects recognized /pal/ faster in "pal-mier" than in "pa-lace." In contrast, a comparable experiment with English speakers suggests no such evidence for syllabifying segmentation (Cutler et al. 1986). That is, English speakers were equally fast at recognizing /pa/ or /pal/, whether listening to "pa[l]ace" or to "palpitate." This was true despite the fact that one would predict an advantage for /pal/ in "palpitate," where ambisyllabicity is not a problem. Cutler et al. went on to find that English speakers also do not show evidence for syllabification when presented with French words, despite its unambiguous syllable boundaries, but that French speakers do syllabify English (though with a stronger effect, as expected, for "palpitate" over "palace"). On the basis of these data, Mehler et al. conclude that alternative word segmentation routines are available to the human language processor, and hypothesize that because syllable segmentation is less efficient for English, it is not the system that is used.[3]

A series of studies with adults in Treiman and Zukowski (1990) also suggest that syllabification in English is not fixed, but fluid. In a variety of word games requiring adults to make a decision regarding where the word divides into syllables, several principles of syllabification were evident, and often competing. The authors suggest that one possible response to their findings is to "argue that there exists no discrete level of representation [in English] that corresponds to the syllable. . .syllables are not primary linguistic units but result from other interacting factors [stress, phonological legality, sonority. . .]" (p. 82).

Other evidence placing the syllable in question derives from a shift in interpretation. Results previously taken as strong support for the internal structure of the syllable, particularly syllable onsets, are now being reinterpreted as evidence for the internal structure of the word (e.g., word onsets). In particular, adult speech errors and tip-of-the-tongue phenomena suggest that the primary cut below the level of the word is not between syllables but between the word onset and the remainder of the word (Berg 1989; Browman 1978; Davis 1989; Shattuck-Hufnagel 1983). For example, Browman (1978) and Shattuck-Hufnagel (1983) report that syllable-sized units exchange rarely in either spontaneous or elicited speech errors (e.g., "Al Lucinder" for "Lou Alcinder"). Whereas syllable-sized units make up less than 3% of all the exchange errors discussed in Shattuck-Hufnagel (1983), word onset exchanges (e.g., "breathing and smoking" to "smeething and broking") constitute as much as 91% of the exchange errors presented in Shattuck-Hufnagel (1987). Significantly, Browman (1978) and Shattuck-Hufnagel (1983) note that most exchanges involve word onsets rather than just any syllable onset. When errors occur that do not involve the word onset, the source is often the onset of the stressed syllable, again invoking word level organization (e.g., "pomato" for "potato," influenced by tomato) (Browman 1978; see also Browman and Goldstein 1990). They

---

[3]Recent results buttress the conclusion that various word segmentation procedures are possible. A study of Dutch, which like English is ambisyllabic, finds that Dutch listeners nonetheless treat it in a French-like manner (i.e., they are faster at recognizing syllabic subdivisions of words)(Zwitserlood et al. 1993). Zwitserlood et al. suggest that segmentation behavior may vary across languages because "languages vary with respect to their phonological structure and, as a consequence, with respect to the knowledge listeners may use in structuring the speech input," p. 270. They point out that English and Dutch differ in the nature of ambisyllabicity in terms of the language specific rules that determine which consonants can become ambisyllabic.

summarize, "cohesion in speech production errors appears to be defined with respect to the word. The featurally cohesive units are not the same everywhere in the word, nor are they segments, or even onsets of syllables" (Browman and Goldstein 1990, p. 421).

In recent work with adults, Treiman and her colleagues have taken a more moderate stance on whether words are represented by a syllable-based structure or a word-based structure. Mixed results have been obtained when adults are presented with tasks involving multisyllabic non-words. For example, supporting their perspective, adult listeners are better able to play word-games with onsets of an embedded syllable than with corresponding codas (Treiman et al. 1995). That is, for words with a C_1V-C_2VC_3-C_4VC_5 structure, they can more readily learn the rule $C_2 \rightarrow$ /g/ (e.g., / ʃəˈpolhað / $\rightarrow$ / ʃəˈgolhað /) than the rule $C_3 \rightarrow$ /g/ (e.g., / ʃəˈpolhað / $\rightarrow$ / ʃəˈpoghað /). Accordingly, the authors argue that the proposed onset-rime division of syllables is not restricted to monosyllabic words, but is also supported in medial syllables of multisyllabic words (see also Fowler, Treiman, and Gross [1993]).[4] Yet, in other conditions (e.g., Treiman, Zukowski, and Richmond-Welty 1995, E 2), only one of two groups of participants showed the predicted pattern. Pertinent to the present discussion, in a further study by Bruck, Caravolas, and Treiman (1995) in which adult participants had to compare pairs of stimuli, results were inconsistent for two experiments with non-word pairs that shared either an entire stressed final syllable (e.g., /horˈten/ - /Nɛgˈten/) or that shared rimes of stressed final syllables (also rhymes) (e.g., /mɪˈtark/ - /soˈdʒark/). The authors argued that syllables play a role in the initial processing of speech, but conceded that there also seem to be effects of word rhyme. Though less extreme than earlier statements with respect to the adequacy of the syllable-structure hypothesis, such comments fail to address the intersection between syllable structure and word structure.

A reexamination of the status of the syllable in early phonological awareness

Despite the apparent salience of the syllable in contrast to the segment in emerging phonological awareness, reports of rhyme and alliteration abilities in very young children suggest other possible entry points of metaphonological analysis. Keeping word-based or-

---

[4]From a word-based perspective, because the words in this experiment were medially stressed, the interpretation is not clear. The outcome of Treiman et al. (1995) may reflect the syllable structure of the embedded syllable; alternatively, it may speak to the salience of a proposed word-level unit, the onset of the stressed syllable.

ganization in mind as an alternative way of looking both at early phonological awareness and at lexical representation, we can now reexamine the role of the syllable in the development of phonological awareness with a more critical eye. Several concerns have led us to question whether the syllable is the most accessible unit, below the word, for young children.

First, as now noted by a number of critics, much of the evidence taken to support the salience of syllabic structure in early phonological awareness is ambiguous because of heavy reliance on monosyllabic stimuli. For example, in response to the Treiman and Zukowski (1991) study, Carlisle (1991) and Read (1991) cautioned that because only monosyllabic words were used as stimuli in the onset-rime condition, little is known regarding the status of onsets and rimes in multisyllabic words or in unstressed syllables. Read proposed that it would be helpful to examine young children's performance on words sharing syllables versus parts of syllables in unstressed portions of words (e.g., re*fer*/re*mit* versus pre*fer*/cr*eate*) in order to test whether the hierarchy of awareness proposed by Treiman and Zukowski still would be evident.

Second, studies testing whether children find syllables easier to detect than onsets or rimes have sometimes confounded unit size and linguistic status, making it difficult to interpret the results. Treiman and Zukowski (1991) acknowledge this confound in their first experiment, noting the fact that the syllables were longer than the onsets and rimes, which were, in turn, longer than the phonemes. In two further experiments, they separated these variables, designing conditions in which units of the same size could function at two different linguistic levels. In their second experiment they compared sensitivity to single phoneme onsets with awareness of single phonemes that were part of onset clusters (e.g., *p*acts, *p*eel vs. *p*lan, *p*row), finding that onsets (even if composed of a single phoneme) are more salient than phonemes that do not themselves constitute an onset. However, in the third study, comparing performance on tasks involving syllables and parts of syllables (e.g., re*treat*, en*treat* vs. ac*claim*, in*flame*), they obtained equivalent performance on syllables and parts of syllables (consisting of rimes, and in some cases rimes with additional phonemes). As Treiman and Zukowski comment, this outcome suggests that size, as opposed to linguistic status, may have determined the superiority for syllables seen in their first experiment.

An experiment by Walley, Smith, and Jusczyk (1986) also suggests that size, or at least the number of shared constituents, influences the ease with which children detect phonological commonalities across words. In their study, kindergartners' and second graders' auditory classifications of two-syllable nonsense words were examined to evaluate whether children's ability to classify together utterances that share whole syllables (e.g., /*n*utae/, /*n*uli/) would emerge prior to their ability to classify utterances that share single phonemes (e.g., /*n*uli/, /*n*ato/) or more than one phoneme not conjoined within a syllable (e.g., /*sona*/, /*siba*/); for all comparisons, stress was kept constant across the two syllables. This study failed to support the developmental sequence from syllable to phoneme or to indicate any special significance of the syllable per se. Instead, the factors that affected the perception of similarity in speech sounds were a combination of the number of phonemes shared across two words and position. For example, though the participants generally performed best on pairs sharing initial syllables, children were not as likely to link pairs sharing final syllables as they were to link pairs sharing the word onset and word final phonemes (e.g., /*sona*/, /*siba*/).

These concerns, emphasized in Brady, Gipstein, and Fowler (1992), prompted Treiman and Zukowski (1996), in a replication and extension of their earlier work, to focus on size of the shared unit as a potential factor in the ease of judging whether two words "share sounds." When preschool and kindergarten children were comparing trisyllabic words in which the medial syllable was stressed, they were more accurate at recognizing shared medial syllables (e.g., /və'gænli/ - /su'gænmo/) than shared medial syllable rimes (e.g., /mo'varnli/ - /du'zarnbə/) even when the length of the shared portions in both conditions were matched for number of phonemes. The authors concluded that although size of the shared portion can be a factor in children's performance, their results confirm the relevance of syllable structure for awareness. While this study confronted the issue of size, it should be noted that the results did not uniformly indicate syllable structure as a primary level of awareness. One of the experiments reported (E. 2) compared sensitivity to syllables in final position (e.g., re*treat*, en*treat*) with ability to detect shared rimes in final stressed syllables (e.g., oppr*essed*, undr*essed*) (i.e., rhymes). In this instance, children were equally sensitive to both. Similar to their handling of their studies of adults described earlier, Treiman and Zukowski state that, "discounting the confounding effect of rhyme, the results support the linguistic status hypothesis in the case of syllables" (p. 210). This remark evades the very issue of how the emergence of awareness of rhymes and of awareness of syllables layer in normal development.

Accordingly, our final concern with granting the syllable primacy in the development of phonological awareness is the lack of

explicit comparisons with other candidate units, using comparable methodology. The Treiman and Zukowski (1996) study had a
single rhyming condition with multisyllabic stimuli (and obtained results that question a strong syllable structure hypothesis), but did not address the role of stress in other portions of the
word. The study did not allow explicit comparison of syllable
rime and word rhyme as a test of the role of syllable structure in
emerging awareness.

The challenge of making comparisons across conditions also
is evident in a recent study looking at the development of phonological sensitivity in two- to five-year-old children (Lonigan et al.
1998). This investigation included measures of oddity detection
both for rhyme (e.g., fish, dish, book) and for alliteration (e.g.,
bed, hair, bell), but very different types of measures of blending
(e.g., "What word do you get when you say *bro. . .ther* together?")
and of elision (e.g., "Now say battle without the *til*") to assess
awareness of syllables. In this case the differences in measures contribute to problems in interpreting the results. In the sample of
two-year olds, for example, 26% scored above chance on rhyme
oddity although only 9% could blend syllables and only 6% could
delete them in the elision measure. Whether these results reflect
earlier development of rhyming skills or the greater conceptual
ease of the oddity task is difficult to judge.

In the Walley, Smith, and Jusczyk (1986) study described earlier, to reconcile their findings with studies that stress the role of
the syllable, they argued that their task may have tapped a less explicit level of awareness than, for example, the segmentation or
manipulation tasks that are more commonly used. Walley, Smith,
and Jusczyk propose that the syllable may play a special role only
in the context of certain types of phonological awareness tasks
that require more explicit, or conscious, awareness. Dowker (1989)
echoes this theme, noting that spontaneous rhyming and alliterative ability, although forms of phonological awareness, are clearly
not identical to the ability to carry out specific requirements in
phonological awareness tasks. She also cites Lundberg (1978) as
stressing the differences between the implicit level of phonological
awareness implied in spontaneous sound play and the explicit
level tapped in traditional phonological awareness tasks that require conscious analysis of words into their constituent elements.
In sum, although there has been considerable evidence that preschoolers are sensitive to both the syllable and the word rhyme,
most of the support for each comes from very distinct traditions of
methods. This circumstance makes it difficult to bridge the approaches and to ascertain which phonological unit, the syllable or

the rhyme, is easier for young children to discover and which theoretical perspective, syllable-based or word-based, is supported.

GOALS

Asking whether initial phonological awareness conforms with syllabic structure or word structure, our first goal was to make a direct comparison between children's awareness of the syllable and the word-level rhyme, using comparable methods. A second question relating to the role of syllabic structure in metaphonological development concerns whether syllable rimes function as constant linguistic units. To address these questions, we designed a study of four- and five-year olds' sensitivity to three different kinds of phonological units: Rhyme, Syllable, and Rime. These units were presented in disyllabic words so that syllable status could be distinguished from word-level factors. Playing a puppet game, children were asked to judge whether pairs of words shared some of the same sounds.

The Rhyme condition assessed children's ability to identify word pairs that share the stressed vowel and the rest of the word. Half of the items in this condition rhymed only within the second syllable (e.g., sal*oon*-bab*oon*) and an equal number rhymed from immediately following the word onset (e.g., m*ountain*-f*ountain*). Thus, an attempt was made to control for the effects of position of the rhyme. However, it is acknowledged that in items such as m*ountain*-f*ountain*, larger shared segments (i.e, longer strings of phonemes) as well as multiple shared linguistic units (i.e., syllables as well as rhymes) are included, raising the possibility that more than one factor may contribute to the children's performance on this subcondition.

The Syllable condition measured children's awareness of syllables. Half of the items consisted of word pairs that share the first syllable (e.g., *gar*den-*gar*lic) and half consisted of word pairs sharing the second syllable (e.g., tea*cher*-na*ture*).

Finally, the Rime condition examined children's awareness of syllable rimes that are in the stressed but initial syllable (e.g., p*en*cil-t*en*der) and syllable rimes that are in the final but unstressed syllable of disyllabic words (e.g., wiz*ard*-sheph*erd*). The goal in limiting the syllable rime stimuli to these types of pairs was to avoid, for purposes of comparison, syllable rime pairs that are also word rhymes (i.e., for disyllabic words, rimes occurring in the final, stressed syllable). All items in the Syllable and Rime conditions were made up of words in which the first syllable was stressed in order to keep the permutations of conditions to a practical number and to minimize confounding these conditions with rhyme.

By employing these three conditions, we hoped to gain information about factors contributing to the development of phonological awareness. If the hypothesized syllabic hierarchy within the word is the basis for explicit phonological awareness, all other things being equal, the primary unit that children would become aware of would be the syllable. Performance on the rhyme condition in which more than a syllable is shared (e.g., m*ountain*-f*ountain*) might be expected to be even better than performance on shared single syllables (e.g., *gar*den-*gar*lic), but one would anticipate full-shared syllables to be more salient than shared partial syllables (e.g., Syllable: tea*cher*-na*ture*; Rhyme: sal*oon*-bab*oon*). If, instead, children are more successful in the Rhyme condition than in the Syllable condition, especially when the number of phonemes are equal, this outcome would support a word-based unit as the easier subword level of analysis, rather than a syllable-based unit. A stringent test of this hypothesis would predict that Rhyme would be more salient than Syllable even when the two are matched for stress and length, as in *gar*den-*gar*lic versus sal*oon*-bab*oon*.

The second test of the importance of the syllable-onset-rime hierarchy in the development of phonological awareness will come from a comparison of the Rhyme and Rime conditions in the second syllable (e.g., sal*oon*-bab*oon* vs. wiz*ard*-shep*herd*). As noted above, in both cases the shared material constitutes rimes. If syllable structure is the overriding factor, no difference would be expected on these two conditions. If, instead, the rhyming items are easier for the children, this too would suggest that word-level factors are important.

Our study was designed to examine the impact of structural units (i.e., the syllable and the rhyme) in phonological awareness, working under the assumption that linguistic organization provides the basis for the development of metaphonological awareness. We acknowledge, however, that other linguistic factors, specifically size and stress, may prove to be more relevant. In coming to appreciate that words have sounds in common, it may be easier for a child to notice larger chunks of shared information than smaller chunks; that is, a child might recognize the shared sounds in m*ountain*-f*ountain* more easily than in sal*oon*-bab*oon*. Stress may also enhance accessibility, with children becoming aware of units with shared stressed vowels regardless of the size or status of the segment. So, for example, the stressed rimes in sal*oon*-bab*oon* should then be more salient than full syllables that are unstressed (e.g., tea*cher*-na*ture*).

METHOD

Participants

The participants included 195 children (100 girls and 95 boys) from fifteen nursery schools, day-care centers, and private schools serving primarily middle-class children. They included 102 children in the four-year-old group (mean age = 54.22 months, SD = 3.31, range = 46-59 months) and 93 five-year olds (mean age = 64.14 months, SD = 3.38, range = 60-71 months).

A total of 249 consent forms were returned. Seven children did not choose to participate, and two who did would not speak to the examiner; these nine children therefore could not be included in the study. Certain eligibility requirements eliminated six additional children: four children who spoke languages other than English as their primary language and two who had diagnosed hearing problems. (Information regarding primary language spoken in the home and hearing problems was gathered from a parent questionnaire returned with consent forms.) An additional 39 did not pass a pretest demonstrating understanding of the task requirements. This is discussed further below. The remaining 195 children met all the criteria for participation in the study. One additional piece of information, the educational level of subjects' mothers, was monitored, not for screening purposes, but to allow a closer examination of whether the children in the different conditions came from comparable home environments. This particular variable was assessed because the educational background of the mother appears to be related to children's language development (e.g., Snow 1991).

Each study participant served in one condition—Rhyme, Syllable or Rime. An effort was made to balance the number of children from each school participating in each condition, since schools and centers may differ in the emphasis of language activities, thereby facilitating development of phonological awareness to different degrees (Wilkinson 1991). Table I provides a summary of subject characteristics.

Measures

Phonological Awareness Pretest. A brief training procedure, drawn from the method used by Treiman and Zukowski (1991), introduced the child to a pretest. It was explained and demonstrated

Table I. Subject Characteristics by Age and Condition

	Condition	n	Females/ males	Mother education[a] (Mode)	Age, in mos. M	(SD)	Age range
Four-year-old group	Rhyme	34	16/18	5	53.68	(3.60)	46-59
	Syllable	35	22/13	5	53.66	(3.04)	49-59
	Rime	33	18/15	4	53.36	(3.05)	48-59
	Total	102	56/46	5	53.57	(3.23)	46-59
Five-year-old group	Rhyme	31	12/19	4	65.10	(3.29)	60-71
	Syllable	31	20/11	5	63.19	(3.43)	60-71
	Rime	31	12/19	5	64.13	(3.24)	60-71
	Total	93	44/49	5	64.14	(3.32)	60-71
All conditions, both age groups		195	100/95	5	58.61	(3.27)	46-71

[a]Based on a scale in which 1 = some high school; 2 = high school graduate; 3 = some college; 4 = college graduate; 5 = graduate or professional school

that the puppet held by the examiner was "happy" when it heard words that had some of the same sounds (*cat-sat*), but "sad" when it heard words that did not have any of the same sounds (*bed-rake*). The child had to listen to pairs and say if they make the puppet "happy" or "sad." If the child did not seem to understand, further examples were given. The child's understanding was then tested using four word pairs (*bay-ray*, *more-pack*, *land-sand*, and *lake-grass*). (All of the word pairs presented in the pretest and in the other conditions were spoken by the examiner with care being taken to pronounce the designated portions in the same way.) Children who answered three of the four test items correctly proceeded to one of the three conditions of the phonological awareness task described below. Children who did not pass the pretest were praised and thanked for participating in the study, and escorted back to the classroom. A total of 39 children failed to pass the pretest. More four-year olds ($n = 32$) than five-year olds ($n = 7$) did not pass the pretest, X^2 (1, $n = 39$) = 7.42, $p < .05$. (See Appendix A for summary characteristics of those who did not pass.)[5]

---

[5]Initially, the examiner immediately proceeded to the four pretest items following one positive and one negative example. However, this protocol resulted in a large portion of subjects (19 of the first 68 subjects, or 28 percent) not passing the pretest. The reason for this appeared to be related, in large part, to a lack of comprehension of the task. It was at this point that we changed the protocol to allow for additional pretraining for those who did not appear to understand the task (i.e., up to four additional pairs of examples were presented). Whether or not subjects displayed understanding of the four additional examples, the examiner proceeded to the pretest items. Following these changes in procedure, an additional 127 children were tested. Twenty children out of 127 (16 percent) failed both the six training examples and the pretest, and were thus eliminated from the study.

Phonological Awareness Task. This task, consisting of eighteen trials, followed the same format as the pretest described earlier. Prior to each of the conditions, four examples (two positive pairs and two negative pairs) were given to demonstrate to the child what kinds of words made the puppet happy or sad. (Examples of positive items: Rhyme condition—n*umber*-l*umber*, cart*oon*-racc*oon*; Syllable condition—*cargo*-*car*pet, bu*gle*-wi*ggle*; Rime condition—*farmer*-*gar*lic, leop*ard*-haz*ard*). The examiner then presented the word pairs, asking the child to indicate after each pair whether the puppet would be happy or sad. The positive and negative items were presented in a single randomized order. (See Appendix B for a full list of the test items in each of the three conditions.) Four scores were calculated for each child: (1) number of the negative trials correctly eliciting a "sad" response (maximum = 6); (2) the number of pairs correctly judged for items sharing 'sounds' at the beginning of the word (maximum = 6); (3) the number of trials correctly judged as sharing sounds in the second syllable of the word (maximum = 6); and (4) the sum of these accurate responses to positive trials (maximum = 12).

Prereading/Reading Tests. Reading and letter knowledge were assessed to determine whether the reading skills of the children were comparable across the three conditions and between age-groups. Measuring reading skills also allowed us to evaluate the relationship between reading level and phonological awareness as measured in the current study. Selected subtests from the Woodcock Reading Mastery Tests-Revised (WRMT-R), Form G (Woodcock 1987) were administered to each child, including Letter Identification (the supplementary letter checklist that includes capital and lower case letters), Word Identification (i.e., reading real words), and Word Attack (i.e., reading pseudowords). Raw scores were used for data analyses.

Procedure

Each child was tested individually in a single 10-minute session by the first author in a quiet space in his or her school or center. The session began with the pretest. Next, nine trials of one of the phonological awareness tasks were administered to each child who passed the pretest. In order to avoid the children becoming bored with the task, we then changed activities and administered the prereading/reading assessment. Then, after a brief review of the "puppet game," the child was given nine more trials of the phonological awareness task. The order of the first and second nine items was alternated with each child. A pilot study had confirmed that the test procedure was suitable for four-year olds and five-year olds.

RESULTS

First, a series of analyses of variance were conducted to obtain pertinent information regarding comparability of experimental groups on background variables. No significant differences were found across the three experimental conditions for mothers' education, age of subjects, or reading ability. (See table II for a summary of reading scores for the two age groups). As one would anticipate, there was a significant effect of age on reading attainment for Letter Identification, $F(1,189)= 13.78$, $p < .05$; for Word Identification, $F(1,189) = 6.82$, $p < .05$; and for Word Attack, $F(1,189)= 4.23$, $p < .05$. Likewise, children designated "readers" (i.e., those with a score of at least three on the Word Identification subtest, $n = 34$) performed significantly better on the phonological awareness measures than did the other participants, $F(2,189) = 39.87$, $p < .001$). However, there was no interaction between reading ability (readers versus nonreaders) and condition (Rhyme, Syllable, and Rime).

Having established that the subjects included in the different conditions were comparable with respect to potentially relevant variables such as reading skill and age, it was next of interest to examine accuracy as a function of condition (Rhyme, Syllable, Rime) and of position of the shared unit (i.e., first or second syllable). At the same time, the data were analyzed to determine whether age had an effect on scores. (Table III provides mean scores for each condition, by age group.)

To ascertain whether children performed differently on the three conditions, three 2 X 3 (Age X Condition) Anovas were carried out using: (1) the scores for the positive trials (i.e., when the pair "shared sounds"); (2) the scores for the negative trials (i.e., when no "sounds" were in common); and (3) the total score (i.e., a combined score for the positive and the negative pairs). For all three sets of scores, significant condition effects were obtained: Positive, $F(2,189) = 28.96$, $p < .0001$; Negative, $F(2,189) = 9.28$, $p < .0001$; Total, $F(2,189) = 39.75$, $p < .0001$. Follow-up analyses

Table II. Woodcock Reading Mastery Test-Revised Subtest Scores[a] by Age-Group

	n	Letter Identification		Word Identification		Word Attack	
		M	(SD)	M	(SD)	M	(SD)
Four-year olds	102	29.56	(16.52)	1.00	(5.27)	.21	(1.50)
Five-year olds	93	37.69	(13.70)	3.94	(9.91)	.99	(3.46)

[a]Raw scores for the number correct.

Table III.   Phonological Awareness Scores for Each Condition, by Age-Group

Condition	Age Group	Positive[a] Pairs M	(SD)	Negative[b] Pairs M	(SD)
Rhyme	4	10.50	(2.23)	5.35	(1.07)
	5	10.35	(2.59)	5.42	(1.26)
Syllable	4	8.34	(2.29)	4.49	(1.74)
	5	8.80	(3.11)	5.23	(0.96)
Rime	4	6.52	(3.42)	4.06	(1.73)
	5	6.74	(3.20)	4.45	(1.80)

[a]maximum score = 12

[b]maximum score = 6

(Fisher's Protected LSDs) yielded significant differences between all three conditions (Rhyme, Syllable, Rime) for each of the three types of scores (Positive, Negative, Total). Performance in the Rhyme condition was significantly better than in the Syllable condition, and performance in the Syllable condition was significantly better than in the Rime condition. As one might anticipate, when the targeted "shared sounds" were easier for children to discern, the absence of a shared constituent was likewise recognized more easily. Accordingly, performance on the Negative trials complemented the performance on the Positive trials.

Age effects were not obtained for either the Total scores (four-year-old mean = 12.99; five-year-old mean = 13.66) or for the Positive pairs (four-year-old mean = 8.45; five-year-old mean = 8.63), nor were there age by condition interactions. However, on the Negative items the less accurate performance by the four-year olds was marginally significant (four-year-old mean = 4.63; five-year-old mean = 5.03), $F(1,189) = 3.76$, $p = .054$, though there was not a significant age by condition interaction.

We were somewhat surprised that the group scores for the five-year olds were not significantly greater on the Total or Positive Scores than the scores for the four-year olds. One possibility was that there was not a sufficient difference in age between the two groups. Due to a high concentration of older four-year olds and younger five-year olds in our sample, only a four month gap was present between the modal ages of the children in the two age groups. To see if the small difference in age was responsible for the lack of an age effect, a follow-up analysis of variance was performed on the Total scores using only the younger four-year olds (46 to 54 months, $n = 57$) and older five-year olds (64 to 71 months, $n = 41$). Still, no age effect was found. We suspect that this was because the selection procedure eliminated many four-year olds who could not do the pretest; we project that if our task had required the child to isolate phonemes, an age effect would have been found. The present study targeted only awareness of larger phonological components.

It was next of interest to determine whether the ease of detecting shared similarities of a phonological unit was influenced by whether it occurred in the first or second syllable of a word. A 2 x 3 x 2 repeated measures design was employed to analyze whether there was a significant difference between performance on items involving shared units in the first syllable and items involving shared units in the second syllable. Positive scores on the two different positions served as within-subjects factors, and the three conditions and two age-groups served as between subjects factors. Again, we obtained a significant condition effect, $F(2,191) = 29.38$, $p < .0001$, no age effect, and no age by condition interaction. The new focus in this analysis was on the effects of position. A significant Position effect was found, $F(1, 191) = 3.94$, $p < .05$, as was a Position by Condition interaction, $F(2,191) = 5.28$, $p < .01$. (Age did not interact with Position). Simple effects tests demonstrated a significant position effect for the Syllable condition, but not for the Rhyme and Rime conditions. In the Syllable condition, children in both age groups scored higher on trials involving words that shared the first (stressed) syllable (e.g., *gar*den-*gar*lic) than on pairs sharing the second (unstressed) syllable (e.g., tea*cher*-na*ture*).

In order to assess whether children's patterns of performance reflect word-based or syllable-based organization, we next focused on comparisons across subconditions using follow-up Fisher protected LSD tests. In first position subconditions, Rhyme (e.g., *moun*tain-*foun*tain) was significantly easier than Syllable (e.g., *gar*den-*gar*lic), which, in turn, was significantly easier than the Rime subcondition (e.g., *pen*cil-*ten*der). In second position, children more accurately identified Rhymes that are portions of syllables (e.g., sal*oon*, bab*oon*) than they did fully shared Syllables (e.g., tea*cher*, na*ture*). Because that advantage might be attributed to stress differences, we also did one non-orthogonal comparison using a t-test to examine how performance on second syllable rhymes (e.g., sal*oon*-bab*oon*) compared to performance on first position (stressed) syllables (e.g., *gar*den-*gar*lic). The Rhyme task was again found to be easier (t (129) = –2.03, $p = .04$), despite the fact that the syllable stimuli were stressed and necessarily incorporated the word onset. Paralleling the results for the first position subconditions, children did significantly better on the second position Syllable pairs (e.g., tea*cher*-na*ture*) than on the second position Rime stimuli (e.g., shep*herd*-haz*ard*). A further comparison concerned rhymes versus rimes in second syllable position (e.g., sal*oon*-bab*oon* vs. sheph*erd*-haz*ard*). Here again, a Fisher Protected LSD test confirmed a significant advantage for the Rhyme items, supporting the need to differentiate between different kinds of rime units.

Lastly, because we observed a trend for rhymes following the onset (e.g., m*ountain*-f*ountain*) to be easier for the children than rhymes at the end of the word (e.g., sal*oon*-bab*oon*), we were interested in whether unit size may have exerted an influence on the pattern of results. The stimuli were not designed to control for this and we wanted to check the extent to which the results mirror the relative size of the stimuli in the six subconditions (Rhyme, Syllable, and Rime in first and second syllables). To assess unit size, the number of phonemes in the shared segments were tallied. Long, stressed vowels were counted as two phonemes (e.g., /iy/ in caff*eine*-mach*i*ne). Since there is some debate as to whether syllabic /r/, /l/, and /n/ (e.g., as in napk*in*-gard*en*) constitute one phoneme (e.g., n) or two (e.g., ɛn), unit size was calculated both ways. (Table IV provides subconditions and phonological awareness scores listed in the order of unit size.) Spearman r correlations between the mean number of phonemes per unit and the phonological awareness scores yielded a coefficient of .72 when the "one-phoneme" method of counting syllabic phonemes was used and a correlation

Table IV. Subconditions Listed in Order of Unit Size, Phonological Awareness Scores[a], and Rank Order of Mean Phonological Awareness Scores

A. Syllabic /r/, /l/, and /n/ counted as *one* phoneme

Subcondition	Mean # of Phonemes	Mean Phonological Awareness Score	Rank Order: Phonological Awareness Scores
Rhyme—Position 1	3.83	5.28	1
Syllable—Position 1	3.17	4.61	3
Rhyme—Position 2	3.00	5.15	2
Syllable—Position 2	2.33	3.92	4
Rime—Position 1	1.83	3.23	6
Rime—Position 2	1.67	3.39	5

B. Syllabic /r/, /l/, and /n/ counted as *two* phonemes

Subcondition	Mean# of Phonemes	Mean Phonological Awareness Score	Rank Order: Phonological Awareness Scores
Rhyme—Position 1	4.83	5.28	1
Syllable—Position 1	3.17	4.61	3
Syllable—Position 2	3.17	3.92	4
Rhyme—Position 2	3.00	5.15	2
Rime—Position 2	2.33	3.39	5
Rime—Position 1	1.83	3.23	6

[a]on Positive Trials

of .63 for the "two-phoneme" method. These values demonstrate a strong positive relationship between these two factors. That is, in general, the greater the number of phonemes in the shared units, the higher the phonological awareness scores. Yet, there were interesting exceptions that will be noted in the discussion.

Hierarchical multiple regression was used to determine if the condition variable (Rhyme, Syllable, Rime) improved the prediction of phonological awareness scores beyond that predicted by length. Several analyses were carried out with similar patterns of results. We present here the results of only the most stringent test. In that test, in order to hold stress constant, phonological awareness of the first position subconditions was the criterion variable. In these subconditions, all 18 pairs shared a stressed vowel in the first syllable (e.g., m*ountain*-f*ountain*, g*ar*den-g*ar*lic, p*encil*-t*ender*). To be on the conservative side, we employed the one phoneme method of calculating length, as it had correlated more highly with performance than had the two phoneme method. Using this technique, length accounted for 62% of the variance when it was entered first and condition accounted for an additional 17% of the variance: the r^2 change value was significant, $F(1,16) = 14.19$, $p < .001$. In contrast, when condition was entered first, it accounted for 79% of the variance; no further variance was accounted for by length.

DISCUSSION

Linguistically motivated research on early phonological awareness has demonstrated that awareness of the syllable unit emerges before awareness of the subsyllabic units of onset and rime. Other research, however, looking at language play and language awareness from a developmental perspective, has documented the ability to recognize and produce rhymes in children as young as two years of age. The present study was motivated by these developmental findings to reconsider the role of the syllable in emerging phoneme awareness. We asked, too, whether rimes, as a hypothesized sub-unit of syllables, function as constant units of phonological awareness. That is, we investigated whether the evidence for the rime obtained with monosyllabic words would hold up if multisyllabic stimuli were used in which rimes can be presented in both stressed and unstressed syllables. Four-year-old and five-year-old children were tested on phonological awareness in three conditions using disyllabic stimuli: Rhyme, Syllable, and Rime. Our results indicate that word-level rhymes are particularly salient for young children, much more so than are syllables and syllable rimes.

Concerning the relative ease of Rhymes versus Syllables, Rhymes were significantly easier to detect both for first and second syllable position comparisons. The results for pairs sharing elements in the first syllable (e.g., m*ountain*-f*ountain* vs. *gar*den-*gar*lic) are interesting because they suggest that rhyme is even easier than word onset for young children to detect. In addition, the findings for the second syllable pairs (e.g., sal*oon*-bab*oon* vs. tea*cher*-na*ture*) are compelling because the portions of the words shared in the Rhyme and Syllable stimuli were fairly comparable in length, indicating that the relative ease of the Rhymes was not simply a function of size. The salience of rhyme is further indicated by the finding that second syllable Rhymes (e.g., sal*oon*-bab*oon*) were even easier for children to recognize than were (stressed) Syllables shared at the beginning of words (e.g., *gar*den-*gar*lic). This result would be problematic for an analysis based strictly upon hierarchic linguistic units: in linguistic terms it would mean the stressed rime (e.g., sal*oon*-bab*oon*) is more salient than the stressed syllable. The outcome with this experimental measure corroborates the previous observational data obtained with young children demonstrating the early accessibility of rhyme (e.g., Dowker 1989) and supports the claim that rhyme awareness is the earliest stage of metaphonological development (e.g., Bryant et al. 1990).

Our evidence also underscores difficulties with positing rime as a constant unit of subword analysis. In the present study, the use of disyllabic stimuli allowed the differentiation of stressed and unstressed rimes (e.g., Rhymes vs. Rimes), yielding strikingly different results. Thus the Rhymes and Rimes in second syllable position (e.g., sal*oon*-bab*oon* vs. shep*herd*-haz*ard*) both constitute rimes, yet they were designed to differ in stress. The children's performance on the unstressed Rimes was significantly worse. Comparison of Rhymes and Rimes in the first syllable position (e.g., m*ountain*-f*ountain* vs. p*en*cil-t*en*der) makes a different point. In this contrast both targets incorporate stressed vowels, but the shared portion in the Rhymes constitutes a word-level rhyme, extending to the final word edge, while in the Rime stimuli the shared portion was restricted to the first syllable. As anticipated, performance on the Rhyme stimuli was much superior.

These results confirm doubts, raised in Treiman and Zukowski (1991), about the adequacy of the syllabic hierarchy as a framework for explaining the acquisition of phonological awareness. As noted in our introduction, Treiman and Zukowski (1991) observed comparable performance on full syllables and on parts of syllables (e.g., re*treat*, en*treat* vs. ac*claim*, in*flame*), rather than obtaining the hypothesized advantage for the full syllabic units (see Treiman and Zukowski [1996] for a replication of this same result). We find a further exception to the syllable hypothesis in a study by Fox and Routh (1975), often cited as providing strong evidence for superior performance by young children on syllables versus phonemes. In the experiments reported in Fox and Routh, children were asked to "say a little bit of" a word. Fox and Routh describe two scoring procedures used for the syllable task (e.g., "say a little bit of *window*"): First, the number of words segmented in any way (e.g., "indow" or "o") and second, the number segmented at the conventional syllable boundary (e.g., "dow") (*our examples*). By age four, children were able to segment words according to the first procedure. However, the authors note that even the oldest children (seven-year olds) had not acquired accuracy using canonical syllabification. Surprisingly, these older children were *more* accurate on the phoneme segmentation task than on canonical syllable segmentation, and the syllable task proved to be an even more potent index of reading skill. In other studies purportedly demonstrating syllable awareness, the children are asked only to tap out the correct number of syllables (e.g., Liberman et al 1974; Mann and Liberman 1984). We speculate that children may base their responses on the salient portions of speech signals associated with the vowel nuclei rather than on canonical syllables. Read (1978) likewise comments that, " the syllable . . . has resisted satisfactory delimitation, but there is a simple acoustic criterion for the number of syllables, if not for their boundaries" (p. 73). In short, the apparent consistency in the prior literature concerning the relative ease of segmentation tasks may have stemmed from an overreliance on monosyllabic stimuli in which multiple factors are confounded and on the use of measures for which the interpretation is ambiguous. Consequently, even before the present results, the case for the primacy of the syllable was questionable.

Further evidence that rhyme awareness precedes awareness of syllables derives from several prediction studies reporting that syllable measures in kindergarten are better predictors of later reading success than are measures of rhyme. We speculate that this may be a function of the fact that rhyme awareness is generally at ceiling by this age (e.g., Bowey and Frances 1991; Stanovich, Cunningham, and Cramer 1984). In contrast, syllable and phoneme segmentation are good predictors because awareness of these elements is still developing in kindergarten.

Three caveats are necessary here. First, it must be noted that not all children have achieved rhyme awareness in the preschool years. For example, in our study, a sizeable proportion of four-year olds were not able to pass the pretest that involved a simple rhyme task. Similarly, rhyme awareness may not yet be acquired by kindergarten children who are disadvantaged or language delayed (e.g., Brady et al. 1994; Lonigan et al. 1998; Robertson 1997; Warrick and Rubin 1992). Hence, rhyme may prove to be a sensitive predictor in younger or at-risk groups of children.[6] The second caveat relates to the particular measure itself and the developmental age of the child. As the discussion of the Fox and Routh (1975) research implied, the nature of a syllable task will influence the stage at which children can carry it out successfully. Therefore, the success of different measures for prediction purposes will depend upon both the developmental level of the children assessed and upon the actual task employed (cf., Bowey and Frances 1991). Third, we also need to qualify our conclusions, stressing that they pertain only to the development of phonological awareness for children who speak English. One would anticipate that for languages organized in terms of different structural principles than those for English, emerging awareness of the phonological structure would differ accordingly (Caravolas and Bruck 1993). For example, in languages such as French that are syllable timed (Cutler et al 1986), syllable organization may play a more pivotal role in metaphonological development.

Explaining the salience of word-level rhyme

Because the results obtained in this study highlight the early salience of word-level rhyme, at least for English, it is now worth considering the basis for the early recognition and production of rhymes by young children. Two possibilities come to mind, and both may apply: first, rhymes may constitute a structural unit germane to linguistic processing; and second, rhymes may incorporate other attributes such as stress, unit size, and word position that may help focus attention and heighten the detectability of rhyme. We will consider each of these in turn.

In the introduction, we presented a view that intra-word analyses are based on word-level organization rather than on syllable-based organization, with special status accorded to the word-onset (Browman and Goldstein 1990; Shattuck-Hufnagel

---

[6]For younger or at-risk groups, the development of phonological sensitivity is likely to be at an earlier stage. Research with older reading-disabled children confirms that their phoneme awareness skills are comparable to those of younger reading-age matched participants (Metsala, 1999).

1987). Although the rhyme has not been discussed as a candidate for a word-level unit, one could argue that the rhyme constitutes the structural subdivision of the word complementing the word onset or, to be more accurate, the stressed onset. We are intrigued with this possibility. The evidence that children can not only detect rhymes, but can also generate rhyme patterns (e.g., Dowker 1989), may indicate an appreciation of the overall structure of the rhyme unit.

If rhyme and onset are important linguistic units for young children, it does not appear to be the case that the child discovers them simultaneously. As noted in the introduction, research on children's speech indicates that the onset is somewhat late to develop as a salient unit of word organization especially if the first syllable is not stressed. For example, when producing multi-syllabic words, it is common for young children to drop the portion of the word including the word onset and to preserve the second, stressed syllable, incorporating the rhyme (e.g., /raef/ for *giraffe*) (e.g., Echols and Newport 1992). Correspondingly, it does not appear that the word onset is available at a metalinguistic level to young children at as early an age as rhyme is. As Treiman and Zukowski (1991) reported, shared rimes (in fact, rhymes) tend to be easier to recognize than are shared onsets. This outcome is consistent with studies reporting that the ability to detect word onset emerges later than sensitivity to other phonological segments such as rhymes and syllables (e.g., Stanovich, Cunningham, and Cramer 1984; Treiman and Zukowski 1991). Although the present study did not explore the availability of word onsets to young children, one result was telling. We found both Rhyme subconditions (e.g., m*ountain*-f*ountain*; sal*oon*-bab*oon*) to be easier than even the first stressed Syllable (e.g., *gar*den-*gar*lic), despite the presence of a word onset in the Syllable condition.

Although less accessible than the rhyme, the word onset (when it is a single phoneme), does seem to be the easiest single phoneme within the word for children to isolate and identify. As mentioned in the beginning of this chapter, the frequent use of alliteration in children's literature and the spontaneous use of alliteration by young children indicate the salience of the word onset even before formal instruction in reading has begun. Likewise, tasks requiring segmentation between the word onset and the remainder of the word have been found to be strong predictors in kindergarten of subsequent success in reading (e.g., Share et al. 1984). In short, the literature on early phonological development and on the emergence of phonological awareness has numerous indications that word level rhymes and onsets are relevant linguistic units for young children. We submit that the rhyme and onset can plausibly be viewed as word-based structures. Yet, it appears that the rhyme may play an even more central role in early lexical organization, and that it is available as a metalinguistic unit at an earlier age.

The alternative explanation for children's superior performance in the Rhyme condition rests on other linguistic factors, including stress, duration, and position. We did not set out to evaluate the role these factors might play so the stimuli have shortcomings for addressing these issues. With this caution in mind, we will first consider whether the impact of the stressed vowel, with its attendant acoustic salience, explains the results. Clearly, performance on pairs sharing stressed segments tended to be superior. The three easiest conditions (the two Rhyme subconditions and the first syllable subcondition) all included the stressed vowel. Within the Rhyme condition, no significant difference was found between the first and second position rhymes, demonstrating the salience of rhyme (or the stressed vowel) independent of the size of the shared segment. In the Syllable condition, children performed better when the shared unit was the first (stressed) syllable (e.g., *gar*den-*gar*lic), rather than the second (unstressed) syllable (e.g., tea*cher*-na*ture*). Similarly, Treiman and Zukowski (1991) failed to obtain a position effect for syllables when stress was balanced across first and second positions, or, in Treiman and Zukowski (1996), an effect for syllables when stressed final syllables were contrasted with stressed rimes (rhymes) in the final syllable. Both outcomes support our interpretation that the difference in detectability found in the present study was due to stress.

Further evidence consistent with the stress account is the comparison of performance on Rhyme versus Rime measures. Children performed significantly better on items involving shared rhymes in the second portion of the word than on shared rimes in the same position. Given that stress constitutes a major contrast in this comparison, a strong case can be made for the impact of the stressed vowel on the salience of phonological segments. As mentioned above, this particular effect raises a question regarding the generalizability of the concept of rime. The English language, with numerous multisyllabic words, necessarily includes many rime units that are unstressed, and these are apparently less accessible than those that are stressed.

However, one outcome from the present study hints that rhyme status, and the corresponding availability of rhyme units, goes beyond the presence of a stressed vowel. Performance on the

Rimes in first position (e.g., pe*n*cil-te*n*der) was fairly low, despite the fact that a stressed vowel was incorporated in the shared segment. We are also struck by the evidence that even very young children can sometimes generate rhyme patterns, indicating an appreciation of the overall structure of the rhyme unit, not merely the stressed vowel (Dowker 1989). It is even possible that rhyme generation may precede a consistent ability to recognize rhyme patterns in a formal task.

A second factor that appears to influence early phonological awareness performance is the size of the shared portion. Strong correlations between number of shared phonemes and phonological awareness scores were obtained for both of the methods of counting phonemes. In addition, in multiple regression analyses, length accounted for a large portion of the variance in phonological awareness scores. This pattern is in agreement with the findings from other studies (e.g., Treiman and Zukowski 1991; Walley, Smith, and Jusczyk 1986) that support the number of segments in common as one of the factors affecting performance on phonological awareness tasks. On the other hand, it was somewhat surprising that no significant difference was observed between performance on the rhymes beginning in the first syllable and on those in the second syllable, despite the notable size difference. Either a ceiling effect may be obscuring the distinction between these two subconditions or the salience of the rhyme/stress may override the effect of unit size. Other results, described earlier, indicate that unit size alone is not the major determinant of the results obtained (see also Treiman and Zukowski [1996]). For example, awareness scores were significantly better on second position Rhymes than on the second position Syllables, though a comparison of mean number of phonemes in each demonstrates that the items making up rhymes in the second position contained equal or fewer phonemes. Similarly, the mean number of shared phonemes in the Rhyme and Rime conditions in the second position was nearly the same, yet performance on these subconditions was markedly different. In multiple regression analyses, entering length first (with stress constant across conditions), a significant amount of variance was accounted for by linguistic status (Rhyme, Syllable, Rime). These results point to the impact of rhyme as a salient unit, beyond quantity of shared material.

One difficulty in evaluating the role of size concerns the issue of how size should be estimated. Here we defined it as the number of shared phonemes and ran into problems with how phonemes are to be counted. A further possibility is that it is not the number of shared phonemes that is relevant, but the actual duration of the shared portions.[7] Should duration turn out to be the relevant dimension, several predictions would follow about what kinds of phonemic patterns young children first acquiring phonological awareness should find easier to detect. For example, rhymes containing long vowels before voiced consonants (e.g., *made-spade*) might be notably easier than those with short vowels before voiceless consonants (e.g., *hit-mit*).

A third possible factor relates to position within the word. We have already mentioned the accessibility of word onsets for young children, as indicated by alliteration. There are several reasons to think that word final position is also salient to young children. For example, as noted in the introduction, teachers have long observed that beginning readers and spellers often perform better on the ends of words than on the middle position (ig., spelling "bd" for *bed*), indicating the relatively easier detection of word edges (Treiman 1993; see also Treiman et al. 1995). Similarly, recent studies of language production (Echols l993; Echols and Newport 1992) report that for spontaneous utterances and elicited imitations, very young children (under 2 years) more often pronounce the final portion of the word accurately, whether or not it is stressed. Similarly, Vihman's (1981) work on children's malapropisms finds that the preserved segments of words tend to be from the ends of the target items.

To illustrate how these various factors (stress, unit size, word position) may have interacted to influence performance, we charted factors present in each of the conditions we tested (see table V). The results clearly show a disadvantage for the Rime stimuli, mirroring the poor performance on the Rime condition. Looking at the confluence of factors for the Rhyme and Syllable conditions, the obtained pattern of results is again seen (i.e., rhyme > syllable) suggesting we need to further explore the role of these linguistic factors in the development of phonological awareness. To assess fully the basis for the advantage of rhymes, it would be necessary to create stimuli in which the linguistic unit and the other factors are manipulated independently. For example, would first syllable rimes (e.g., pencil-tender) be more easily detected if the size of the unit were increased (e.g., sandwich-handsome)? Similarly, though rhyme necessarily incorporates both the vowel and word final position, do young children just discovering rhyme perhaps find long rhymes easier to recognize than short rhymes?

---

[7]"Sonority" or "prominence" has been identified as a feature of stress carried by certain syllables. In a study of what acoustic attributes specify sonority, it was found that absolute duration of the stressed segment(s) is an important cue (Price1980).

Table V. Stimuli Characteristics in the Rhyme, Syllable, and Rime Conditions

Subcondition	Stress[a]	Word Edge[a]	Final Unit Size[b]	Total
Rhyme				
first position: m*ountain*-f*ountain*	1	1	2 (3)	4 (5)
second position: sal*oon*-bab*oon*	1	1	2 (2)	4 (4)
Syllable				
first position: *garden*-*garlic*	1	0	2 (2)	3 (4)
second position: tea*cher*-na*ture*	0	1	1 (2)	2 (3)
Rime				
first position: p*encil*-t*ender*	1	0	0 (1)	1 (2)
second position: wiz*ard*-sheph*erd*	0	1	0 (0)	1 (1)

[a]Stress: a score of zero indicates the absence of stress, one indicates the presence. Word edge: a score of zero indicates the absence of a final word edge, one indicates the inclusion of a common word final edge. (Note, the decision to count only shared word final edges was based on the evidence mentioned earlier that these are salient to very young children, whereas there is little evidence of an advantage for word beginnings. If beginning word edges were included, only the score for the first position syllable condition would change.)

[b]In the first column, unit size is based on means for the one-phoneme method listed in table IV. In the second column (in parentheses), the two-phoneme method of counting is represented. For both, a size of four(+) phonemes was given a score of 3; a size of three phonemes was given a score of 2, a size of two phonemes was given a score of 1, and a size below two phonemes was given a score of 0. This arbitrary scoring system was chosen for the present purposes to reflect the distribution of size values without excessively weighting the contribution of unit size in comparison to the other word characteristics considered here.

In sum, the importance of phoneme awareness in reading development has raised interest in how children progress from lacking phonological awareness in their early years to attaining insights gradually about the phonemic structure of words. The results of the present study suggest that the syllable hierarchy hypothesis may not be the correct framework for explaining the early development of phonological awareness in English. They demonstrate that rhyme is an easier, and probably earlier, subword unit of phonological awareness for young children to identify. The present data, obtained using a phonological awareness measure, can be explained by two alternative though not incompatible accounts: (1) In accord with recent work on lexical organization, word-level units (i.e., rhyme) may warrant important status. (2) Certain properties of words (e.g., stress, size of shared segments) may facilitate children's abilities to analyze word structure. By either account, the results of this study point to the need to use the syllable/onset/rime terminology cautiously, particularly for monosyllabic words in which word-level units (word onset/rhyme) overlap with syllable-level units (onset/rime).

In practical terms, for very young children, activities that target rhyme and awareness of onsets (i.e., alliteration) appear to be sensible starting points for drawing attention to the sound structure of words. On the other hand, whether extensive instruction in rhyme is a necessary component of phoneme awareness instruction beyond the first month of kindergarten is yet to be resolved. At least two successful approaches to phoneme awareness instruction (Lindamood and Lindamood 1998; Ball and Blachman 1991) deliberately sidestep extensive rhyming games as unnecessary and as possibly even confusing their efforts in kindergarten or first grade to direct the child's attention to phoneme-level segments. Consistent with the sequence of development observed in our research, other programs begin with rhyming (including of multisyllabic words) as the earliest step, and then move on to segmenting of syllables and phonemes (Catts and Vartiainen 1993; Robertson and Salter 1997; Torgesen and Bryant 1994).

We have made considerably less progress regarding whether, where, and how to direct children's attention to the syllable structure of words. It clearly is not as "natural" as rhyming for the entry level to awareness, but it does seem a logical step in helping children to learn to segment words into the sublexical components (e.g., Fox and Routh 1975). For this goal, counting and clapping tasks are both engaging and apparently helpful. Yet, the role of the syllable in the development of awareness and in learning to read needs to be investigated further. It may be that awareness of syllables at an explicit level, as opposed to a grosser appreciation of syllabic gestures in the syllable counting or clapping tasks, pertains to the syllable division skills honed as English-speaking children move into reading multisyllabic words in second and third grades (e.g., Aronoff and Koch 1996; Johnson and Bayrd 1993; Stanback 1992).

ACKNOWLEDGMENTS

First, we thank Carol Fowler, and Michael Studdert-Kennedy for their insightful and valuable comments on earlier versions of the paper, and Catherine Browman for several helpful discussions. Second, we are grateful to Krista Robertson for her assistance rescoring and reanalyzing the data. Third, we appreciate helpful methodological suggestions from Jerry Cohen and Len Katz. We also wish to extend thanks to the directors, staff, parents, and children of the fifteen schools and centers where the data was collected. Lastly, we are grateful for the grant support that made this project possible: National Institutes of Health grant HD-01994 to Haskins Laboratories and grant NSS2-S07-RR07086-14 to the University of Rhode Island from the National Center for Research Resources.

This paper is based on the doctoral dissertation of the first author, conducted under the supervision of the second author. The results were presented at the American Educational Research Association meeting held in San Francisco, April, 1992.

REFERENCES

Adams, M. J. 1990. *Beginning to Read*. Cambridge, MA: MIT Press.

Aitchison, J., and Straf, M. 1981. Lexical storage and retrieval: A developing skill? *Linguistics* 19(7–8):751–95.

Aronoff, M. and Koch, E. 1996. Context-sensitive regularities in English vowel spelling. *Reading and Writing: An Interdisciplinary Journal* 8:261–65.

Ball, E. W. and Blachman, B. 1991. Does phoneme awareness training in kindergarten make a difference in early word recognition and developmental spelling? *Reading Research Quarterly* 26:49–66.

Blachman, B. (ed.) 1997. *Foundations of Reading Acquisition and Dyslexia*. Mahwah, NJ: Lawrence Erlbaum Associates.

Berg, T. 1989. On the internal structure of polysyllabic monomorphemic words: The case for superrimes. *Studia Linguistica* 43:5–32.

Bowey, J., and Francis, J. 1991. Phonological analysis as a function of age and exposure to reading instruction. *Applied Psycholinguistics* 12:91–121.

Brady, S., Gipstein, M., and Fowler, A. 1992. Phonological awareness in four- and five-year old children. Paper presented at the American Educational Research Association, San Francisco, April.

Brady, S. and Shankweiler, D. (eds.) 1991. *Phonological Processes in Literacy: A Tribute to Isabelle Y. Liberman*. Hillsdale, NJ: Lawrence Erlbaum Associates.

Brady, S., Stone, B., Fowler, A., and Winbury, N. 1994. Training phonological awareness: An intervention study with inner-city children. *Annals of Dyslexia* 44:26–59.

Browman, C. P. 1978. Tip of the tongue and slip of the ear: Implications for language processing. *University of California Working Papers in Phonetics* 42.

Browman, C. and Goldstein, L. 1990. Representation and reality: Physical systems and phonological structure. *Journal of Phonetics* 18:411–24.

Bruck, M., Caravolas, M., and Treiman, R. 1995. Role of the syllable in the processing of spoken English: Evidence from a nonword comparison task. *Journal of Experimental Psychology: Human Perception and Performance* 21:469–79.

Bruck, M. and Treiman, R. 1990. Phonological awareness in normal children and dyslexics: The case of initial consonant clusters. *Journal of Experimental Child Psychology* 50:156–78.

Bryant, P. E., and Bradley, L. 1985. *Children's Reading Problems: Psychology and Education*. Oxford: Basil Blackwell.

Bryant, P. E., Bradley, L., MacLean, M., and Crossland, J. 1989. Nursery rhymes, phonological skills and reading. *Journal of Child Language* 16:407–28.

Bryant, P. E., MacLean, M., Bradley, L., and Crossland, J. 1990. Rhyme, alliteration, phoneme detection and learning to read. *Developmental Psychology* 26:429–38.

Caravolas, M. and Bruck, M. 1993. The effect of oral and written language input on children's phonological awareness: A cross-linguistic study. *Journal of Experimental Child Psychology* 55(1):1–30.

Carlisle, J. F. 1991. Questioning the psychological reality of onset-rime as a level of phonological awareness. In *Phonological Processes in Literacy: A Tribute to Isabelle Y. Liberman*, eds. S. Brady and D. Shankweiler. Hillsdale, NJ: Lawrence Erlbaum Associates.

Catts, H. and Vartianen, T. 1993. *Sounds Abound*. East Moline, IL: LinguiSystems.

Chaney, C. 1992. Language development, metalinguistic skills, and print awareness in 3-year-old children. *Applied Psycholinguistics* 13:485–514.

Chaney, C. 1998. Preschool language and metalinguistic skills are links to reading success. *Applied Psycholinguistics* 19:433–46.

Chukovsky, K. 1968. *From Two to Five* (Translation of the 1959 ed.). Berkeley: University of California Press.

Clements, G. N., and Keyser, S. J. 1983. *CV Phonology: A Generative Theory of the Syllable*. Cambridge, MA: MIT Press.

Content, A., Kolinsky, R., Morais, J., and Bertelson, P. 1986. Phonetic segmentation in prereaders: Effect of corrective information. *Journal of Experimental Child Psychology* 421:47–72.

Cutler, A., Mehler, J., Norris, D., and Segui, J. 1986. The syllable's differing role in the segmentation of French and English. *Journal of Memory and Language* 25:385–400.

Davis, S. 1989. On a non-argument for the rhyme. *Journal of Linguistics* 25:211–17.

DeFrancis, J. 1991. *Visible Speech: The Diverse Oneness of Writing Systems*. Honolulu: University of Hawaii Press.

Dowker, A. 1989. Rhyme and alliteration in poems elicited from young children. *Journal of Child Language* 16:181–202.

Echols, C. 1993. A role for stress in early speech segmentation. Paper presented at the international conference "Signal to Syntax: Bootstrapping from Speech to Grammar in Early Acquisition," Providence, RI., February.

Echols, C. H. and Newport, E. 1992. Stress and position in first words. *Language Acquisition* 2:189–220.

Fowler, A. E. 1991. How early phonological development might set the stage for phoneme awareness. In *Phonological Processes in Literacy: A Tribute to Isabelle Y. Liberman*, eds. S. Brady and D. Shankweiler. Hillsdale, NJ: Lawrence Erlbaum Associates.

Fowler, C. A., Treiman, R. and Gross, J. 1993. The structure of syllables and polysyllables. *Journal of Memory and Language* 32:115–40.

Fox, B., and Routh, D. K. 1975. Analyzing spoken language into words, syllables, and phonemes: Developmental study. *Journal of Psycholinguistic Research* 4:331–42.

Fudge, E. C. 1969. Syllables. *Journal of Linguistics* 5:253–86.

Fudge, E. 1987. Branching structure within the syllable. *Journal of Linguistics* 23:359–77.

Fudge, E. 1989. Syllable structure: A reply to Davis. *Journal of Linguistics* 25:219–20.

Gleitman, L. R. and Rozin, P. 1973. Teaching reading by use of a syllabary. *Reading Research Quarterly* 8(4):447–83.

Gleitman, L. R. and Rozin, P. 1977. The structure and acquisition of reading: Relation between orthography and the structured language. In *Toward a Psychology of Reading*, eds. A. S. Reber and D. L. Scarborough. Hillsdale, NJ: Lawrence Erlbaum Associates.

Hooper, J. 1972. Language 48:525–40.

Johnson, K. and Bayrd, P. 1993. *Megawords 1: Multisyllabic Words for Reading, Spelling, and Vocabulary*. Cambridge, MA: Educators Publishing Service.

Kahn, D. 1976. *Syllable-based Generalizations in English Phonology*. Bloomington, IN: Indiana University Linguistics Club.

Liberman, A.M. 1992. The relation of speech to reading and writing. In *Orthography, Phonology, Morphology, and Meaning*, eds. R. Frost and L. Katz. Amsterdam: North-Holland Elsevier.

Liberman, A. M., Cooper, F. S., Shankweiler, D., and Studdert-Kennedy, M. 1967. Perception of the speech code. *Psychological Review* 24:431–61.

Liberman, I. Y. 1973. Segmentation of the spoken word and reading acquisition. *Bulletin of The Orton Society* 23:65–77.

Liberman, I. Y., Shankweiler, D., Fischer, F. W., and Carter, B. 1974. Explicit syllable and phoneme segmentation in the young child. *Journal of Experimental Child Psychology* 18:201–12.

Liberman, I. Y., Shankweiler, D., and Liberman, A. M. 1989. The alphabetic principle and learning to read. In *Phonology and Reading Disability*, eds. D. Shankweiler and I. Y. Liberman. Ann Arbor, MI: University of Michigan Press.

Liberman, I. Y., Shankweiler, D. Liberman, A. M., Fowler, C., and Fischer, F. W. 1977. Phonetic segmentation and recoding in the beginning reader. In *Toward a Psychology of Reading*, eds. A. S. Reber and D. L. Scarborough. Hillsdale, NJ: Lawrence Erlbaum Associates.

Lindamood, P. and Lindamood, P. 1998. *The Lindamood Phoneme Sequence Program for Reading, Spelling and Speech (3rd Edition)*. Austin, TX: PRO-ED.

Lonigan, C. J., Burgess, S. R., Anthony, J. L., and Barker, T. A. 1998. Development of phonological sensitivity in 2- to 5-year-old children. *Journal of Educational Psychology*, 90: 294–311.

Lundberg, I. 1978. Aspects of linguistic awareness related to reading. In *The Child's Conception of Language*, eds. A. Sinclair, R. J. Jarvella, and W. J. M. Levelt. Berlin: Springer-Verlag.

MacKay, D. G. 1972. The structure of words and syllables: Evidence from errors in speech. *Cognitive Psychology* 3:210–27.

MacLean, M., Bryant, P., and Bradley, L. 1987. Rhymes, nursery rhymes, and reading in early childhood. *Merrill-Palmer Quarterly* 33:255–81.

Mann, V. A., and Liberman, I. Y. 1984. Phonological awareness and verbal short-term memory: Can they presage early reading problems? *Journal of Learning Disabilities* 17(10):592–99.

Mehler, J., Dommergues, J., Frauenfelder, U., and Segui, J. 1981. The syllable's role in speech segmentation. *Journal of Verbal Learning and Verbal Behavior* 20:298–305.

Metsala, J.L. 1999. The development of phonemic awareness in reading-disabled children. *Applied Psycholinguistics* 20: 149–58.

Morais, J. Bertelson, P., Cary, L., and Alegria, J. 1986. Literacy training and speech segmentation. *Cognition* 24:45–64.

Price, P. J. 1980. Sonority and syllabicity: Acoustic correlates of perception. *Phonetica* 37:327–43.

Read, C. 1978. Children's awareness of language, with emphasis on sound systems. In *The Child's Conception of Language*, eds. A. Sinclair, R. J. Jarvella, and W. J. M. Levelt. New York: Springer-Verlag.

Read, C. 1991. Access to syllable structure in language and learning. In *Phonological Processes in Literacy: A Tribute to Isabelle Y. Liberman*, eds. S. Brady and D. Shankweiler. Hillsdale, NJ: Lawrence Erlbaum Associates.

Robertson, C. and Salter, W. S. 1997. *The Phonological Awareness Kit*. East Moline, IL: LinguiSystems.

Robertson, K. 1997. Phonological awareness and reading achievement of children from differing socio-economic status. Unpublished doctoral dissertation, University of Rhode Island, Kingston, RI.

Selkirk, E. O. 1982. The syllable. In *The Structure of Phonological Representations (Part II)*, eds. H. Van der Hulst and N. Smith. Dordrecht: Foris.

Share, D., Jorm, A., MacLean, R., and Matthews, R. 1984. Sources of individual differences in reading acquisition. *Journal of Educational Psychology* 76:1309–24.

Shankweiler, D. 1992. Surmounting the consonant cluster in beginning reading and writing: A segmentation problem. Paper presented at the American Educational Research Association, San Francisco, CA, April.

Shattuck-Hufnagel, S. 1983. Sublexical units and suprasegmental structure in speech production planning. In *The Production of Speech*, ed. P. F. MacNeilage. New York: Springer-Verlag.

Shattuck-Hufnagel, S. 1987. The role of word-onset consonants in speech production planning: New evidence from speech error patterns. In *Motor and Sensory Processes of Language*, eds.E. Keller and M. Gopnik. Hillsdale, NJ: Lawrence Erlbaum Associates.

Snow, C. E. 1991. *Unfulfilled Expectations: Home and School Influences on Literacy*. Cambridge, MA: Harvard University Press.

Snow, C. E., Burns, M. S., and Griffin, P. 1998. *Preventing Reading Difficulties in Young Children*. Washington, DC: National Academy Press.

Stanback, M. 1992. Syllable and rime patterns for teaching reading: Analysis of a frequency-based vocabulary of 17,602 words. *Annals of Dyslexia* 42:196–221.

Stanovich, K. E., Cunningham, A. E., and Cramer, B. B. 1984. Assessing phonological awareness in kindergarten children. *Journal of Experimental Child Psychology* 38:175–90.

Studdert-Kennedy, M. 1987. The phoneme as a perceptuomotor structure. In *Language, Perception, and Production*, eds. A. Allport, D. MacKay, W. Prinz, and E. Scheerer. New York: Academic Press.

Torgesen, J. K. and Bryant, B. R. 1994. *Phonological Awareness Training for Reading*. Austin, TX: PRO-ED.

Treiman, R. 1983. The structure of spoken syllables: Evidence from novel word games. *Cognition* 15:49–74.

Treiman, R. 1985. Onsets and rimes as units of spoken syllables: Evidence from children. *Journal of Experimental Child Psychology* 39:161–81.

Treiman, R. 1986. The division between onsets and rimes in English syllables. *Journal of Memory and Language* 25:476–91.

Treiman, R. 1989. The internal structure of the syllable. In *Linguistic Structure and Language Processing*, eds. G. Carlson and M. Tanenhaus. Dordrecht, the Netherlands: Reidel.

Treiman, R. 1993. *Beginning to Spell*. New York: Oxford University Press

Treiman, R., and Baron, J. 1981. Segmental analysis ability: Development and relation to reading ability. In *Reading Research: Advances in Theory and Practice*, eds. G. E. MacKinnon and T. G. Waller. New York: Academic Press.

Treiman, R. and Danis, C. 1988. Short-term memory errors for spoken syllables are affected by the linguistic structure of the syllables. *Journal of Experimental Psychology: Learning, Memory, and Cognition* 14:145–52.

Treiman, R., Fowler, C. A., Gross, J., Berch, D., and Weatherston, S. 1995. Syllable structure or word structure? Evidence for onset and rime units with disyllabic and trisyllabic stimuli. *Journal of Memory and Language* 34: 132–55.

Treiman, R., and Zukowski, A. 1990. Toward an understanding of English syllabification. *Journal of Memory and Language* 29: 66–85.

Treiman, R. and Zukowski, A. 1991. Levels of phonological awareness. In *Phonological Processes in Literacy: A Tribute to Isabelle Y. Liberman*, eds. S. Brady and D. Shankweiler. Hillsdale, NJ: Lawrence Erlbaum Associates.

Treiman, R., Zukowski, A. and Richmond-Welty, E.D. 1995. What happened to the "n" of sink? Children's spellings of final consonant clusters. *Cognition* 55:1–38.

Treiman, R. and Zukowski, A. 1996. Children's sensitivity to syllables, onsets, rimes, and phonemes. *Journal of Experimental Child Psychology* 61:193–215.

Van Kleeck, A., and Schuele, C. M. 1987. Precursors to literacy: Normal development. *Topics in Language Disorders* 7:13–31.

Vennemann, T. 1988. The rule dependence of syllable structure. In *On Language: Rhetorica, Phonologica, Syntactica: A Festschrift for Robert P. Stockwell From His Friends and Colleagues*, eds. C. Duncan-Rose and T. Vennemann. London: Routledge.

Vihman, M. M. 1981. Phonology and the development of the lexicon: Evidence from children's errors. *Journal of Child Language* 8:239–64.

Wagner, R. K., and Torgesen, J. K. 1987. The nature of phonological processing and its causal role in the acquisition of reading skills. *Psychological Bulletin* 101:192–212.

Walley, A. C. 1993. The role of vocabulary development in children's spoken word recognition and segmentation ability. *Developmental Review* 13:286–350.

Walley, A. C., Smith, L. B., and Jusczyk, P. W. 1986. The role of phonemes and syllables in the perceived similarity of speech sounds for children. *Memory and Cognition* 14:220–29.

Warrick, N., and Rubin, H. 1992. Phonological awareness: Normally developing and language delayed children. *Journal of Speech-Language Pathology and Audiology* 16(1):11–20.

Wilkinson, C. 1991. A study of the emergence of phonological awareness as influenced by type of nursery school program, parent-teaching, and age. Unpublished doctoral dissertation, Bryn Mawr College, Bryn Mawr, PA.

Woodcock, R. W. 1987. *Woodcock Reading Mastery Tests—Revised.* Circle Pines, MN: American Guidance Service.

Zwitserlood, P. Schriefers, H., Lahiri, A., and van Donselaar, W. 1993. The role of syllables in the perception of spoken Dutch. *Journal of Experimental Psychology: Learning, Memory, and Cognition* 19(2):260–71.

APPENDIX A
Summary Characteristics of Those Who Did Not Pass Pretest

Age-group	n^a	Percentage of total given pretest	Females/ males	Mother Ed.[b] (Mode)	Age, in mos. M	(SD)
Four-year olds	32	14	9/23	5	52.31	(4.26)
Five-year olds	7	3	2/5	4.5[c]	64.43	(4.04)

[a]Fourteen of the four-year olds and five of the five-year olds were given the initial procedure. Eighteen of the four-year olds and two of the five-year olds were given the revised procedure.

[b]Based on a scale in which 1 = some high school; 2 = high school graduate; 3 = some college; 4 = college graduate; 5 = graduate or professional school.

[c]There were equal numbers of mothers at these two educational levels.

APPENDIX B

Test Stimuli[a]

Rhyme		Syllable[b]		Rime	
Rhyme Following Word Onset:		First (Stressed) Syllable Shared:		Rime in First (Stressed) Syllable:	
1. HANDLE	CANDLE	1. GARDEN	GARLIC	1. BARBER	MARKET
2. BUTTER	CUTTER	2. BARLEY	BARGAIN	2. BUILDER	SILKY
3. MOTION	LOTION	3. FURTHER	FURNACE	3. PENCIL	TENDER
4. DIMPLE	SIMPLE	4. BANJO	BANDIT	4. TURTLE	THERMOS
5. MOUNTAIN	FOUNTAIN	5. WINTER	WINDOW	5. PASTURE	BASKET
6. SOCCER	LOCKER	6. CRADLE	CRAYON	6. BISCUIT	WHISPER
Rhyme in Second Syllable:		Second (Unstressed) Syllable Shared:		Rime in Second (Unstressed) Syllable:	
7. SALOON	BABOON	7 GABLE	BABBLE	7. WIZARD	SHEPHERD
8. TONIGHT	POLITE	8. TEACHER	NATURE	8. CARRIAGE	LUGGAGE
9. MACHINE	CAFFEINE	9 CURTAIN	MOUNTAIN	9. EXPERT	CONCERT
10. BEHIND	UNWIND	10. STATION	LOTION	10. NAPKIN	GARDEN
11. GUITAR	BAZAAR	11. NOTICE	LETTUCE	11. PALACE	TENNIS
12. CEMENT	INVENT	12. WIZARD	HAZARD	12. WAGON	MELON
Nothing Shared:		Nothing Shared		Nothing Shared	
13. BUNNY	SUPER	13. CARROT	SIMPLE	13. WORKER	EMPTY
14. NUMBER	PILLOW	14. NUMBER	WAFFLE	14. NUMBER	DOLPHIN
15. WAFFLE	CIRCUS	15. DESERT	PILLOW	15. DESERT	PILLOW
16. SUMMER	BANJO	16. HANDLE	FOREST	16. FOREST	HANDLE
17. GIRAFFE	BEGIN	17. WELCOME	FANCY	17. ARTIST	WELCOME
18. THIRTEEN	CABOOSE	18. BANJO	SALAD	18. POWDER	BANJO

[a]Note the order of test items within each condition was randomized.

[b]Although, as discussed in the text, disagreement exists about the location of syllable boundaries, for this task, the experimenter was careful to pronounce the stimuli to conform to the boundaries indicated.

Chapter • **9**

A Case for Early Onset-Rime Sensitivity Training in At-Risk Preschool and Kindergarten Children

Judith A. Bowey

This chapter makes a case for introducing phonological sensitivity training to preschool children who are at risk for later reading difficulties. It is argued that these programs should focus on the development of mastery of phonological sensitivity tasks at the onset-rime level, with particular emphasis on singleton onsets. Such training is likely to orient children toward sound structure and, in conjunction with limited letter instruction, may support some insight into the alphabetic principle. At the same time, activities that enhance onset-rime sensitivity appear well suited to the broader goals of preschool education. Further work will be required at the kindergarten level to develop these skills further, but it is unlikely that this instruction will be successful unless onset-rime sensitivity tasks have been truly mastered.

THE DEVELOPMENT OF PHONOLOGICAL SENSITIVITY

The term *phonological awareness* has been widely used as an umbrella term covering performance on a diverse range of metalinguistic tasks that require children to focus attention on the phonological structure of spoken language. To divorce the concept from notions of conscious awareness, Stanovich (1992) suggested that the term *phonological awareness* be replaced by *phonological sensitivity*.

Phonological sensitivity can then be viewed as a continuum, ranging from "deep" to "shallow" sensitivity. Tasks that require children to manipulate the smallest units of sounds—phonemes— may be regarded as assessing deep phonological sensitivity. Such tasks include phoneme segmentation, requiring the explicit analysis of a spoken word into its constituent phonemes, or phoneme deletion, requiring deletion of a word-final phoneme. These tasks unambiguously require the manipulation of individual phonemes within spoken words. Shallow phonological sensitivity is generally assessed by tasks requiring phonological similarity or difference judgments, generally in relation to larger phonological units. They may assess rhyme recognition, for instance by asking children to pick the two rhyming words, or to detect the non-rhyming word, in a spoken sequence (e.g., *pink, think, blank*). The latter is generally referred to as a phonological "oddity" task. These particular examples of deep and shallow phonological sensitivity tasks differ in terms of both the nature of the task and the phonological unit on which the task focuses.

Most linguists regard the English syllable as having a hierarchical structure. The onset is the optional consonant or consonants preceding the vowel within a syllable (e.g., /m/ in *mash*, /tr/ in *trash*). The rime is the obligatory vowel and optional consonant or consonants following the vowel (e.g., the diphthong /aɪ/ in *eye*, and /aɪs/ in *ice*). Where the onset or rime comprise only a single phoneme, sub-syllabic and phonemic units coincide. For instance, /m/ in *mash* is both a phoneme and a singleton onset and the diphthong /aɪ/ in *pie* is both a phoneme and a rime. Children can perform phonological sensitivity tasks requiring the same cognitive operation (e.g., sound deletion, sound judgment) at the level of onsets and rimes before they can perform parallel tasks at the phoneme level (e.g., Bowey 1994; Bowey and Francis 1991; Kirtley et al. 1989; Rosner and Simon 1971; Treiman and Zukowski 1996).

Children and adults who cannot read an alphabetic script typically cannot perform deep phonological sensitivity tasks. For instance, Morais et al. (1979; see also Morais et al. 1986) found that most Portuguese adults who had not been taught to read experienced great difficulty in deleting a singleton onset from a word to produce another word. They experienced even more difficulty when they had to delete a singleton onset from a non-word to produce another non-word. Similarly, illiterate adults experienced great difficulty in adding a singleton onset to a word to produce another word, or to a non-word to produce another non-word. Ex-illiterates who had been taught to read as adults found all of these tasks easier. These results have been replicated in Chinese adults who can read only the logographic Chinese script (Read et al. 1986).

With considerable variability, children within kindergartens in the United States are introduced to reading instruction, so that a substantial proportion are already "beginner" readers. For instance, Vellutino and Scanlon (1987) reported that 10% to 20% of children could identify over ten common sight words by the end of kindergarten. Midway through the kindergarten year, there is already a modest correlation between phonological sensitivity and word reading ability (Wagner, Torgesen, and Rashotte 1994). This variable introduction to reading instruction within both homes and kindergartens probably accounts for findings that some children enter first grade with deep phonological sensitivity.

Nevertheless, low levels of performance on deep phonological sensitivity tasks are typical even in middle-class children tested towards the end of the kindergarten year in the United States. These children find singleton onset deletion tasks very difficult, with mean performance of about 25% correct (Stanovich, Cunningham, and Cramer 1984). Only 17% of kindergarten children tested by Liberman et al. (1974) were able to segment spoken words into phonemes reliably. In contrast, 48% could segment spoken words into syllables. Even at the end of first grade, only 70% of children succeeded on the phoneme segmentation task. In Denmark, floor levels of phoneme segmentation ability were observed in 37% of 155 Danish 7-year olds early in first grade (Lundberg, Frost, and Peterson 1988).

Greater success is observed for alphabetically illiterate individuals on tasks requiring shallow phonological sensitivity. When required to indicate which of four pictures had a name that rhymed with a given picture name, illiterate Portuguese adults obtained scores of 63.8% correct (Morais et al. 1986). Adults with similar backgrounds who had been taught to read scored better on this rhyme detection task, although their performance varied with their reading ability.

Parallel findings have been observed with children. Of a group of 3-year olds, 21% scored above chance in a rime oddity task in which they indicated which one of three picture names did not rhyme with the other two (MacLean, Bryant, and Bradley 1987). Eight months later, 44% obtained an above-chance score. Fairly high levels of success on similar tasks have been observed in 5-year olds on rime oddity tasks, even without picture cues and with data from "novice" readers excluded (Bowey 1994). As is the case with adults, performance on shallow phonological sensitivity tasks increases dramatically following exposure to alphabetic reading instruction. Children just below and just above the school cut-off age and differing only in exposure to reading instruction show markedly different rime and onset oddity performance (Bowey and Francis 1991).

Performance on shallow phonological sensitivity tasks is associated with markers of "at-risk" status, such as socioeconomic status. For instance, Wallach et al. (1977) developed a simple phonological identity judgment task requiring children to identify spoken words sharing a singleton onset. On this 15-item task, 84% of middle-class children made one error or less; this was true of only 7% of children from low-income backgrounds. In their study of disadvantaged inner-city kindergartners, Brady et al. (1994) reported that, toward the end of the kindergarten year, 57% of children in a control group could not produce a single word that rhymed with a stimulus word. Ceiling effects were observed in middle-class children on a very similar task (Stanovich et al. 1984). Similarly, MacLean, Bryant, and Bradley (1987) observed a correlation between maternal educational level and rime oddity performance of .55 in 4-year olds. I (Bowey 1995a) observed a correlation of .47 between paternal occupational status and singleton onset and rime identity in a large group of 5-year olds, from which "novice" readers were excluded.

PHONOLOGICAL SENSITIVITY HELPS CHILDREN LEARN TO READ ALPHABETIC SCRIPTS

Alphabetically literate adults find it very easy to focus on phonemic units. The phonemic structure of spoken language is not as apparent to alphabetically illiterate individuals (see above). This is not surprising when the nature of the phoneme is considered. Phonemes are abstract categories; they cannot be isolated precisely in the acoustic waveform (see Liberman and Liberman 1990). Many phonemes cannot be produced in isolation; they are certainly not produced in isolation within the context of a spoken word. Information about the phoneme /t/ is partly conveyed by the surrounding phonemes; these are co-articulated. Through co-articulation, a single segment of sound contains information about several phonemes. Thus, the word *top* has three phonetic segments, but only one acoustic segment. Because phonemes are encoded within larger units, their precise form varies with the surrounding phonological context. Phonemes are perceived automatically, below the level of conscious awareness. Thus, because the distinctions are not used to convey meaning differences, most English speakers are unaware that /t/ is different in *top* and *stop*, let alone in *top* and *teeth*.

English is an alphabetic language, albeit one that is not perfectly regular. In alphabetic languages, letters symbolize phonemes. The advantage of such writing systems is that words can be decoded without prior experience, provided that they are regular.[1] Mastery of reading an alphabetic script thus entails the ability to use letter-sound correspondences to pronounce unfamiliar items *de novo* through phonological recoding of print to sound (Liberman et al. 1977). This ability both allows new items to be read accurately and provides a mechanism for self-teaching; for Share (1995), phonological recoding is the *sine qua non* of reading an alphabetic script. Children who can make accurate and effortless phonological identity judgments are more likely to notice phonological similarities in a range of contexts and thus to detect print-sound correspondences spontaneously, thereby increasing their own phonological recoding skill (see Bowey 1995b).

Clearly, phonological recoding presupposes insight into the alphabetic principle, (the knowledge that letters represent sounds) so that "whenever a particular phoneme appears in a word, and in whatever position, it can be represented by the same letter" (Byrne and Fielding-Barnsley 1989, p. 313). Comprehension of the alphabetic principle is a necessary, but not a sufficient, condition for mastery of alphabetic reading. For instance, children may understand the alphabetic principle, but know insufficient letter-sound correspondences to read a particular word, or be unable to blend sounds to form a word.

Children should find it easier to understand the alphabetic principle if they already understand that spoken words comprise a series of sound segments that map onto letters (Liberman et al. 1977). Otherwise, they may find it difficult to understand that letters represent sounds. In addition, an understanding that the initial sounds of *mat* and *mow* are conceptually equivalent, as is the final sound of *plum*, may help them understand why the letter *m* is used in the printed form of all three words (Byrne and Fielding-Barnsley 1989). Without this understanding, the fact that *mat* and

---

[1]Although estimates vary, approximately 80% of English words can be considered regular for reading purposes (Woodcock 1987). Note that irregular words are not arbitrarily spelled. In the word *deaf*, only the vowel is irregular. Thus, readers can also use context or attempt variable vowel pronunciations to assist them in reading irregular words.

mow both begin with the letter *m* may be regarded as coincidental. If the principle that letters represent sound is not understood, then children may be reduced to learning words as visually distinct patterns. Very few 5-year olds taught to read by "whole-word" techniques are able to read unfamiliar words that have not been directly taught (Seymour and Elder 1986).

The view that children who are able to focus attention on the phonological structure of spoken words will be better equipped to understand the alphabetic principle and to deduce letter-sound correspondences is not specific about the precise level of phonological sensitivity required. However, this view does generate two clear predictions, that school entrants' phonological sensitivity will predict subsequent reading success, and that increasing phonological sensitivity in children just entering school will facilitate the process of learning to read an alphabetic script.

Many of the studies showing that phonological sensitivity predicts subsequent reading development did not control for the auto-regressive effects of prior reading ability (see Bowey and Francis 1991; Wagner et al. 1994). However, there are sufficient studies that have controlled for such effects for us to be confident that children who commence formal reading instruction with greater phonological sensitivity will become better readers than those with less (e.g., Bradley and Bryant 1983; Muter et al. 1997; Wagner et al. 1997). In fact, Wagner et al. (1997) recently reported that a kindergarten latent measure of phonological sensitivity, derived from measures of segmentation and blending of both phoneme and onset-rime units, predicted second-grade word reading independently of the auto-regressive effects of kindergarten reading, vocabulary, and latent verbal working memory and rapid symbol naming speed measures.

We do not, at this stage, know what level of phonological sensitivity is required for alphabetic reading success (Blachman 1997; Stanovich 1992). In predictive studies that have only included school entrants who could not read, both deep phonological sensitivity (Muter et al. 1997) and shallow phonological sensitivity (Bradley and Bryant 1983) predict subsequent word reading ability. Although the relative strength of phoneme versus rime sensitivity as predictors of subsequent reading ability is disputed (Bryant et al.1990; Muter et al. 1997), no valid conclusions concerning this issue can be drawn from any published studies, because phonological unit and task requirements have been confounded (Bryant 1998). Nor is a clear answer likely to emerge; when pairs of tasks are equivalent in cognitive requirements, the relative strength of phoneme versus onset-rime sensitivity as predictors of word-level reading varies, depending on the presence of ceiling ease and floor effects (Bowey in preparation).

Furthermore, even if performance on deep phonological sensitivity tasks at the end of kindergarten predicts subsequent reading ability, Liberman et al.'s (1974) finding that only 17% of children at the end of kindergarten could segment spoken words into phonemes reliably implies that deep phonological sensitivity cannot be a prerequisite for reading instruction (see also Ehri 1979). As Stanovich (1992) suggested, "Deep phonological sensitivity . . . appears not to be an absolute prerequisite to reading progress, but is itself fostered by the analytic attitude developed during the initial learning of an alphabetical orthography" (p. 318). Unless specifically taught, deep phonological sensitivity appears to develop concomitantly with alphabetic reading instruction, probably as a result of insight into the alphabetic principle, i.e., the tacit understanding that letters represent the sounds of spoken language at the phoneme level (Bowey and Francis 1991; Ehri 1979; Lukatela et al. 1995; Morais 1990; Stanovich 1992).

The training study of Lundberg, Frost, and Peterson (1988) convincingly demonstrated that increasing phonological sensitivity experimentally in preliterate children, in isolation from letter knowledge, selectively enhances later reading and spelling achievement. Although Danish children do not commence formal schooling until the age of 7 years, they are seldom provided with informal literacy instruction by parents or older peers. It is thus unusual for Danish children to be able to read before formal schooling begins. At the end of the kindergarten year, only two of 135 children in Lundberg, Frost, and Peterson's "no treatment" control group showed any word-reading ability.

At the beginning of the kindergarten year, the few differences between the experimental and control groups favored the control group. However, following an intensive eight-month phonological sensitivity training program, the experimental group scored significantly higher than the control group on each post-test measure of phonological sensitivity; with the exception of phoneme blending, these scores were dramatically higher. Improvement was most marked on the phoneme sensitivity tests, although the experimental group was well short of ceiling. Three months later, at the beginning of first-grade, children were given a series of five phonological sensitivity tasks that had not been explicitly taught within the experimental program. The experimental group did better on each.

The larger gains in phonological sensitivity made by the experimental group enhanced later reading and spelling achievement.

Although midway through first grade there was no between-group difference in reading performance, early in second grade the experimental group was reading significantly better than the control group. Even stronger gains were made in spelling. Slight differences in a mathematics test administered in first grade favored the control group, indicating that gains in spelling and later reading were unlikely to have reflected "Hawthorne" effects or differential academic ability.

Although the Lundberg, Frost, and Petersen study is a landmark in demonstrating unambiguously that phonological sensitivity contributes directly to subsequent reading ability, it is difficult to generalize from that study. The children were considerably older than U. S. kindergarten children. More importantly, it is not possible to determine conclusively from this study which aspect(s) of phonological sensitivity enhanced later reading achievement, although, clearly, the greater gains in phoneme sensitivity suggest that this may have contributed most.

Further support for the notion that phonological sensitivity contributes to alphabetic reading success comes from studies showing how phonological sensitivity can interact with letter knowledge to assist a child in developing insight into the alphabetic principle. It appears that normally developing children with high letter name knowledge and reasonable levels of phonological sensitivity sometimes gain some insight into the alphabetic principle before they are explicitly taught to read.

The ability to notice similarities between letter names and the sound sequences of printed words may assist children in attaining a rudimentary understanding of the alphabetic principle and in learning to recognize and spell printed words. Ehri and Wilce (1985) found that only 5-year olds with high letter name and sound knowledge were able to take advantage of phonetic cues by learning to read words like RM (arm) or NE (knee) faster and better than they learned to read words printed in visually distinctive fonts, but where the letters themselves were misleading phonetic cues to word identity (see also Scott and Ehri 1990; Treiman and Rodriguez in press). Even when only children who had learned both types of word to criterion were considered, they were more likely to remember the first letter of words like RM. Similarly, Treiman, Tincoff, and Richmond-Welty (1996) found that preschoolers (mean age 5;5 years), asked to say the first letter of a spoken word, gave the letter *b* for words like *beach* 68% of the time (cf. 2% for words like *wait*).

Children may also use their phonological segmentation skills to use letter names to help them remember some letter-sound correspondences (Ehri 1983). Treiman, Weatherstone, and Berch (1994) reported that preschoolers (mean age 5;2 years) were better able to supply the first or last letter of a spoken nonsense word when the letter name began with the letter's sound (e.g., *b*, *d*, *t*) than when the letter's sound occurred as the final consonant of its VC name (e.g., *f*, *l*, *m*). They were worst at supplying the initial letter when the letter sound did not occur within its name at all (e.g., *g*, *h*, *w*, *j*; see also Treiman et al. 1996).

Once children have acquired the alphabetic insight, some may use their understanding of phoneme identity and their knowledge of whole printed words to derive letter-sound correspondences. For example, they may infer from the printed word *bat* that the sound value of *b* in printed words is /b/. Children's segmentation skills may even help them derive some letter-sound correspondences from letter names. Using their knowledge of the letter *y*'s name (/waɪ/) to wrongly derive its sound, preschool and kindergarten children gave *y* as the first letter of items that began with /w/ approximately 17% of the time (Treiman et al. 1994). Only 2% of other words were misspelled with *y* at the beginning. This error had all but disappeared by first grade.

There are independent grounds for suggesting that letters be incorporated into phonological sensitivity training programs, even those designed for quite young children. Although the effects have been small in the analogue training studies that have specifically manipulated this factor, the available evidence suggests that phoneme sensitivity training is more effective when letters are used to represent the sounds (Haddock 1976; Hohn and Ehri 1983; Marsh and Mineo 1977). The incorporation of letters in this way boosts children's knowledge of letter-sound values and potentially can help them acquire the alphabetic principle (see Ball and Blachman 1988, 1991). In addition, it familiarizes children with conventional letters, a process that is likely to help them attach names and sound values to them when they are later encountered within formal reading instruction (Ehri 1983). Thus, whatever the size of the phonological unit being emphasized in phonological sensitivity training, it would seem worthwhile to include letter name teaching as a general part of the program, and to provide letter-sound instruction for singleton onsets, even in preschool programs.

TRAINING PROGRAMS IN PRESCHOOL SETTINGS

Byrne and Fielding-Barnsley (1989) found that preliterate 4-year olds' ability to recognize the identity of singleton onsets in spoken words, i.e., to judge whether or not the spoken words *mat* and *sat* begin with the same sound, when combined with knowledge of these words in print and the two onset-print correspondences, was sufficient for children to gain insight into the alphabetic principle. This was assessed in a reading analogue task in which children were shown script representations of unfamiliar items one item at a time, and asked whether, for instance, the printed word *mow* said /mo/ or /so/ (Byrne and Fielding-Barnsley 1989). That this training truly produced comprehension of the alphabetic principle was demonstrated by children's performance in a further transfer test that required them to select between printed forms of words such as *plum* and *plus*. Eight of 11 children generalized their understanding of singleton onset identity to phoneme identity, recognizing that the *m* in *plum* represented the same sound as the *m* in *mat*.

Drawing on this work, Byrne and Fielding-Barnsley (1991b) published a teaching program, entitled Sound Foundations, suited to preschool and kindergarten children. This program teaches phoneme identity, the understanding that spoken words such as *sun* and *sail* or *broom* and *drum* share common sounds. Sound Foundations focuses on nine phonemes (including two vowels), although others are eventually taught. For each phoneme there is a poster, with pictures whose names begin with that sound. For each consonant there is also a poster with pictures whose names end with that sound. Children are introduced to the letter representing the sound, and told that it "says" the sound. Worksheets for each phoneme contain outline drawings of objects and characters, and children are asked to locate and color the items whose names begin (or, on other worksheets, end) with the designated phoneme. Card games require children to identify initial (or end) sounds.

Byrne and Fielding-Barnsley (1991a) reported an evaluation of this program, given in 12 weekly, 25- to 30-minute sessions to groups of four to six preschool children (mean age 4;7 years). Although both the experimental Sound Foundations group and a control group, given a training program involving story reading, posters, and semantic categorization tasks and games, showed improved phoneme identity performance from pretest to post-test, the increase was much greater for the experimental group, which performed close to ceiling on trained items. The experimental group also improved more on untrained phonemes. With 32 of 48 items correct, 95% of children in the experimental group (cf. 32% in the control group) "passed" the phoneme identity task at post-test. With 9 of 12 trials correct, 48% of children in the experimen-

tal group (cf. 15% in the control group) "passed" a reading analogue task similar to that of Byrne and Fielding-Barnsley (1989).

Follow-up evaluations showed that, at the end of kindergarten[2]
(Byrne and Fielding-Barnsley 1993), the Sound Foundations group
scored higher than the control group in phoneme identity and in
non-word reading. Both groups scored near ceiling on initial
phoneme identity, differing only in final phoneme identity. On
phoneme deletion, Woodcock Word Identification (Woodcock
1987), and spelling, the two groups scored at the same level. At the
end of grade 1, the Sound Foundations group scored higher than
the control group only on non-word reading (Byrne and Fielding-
Barnsley 1995). The two groups scored at the same level on regular
and irregular word reading, regular and irregular word spelling, letter sound knowledge, and phoneme identity. (Letter sound knowledge and phoneme identity scores were close to ceiling.) At the end
of grade 2, the Sound Foundations group was better at reading three
separate lists of non-words and at reading comprehension, although
the control group was equivalent on word reading and listening
comprehension (Byrne and Fielding-Barnsley 1995). In grade 3, the
Sound Foundations group maintained their non-word reading superiority, but were no better than the control group on irregular word
reading or reading and listening comprehension (Byrne 1998). In
fifth grade, the Sound Foundations group scored higher than the
control group on the reading of irregular words and non-words
(B. Byrne personal communication, June 7, 1999). They scored similarly on the Woodcock Word Identification test.[3]

This series of studies suggests that approximately 6 hours of
early Sound Foundations instruction, focusing on initial and final
phoneme identity, may have an enduring effect on the development

---

[2]The age at which 5-year olds are taught to read and the nomenclature given
to the preschool years varies from state to state in Australia. Of the Australian studies
cited in this chapter, Byrne's were carried out in New South Wales (NSW), Ballinger's
in Victoria, and mine in Queensland. In NSW and Victoria, the year immediately before first grade corresponds approximately to kindergarten in the United States, and
usually includes formal reading instruction. In Queensland, no formal or informal
reading instruction is included in the year preceding first grade. Indeed, attendance
during this year is optional.

[3]In general, the third-grade and fifth-grade data revealed significant group effects only when individual data points were analyzed. Earlier evaluations analyzed
group means. Analysis using training group means as units of analysis is a more conservative technique, and is preferable when there are many training groups. However,
many of the training studies reported in this chapter also analyzed individual data
points. In some cases, where the total numbers are large, this may over-estimate training effects (e.g., Blachman et al. 1994; Lundberg, Frost, and Peterson 1988). In some
cases, these analyses are nevertheless appropriate; where the total number of training
groups is small, the analysis of group means may underestimate training effects (e.g.,
Blachman et al. 1994; Morgan and Willows 1996; Sumbler and Willows 1996).

of later reading skills. Nevertheless, we cannot be sure that it was the phoneme identity component of Sound Foundations that contributed to later reading success. Since approximately half of the program taught singleton onset identity and, at post-test, both the experimental and the control groups managed singleton onset identity judgments much better than final phoneme judgments (Byrne and Fielding-Barnsley 1991a), it is possible that the effects primarily reflected the onset identity or letter-sound components of the phonological sensitivity training.

When taught by regular teachers working from the Sound Foundations manual with groups of about 20 children (mean age 4;6 years), the implementation of the program varied from preschool to preschool (Byrne and Fielding-Barnsley 1995). Two preschools used the program for six weeks, teaching two phonemes a week, and a third preschool used the program for 12 weeks, also teaching 12 phonemes in all. All schools emphasized initial phonemes; teachers at two of the three preschools did not teach final phonemes at all. When the phoneme identity test used by Byrne and Fielding-Barnsley (1991a) was administered at post-test, 51% of children were classified as "passing" the phoneme identity task, with 32 of 48 items correct (cf. 95% of children in the original Sound Foundations group and 32% in the original control group). There were no pretest differences in the numbers of children passing this test (about 20% in each group).

Byrne et al. (1997) identified preschoolers at risk for reading difficulties by virtue of the presence of significant reading difficulties in either a parent or an older sibling. These children (mean age of 4;8 years) scored lower than the 128 children in the original Sound Foundations evaluation study (Byrne and Fielding-Barnsley 1991a) on both rhyme recognition and the Peabody Picture Vocabulary Test-Revised (PPVT-R, Dunn and Dunn 1981). Forty at-risk children completed the Sound Foundations program, supplemented by intensive letter instruction and "interactive reading" (see Whitehurst et al. 1994) components. This program was taught in groups of one to six children, in sessions totaling 40 minutes per week for 16 to 20 weeks. The training program significantly increased children's phoneme identity and rhyme recognition, letter knowledge, and understanding of print. Because different tests were used and the programs differed in intensity, it was not possible to compare directly these children's phoneme identity scores at post-test with the children from the larger evaluation study, although Byrne et al. interpreted their performance as being lower than that of the normal intervention group. Nevertheless, the at-risk trained children performed just as well as the original intervention group (Byrne and Fielding-Barnsley 1991b) on a reading analogue task testing understanding of the alphabetic principle, although this finding was attributed to the more intensive letter instruction given to the at-risk group. The latter finding reinforces the earlier suggestion regarding the importance of letter instruction within phonological sensitivity training programs.

Whitehurst et al. (1994) added interactive reading and phonological sensitivity components to "standard" Head Start programs given to 4-year olds. The phonological sensitivity program consisted of an adaptation of Sound Foundations. Teacher compliance with the program varied. On the first day of each week, when a new sound was introduced and children were given a phoneme identity activity, compliance was nearly universal. However, the use of the suggested extension activities was highly variable. Results indicated that the modified Sound Foundations program did enhance performance on a test examining skills taught directly in the program, the ability to identify sounds and letters. In this test, children had to isolate the first sound of the name of a pictured object and indicate the letter corresponding to that sound. However, there was no generalization beyond that task to other aspects of phonological sensitivity.

Ballinger (1998) evaluated Sound Foundations within a group of disadvantaged children (aged 4;9 years) attending preschools located in inner suburbs of Melbourne, Australia. Only children whom teachers rated as having extremely poor English language proficiency were excluded from the study. The final sample included 12% of children with English as a second language. The mean standard score on the PPVT-R was 85. An experimental group of 201 children was given the Sound Foundations program by their regular teachers over a 12-week period. Each school was then given a Sound Foundations kit, and teachers were given a 90-minute training session on how to implement the program. Training focused on five consonants. Although teachers were asked to teach one sound in one position per week and were encouraged to follow the lesson plan in the Sound Foundations manual, they varied in the extent to which they implemented the program. Three teachers implemented the program fully, one did not complete it in the time allowed, and two others focused only on beginning sounds because their attempts to teach phonemes in final positions met with failure and were judged too difficult for the children.

Extensive pretesting showed that, although the experimental group scored significantly higher than the control group on letter-sound recognition and PPVT-R standard scores (means of 89 and 80, respectively), no differences were found in phonological sensitivity. With pretest PPVT-R and letter-sound knowledge co-varied, there was no difference between the control and experimental groups in either initial or final phoneme identity at post-test. Even after training, children in both groups scored close to chance levels on final phoneme identity tasks, for both trained and untrained items.

In summary, when Sound Foundations is implemented with children at risk for later reading difficulties, the results are generally disappointing (Ballinger 1998; Byrne et al. 1997; Whitehurst et al. 1994). These findings suggest that either more intensive or more prolonged teaching is required, possibly supplemented by additional activities such as letter instruction and interactive reading (see Whitehurst et al. 1994). In addition, programs that include a variety of phonological sensitivity tasks are more likely to produce mastery and transfer (Whitehurst et al. 1994).

More generally, these studies also suggest that promising results obtained in controlled evaluation studies administered by research personnel may be diluted when programs are administered in more ecologically valid conditions by regular teachers. This may partly stem from modifications made to the program, although some modifications are made because of children's perceived difficulties with aspects of the program.

SUCCESSFUL KINDERGARTEN TRAINING PROGRAMS

When taught to somewhat older kindergarten children who are usually concurrently exposed to some reading instruction, experimental phonological sensitivity training programs administered directly by research personnel have generally produced enhanced phonological sensitivity (Torgesen, Morgan, and Davis 1992; Torgesen and Davis 1996), with gains generalizing to reading (Ball and Blachman 1988, 1991; Cunningham 1990; O'Connor, Jenkins, and Slocum 1995). Furthermore, these programs have been successful in disadvantaged children taught by regular teachers (Blachman et al. 1994; Brady et al. 1994; Morgan and Willows 1996). Notably, most of these programs also taught letters. Only two of these programs will be reviewed here; both integrated letter-sound instruction within phonological sensitivity training (Ball and Blachman 1988, 1991; Blachman et al. 1994; Morgan and Willows 1996; Sumbler and Willows 1996).

Ball and Blachman (1988, 1991) evaluated an intensive phonological sensitivity training program, in which small groups of five kindergarten children (mean age 5.7 years) were given 20-

minute phoneme segmentation lessons four times per week for seven weeks. The teaching of nine letter-sound correspondences was integrated with segmentation training. For instance, children were taught to segment spoken words by representing each sound with a disc. After three weeks, letters were written on individual tiles. These tiles were included in the segmentation activities twice weekly. The children had already been taught the names and sounds of nine letters that generate a large number of real consonant-vowel-consonant (CVC) words (*a, m, t, i, s, r, f, u, b*), partly through a series of games that reinforced letter-name and letter-sound knowledge. The use of letter tiles effectively taught the alphabetic principle within the context of phoneme segmentation activities.

Relative to a "language activities" control group, given the same letter knowledge training, and a "no treatment" control group, children in the experimental training group scored significantly higher on the phoneme segmentation post-test. The greatest gains were made on items containing phonemes that had been taught in the program (mean gain of 37% from pretest) and the least on the unfamiliar items (mean gain of 21%). All groups performed at the same level on letter name knowledge, reflecting the generally high levels of letter knowledge in all groups even at pretest (mean of 71% letter names correct). The experimental and language activities groups made much greater gains in letter-sound knowledge, but only the experimental training group made significant transfer to concurrent reading and spelling. Children in this group were also able to read 52% of 21 simple regular VC and CVC words generated from the graphemes taught in the letter-sound components of the experimental and language activities groups' training. In neither control group could children read a substantial number of those words. The children in the experimental training group were also able to transfer this knowledge of the alphabetic principle to other words, scoring higher on the Woodcock Word Identification test and on a simple spelling test.

In addition to excluding from their study children who had already begun to read, Ball and Blachman (1988, 1991) excluded those with standard PPVT-R scores more than 1.5 standard deviations below the mean. To some degree, this restricts the ability to generalize their findings. The remaining children obtained a mean standard score of 101 on the PPVT-R. At pretest, halfway through the school year, they knew about 71% of letter names and about 34% of letter-sound correspondences.

Blachman et al. (1994) investigated the effectiveness of a very similar program implemented by regular teachers or teaching assistants to kindergarten children from four low-income inner-city schools, in which approximately 85% of children received free or supported lunches. As in the earlier Ball and Blachman (1991) study, children who could already read ($n = 2$, in this study) and children with standard PPVT-R scores more than 1.5 standard deviations below the mean, were excluded from the study. So, too, were children with severe articulation difficulties and children who could not yet demonstrate the one-to-one correspondence required in phoneme counting tasks. The children in the final study knew about 40% of letter names at pretest, and obtained a mean standard score of 91 on the PPVT-R.

Children from two of the schools were assigned to a control group, which received the regular kindergarten program, including whole class instruction in letter names and sounds. Children from the other schools were assigned to an experimental treatment group. Teachers and teacher aides participated in 7 two-hour workshops that introduced the rationale for teaching phonological sensitivity, and gave opportunities to practice the activities and to ask questions about the program. In their 11-week training program, working with groups of four to five children in 15- to 20-minute sessions four times a week, children in the experimental group were effectively taught both phoneme segmentation and the alphabetic principle (see Ball and Blachman 1991). During the eighth week of instruction, selected children who had mastered several letter names and sounds were given enough letter tiles to produce real CVC words (e.g., *bit*) during these segmentation activities.

At post-test, children in the experimental group scored significantly higher than the control group on phoneme segmentation and letter name and sound knowledge, and made significant transfer to concurrent reading and spelling. Children in this group could read more two- and three-phoneme regular words and more non-words, and scored higher on an invented spelling test (see also Tangel and Blachman 1992), although these gains did not show up on the standardized Woodcock Word Identification test. Stronger transfer to reading may have been observed if the training program had incorporated blending.

Jolly Phonics (Lloyd 1992, 1998) is a commercially published phonics approach to reading (and reading readiness) training that uses a playful and flexible approach to teach phoneme segmentation and blending skills, letter names, and letter-sounds, and to use letter sounds to read and spell words, using a progressively larger pool of letters and sounds. For instance, children are first taught activities including the sounds and letters corresponding to the letters *s, a, t, i, p,* and *n,* introduced with actions that help children remember both the sounds and key words beginning with the sound. The actions and letters permit a variety of phonemic analysis and blending games to be played with actions and letters. Children eventually learn 42 phonemes and corresponding letters or letter combinations.

When compared with "whole language" literacy programs, Jolly Phonics produces superior reading and spelling in older kindergartners (mean age of 5;11 years) (Sumbler and Willows 1996). Although the children in the Jolly Phonics and control classrooms were equivalent in pretest letter name and letter sound knowledge, the Jolly Phonics group scored higher on both measures at post-test. The Jolly Phonics group also scored higher on all post-test measures, including standardized Reading and Spelling tests of the WRAT-3 and the Woodcock Word Attack test. The latter requires children to apply letter-sound correspondences to unfamiliar non-words. Importantly, these gains were also significant, relative to a control group, for children in the bottom quartile of pretest letter name knowledge.

The Jolly Phonics program has also proven highly successful when taught by classroom teachers to children (mean age of 4;11 years) attending schools in low-income areas (Morgan and Willows 1996). Moreover, the children given Jolly Phonics performed at the same level on these tasks at post-test, regardless of native language status.

INDIVIDUAL DIFFERENCES IN RESPONSIVENESS TO TRAINING

We have seen that the gains in phonological sensitivity and reading produced by training programs, especially those implemented within kindergarten programs, have not been limited to normally developing children. Nevertheless, it is not unusual for researchers to report that, despite intensive training, a sizeable proportion of children who are at risk for later reading failure show no appreciable gains in phonological sensitivity (Byrne et al. 1997; Torgesen, Morgan, and Davis 1992; Torgesen and Davis 1996; cf. O'Connor, Jenkins, and Slocum 1995).

Byrne and Fielding-Barnsley (1991a) noted that, after 12 weeks of Sound Foundations training, all but 5% of preschool children "passed" the phoneme identity task. However, 32% of at-risk preschoolers showed no growth in phoneme identity after Sound Foundations training, and a further 20% showed only partial improvement (Byrne et al. 1997). Greater success was reported with older children by O'Connor, Jenkins, and Slocum (1995). They gave intensive phonological sensitivity training to kindergarten children with scores of 0% to 20% on a pretest measure of blending and segmentation, in which two thirds of the items tested onset-rime blending or segmentation. On post-test measures of blending and segmentation and a reading analogue task, these children scored higher than a "low skill" letter-sound control group and as well as a "high skill" control group comprising nonreaders who did well on the pretest phonological sensitivity measure. This training was effective for most children. Of 18 (27%) children who still obtained low scores on the post-test blending and segmentation test, all but three were in the control group.[4] However, since quite high scores could be obtained on this measure by children who could only blend and segment onsets and rimes, the training may only have boosted onset-rime manipulation skills.

It would be reasonable to expect that lack of responsiveness to phonological sensitivity training may reflect low initial phonological sensitivity. Low levels of phonological sensitivity have certainly been reported within studies of disadvantaged children (see above). When Torgesen and Davis (1996) gave a 12-week phonological sensitivity training program to disadvantaged kindergarten children, 35% of the training group showed no growth in segmentation ability, and 10% showed no growth in blending. At pretest, 57% of the training group obtained floor scores on phoneme segmentation and 43% obtained floor scores on phoneme blending. In both tests, credit was given for partially correct responses, including onset-rime segmentation responses. The low pretest ability observed by Torgeson and Davis is not unique. Brady et al. (1994) reported that, at pretest, disadvantaged kindergarten children scored at floor on phoneme deletion and segmentation tasks.

There has been little direct exploration of predictors of responsiveness to phonological sensitivity training. We have seen that, for their experimental group as a whole, Lundberg, Frost, and Peterson (1988) found that extensive kindergarten phonological sensitivity training produced gains in phonological awareness that

---

[4]In fact, O'Connor, Jenkins, and Slocum (1995) had two training groups. One was given phoneme segmentation and blending activities and the other (the "global" training group) received more variable training. Although there was no difference between the two training groups on the reading analogue task, only the former group out performed the no treatment control group on the reading analogue task. O'Connor, Jenkins, and Slocum analyzed their data using group means. Since the number of experimental groups was small, this may have underestimated training effects. Of the children who remained "low skill," two were in the blend-segment treatment and one was in the global training group.

transferred to subsequent reading and spelling achievement. However, for the children in the lowest quartile on the pretest composite phonological sensitivity measure, the difference in reading and spelling achievement between the experimental and control group was smaller than for children in the highest quartile (Lundberg 1988). It is not clear whether the children in the lowest quartile failed to benefit from the phonological sensitivity training per se, or failed to transfer gains to literacy tasks.

Byrne (1998) found that pretest phoneme identity predicted post-test phoneme identity within the normal training group. However, the at-risk children who benefited from Sound Foundations training scored no higher on pretest phoneme identity than those who showed no improvement (Byrne 1998).

Torgesen and Davis (1996) reported that the strongest predictor of growth in segmentation in their training group was pretest non-word spelling, a measure that presupposes segmentation in the context of writing and some insight into the alphabetic principle. Pretest general verbal ability, most measures of phonological sensitivity, and letter name knowledge also predicted growth in segmentation. Although pretest segmentation did not predict growth in phoneme segmentation, this may reflect floor effects (see above). Explaining 26% of the true variance, the model that best predicted growth in segmentation included non-word spelling and general verbal ability. Non-word spelling, one measure of pretest phonological sensitivity, and continuous digit naming rate, each predicted growth in blending in the trained group. Pretest blending did not. Again, this may reflect floor effects. Accounting for 96% of the true variance in growth, the model that best predicted growth in blending included non-word spelling and digit naming rate.

Further work clearly remains to discover the origins of individual differences in responsiveness to phonological sensitivity programs. Such research is still in its infancy.

IS PHONOLOGICAL SENSITIVITY CONSTRAINED BY PHONOLOGICAL DEVELOPMENT?

Findings that a substantial proportion of children at risk for later reading difficulties may not respond to training that focuses on deep phonological sensitivity (requiring the manipulation of phonemes) is quite consistent with the view that children's vocabularies may not be organized initially as a sequence of individual phonemes but may instead be encoded and retrieved as more holistic patterns.[5]

As was noted earlier, phonemes are abstract categories; they do not "exist" in the acoustic waveform. In discussing adult speech perception, Pisoni and Luce (1987) argued that much of variability at the phonetic level is inherently rule governed, so that the process of deriving abstract phonemic representations from the acoustic-phonetic waveform is itself simplified through the use of tacit phonological and morphological knowledge. In a mature linguistic system, word recognition then becomes a process of generating a rule-governed phonological representation from the acoustic-phonetic information in the waveforms and matching this pattern to patterns previously stored in memory (for words), or to patterns generated by rule (for non-words). The quality of the output of the speech perception module depends on phonological development (Fowler 1991; Walley 1993; see below). The output can then be exploited for memory or other cognitive tasks, including those assessing phonological sensitivity (Mattingly 1991).

Because a fully specified phonemic representation is a much more efficient method of encoding, storing, and retrieving phonological information (Pisoni and Luce 1987), the expanding vocabulary eventually creates pressure for more economical phonological representations of lexical items, eventually producing segmental or phonemic representations (see Fowler 1991; Metsala and Walley 1998; Walley 1993). In other words, as children's vocabularies expand, the mental representations of words evolve slowly to segmental (phonemic) representations that appear to be superimposed upon earlier representations (see also Aslin and Smith 1988; Menyuk and Menn 1979; Metsala in press; Metsala and Walley 1998; Studdert-Kennedy 1987; Walley 1993).

According to this view, the phonological representation of vocabulary items becomes increasingly phonemically organized throughout early and even middle childhood, but different items may be differently specified both within and between children, as a function of the word's familiarity and the density of its phonological neighborhood (Fowler 1991; Metsala 1997; Metsala and Walley 1998; Walley 1993). Thus, familiar items eventually be-

---

[5]Production does not necessarily reflect the phonological representation of words within the input lexicon, particularly in very young children. We may need to distinguish between input and output lexicons, which can mutually influence each other, although impairments in the input lexicon will result in inaccurate output. Units of production may differ from units of perception. This distinction is not elaborated upon in the text.

come phonemically specified in all children, but phonologically complex and relatively unfamiliar words are less likely to be fully specified as soon. The vocabulary of even 7-year olds contains a much lower proportion of highly confusable items than that of adults (Charles-Luce and Luce 1990). It may thus be assumed that the process of lexical reorganization extends over a protracted period, particularly for children with smaller vocabularies or with more specific phonological processing difficulties.

Performance on any task that relies on accurate phonological representations being available (e.g., speech perception, non-word repetition, phonological sensitivity) would be enhanced "by segmental analysis and by refined, well-articulated prototypes of those segments to which the input must be compared" (Fowler 1991, p. 108). Furthermore, the quality of phonological representation in perception and production may influence the ease with which sensitivity to these structures is achieved (Fowler 1991; Metsala and Walley 1998; Walley 1993), as is suggested by work showing that drawing children's attention to both articulation (see Lewkowicz 1980) and speech perception (Hurford 1990) may itself enhance phoneme sensitivity. Consistent with this hypothesis are findings that preschoolers' productive phonology is closely tied to the development of phonological sensitivity in children from 3 to 5 years (Webster and Plante 1995) and that children of this age show superior phonological sensitivity for items proposed by the lexical restructuring hypothesis to be among the first to be phonemically represented within children's vocabularies (Metsala in press).

It is well known that older poor readers perform poorly on a range of superficially different tasks that require the efficient processing of phonological material (see Brady 1991; Share 1995; Wagner et al. 1997). The current account of phonological development suggests that these tasks may reflect an underlying phonological processing ability that may in turn reflect the quality of speech representation (see Fowler 1991). In other words, children with reading difficulties or at risk for later reading difficulties generally have less mature phonological processing abilities than normally developing children, even when assessed in tasks that do not require phonological sensitivity (see also Wagner et al. 1997). This view would suggest that children who are at risk for later reading difficulties are more likely to be delayed in constructing phonemically based representations of words in their (possibly smaller) vocabularies, resulting in lower initial phonological sensitivity (Fowler 1991; Metsala and Walley 1998; Walley 1993) and lower responsiveness to training programs that aim at teaching phoneme segmentation and blending, tasks that normally developing preschool and kindergarten children find difficult even in the context of training studies (Brennan and Ireson 1997; Byrne and Fielding-Barnsley 1990; Torgesen, Morgan, and Davis 1992).

Although it is consistent with available evidence, more research is required to test this account of individual differences in responsiveness to phonological sensitivity training.

THE CASE FOR BEGINNING WITH ONSET AND RIME SENSITIVITY TRAINING

Regardless of the origins of lower responsiveness to phoneme segmentation and blending training of some children who are at risk for reading difficulties, these children may well be more responsive to programs that not only focus initially on more accessible singleton onset and rime units, but progress to phoneme sensitivity only when onset and rime tasks are thoroughly mastered. Preschool activities designed to highlight onset and rime can be easily introduced in game format, and provide successful and enjoyable experiences that are consistent with the broader aims of preschool education. The importance of early enjoyment and success on these tasks cannot be underestimated.

Such programs are indeed less ambitious, but are likely to succeed in orienting children to focus attention on the sound structure of language. This is the hallmark of metalinguistic functioning (Bowey 1988), and thus represents a critical skill that needs to be mastered prior to the development of deep phonological sensitivity tasks like segmentation and blending. For preschoolers who are at risk for later reading difficulties, this may be a sufficient goal, especially given that other useful activities should probably be included in any intervention program (see also Blachman 1997; Whitehurst et al. 1994). If children have not mastered tasks requiring them to focus on singleton onsets, they will not succeed on tasks requiring them to segment onset and rimes into constituent phonemes. It is no accident that most phonological sensitivity training programs begin with onset-rime activities (e.g., Brady et al. 1994; Torgesen et al. 1992; Torgesen and Davis 1996). Training programs that include a variety of tasks are more likely to produce mastery and transfer.

Complete mastery of tasks involving singleton onsets at preschool level will provide a secure foundation both for subsequent kindergarten programs that explicitly integrate the teaching of letter-sound correspondences with phoneme segmentation and blending in enjoyable game-oriented activities (e.g., Ball and Blachman 1988; Lloyd 1998) and for first-grade reading instruction programs that explicitly integrate the teaching of reading with phoneme segmentation and blending (e.g., Cunningham 1990; Lloyd 1998). Because phoneme blending appears easier to teach (Torgesen and Davis 1996), and because it demonstrates that spoken words can be thought of as a sequence of sounds, such activities should be included in any phoneme-oriented training program, possibly before phoneme segmentation tasks are introduced (but after onset-rime segmentation).

One obvious issue that arises in suggesting that preschool and kindergarten children who are at risk for reading difficulties should first be taught to focus on onset and rime units, and only progress to phoneme sensitivity when onset-rime tasks are thoroughly mastered, is whether or not onset-rime training can itself promote understanding of the alphabetic principle. In this context, it may be noted that several of the early analogue training studies that are frequently cited as showing that phoneme sensitivity enhances reading skill, actually taught children to manipulate onsets and rimes (e.g., Fox and Routh 1984; Treiman and Baron 1983). Because it focused on teaching recognition of singleton onset identity, much of the experimental work of Byrne and Fielding-Barnsley (1989, 1990; see above) can be similarly interpreted.

Fox and Routh (1984) taught kindergarten children who had obtained low pretest scores on a phonological segmentation task to segment and blend onsets and rimes. At post-test, all children were first taught to associate sounds with five letter-like visual forms, representing three onsets and two rimes, and then were asked to read a set of six CVC words. Children who had been taught to segment and blend onsets and rimes performed better than a "no treatment" control group on this task; 80% were able to learn to "read" these words to criterion. The latter finding complements the work of Fox and Routh (1976). Relative to the control group, onset-rime blending training boosted 4-year olds' performance in a reading analogue task only if children were already proficient segmenters.

It is also arguable that some of the gains in subsequent reading shown by children given extensive Sound Foundations training are attributable to the intensive teaching of singleton onset identity (see above). In small-scale experimental studies, Byrne and Fielding-Barnsley (1989, 1990) found that it was equally easy to teach preschoolers individually to segment the first and last phonemes of CVC words, and that preschoolers generalized from singleton onsets to final phonemes. However, these results may not generalize. In their evaluation of Sound Foundations within normally developing preschoolers, the experimental and control groups both managed initial phonemes (corresponding to singleton onsets) much better than final phonemes at post-test (Byrne and Fielding-Barnsley 1991a).

It is not yet known whether onset-rime training generalizes to phoneme sensitivity tasks. This is unlikely to be so. Cary and Verhaeghe (1994) found that prereaders (mean age 5;5 years) from Portuguese kindergartens serving children from shanty towns who had been taught to segment and blend phonemes could also segment and blend syllables. However, children taught to segment and blend syllables could not segment and blend phonemes.

Although it may well be both useful and educationally appropriate to teach preschoolers at risk for later reading difficulties onset-rime sensitivity (especially in tasks involving singleton onsets), so that they learn to focus their attention on sound, as well as on meaning, it should not be assumed that this ability will generalize to phonemes without explicit phoneme sensitivity training, either within kindergarten or within first-grade reading instruction (Cunningham 1990; Lloyd 1998; see also Ehri 1979). It should also be noted that, although children who can recognize common singleton onsets may better acquire the rudiments of the alphabetic principle (Byrne and Fielding-Barnsley 1989), there is no secure evidence that reading instruction should be adjusted to focus on orthographic onset and rime units (see Bowey 1999).

REFERENCES

Aslin, R. N., and Smith, L. B. 1988. Perceptual development. *Annual Review of Psychology* 39:435–73.

Ball, E. W., and Blachman, B. 1988. Phoneme segmentation training: Effect on reading readiness. *Annals of Dyslexia* 38:208–25.

Ball, E. W., and Blachman, B. 1991. Does phoneme awareness training in kindergarten make a difference in early word recognition and developmental spelling. *Reading Research Quarterly* 26:49–66.

Ballinger, K. 1998. Evaluation of a pre-reading skills program designed to teach at-risk preschoolers phoneme awareness. Unpublished doctoral dissertation, LaTrobe University.

Blachman, B. A. 1997. Early intervention and phonological awareness: A cautionary tale. In *Foundations of Reading Acquisition and Dyslexia: Implications for Early Intervention*, ed. B. Blachman. Mahwah, NJ: Erlbaum.

Blachman, B. A., Ball, E. W., Black, R. S., and Tangel, D. M. 1994. Kindergarten teachers develop phoneme awareness in low-income, inner-city classrooms: Does it make a difference? *Reading and Writing* 6:1–18.

Bowey, J. A. 1988. *Metalinguistic Functioning in Children.* Geelong, Australia: Deakin University Press.

Bowey, J. A. 1994. Phonological sensitivity in novice readers and non-readers. *Journal of Experimental Child Psychology* 58:134–59.

Bowey, J. A. 1995a. Socioeconomic status differences in preschool phonological sensitivity and first-grade reading achievement. *Journal of Educational Psychology* 87:476–87.

Bowey, J. A. 1995b. On the contribution of phonological sensitivity to phonological recoding. *Issues in Education* 1:65–69.

Bowey, J. A. 1999. The limitations of orthographic rime analogies in beginners' word reading: A reply to Goswami (1999). *Journal of Experimental Child Psychology* 72:220–31.

Bowey, J. A. in preparation. Onset-rime and phoneme sensitivity as predictors of school entrants' subsequent reading achievement.

Bowey, J. A., and Francis, J. 1991. Phonological analysis as a function of age and exposure to reading instruction. *Applied Psycholinguistics* 12:91–121.

Bradley, L., and Bryant, P. E. 1983. Categorizing sounds and learning to read — A causal connection. *Nature* 301:419–21.

Brady, S. A. 1991. The role of working memory in reading disability. In *Phonological Processes in Literacy: A Tribute to Isabelle Y. Liberman,* eds. S. A. Brady and D. Shankweiler. Hillsdale, NJ: Erlbaum.

Brady, S., Fowler, A., Stone, B., and Winbury, N. 1994. Training phonological awareness: A study with inner-city kindergarten children. *Annals of Dyslexia* 44:26–59.

Brennan, F., and Ireson, J. 1997. Training phonological awareness: A study to evaluate the effects of a program of metalinguistic games in kindergarten. *Reading and Writing* 9:241–63.

Bryant, P. 1998. Sensitivity to onset and rhyme does predict young children's reading: A comment on Muter, Hulme, Snowling, and Taylor (1997). *Journal of Experimental Child Psychology* 71:29–37.

Bryant, P. E., MacLean, M., Bradley, L. L., and Crossland, J. 1990. Rhyme, alliteration, phoneme detection, and learning to read. *Developmental Psychology* 26:429–38.

Byrne, B. 1998. *The Foundation of Literacy: The Child's Acquisition of the Alphabetic Principle.* Hove, UK: Psychology Press.

Byrne, B., and Fielding-Barnsley, R. 1989. Phonemic awareness and letter knowledge in the child's acquisition of the alphabetic principle. *Journal of Educational Psychology* 81:313–21.

Byrne, B., and Fielding-Barnsley, R. 1990. Acquiring the alphabetic principle: A case for teaching the recognition of phoneme identity. *Journal of Educational Psychology* 82:805–12.

Byrne, B., and Fielding-Barnsley, R. 1991a. Evaluation of a program to teach phonemic awareness to young children. *Journal of Educational Psychology* 83:451–55.

Byrne, B., and Fielding-Barnsley, R. 1991b. *Sound Foundations.* Artamon, Australia: Leyden.

Byrne, B., and Fielding-Barnsley, R. 1993. Evaluation of a program to teach phonemic awareness to young children: A 1-year follow-up. *Journal of Educational Psychology* 85:104–11.

Byrne, B., and Fielding-Barnsley, R. 1995. Evaluation of a program to teach phonemic awareness to young children: A 2- and 3-year follow-up and a new preschool trial. *Journal of Educational Psychology* 87:488–503.

Byrne, B., Fielding-Barnsley, R., Ashley, L., and Larsen, K. 1997. Assessing the child's and the environment's contribution to reading acquisition: What we do know and what we don't know. In *Foundations of Reading Acquisition and Dyslexia: Implications for Early Intervention*, ed. B. Blachman. Mahwah, NJ: Erlbaum.

Cary, L., and Verhaeghe, A. 1994. Promoting phonemic analysis ability among kindergartners: Effects of different training programs. *Reading and Writing* 6:251–78.

Charles-Luce, J., and Luce, P. A. 1990. Similarity neighborhoods of words in young children's lexicons. *Journal of Child Language* 17:205–15.

Cunningham, A. E. 1990. Explicit versus implicit instruction in phonemic awareness. *Journal of Experimental Child Psychology* 50:429–44.

Dunn, L. M., and Dunn, L. M. 1981. *Peabody Picture Vocabulary Test — Revised* (3rd ed.). Circle Pines, MN: American Guidance Service.

Ehri, L. C. 1979. Linguistic insight: Threshold of reading acquisition. In *Reading Research Revisited*, eds. T. G. Waller and G. E. MacKinnon. Columbia, OH: Merrill.

Ehri, L. C. 1983. A critique of five studies related to letter-name knowledge and learning to read. In *Reading Research: Advances in Theory and Practice*, eds. L. M. Gentile, M. L. Kamil, and J. Blanchard. New York: Academic Press.

Ehri, L. C., and Wilce, L. S. 1985. Movement into reading: Is the first stage of printed word learning visual or phonetic? *Reading Research Quarterly* 20:163–79.

Fowler, A. E. 1991. How early phonological development might set the stage for phonemic awareness. In *Phonological Processes in Literacy: A Tribute to Isabelle Y. Liberman*, eds. S. A. Brady and D. Shankweiler. Hillsdale, NJ: Erlbaum.

Fox, B., and Routh, D. K. 1976. Phonemic analysis and synthesis as word attack skills. *Journal of Educational Psychology* 68:70–74.

Fox, B., and Routh, D. K. 1984. Phonemic analysis and synthesis as word attack skills: Revisited. *Journal of Educational Psychology* 76:1059–64.

Haddock, M.1976. Effects of an auditory and an auditory-visual method of blending instruction on the ability of prereaders to decode synthetic words. *Journal of Educational Psychology* 68:825–31.

Hohn, W. E., and Ehri, L. C. 1983. Do alphabet letters help prereaders acquire phonemic segmentation skill? *Journal of Educational Psychology* 75:752–62.

Hurford, D. P. 1990. Training phonemic segmentation ability with a phoneme discrimination intervention in second- and third-grade children with reading disabilities. *Journal of Learning Disabilities* 23:564–69.

Kirtley, C., Bryant, P. E., MacLean, M. J., and Bradley, L. L. 1989. Rhyme, rime and the onset of reading. *Journal of Experimental Child Psychology* 48:224–45.

Lewkowicz, N. 1980. Phonemic awareness training: What to teach and how to teach it. *Journal of Educational Psychology* 72:686–700.

Liberman, I. Y., and Liberman, A. M. 1990. Whole language versus code emphasis: Underlying assumptions and their implications of reading instruction. *Annals of Dyslexia* 40:51–76.

Liberman, I. Y., Shankweiler, D., Fischer, F. W., and Carter, B. 1974. Explicit syllable and phoneme segmentation in the young child. *Journal of Experimental Child Psychology* 18:201–12.

Liberman, I. Y., Shankweiler, D., Liberman, A. M., Fowler, C., and Fischer, F. W. 1977. Phonetic segmentation and recoding in the beginning reader. In *Toward a Psychology of Reading*, eds. A. S. Reber and D. L. Scarborough. New York: Wiley.

Lloyd, S. 1992. *The Phonics Handbook*. Chigwell: England: Jolly Learning.

Lloyd, S. 1998. *The Phonics Handbook*. (3rd ed.). Chigwell: England: Jolly Learning.

Lukatela, K., Carello, Shankweiler, D., and Liberman, I. Y. 1995. Phonological awareness in illiterates: Observations from Serbo-Croatian. *Applied Psycholinguistics* 16:463–87.

Lundberg, I. 1988 . Preschool prevention of reading failure: Does training in phonological awareness work? In *Preschool Prevention of Reading Failure*, eds. R. L. Masland and M. W. Masland. Parkton, MD: York Press.

Lundberg, I., Frost, J., and Peterson, O. -P. 1988. Effects of an extensive program for stimulating phonological awareness in children. *Reading Research Quarterly* 23:263–84.

MacLean, M., Bryant, P., and Bradley, L. 1987. Rhymes, nursery rhymes, and reading in early childhood. *Merrill-Palmer Quarterly* 33:255–81.

Marsh, G., and Mineo, R. J. 1977. Training preschool children to recognize phonemes in words. *Journal of Educational Psychology* 69:748–53.

Mattingly, I. G. 1991. Modularity, working memory, and reading disability. In *Phonological Processes in Literacy: A Tribute to Isabelle Y. Liberman*, eds. S. A. Brady and D. Shankweiler. Hillsdale, NJ: Erlbaum.

Menyuk, P., and Menn, L. 1979. Early strategies for the perception and production of words and sounds. In *Language Acquisition*, eds. P. Fletcher and M. Garman. Cambridge, England: Cambridge University Press.

Metsala, J. L. 1997. An examination of word frequency and neighborhood density in the development of spoken word recognition. *Memory & Cognition* 25: 47–56.

Metsala, J. L. in press. Young children's phonological awareness and nonword repetition as a function of vocabulary development. *Journal of Educational Psychology*.

Metsala, J. L., and Walley, A. C. 1998. Spoken vocabulary growth and the segmental restructuring of lexical representations: Precursors to phonemic awareness and early reading ability. In *Word Recognition in Beginning Literacy*, eds. J. L. Metsala and L. C. Ehri. Mahwah, NJ: Erlbaum.

Morais, J. 1990. Phonological awareness: A bridge between language and literacy. In *Phonological Awareness in Reading*, eds. D. J. Sawyer and B. J. Fox. New York: Springer-Verlag.

Morais, J., Bertelson, P., Cary, L., and Alegria, J. 1986. Literacy training and speech segmentation. *Cognition* 24:45–64.

Morais, J., Cary, L., Alegria, J., and Bertelson, P. 1979. Does awareness of speech as a series of phones arise spontaneously? *Cognition* 7:323–31.

Morgan, J., and Willows, D. 1996. Early phonological awareness training for at-risk children in junior kindergarten. Paper presented at the National Reading Conference, Charleston, SC, December.

Muter, V., Hulme, C., Snowling, M., and Taylor, S. 1997. Segmentation, not rhyming, predicts early progress in learning to read. *Journal of Experimental Child Psychology* 65:370–96.

O'Connor, R. E., Jenkins, J. R., and Slocum, T. A. 1995. Transfer among phonological tasks in kindergarten: Essential instructional content. *Journal of Educational Psychology* 87:202–17.

Pisoni, D. B., and Luce, P. A. 1987. Acoustic-phonetic representations in word recognition. *Cognition* 25:21–52.

Read, C., Zhang, Y. -N., Nie, H. -Y., and Ding, B. -Q. 1986. The ability to manipulate speech sounds depends on knowing alphabetic writing. *Cognition* 24:31–44.

Rosner, J., and Simon, D. P. 1971. The auditory analysis test: An initial report. *Journal of Learning Disabilities* 4:384–92.

Scott, J. A., and Ehri, L. C. 1990. Sight word reading in prereaders: Use of logographic vs. alphabetic access routes. *Journal of Reading Behavior* 22:149–66.

Seymour, P. H. K., and Elder, L. 1986. Beginning reading without phonology. *Cognitive Neuropsychology* 3:1–56.

Share, D. L. 1995. Phonological recoding and self-teaching: *Sine qua non* of reading acquisition. *Cognition* 5:151–218.

Stanovich, K. E. 1992. Speculations on the causes and consequences of individual differences in early reading acquisition. In *Reading Acquisition*, eds. P. Gough, L. Ehri, and R. Treiman. Hillsdale, NJ: Erlbaum.

Stanovich, K. E., Cunningham, A. E., and Cramer, B. B. 1984. Assessing phonological awareness in kindergarten children: Issues of task comparability. *Journal of Experimental Child Psychology* 38:175–90.

Studdert-Kennedy, M. 1987. The phoneme as a perceptuomotor structure. In *Language Perception and Production*, eds. A. Allport, D. MacKay, W. Prinz, and E. Scheerer. London: Academic Press.

Sumbler, K., and Willows, D. 1996. Phonological awareness and alphabetic coding instruction within balanced senior kindergartens. Paper presented at National Reading Conference, Charleston, SC, December.

Tangel, D. M., and Blachman, B. A. 1992. Effect of phoneme awareness instruction on kindergarten children's invented spelling. *Journal of Reading Behavior* 24:233–61.

Torgesen, J. K., and Davis, C. 1996. Individual differences variables that predict response to training in phonological awareness. *Journal of Experimental Child Psychology* 63:1–21.

Torgesen, J. K., Morgan, S. T., and Davis, C. 1992. Effects of two types of phonological awareness training on word learning in kindergarten children. *Journal of Educational Psychology* 84:364–70.

Treiman, R., and Baron, J. 1983. Phonemic-analysis training helps children benefit from spelling-sound rules. *Memory & Cognition* 11:382–89.

Treiman, R., and Rodriguez, K. in press. Young children use letter names in learning to read words. *Psychological Science*.

Treiman, R., Tincoff, R., Richmond-Welty, E. D. 1996. Letter names help children to connect print and speech. *Developmental Psychology* 32:505–14.

Treiman, R., Weatherstone, S., and Berch, D. 1994. The role of letter names in children's learning of phoneme-grapheme relations. *Applied Psycholinguistics* 15:97–122.

Treiman, R., and Zukowski, A. 1996. Children's sensitivity to syllables, onsets, rimes, and phonemes. *Journal of Experimental Child Psychology* 61:193–215.

Vellutino, F. R., and Scanlon, D. M. 1987. Phonological coding, phonological awareness, and reading ability: Evidence from a longitudinal and experimental study. *Merrill-Palmer Quarterly* 33:321–63.

Wagner, R. K., Torgesen, J. K., and Rashotte, C. A. 1994. Development of reading-related phonological processing abilities: New evidence of bidirectional causality from a latent variable longitudinal study. *Developmental Psychology* 30:73–87.

Wagner, R. K., Torgesen, J. K., Rashotte, C. A., Hecht, S. A., Barker, T. A., Burgess, S. R., Donahue, J., and Garon, T. 1997. Changing relations between phonological processing abilities and word-level reading as children develop from beginning to skilled readers: A 5-year longitudinal study. *Developmental Psychology* 33:468–79.

Wallach, L., Wallach, M. A., Dozier, M. G., and Kaplan, N. E. 1977. Poor children learning to read do not have trouble with auditory discrimination but do have trouble with phoneme recognition. *Journal of Educational Psychology* 69:36–39.

Walley, A. C. 1993. The role of vocabulary development in children's spoken word recognition and segmentation ability. *Developmental Review* 13:286–350.

Webster, P. E., and Plante, A. S. 1995. Productive phonology and phonological awareness in preschool children. *Applied Psycholinguistics* 16:43–57.

Whitehurst, G. J., Epstein, J. N., Angell, A. L., Payne, A. C., Crone, D. A., and Fischel, J. E. G. 1994. Outcomes of an emergent literacy intervention in Head Start. *Journal of Educational Psychology* 86:542–55.

Woodcock, R. W. 1987. *Woodcock Reading Mastery Tests — Revised.* Circle Pines, MN: American Guidance Service.

Chapter • **10**

What Do You Get if You Add /mmm/ to Ice? Training Phoneme Awareness in Kindergarten: *An Intervention Study with Children of Dyslexic Parents*

For some children, learning to read becomes a life-long struggle, and there is no obvious explanation for their problems. They do not have severe attention deficits, problems in the primary sensory apparatus, or more global language problems. These children suffer from developmental dyslexia, and they are not good at using the alphabetic nature of the writing system. In alphabetic writing systems, the main principle is that each phoneme is represented by a grapheme, and that the phoneme is represented by the same grapheme each time it occurs. In these writing systems, unknown words can be read by giving each letter a sound. This process is called phonological coding and lack of this ability is the core difficulty in dyslexia (cf. Rack, Snowling, and Olson 1992). Children with dyslexia have difficulties when reading words they have not seen before because they cannot use the phonological coding strategy.

During the last decades, several studies have tried to find the main causes of poor phonological coding. Some of these were longitudinal studies in which the children were followed from before initial reading instruction until they had received reading instruction for at least one or two years (cf. Scarborough 1989, 1990). The main aim of these longitudinal studies was to find the language measures that were the best predictors of reading development, but these can only be assessed if some of the children in the study have difficulties in learning to read. Dyslexia runs in families. If a child has a dyslexic parent, the risk of becoming reading disabled is increased by a factor of four or higher compared with children of normally reading parents (Gilger, Pennington, and Defries 1991). Therefore, one way to follow a group of children who are at risk of having reading difficulties is to follow children who have at least one parent with dyslexia.

Scarborough was the first to report on a longitudinal study with children of dyslexic parents (Scarborough 1989, 1990). In her study, the children were followed from the age of 30 months until second grade. Scarborough found differences between the children who became dyslexic at 30 months of age and children who became good readers (Scarborough 1990). The children who became dyslexic made more pronunciation errors and produced shorter and syntactically less complex utterances. At the age of five, the children who became dyslexic performed less well on phoneme awareness, letter knowledge, and vocabulary. In many longitudinal studies, phoneme awareness and letter knowledge have been shown to be very strong predictors of future reading development (cf., Scarborough 1998, and Elbro 1996).

PHONEME AWARENESS AND READING DEVELOPMENT

One of the most important causes of phonological coding difficulties (cf. Lyon 1995, and Rack, Snowling, and Olson 1992) is the lack of awareness of the phoneme-sized segments in speech (cf. Elbro 1996, and Scarborough 1998 for a review).

In this chapter, the term *phonological awareness* is used to describe a child's ability to shift attention from the meaning of a word to the phonological form of a word (Tornéus 1987). For example, a phonological awareness task could be comparing the length of two words, counting syllables in a word, finding words that rhyme, or finding words that have the same initial sound. *Phoneme awareness*, on the other hand, is the ability to identify and manipulate segments of phoneme size. Although phonological awareness is developed at the age of three or four, long before learning to read (Bryant, Maclean, and Bradley 1990), phoneme awareness usually develops as the result of language games in kindergarten or of initial reading instruction (Bowey and Francis 1991).

Initial reading instruction is an efficient way to train children's phoneme awareness. During the first year of reading instruction, children's phoneme awareness increases more than during the kindergarten year (Bowey and Francis 1991). On the other hand, children who have poor phoneme awareness at the beginning of reading instruction are at risk of developing reading difficulties (Wagner, Torgesen, and Rashotte 1994). Poor phoneme awareness seems to be a core difficulty in dyslexia and it does not disappear as children grow and learn to read. A study with reading disabled adults found that these adults had poor phoneme awareness compared with normal readers at the same reading level on a sentence reading task (Elbro, Nielsen, and Petersen 1994).

These studies indicate that a certain degree of phoneme awareness is necessary in order to learn to read. A number of training studies have been conducted to see if reading difficulties can be prevented by giving children special training during the year in kindergarten. Most of these studies were with unselected children (e.g., Lundberg, Frost, and Petersen 1988 or Ball and Blachman 1991). These studies showed that children's phoneme awareness could be improved during training in kindergarten and that there was a positive effect on their later reading ability.

Studies Comparing Different Ways to Train Children in Phoneme Awareness

Because several studies with unselected children have shown that phoneme awareness and reading level can be improved, the next step was to find the most efficient way to improve children's phoneme awareness and, through that, their reading level. Therefore, several studies were carried out in which different training programs were compared. One of the main topics was whether letters ought to be included in the training program. Bradley and Bryant (1985) compared two different training programs, one that included letters and one that did not. One training program introduced the phonemes and letters simultaneously and the other program introduced only the phonemes. Children who received training that included both letters and phonemes made better gains in reading than did children who received training that included only phonemes.

Cary and Verhaeghe (1994) did a longitudinal study in which they compared two different training programs. The purpose of their study was to compare the training effect on children's phoneme awareness when training focused on different linguistic units. The first program included training in phonemes and the second program included training in syllables. They then compared the progress of the two groups of children in phoneme awareness. The children who had received training that included phonemes showed progress in phonemic analysis ability. The children who had received training in syllables did not show any progress in phonemic analysis ability. Nevertheless, both groups of children showed progress in syllabic analysis. So the group trained with phonemes generalized their awareness to supra-phoneme units, while the group trained with syllables could not generalize their syllabic awareness to the phoneme level. Cary and Verhaeghe's study indicates that it is not possible to improve children's phoneme awareness by training units other than phonemes.

Schneider et al. (1997) replicated the study of Lundberg, Frost, and Petersen (1988) with German children. Their study with children in Munich showed that it is important that phoneme awareness training be consistent. A total of 22 different classes were trained in phoneme awareness. Only nine of the classes were trained consistently. The other 13 did not spend as much time as necessary on the program and did not finish the program. The consistently trained group outperformed the control group on four out of six measures of phoneme awareness at the end of kindergarten. The consistently trained children also outperformed the control group on measures of reading and spelling at the end of first grade. The inconsistently trained group did not perform better than the control group on phoneme awareness at the end of kindergarten or on measures of reading and spelling at the end of first grade. The results from this study show that it is important to spend the necessary time on phoneme awareness training and to ensure that the phoneme awareness training is consistent.

Phoneme Awareness Training in At-risk Children or Children with Reading Disabilities

The training studies described in the last section involved unselected children. But what about children with reading difficulties and children at risk of having reading difficulties? Do they also profit from phoneme awareness training?

Age is important to the success of phoneme awareness training. Olson et al. (1997) trained older children with reading disabilities in phoneme awareness. The children's phoneme awareness improved and they were better non-word readers. But it had no effect on the children's reading of real words or on reading comprehension. This lack of transfer tells us that it is difficult to change bad habits and that prevention is easier than cure.

Training studies with unselected kindergarten children have generally been fairly successful (see, for example, Lundberg, Frost, and Petersen 1988, and Ball and Blachmann 1991). The children taking part in these studies became better readers than the children in the control groups. But what about the children who have very poor phoneme awareness at the beginning of kindergarten? Do they also profit from phoneme awareness training? In Torgesen, Wagner, and Rashotte's study (1994), 60 children with low phoneme awareness were given a 12-week training program in phoneme awareness. Training was given to the children in small groups of three or four. There was a positive effect of the training. The trained group outperformed a control group (40 children with low phoneme awareness) on a segmentation task. However, the children's skills in the trained group varied greatly and about 30% of the children got very poor scores on the segmentation task.

So far, Byrne et al. (1997) have been the only researchers to report a training study with children of dyslexic parents. In Byrne's study, the training program by Byrne and Fielding-Barnsley (1991) was used. The children of dyslexic parents were trained in small groups (from one to six children) and the training lasted for about 40 minutes per week for 16 to 20 weeks. A group of children of normally reading parents was given the same training. In both of the trained groups there was significant improvement in phoneme awareness. However, 32% of the children of dyslexic parents showed no progress in phoneme awareness, while this was the case for only 5% of the random-sample children of normally reading parents. At the moment, no results about the children's reading and spelling have been published in Byrne's study, so it is too early to say whether there will be the same differences in the children's reading and spelling as in their phoneme awareness. But Byrne's and Torgesen's training studies show that it is more difficult to improve at-risk children's phoneme awareness than that of unselected children.

What Is Important for the Development of Phoneme Awareness?

Recently, some studies have tried to discover language abilities that are important for the development of phoneme awareness.

Several researchers have hypothesized that the quality of the phonological representations in the mental lexicon is of great importance for the development of phonological awareness (cf. Elbro 1996; Fowler 1991; or Swan and Goswami 1997). However, the researchers disagree about in what way the phonological representation of the children with poor phoneme awareness is inadequate (Elbro 1996). Together with Borstrøm and Elbro, I have previously suggested that the phonological representations of children with poor phoneme awareness might be inadequate because they are indistinct. For instance, [teləviʒən] is more distinct than[teliʒən]. If phonological representations are stored and retrieved in an indistinct manner, it may be relatively difficult to perform phonological operations on these representations. For further description and discussion of this hypothesis see Elbro (1996). A special test was designed to measure the distinctness of the children's phonological representations.

THE COPENHAGEN DYSLEXIA STUDY

Aims of the Study

The Copenhagen Dyslexia Study followed children of dyslexic and normally reading parents from the beginning of kindergarten until third grade. The study was a combined prediction and intervention study.

The aim of the prediction part of the study was to assess the relative strengths of linguistic predictors of dyslexia. The study included several language measures that have previously been found to be very strong and independent predictors of dyslexia, together with a new measure of the distinctness of the phonological representations.

The aim of the intervention part of the study was to see if children, even children of dyslexic parents, could be trained in phoneme awareness during kindergarten, and whether such training might facilitate initial reading development. Our hypothesis was that the phoneme awareness training would reduce the incidence of dyslexia in the group of children of dyslexic parents. The main focus here will be the intervention part of the study.

Method

Subjects.   Subjects for this study were children of dyslexic and normally reading parents. The children started kindergarten in August 1993 or August 1994. In Denmark, children begin kindergarten at the age of six, but reading instruction does not start until first grade when most of the children have reached the age of seven. This fact makes it possible to test language abilities of children before initial reading instruction and to do an intervention study in kindergarten with children who have not yet had any reading instruction.

Our first step was to recruit children of dyslexic parents. We used many different channels in our recruitment. We made public announcements in newspapers, on the radio, and on television. We also contacted teachers who taught adults with dyslexia, as well as speech and reading consultants in the greater Copenhagen area. We spent six months recruiting families for the study. Our first contacts with the families were telephone interviews with parents with reading difficulties.

Parents were asked about the nature of their reading disabilities. An appointment for a home interview was made if they had difficulties that had lasted for more than a year, consisted of more than low reading speed, and had been identified by an adult (teacher or parent). These were the same criteria as those used by Scarborough (1990).

In a home interview, parents were asked about their own reading habits and their reading habits in connection with their child. The home interview also included different tests of the parents' reading abilities (for a further description see Elbro, Nielsen, and Petersen 1994). There were two measures of phonological recoding in the adult test battery. One measure was the reading of non-words and the other was the reading of pseudo-homophones, like the one Olson first used (Olson 1985). A composite score was derived from the scores of the two phonological coding tests, and, to be included in the study as a dyslexic parent, the average composite score had to be at least one standard deviation lower than the mean score of normally reading parents. So to be included as a dyslexic parent in the study, parents had to have a history of reading difficulties and poor performance on the phonological coding tests.

It was not difficult to recruit the children of normally reading parents. We contacted six different schools in the greater Copenhagen area and they all wanted to participate in the project. All the parents were interviewed by telephone and those who reported reading difficulties were tested in their homes. If they turned out to have reading difficulties, their children were included in the group of children of dyslexic parents. If there was a mismatch between the parents' self-reported reading history and the objective findings, the family was excluded from the project. The families were also excluded from the study if the affected parent scored below the 10th percentile on a vocabulary test, indicating a more global language problem.

Children were excluded from both groups if Danish was not their first language, if two or more languages were spoken in their homes, or if the child already showed signs of general learning or language disabilities before kindergarten.

A total of 154 children remained in the study from before kindergarten until the end of second grade. In all, 93 of the children started kindergarten in 1993, and 61 started kindergarten in 1994. There were 88 children of dyslexic parents and 66 children of normally reading parents.

The children were tested every summer. The first time was just before they started kindergarten, and the last time was at the beginning of the third grade. For practical reasons, the children of dyslexic parents were tested in their homes while the children of normally reading parents were tested at their respective schools. The testing lasted somewhere between one and three hours with breaks whenever the child needed them.

The Intervention Study of the Copenhagen Dyslexia Project

When Danish children start kindergarten at the age of 6, they cannot read. The kindergarten teacher is not supposed to teach children any academic skills. So Danish children spend their first year at school without any formal reading instruction. These factors make Danish kindergartens well suited for intervention studies such as ours. Lundberg, Frost, and Petersen's intervention study (1988) has made kindergarten teachers aware of the importance of improving children's linguistic awareness. Nursery rhymes and syllable games are often played in Danish kindergartens. However, when it comes to developing the children's phoneme awareness, many kindergarten teachers said that they did not play such games. We interviewed the kindergarten teachers in this study. A total of 77 teachers were interviewed, and 73 said that they played with rhymes in their classes. Only 37 of them said that they included activities with segments of phoneme size and only 25 said that they included written letters in their language games.

This intervention study included four groups of children. A group of 51 of the children of dyslexic parents followed the usual training in their kindergartens while 36 children of dyslexic parents were given our phoneme awareness training. The children of normally reading parents were also divided into two groups, 53 children who followed the usual training in their kindergartens and 19 children who were given our phoneme awareness training.

The children of dyslexic parents came from many different classrooms (71 different classes) and the children of normally reading parents came from six different classrooms. The two control groups (children of dyslexic and normally reading parents who followed the usual training in their kindergarten) received the usual training in linguistic awareness.

The two experimental groups received our phoneme awareness training program. The regular kindergarten teacher administered the training program, which lasted for 17 weeks. The children's phoneme awareness and other language abilities were tested at the beginning and the end of the training period and the children's reading level was assessed at the beginning of second and third grade (for further details see Borstrøm and Elbro 1997).

The Training Program in the Copenhagen Dyslexia Project

The phoneme-training program was specially designed for this study (Borstrøm and Petersen 1996). Our aim was to design a program that met the needs of the children with poor language abilities, because our target group was children of dyslexic parents. Therefore, our main criteria when designing the program were that the method should be as effective as possible and focus on the speech units that were particularly crucial for reading acquisition. The program focuses on phonemes from the very beginning, but at a very slow rate of presentation and with much repetition during the 17 weeks. Vowels are introduced in the first two weeks and then the program focuses on consonants and introduces two new consonants every week. Consonants that are introduced during the same week differ as much as possible in how they sound and how they are articulated. Every other week is a repetition week. Each consonant sound is introduced in many different ways in order to give the children as many "hooks" for each sound as possible.

Each sound is first introduced by a nursery rhyme with many words that begin with the sound. Then the teacher and the children discuss what the sound sounds like ([fff] like a wind blowing) and the letter name is introduced while the letter is being written on the blackboard. Then the children find names and other words that begin with the sound. The program also includes articulatory awareness and the children are instructed in how to describe the articulation of the speech sounds. The articulatory awareness instruction was inspired by Lindamood (Lindamood and Lindamood

1975) and, as they did in the Lindamood program, we used pictures of what the mouth looks like when articulating the different sounds.

The main idea of the training is to make the children aware of phonemes by means of minimal pairs. The minimal pairs used in the program are pairs in which the words share rime parts but have different onsets (for example m-ice and n-ice). The words are not written for the children. The teacher draws a box on the blackboard and tells the children that this box means [eil]. Then the teacher adds an initial [m] to get mail. The letter m is written in front of the box. Then the second sound [s] of the week is added to the non-word to get sail. The teacher and the children discuss in what way sail and mail are alike and in what way they differ. By means of words that rhyme the children become aware of the phonemes. There are four different levels of these onset and rime exercises (for further descriptions of the program see Borstrøm and Elbro 1997).

The training program consisted of 17 weeks training for half-an-hour a day. The children were not instructed in small groups as Byrne et al. (1997) and Torgesen, Wagner, and Rashotte (1994) did. The children were instructed in their classroom together with their classmates. This is more in line with the Danish tradition of teaching, but the risk was that it would be less efficient. The children were taught by the kindergarten teachers. The kindergarten teachers were given a 15-hour course in phonetics and phonology at the University of Copenhagen before using the program.

Measures at the Beginning of Kindergarten and at the Beginning of the First Grade

The children were tested with a number of different measures at the beginning of kindergarten and first grade. Not all the measures are described here (for further description of all the measures see Elbro et al. 1998).

Vocabulary. We measured the children's receptive vocabulary using a Danish version of Peabody Picture Vocabulary Test (Dunn and Dunn 1981)

Non-verbal intelligence. The children's non-verbal intelligence was measured by Raven's colored matrices (Raven 1959).

Picture-naming accuracy and speed. The purpose of this task was to see how quickly the children could retrieve the phonological representations of lexical items. This task was a simple naming task with pictures from children's lotto. The pictures are presented in triads of items from the same semantic field to avoid choices of less specific names than intended, for example, "box, box, box" instead of "box, suitcase, basket." There were 6 practice items and 30 test items. The child was asked to name the pictures as quickly and accurately as possible. The score used is a combined accuracy and speed score (number of correctly named pictures per minute).

Verbal short-term memory. As a measure of phonological short-term memory, we used the digit span from the WISC-R (Weschler 1974). We made an extra easy level with two digits because we were afraid that the three-digit level would be too difficult for some children. This means that the scores cannot be compared directly with those from other studies because of the extra level.

Letter naming. A child was shown all the 29 Danish letters and asked to name them one by one. If a child at the beginning of kindergarten knew more than six letters, the child was asked to read some words from a short version of a frequently used Danish word decoding test (OS 400, Søegård and Petersen 1974).

Phonological awareness. There were five different measures of phoneme awareness. In three of them, the child was asked to delete the first part of a word. This test was inspired by Catts (1991). In the first deletion task, a child was asked to delete the first morpheme in six compound words with two free morphemes. In the second deletion task, the child was asked to delete the first syllable (or the first two syllables) in six different words with two or three syllables. In the third deletion task, the child was asked to say what was left if the first sound was removed from a word. There were nine items in this part of the test.

The other kind of phoneme awareness test was an identification test with two different tasks. In the first part of the identification test, the child was asked to find a word (among six pictures) that started with a certain syllable. There were eight items in this task. In the second part of the test, the child was asked to identify words by an initial phoneme instead of a syllable. There were eight items in this task.

Phoneme discrimination. This task is a modification of a phoneme discrimination test, the BKS-test, often used by speech therapists (Kjær 1977). The child was asked to discriminate between minimal pairs (words that differ by a single phoneme) such as *hat* and *cat*. A modified version with background noise was used in this study (the background noise was 12 female voices speaking simultaneously). The words are tape-recorded and played to the child. There were 34 different word pairs.

The distinctness of the phonological representations. The
purpose of this task was to get information about the phonological
representations of the children. The test was designed to obtain a
child's most distinct pronunciation of a word. This was done by
means of a hand-held puppet that did not pronounce words very
well, and the child was supposed to teach the puppet the most distinct pronunciation of a word. The experimenter pronounced the
words at a very low level of distinctness on behalf of the puppet
and the child was asked to tell the puppet how this word was pronounced as clearly and precisely as possible. For example the
Danish word *lokomotiv* ("locomotive") was pronounced [lo'ti'w] by
the puppet. The puppet was a slow learner, so the child had to repeat the word, and following the child's second attempt, the experimenter pronounced the word the way the child had said it
and asked the child if this was the correct way to pronounce the
word. When the child accepted the pronunciation, the experimenter always gave feed-back in the form of the most distinct
variant. There were nine words in this test and the children obtained a distinctness score, which was a measure of how much
they tended to use indistinct forms of the words. The most distinct form of *lokomotiv* would be [lokomo'ti'w] and a correct but
more indistinct pronunciation, for example, could be [logmo'ti'w].
The children also got a pronunciation accuracy score that was a
measure of how many of the words the child pronounced correctly.
If the child, for example, said [lobə'ti'w] instead of [logmo'ti'w]
then the child's answer is not indistinct, it is a pronunciation error
(The items on which the children made pronunciation errors were
not included in the distinctness score). An answer was categorized
as a pronunciation error if this pronunciation of the word could
not be found listed in *Den Store Danske Udtaleordbog* (*The Great
Danish Pronunciation Dictionary*, Brink et al. 1991).

Family background. We have information about the parents' education, job, reading habits, reported reading difficulties,
reported reading to the child, and other issues (see Elbro, Nielsen,
and Petersen 1994). Here the only background variable used is
dyslexia in the family. Elbro, Nielsen, and Petersen have previously described the other background factors and their influence
on the children's reading development (Elbro, Nielsen, and
Petersen 1998).

Measures at the Beginning of Second and Third Grade

At the beginning of second and third grade there were also various
measures of the children's language abilities, but the focus here is

on the various measures of decoding and a measure of the children's spelling ability that were used on the two occasions.

Oral non-word reading.   The child was asked to read aloud a list of 30 non-words. Corrective feed-back was given on the practice items. The 30 test words were presented on three different pages. The task was interrupted if the child did not read any non-words correctly on the current page or if the child failed to read any practice items correctly. The score was the number of correctly read non-words. The non-words were matched with the words in the oral word-reading test.

Identification of pseudo-homophones.   In the case of the pseudo-homophone identification test, the child was asked to decide which of four non-words might sound like a real word if it was pronounced. This test was a silent reading task and consisted of 48 items. There was a picture for every group of four words. The picture illustrated the word for which the correct non-word was a pseudo-homophone. We used a child's score on this task and on the oral non-word reading task to form a composite phonological coding score. The composite score was obtained by adding half the standardized scores from each of the two reading tests.

Oral word-reading.   A child was asked to read aloud a list of 30 words (these words were matched on length, syllable structure, and complexity with the non-word in the oral non-word reading). Corrections were made on the practice items. The 30 test words were presented on three different pages. The task was interrupted if the child did not read any words correctly on the current page or if the child failed to read any practice items correctly. The score was the number of correctly read words.

Silent word-reading.   This test was a silent reading test in which the child was to find a picture that matched a word among four different pictures. There were 400 items in this test and the child was to read as many as possible in 10 minutes. This test is a frequently used Danish word-decoding test (OS 400, Søegård and Petersen 1974).

Reading with the same rime.   This reading measure was included in the test battery only at the beginning of the second grade. In this test, the experimenter read a word aloud and then the child was to read two words that shared a rime with the example word. There were 22 items in this test with 11 different rimes.

Spelling.   The spelling test was included as a measure only at the beginning of third grade. The children were to spell 24 different words. The test was divided into three different levels of difficulty and the testing was stopped if a child did not spell any word correctly at the current level of difficulty.

Results

Some of the analyses have been previously published (Elbro, Borstrøm, and Petersen 1998 and Borstrøm and Elbro 1997). This chapter presents data from the third grade and reading measures other than the two phonological coding measures, and comparisons between the children with poor phoneme awareness who benefit from training and the "hard core" (children with poor phoneme awareness who do not benefit from training).

Do children of dyslexic and normally reading parents differ in preschool abilities? When comparing two groups of children, it is important that the two groups match on age. If one of the groups has older children, then some of the other differences could be due to age. The mean ages of the children of dyslexic and normally reading parents were 6 years and 1 month (SD 0.75) and 6 years and 3 months (SD 0.31) respectively. This difference was not statistically significant. The average non-verbal IQ-scores (measured by Raven's colored matrices, Raven 1959) were close to the 70th percentile for both groups and not statistically significantly different in the two groups.

It is also relevant, when comparing the initial reading development of two groups of children, to compare their language abilities before reading instruction. Our hypothesis was that the children of dyslexic parents had poorer language abilities than children of normally reading parents.

On the measure of receptive vocabulary, the scores of children of dyslexic parents was significantly lower than that of children of normally reading parents (mean 67.01, SD 6.96 and mean 69.58, SD 8.95, $F(1,150) = 6.9$, $p < 0{,}05$). This result was the same as in Scarborough's study (Scarborough 1990).

Children of dyslexic parents were also poorer at letter naming ($F(1,150) = 9.5$, $p < 0.01$), and phonological short-term memory ($F(1,150) = 13.3$, $p < 0.001$). The scores of the children of dyslexic parents were also significantly lower on all the five measures of phoneme awareness.

The children of dyslexic parents also performed less well on two measures of basic language abilities. The first task was the phonological discrimination task ($F(1,150) = 9.5$, $p < 0.001$) and the other was the measure of the phonological representations on which the children of dyslexic parents were less distinct in their pronunciation of the words in the test ($F(1,150) = 13.3, p < 0.001$) and made more pronunciation errors ($F(1,150) = 9.2, p < 0.01$).

The children of dyslexic parents have poorer language abilities than children of normally reading parents. They differ on tasks such as letter naming, short-term memory, and phoneme awareness. Other studies have found these abilities to be important predictors of reading development (see, for example, Wagner and Torgesen 1987).

Because of the poorer language abilities at the beginning of kindergarten, we expected that a greater percentage of the children of dyslexic parents would have difficulties in learning to read. We expected the children of dyslexic parents would have particular difficulties in phonological coding. But we hoped that our 17 weeks of phoneme awareness training in kindergarten could improve the children's phoneme awareness and reduce the incidence of dyslexia in the trained groups.

Effects of training on the children's language abilities. There were four different groups of children in the study: two experimental groups, one with children of dyslexic parents and one with children of normally reading parents, and two control groups, one with children of dyslexic parents and one with children of normally reading parents. The children were tested with the measures of language abilities before and after the training period.

We expected to see effects of training on the measures of letter knowledge (the letters were shown to the children when the phonemes were introduced), phoneme awareness, and syllable awareness. We also expected to see an effect of training on syllable awareness because Cary and Verhaeghe (1994) found transfer effect from the phoneme level to the syllable level in their intervention study. Cary and Verhaeghe found that the children who received training that included phonemes generalized their ability to supra-phoneme units resulting in an improved syllabic analysis ability. The measures of phoneme and syllable awareness were combined scores of the identification task and the deletion task. So, the syllable and phoneme awareness test had the same format. The only difference was the size of the phonological units the children were to manipulate. We did not expect training to have an effect on the children's vocabulary (measured by the Peabody) because of the specificity of the training.

We calculated individual gains as lod-scores (the logarithm of the quotients between the odd-transformed scores at each testing occasion. For further description of this method, see Allerup and Elbro 1998). The gains in the four groups were compared by means of a non-parametric Mann-Whitney U-test. We chose this procedure because many of the data were not normally distributed.

As shown in figure 1, the two experimental groups progressed more than the control groups on a sum score of the two different measures of phoneme awareness. The control group, with children of normally reading parents, had better phoneme awareness than the other groups at the beginning of kindergarten ($z = -2$, $p < 0.05$). But at the end of the training period, the two groups of children of normally reading parents did not differ on the phoneme

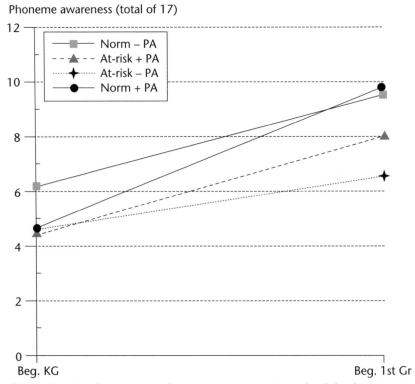

Figure 1.   Development in phoneme awareness in each of the four groups. The children were tested at the beginning and the end of the training period. Norm –PA = Children of normally reading parents who received the usual phoneme awareness training in kindergarten. At-risk +PA = Children of dyslexic parents who received our phoneme awareness training in kindergarten. At-risk –PA = Children of dyslexic parents who received the usual phoneme awareness training in kindergarten. Norm +PA = Children of normally reading parents who received our phoneme awareness training in kindergarten.

awareness tests ($z = -0$–4, non-significant), showing that the experimental group, with children of normally reading parents, gained more in phoneme awareness than the corresponding control group, with children of normally reading parents ($z = -2.5$, $p < 0.05$). The experimental group of children of dyslexic parents gained more in phoneme awareness than the control group of children of dyslexic parents ($z = -2.4$, $p < 0.05$). If we compare the experimental group (children of dyslexic parents) with the control group (children of normally reading parents), there was no difference between the gain in phoneme awareness in the two groups ($z = 0.8$, non-significant). But the control children of dyslexic parents tended to lag behind the control children of normally reading parents. They did not gain so much in phoneme awareness during kindergarten as the control group of children of normally reading parents ($z = 1.8$, near significance $p < 0.1$).

The experimental group of children of dyslexic parents also gained more in letter knowledge during kindergarten than the control children of dyslexic parents ($z = -3.3$, $p < 0.001$) but for the children of normally reading parents there was no difference between the gains of the control group and the experimental group ($z = -1.5$, non significant).

In figure 2, the children's syllable awareness at the beginning of kindergarten and first grade is shown. The syllable awareness was measured with two different tests, which were similar to those at the phoneme level. Surprisingly, there was no significant difference in the gains in syllable awareness between the four different groups ($z > -1.3$, non-significant). So we did not find any sign of a transfer effect from the phoneme level to the syllable level as Cary and Verhaeghe found (Cary and Verhaeghe 1994). As expected, we did not find any significant difference in the gains in receptive vocabulary (measured with the Danish version of the Peabody Picture Vocabulary Test) between the four different groups.

The Hard Core—the Children with Whom We Did Not Succeed

For most of the children of dyslexic parents in the experimental group, the training was a success. On average, they gained more in phoneme awareness than the control group. But a small group of children in the experimental group did not benefit from the training. Their phoneme awareness was poor at the beginning of the training period and it was not significantly better at the end of the training period. These children (from now on called the *hard core*) are defined by having no more than four correct answers in the phoneme awareness test at the beginning of kindergarten and having a difference of

Syllable awareness (total)

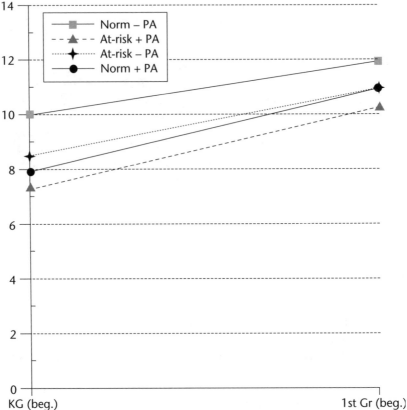

Figure 2. The development of syllable awareness in each of the four groups of children. The children were tested at the beginning and the end of the training period. Norm –PA = Children of normally reading parents who received the usual phoneme awareness training in kindergarten. At-risk +PA = Children of dyslexic parents who received our phoneme awareness training in kindergarten. At-risk –PA = Children of dyslexic parents who received the usual phoneme awareness training in kindergarten. Norm +PA = Children of normally reading parents who received our phoneme awareness training in kindergarten.

no more than two between their phoneme awareness at the beginning and end of the training period. Six of the 36 children of dyslexic parents in the experimental group matched these criteria.

But how is it that some of the children did not benefit from training? A way to find an explanation is to compare the hard core with other children from the experimental group of children of dyslexic parents, who also had a poor phoneme awareness at the beginning of the training period, but who had a difference of three or more between their phoneme awareness at the beginning and end of the training period. Fourteen of the 36 children of dyslexic parents matched the criteria for the comparison group. The two groups of children were compared on the different language measures at the beginning of the training period. The two groups' scores on the different measures were compared by means of the non-parametric Mann-Whitney U-test.

There were no significant differences between the hard core and the rest of the children on receptive vocabulary ($z = -0.8$, non-significant), non verbal intelligence ($z = -1.4$, non-significant), morpheme deletion ($z = -0.9$, non-significant), phoneme discrimination ($z = -0.4$, non-significant), syllable awareness ($z = -1.6$, non-significant), letter knowledge ($z = -1.9$, near-significant), short-term memory ($z = -1.5$, non-significant), and picture naming ($z = -0.9$, non-significant).

The test of the children's phonological distinctness gave us measures of the children's level of distinctness and pronunciation accuracy. The hard core and the rest of the children were compared on distinctness level and pronunciation errors. The hard core made significantly more pronunciation errors ($z = -3.0$, $p < 0.01$) but there was no significant difference between the two groups on the distinctness score ($z = -0.08$, non-significant). Thus, the only difference between the hard core and the children with poor phoneme awareness who benefitted from the phoneme awareness training is their pronunciation accuracy, indicating that the phonological impairment of the hard core was more severe and also affected their spoken language. Children were not included in the study if they had a diagnosis of dysphasia, but maybe these children in the hard core are somewhere in the border area between dysphasia and dyslexia.

Effects of training on the children's reading and spelling. The children's reading was tested with many different measures at the beginning of the second and third grades. The reading data from the beginning of second and third grade are given in table I. Again the group means were compared by means of the non-parametric Mann-Whitney U-test.

Group comparisons of the two groups of children of dyslexic parents showed that the experimental group outperformed the control group on four out of five measures of reading in second grade and on three out of four measures of reading in third grade. There was no difference between the two groups on the spelling test in the third grade.

Table I. The reading abilities for the four groups of children at the beginning of 2nd and 3rd grade. The scores are average scores (the standard deviation is in brackets) on the different reading measures. In 3rd grade there is also a measure of spelling ability. The results from the statistical analyses are displayed in the last four columns (z values from Mann-Whitney U-test).

	At-risk children		Normal		Group Differences (z)			
	Exp	Control	Exp	Control	E1-	E2-	E1-	C1-
	1	1	2	2	C1	C2	E2	C2
2nd grade								
Non-words (max 30)	5.3	3.5	8.3	9.2	-0.8	-0.4	-1.7*	—
	(7.1)	(5.0)	(9.2)	(9.1)				4.5***
Pseudo-homophones	16.8	11.8	19.4	18.7	—	-0.2	-0.6	—
(max 48)	(8.3)	(7.1)	(11.0)	(11.4)	3.0***			3.7***
Real words (max 30)	6.1	4.0	10.2	11.5	-2.0**	-0.03*	-1.7*	—
	(8.1)	(7.0)	(12.1)	(14.3)				4.5***
Real words (max 400)	64.2	51.3	75.1	83.0	-2.1**	-.05	-0.6	—
	(36.9)	(35.9)	(50.3)	(58.4)				3.5***
Rime-words (max 22)	7.4	5.4	8.2	8.6	-1.9*	0.4	-1	—
	(3.5)	(3.6)	(3.3)	(2.5)				4.6***
3rd grade								
Non-words (max 30)	15.5	8.9	16.2	20.1	-1.8*	-0.3	-1.3	-4.4*
	(7.4)	(8.8)	(11.2)	(13.4)				
Pseudo-homophones	25.1	11.8	32.4	30.2	—	-0.6	-1.9*	-3.9**
(max 48)	(10.7)	(7.1)	(13.6)	(13.5)	2.46**			
Real words (max 30)	18.1	13.3	25.6	28.3	-1.7*	-0.4	-1.6	-4.2*
	(16.8)	(15.5)	(18.2)	(19.8)				
Real words (max 400)	134.5	115.3	156.2	168.4	-1.6	-0.5	-1.1	—
	(63.2)	(67.6)	(64.5)	(72.2)				3.5***
Spelling (max 24)	9.7	8.5	14.0	13.2	-0.7	-0.5	-2.1**	—
	(7.0)	(6.2)	(7.4)	(6.9)				3.4***

Note * = $p < 0.1$, ** = $p < 0.05$, *** = $p < 0.01$

Group comparisons of the two groups of children of normally reading parents showed no significant differences in the reading scores of the experimental and control group. These results may be due to the fact that the control children had better performance on letter knowledge and phoneme awareness at the beginning of kindergarten.

The children of dyslexic and normally reading parents in the experimental groups were compared. The children of normally reading parents outperformed the children of dyslexic parents on two out of five measures of reading in the second grade and on one out of four measures of reading in the third grade. The children of normally reading parents in the experimental group also outperformed the experimental group of children of dyslexic parents on the spelling test.

The control groups of children of dyslexic and normally reading parents were also compared, and the children of normally reading parents outperformed the children of dyslexic parents on all measures of reading in second and third grade (The control group of children of normally reading parents also outperformed the control group of children of dyslexic parents on the spelling test). So there was a greater gap between the children of dyslexic and normally reading parents in the control group than in the experimental group. However, this result should be treated with caution because of the better starting point (better letter knowledge and better phoneme awareness) of the control group of children of normally reading parents.

Reading difficulties among children of dyslexic and children of normally reading parents. When defining the two reader groups (those with reading difficulties and those without reading difficulties), we used the two different measures of phonological coding (oral non-word reading and identification of pseudo-homophones). A composite score was used to define dyslexia. This procedure was similar to the one we used when we defined dyslexia in the parental group (Elbro, Nielsen, and Petersen 1994). A cut-off point was chosen that separated approximately 10% of the children of normally reading parents from the rest of the children of normally reading parents. For simplicity, children who scored below this cut-off point will be called dyslexic and children who score above this point will be called normal readers. We are aware that this distinction is categorical and that children may change groups as they progress in school.

As expected, there was a higher incidence of dyslexia among the children of dyslexic parents. At the beginning of second grade, 36% (31 out of 87) of the children of dyslexic parents scored below the cut-off point on the combined phonological coding score compared with 8% (6 out of 72) of the children of normally reading parents. This difference in incidence of dyslexia is statistically significant (chi-square = 16.44, $p < 0.001$). At the beginning of third grade, the difference in incidence of dyslexia in the two groups of children is no longer statistically significant. A total of 18% (15 out of 84) of the children of dyslexic parents scored below the cut-off point compared with 10% (7 out of 68) of the children of normally reading parents.

In order to study the effect of training on the incidence of dyslexia, group comparisons were made between the experimental groups of children of dyslexic and normally reading parents and the control groups of children of dyslexic and normally reading parents.

As displayed in table II, the training program tended to reduce the prevalence of dyslexia in children of dyslexic parents. In all,

Table II.   Displays the number of children in each of the four groups who at the beginning of second and third grade are identified as possibly normal readers or possibly dyslexic (the groups are made on the basis of the composite phonological coding score).

	At-risk children		Normal	
	Exp 1	Control 1	Exp 2	Control 2
Reading status in 2nd grade				
Possibly dyslexic	7 (19%)	24 (47%)	2 (11%)	4 (8%)
Possibly normal	29 (81%)	27 (53%)	17 (89%)	49 (92%)
Reading status in 3rd grade				
Possibly dyslexic	3 (9%)	12 (25%)	2 (11%)	5 (10%)
Possibly normal	32 (91%)	37 (75%)	19 (89%)	44 (90%)

47% of the untrained children of dyslexic parents were classified as possibly dyslexic at the beginning of second grade compared with 19% of the trained children of dyslexic parents. This difference is statistically significant (chi-square = 7.01, $p < 0.01$). However, at the beginning of third grade, the difference in the prevalence of dyslexia between the experimental and control group of children of dyslexic parents is smaller. In the control group of children of dyslexic parents, 25% were classified as possibly dyslexic compared with 9% of the children in the experimental group. This difference is near-significance (chi-square = 3.5, $p < 0.1$).

Comparisons were made between the children of dyslexic and normally reading parents for the two experimental groups and the two control groups. In the two control groups, the prevalence of dyslexia was higher in the control group of children of dyslexic parents than in the control group of children of normally reading parents on both test occasions (at the beginning of second and third grade), and the difference between the prevalence in the two groups was statistically significant. However, this might be due to the fact that the control group of children of normally reading parents was the best group on the measures of language abilities at the beginning of kindergarten. In the two experimental groups, there was no significant difference in the prevalence of dyslexia between the two groups of children on both test occasions, indicating that the training in kindergarten reduces the differences in initial reading development between children of dyslexic and normally reading parents.

Finally, logistic regression analyses were performed to assess the effect of phoneme awareness training. Such an analysis made it possible to see if there was still an effect of training after controlling for the predictors that in a previous analysis were shown to be the strongest linguistic predictors of dyslexia (Elbro et al. 1998). At the first step of the analysis the strongest linguistic predictors of dyslexia were included and in a second step of the analysis, the training condition was added. In a previous study with some of the children, we found that possible dyslexia in the second grade was predicted well by three of the language abilities measured at the beginning of kindergarten. Those measures were phoneme awareness, letter knowledge, and distinctness of phonological representations (Elbro, Borstrøm, and Petersen 1998). Those measures were included at the first step in the logistic regression analysis and the training condition was added as the second step. The addition of the training condition improved the model significantly in both second and third grade (In second grade: Wald = 8.23, $p < 0.01$, in third grade: Wald = 3.98, $p < 0.05$).

DISCUSSION

Torgesen, Wagner, and Rashotte (1994) have reported that it is difficult to improve phoneme awareness in children with poor phoneme awareness. Byrne et al. (1997) also reported rather poor results from their training study with children of dyslexic parents. Byrne's study showed that phoneme awareness training in small groups is more effective than teaching phoneme awareness in whole-classroom settings, where all the children in the class receive phoneme awareness training in one big group (In Denmark there are approximately 20 children in a class). However, our study showed that the phoneme awareness of children of dyslexic parents could be improved in whole-classroom settings. The prevalence of dyslexia in the trained children of dyslexic parents did not differ from the prevalence of dyslexia in the normal control children.

Despite this, there were some children of dyslexic parents who did not improve in phoneme awareness. These children had poor phoneme awareness at the beginning of the training period and the training did not improve their phoneme awareness significantly. Pronunciation of complex words was one area in which these children differed from children with poor phoneme awareness who benefitted from the training. In the test of the children's phonological representations, we distinguished between indistinct and incorrect pronunciation of words. In the description of the results here and the other published articles about the study, we have retained this distinction. But the distinctness and accuracy score can be two different aspects of the same problem, the least impaired children are indistinct and some of the children have such indistinct phonological representations of words that they pronounce them incorrectly.

In any case, the phonological representations of these children are inaccurate/indistinct and this inaccuracy makes it harder for these children to profit from the phoneme awareness training. Perhaps these children need a specially designed training that could improve the quality of their phonological representations before the phoneme awareness training begins.

The difference in the incidence of dyslexia in children of dyslexic parents and children of normally reading parents was statistically significant in second grade, but in third grade this difference was no longer statistically significant. This result indicated that some children of dyslexic parents are slow starters. They need more time to learn to read words by phonological coding. The prevalence of dyslexia in children of dyslexic parents was halved from second to third grade in both the experimental and the control group. Another factor that might have caused good progress in the children of dyslexic parents was our phoneme awareness training in kindergarten. The significant difference in the incidence of dyslexia between children of dyslexic parents and normally reading parents had disappeared only with regard to the children who received the phoneme awareness training. Among the untrained children, there was still a significantly higher incidence of dyslexia in children of dyslexic parents. However, this result should be treated with some caution because the untrained children of normally reading parents had better phoneme awareness and letter knowledge from the beginning. Finally, our study might have made the teachers more aware of the initial reading development of the children of dyslexic parents and perhaps the study meant that special attention from teachers and parents was paid to the children because they were participating in the study.

Our results showed an effect on different measures of reading ability in second and third grade, but it still remains to be seen whether there will be any long-term effects of the training in kindergarten. A follow-up study is being planned that will study the long-term effects on decoding and discover whether there is any effect of phoneme awareness training on children's reading comprehension.

Almost every Danish kindergarten teacher is conscious of the importance of linguistic awareness for initial reading development. Therefore, linguistic awareness is part of the daily routine in almost every kindergarten. Our study showed that what kind of language games the kindergarten teacher plays with the children is of great importance, especially for children at risk of having reading difficulties. The control children in our study received linguistic awareness training. But only a third of the kindergarten teachers in the control classes provided training that included phonemes. Our results showed that the usual linguistic awareness training in kindergarten was ineffective and created a greater gap between the children of dyslexic parents and children of normally reading parents. Children of dyslexic parents need a well-structured training that focuses on the speech units that are crucial for reading acquisition, namely the phonemes. In this study we planned training for only 17 weeks in kindergarten. Reading instruction in the first grade differed for the participating children. One might wonder what results we might have obtained if we had the chance to give the children specially designed reading instruction in the early grades.

ACKNOWLEDGMENTS

The research reported here was supported by grants to Professor Carsten Elbro from the Danish Research Council (No. 5-25-98-85) and from the Rebekka Foundation. I am very grateful for the collaboration and enthusiasm of the children, their families, and the kindergarten-teachers. I am highly indebted to Ina Borstrøm and Carsten Elbro for collaboration on all phases of the project including the training program, data collection, and development of many of the measures. Kikki F. Christensen, Thora H. Fjeldgren, Astrid Haastrup, Tina Henriksen, Birgit Dilling Jandorf, Mette Pedersen and Line Petersen also did data collection and scoring. I would like to thank Carsten Elbro, Ina Borstrøm, and Nathlie Badian for comments on this chapter.

REFERENCES

Allerup, P., and Elbro, C. 1998. Comparing differences in accuracy across conditions or individuals: An argument for the use of Log Odds. *The Quarterly Journal of Experimental Psychology* 51 (A):409– 24.

Ball, E. W., and Blachman, B. A. 1991. Does phoneme awareness training in kindergarten make a difference in early word recognition and developmental spelling? *Reading Research Quarterly* 26:49–66.

Borstrøm, I., and Petersen, D. K. 1996. *På vej til den første læsning. Fonologisk opmærksomhed* ("On the way to initial reading. Phonological awareness"). Copenhagen: Alinea.

Borstrøm, I., and Elbro, C. 1997. Prevention of dyslexia in kindergarten: Effects of phoneme awareness training with children of dyslexic parents. In *Dyslexia: Biology, Cognition and Intervention*, eds. C. Hulme and M. Snowling, London: Whurr.

Bowey, J. A., and Francis, J. 1991. Phonological analysis as a function of age and exposure to reading instruction. *Applied Psycholinguistics* 12:91–121.

Bradley, L., and Bryant, P. 1985. *Rhyme and Reason in Reading and Spelling*. Ann Arbor: University of Michigan Press.

Brink, L. Lund, J., Heger, S., Jørgensen, J. N. 1991. *Den store Danske udtale-ordbog (The Great Danish Pronunciation Dictionary')*. Copenhagen: Munksgaard.

Bryant, P., Maclean, M., and Bradley, L. 1990. Rhyme, language, and children's reading. *Applied Psycholinguistics* 11:237–52.

Byrne, B., and Fielding-Barnsley, R. 1991. Evaluation of a program to teach phonemic awareness to young children. *Journal of Educational Psychology* 83:451–55.

Byrne, B., Fielding-Barnsley, R., Ashley, L., and Larsen, K. 1997. Assessing the child's and the environment's contribution to reading acquisition: What we know and what we don't know. In *Foundations of Reading Acquisition*, ed. B. Blachman, Mahwah, NJ: Erlbaum.

Cary, L., and Verhaege, A. 1994. Promoting phonemic analysis ability among kindergartners: Effects of different training programs. *Reading and Writing: An Interdisciplinary Journal* 6:251–78.

Catts, H. W. 1991. Early identification of dyslexia: Evidence from a follow-up study of speech-language impaired children. *Annals of Dyslexia* 41:163–77.

Dunn, L. M., and Dunn, L. M. 1981. *Peabody Picture Vocabulary Test Revised*. Circle Pines, MN: American Guidance Service.

Elbro, C., Nielsen, I., and Petersen, D. K. 1994. Dyslexia in adults: Evidence for deficits in non-word reading and in the phonological representation of lexical items. *Annals of Dyslexia* 44:205–26.

Elbro, C. 1996. Early linguistic abilities and reading development: A review and a hypothesis about distinctness of phonological representations. *Reading and Writing: An Interdisciplinary Journal* 8:453–85.

Elbro, C., Borstrøm, I., and Petersen, D. K. 1998. Predicting dyslexia from kindergarten. The importance of phonological representations of lexical items. *Reading Research Quarterly* vol 33, 1:36–57.

Fowler, A. E. 1991. How early phonological development might set stage for phoneme awareness. In *Phonological Processes in Literacy: A tribute to Isabelle Y. Liberman*, eds. S. Brady and D. Shankweiler, Hillsdale, NJ: Erlbaum.

Gilger, J. W., Pennington, B. F., and Defries, J. C. 1991. Risk for reading disability as a function of parental history in three family studies. *Reading and Writing: An Interdisciplinary Journal* 3:205–17.

Kjær, B. 1977. *BKS-testen*. Herning: Specialpædagogisk forlag.

Lindamood, C., and Lindamood, P. 1975. *Auditory Discrimination in Depth*. Science Research Associates Division, MacMillan/Mcgraw Hill: Columbus, OH.

Lundberg, I., Frost, J., and Petersen O. P. 1988. Effects of an extensive programme for stimulating phonological awareness in preschool children. *Reading Research Quarterly* 23:263–84.

Lyon, G. R. 1995. Toward a definition of dyslexia. *Annals of Dyslexia* 45:3–27.

Olson, R. K. 1985. Individual and developmental differences in reading disability. In *Reading Research, Advances in Theory and Practice*, vol. 4, eds. G. E. Mackinnon and T. G. Waller. Academic Press, Inc.

Olson, R. K., Wise, B., Johnson, M., and Ring. J. 1997. The etiology and re-mediation of phonologically based word recognition and spelling dis-abilities: Are phonological deficits the "hole" story? In *Foundations of Reading Acquisition*, ed. B. Blachman, Mahwah, NJ: Erlbaum.

Rack, J. P., Snowling, M. J., and Olson, R. K. 1992. The nonword reading deficit in developmental dyslexia: A review. *Reading Research Quarterly* 27:28–53.

Raven, J. C. 1959. *Colored Progressive Matrices: Sets A, AB, B.* Oxford, England: Oxford Psychologists.

Scarborough, H. S. 1989. Prediction of reading disability from familial and individual differences. *Journal of Educational Psychology* 81:101–108.

Scarborough, H. S. 1990. Very early language deficits in dyslexic children. *Child Development* 61:1728–43.

Scarborough, H. S. 1998. Early identification of children at risk for reading disabilities. In *Specific Reading Disability. A View of the Spectrum.* Timonium, MD: York Press.

Schneider, W., Kåspert, P., Roth, E., Visé, M., and Marx, H. 1997. Short- and long-term effects of training phonological awareness in kinder-garten: Evidence from two German studies. *Journal of Experimental Psychology* 66:311–40

Søegård, A., and Petersen, S. P. B. 1974. *Ordstillelæsningsprøve OS 400* ("*Silent word reading test OS 400*"). Copenhagen: Dansk Psykologisk Forlag.

Swan, D., and Goswami, U. 1997. Phonological awareness deficits in de-velopmental dyslexia and the phonological representation hypothesis. *Journal of Educational Psychology.*

Torgesen, J. K., Wagner, R. K., and Rashotte, C. A. 1994. Longitudinal studies of phonological processing and reading. *Journal of Learning Disabilities* 27:276–86.

Tornéus, M. 1987. The importance of metaphonological and metemor-phological abilities for different phases of reading development. Paper presented at the Third World Congress of Dyslexia, Crete.

Wagner, R. K., and Torgesen, J. K. 1987. The nature of phonological pro-cessing and its causal role in the acquisition of reading skills. *Psycho-logical Bulletin* 101:192–212.

Wagner, R. K., Torgesen, J. K., and Rashotte, C. A. 1994. Development of reading-related phonological processing abilities: New evidence of bidi-rectional causality from a latent variable longitudinal study. *Develop-mental Psychology* 30:73–87.

Wechsler, D. 1974. *Wechsler Intelligence Scale for Children - Revised.* New York: Psychological Corporation.

Chapter • 11

Phonemes and Rhyme in the Development of Reading and Metaphonology
The Dundee Longitudinal Study

Lynne G. Duncan and Philip H. K. Seymour

One of the most important issues facing researchers whose aim is to intervene early to prevent reading failure is the extent to which pre-school phonological awareness predicts future reading progress. This has been a topic of intensive study in recent years and two strands of research have emerged, one dealing with awareness of rhyme and the other with awareness of phonemes. Each strand is linked to theories that differ in the emphasis given to rhyme and phonemes in the sequence of reading development (Goswami and Bryant 1990; Ehri 1992; Duncan, Seymour, and Hill 1997).

In 1987, Bryant and Goswami explored the potential of a number of experimental paradigms to produce evidence that could resolve this question. A central theme of their review was the difficulty in distinguishing cause from effect in the relationship between phonological awareness and reading. They identified two paradigms, the predictive longitudinal study and the training study, which, particularly if combined, can produce information about causation. In the study to be reported here, we have employed both of these techniques. We have also added two additional methodologies that provide further clarification: (1) a process analysis of the development of reading and metaphonological awareness in primary school (see Duncan, Seymour, and Hill 1997, in press); and (2) retrospective individual case studies in which we identify children whose reading development is delayed and look back to consider the predictive potential of their performance in nursery school.

The study was conducted in the city of Dundee on the east coast of Scotland. It extended over a three year period. In the first year, the children were enrolled in three public authority nursery schools (age 4 years). They then transferred to primary schools in various parts of the city and encountered formal reading instruction. They were followed through the primary 1 year (age 5 years) and the primary 2 year (age 6 years).

LONGITUDINAL AND TRAINING STUDIES OF RHYME AWARENESS

An early report of a link between rhyming skills and later reading came from a Swedish longitudinal study by Lundberg, Olofsson, and Wall (1980). They described an association between rhyme production in kindergarten and reading in grades 1 and 2 that was independent of intelligence. Bryant and his colleagues have reported similar predictive relationships between pre-school rhyme oddity assessments and reading over intervals of 2 to 4 years (Bradley and Bryant 1985; Bryant et al. 1990). A recent study by Muter et al. (1997), on the other hand, failed to find a significant relationship between early rhyming and reading in primary 1 or 2. In an attempt to resolve this discrepancy, Bryant (1998) suggested that the instructions to produce a word that "rhymes with or sounds like" a target may have encouraged the production of "incorrect" alliterative responses. However, Hulme, Muter, and Snowling (1998) found that the inclusion of the phrase "sounds like" did not lead to an increase in alliterative responses, making this an unlikely explanation of their original null result.

A mixture of findings also characterizes the training studies. Bradley and Bryant (1983) administered a two-year phonological training in both rhyme and alliteration to beginning readers with poor phonological skills. This did not improve the reading skills of the training group relative to a control group trained in conceptual categorization. In another study, also coinciding with formal reading instruction, Greaney, Tunmer, and Chapman (1997) reported that orthographic training in the use of rime analogies significantly improved the word and non-word reading of 8-year-old poor readers when compared to item-specific training. This advantage persisted over a 1 year period for non-word reading but not for word recognition.

Study 1: Effects of Pre-School Rhyme Training on Later Reading

The preceding review highlights the need for a training study that is directed at improving rhyming skills alone. It seems important that this should be a pre-school intervention, as existing training studies have been conducted concurrently with, and hence confounded with, reading instruction. We attempted to address these points by conducting a small-scale study that introduced rhyme to a group of middle-class children in their last year at nursery school.

We first saw the children in October, when we administered a set of pre-intervention measures individually: (a) Letter Knowledge— all lower-case letters were investigated to ascertain what the child knew about the sounds associated with letters; (b) Early Reading Ability—the stimuli were nine of the most common content words from the initial stage of several well-known reading schemes and the child's first name; (c) Rhyme Production—the child helped two puppets, "Fred" and "Ted," to think of rhymes for 10 words; (d) Alliteration Production—similar to rhyme production using puppets called "Sam" and "Sue"; (e) Vocabulary—the short form of the British Picture Vocabulary Scale (BPVS) (Dunn, Dunn, and Whetton 1982).

The interventions took place between December and April. Three separate classrooms in the nursery enabled two interventions and a control condition to be implemented. The two phonological interventions were based on materials adapted from standard nursery activities such as I-spy, Lotto, Snap, and "Simon says": (a) Rhyme intervention—rhyme was introduced through nursery rhymes, action rhymes, and popular rhyming songs and consolidated using rhyming versions of the activities described above; and (b) Alliteration/initial phoneme intervention— initial phonemes were introduced through tongue-twisters and alliterative songs before alliterative versions of the standard activities were initiated. Preliminary meetings with the classroom teachers outlined the intervention: the activities were scheduled to take place 2 to 3 times a week and training materials, once introduced, were freely available to the children. The control group was essentially untreated although the children were exposed to the same range of activities (in their non-phonological form) as part of their normal nursery curriculum.

The assessment battery was re-administered at the end of the interventions (May) and the results can be seen in table I. Of the reading-related and general assessments, only letter-sound knowledge showed a significant change during the training period ($F(1, 37) = 6.19$, $p < .05$) with all three groups improving to a similar extent on this measure.

We examined performance on the alliteration production task for signs of an alliteration training effect. An analysis of covariance was conducted on the post-intervention scores using the pre-intervention scores as the covariate. The between-subjects factor, Group (rhyme, alliteration, control) did not achieve significance ($F(2,37) = 3.08$, $p > .05$) although the effect of the covariate was significant ($F(1,37) = 4.54$, $p < .05$). Unfortunately, the teacher responsible for the alliteration intervention was absent due to illness during part of the training period and this probably accounts for the lack of a measurable effect.

To evaluate the rhyme intervention, a similar analysis of covariance was conducted on the rhyme production scores. This time the effect of Group was significant ($F(2,37) = 15.98$, $p < .001$) as was the effect of the covariate ($F(1,37) = 6.60$, $p < .05$). Newman-Keuls tests showed that the post-intervention difference between the rhyme and the control groups was marginally non-significant ($p = .057$) but that both groups performed significantly better than the alliteration group (see figure 1). It later emerged that the rhyme intervention proved so popular that the control

Table I. Mean Group Performance on Pre- and Post-Intervention Assessments (Standard Deviations in Parentheses)

| | Intervention Groups | | | | Control Group | |
| | Rhyme (N = 13) | | Alliteration (N = 15) | | (N = 13) | |
	Pre	Post	Pre	Post	Pre	Post
CA (years)	4.30	4.96	4.26	4.90	4.10	4.74
	(0.32)	(0.36)	(0.34)	(0.35)	(0.31)	(0.31)
B.P.V.S.	107	109	101	101	108	105
(standardized score)	(12)	(16)	(17)	(16)	(14)	(12)
Letter-Knowledge	4.44	7.99	3.08	8.79	5.32	14.50
(%)	(8.58)	(16.20)	(7.99)	(14.81)	(8.09)	(24.13)
Early Reading Ability	0.00	0.00	0.00	0.00	0.85	0.00
(%)					(3.08)	
Rhyme Production	26.92	93.08	24.67	31.33	30.00	72.31
(%)	(33.26)	(17.02)	(35.83)	(37.20)	(35.36)	(33.95)
Alliteration Production	6.92	20.77	15.33	38.00	11.54	51.54
(%)	(10.32)	(20.19)	(18.85)	(33.85)	(20.75)	(33.63)

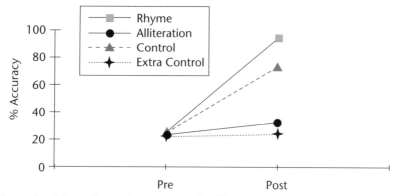

Figure 1.   Mean Group Accuracy in the Rhyme Production Task (including extra control group)

teacher had introduced some of the activities in her own class-room. As a result, the alliteration condition might best be regarded as a treated control against which the continued progress of the two groups with good rhyming skills (rhyme intervention and rhyme-contaminated control) could be assessed. This was borne out by comparing the rhyme production performance of the alliteration training group with that of an additional group who were following the normal curriculum in another nursery school in the city. A re-analysis of the rhyme training effect with this extra control group also produced a significant effect of Group ($F(3,54) = 16.15$, $p < .001$) which Newman-Keuls test indicated was due to the similar and lower performance of the alliteration and extra control groups (see figure 1).

The children were followed longitudinally for the first two years of formal reading instruction. During this time, they encountered a mixed method of instruction that introduced a sight vocabulary together with letter-sound knowledge and phonic exercises. At the end of primary 1 and 2, we measured reading progress using the Word Reading subtest of the British Ability Scales (see table II). To determine whether pre-school rhyme training benefited the acquisition of a reading vocabulary, we performed analyses of co-variance on the BAS Word Reading raw scores with Group (rhyme, alliteration, control) as the between-subjects factor and standardized vocabulary scores from the end of nursery school as a co-variate. There were no significant differences between the groups in reading achievement in either primary 1 or 2 (both $Fs < 1$) and no effect of the covariate in either case (primary 1: $F(1,30) = 3.41$, $p > .05$); primary 2: $F(1,27) = 1.06$, $p > .05$).

Table II.   Mean Reading Progress at the end of Primary 1 and Primary 2
(Standard Deviations in Parentheses)

	Rhyme Training		Alliteration Training		Control	
	P1	P2	P1	P2	P1	P2
	(N = 12)	(N = 12)	(N = 12)	(N = 9)	(N = 10)	(N = 10)
BAS Word Reading	15	49	13	41	18	52
(raw score)	(13)	(23)	(11)	(23)	(16)	(15)

As far as could be determined from this study, an intervention that successfully improved pre-school rhyming skills had no more effect on reading progress than an unsuccessful attempt to train alliterative skills. This raises the question of whether pre-school training in rhyming can produce detectable beneficial effects on subsequent reading development.

LONGITUDINAL STUDIES OF PHONEME AWARENESS

The results of studies that have compared directly the predictive power of pre-school measurements of rhyme and phoneme awareness broadly support these conclusions. Lundberg, Olofsson, and Wall (1980) found that a kindergarten measure of phoneme reversal was a more powerful predictor of grade 1 and 2 reading than a measure of rhyme production. Similarly, Lundberg, Frost, and Petersen (1988) observed that pre-school phoneme awareness emerged as the first step in a multiple regression analysis predicting grade 2 reading. Rhyme awareness did not make a significant contribution. Muter et al. (1997) found no correlation between nursery rhyming or segmentation factors and reading for British primary 1 and 2 children. However, a primary 1 segmentation factor (phoneme identification, phoneme deletion, I.T.P.A. Sound Blending) did correlate with primary 1 and 2 reading. Path analyses revealed an indirect connection between pre-school segmentation and primary 1 reading. Nursery segmentation predicted primary 1 segmentation that was associated with primary 1 reading. A subsequent analysis with primary 2 reading as the dependent variable indicated that nursery and primary 1 segmentation were only indirectly related to primary 2 reading via primary 1 reading.

A problem with all of these studies is that phoneme awareness tasks are often beyond the capability of children until after they have started to learn to read, especially in Britain and the United States where pre-schoolers are only 4 or 5 years old (Bruce 1964; Kirtley et al. 1989). This has led some authors to suggest that phoneme awareness is linked reciprocally to learning to read (Morais, Alegria, and Content 1987; Perfetti et al. 1987; Burgess and Lonigan 1998). Perfetti et al. (1987) demonstrated that beginning readers' phoneme synthesis ability enabled later pseudoword reading but pseudoword reading ability itself was responsible for later phoneme deletion ability.

Several authors have concluded that it is learning about letters that usually initiates this interactive process (Ehri 1992; Johnston, Anderson, and Holligan 1996). This view is supported by longitudinal evidence of a predictive relationship between early letter knowledge and phoneme awareness and later reading (Stuart and Coltheart 1988; Foorman et al. 1991; Johnston, Anderson, and Holligan 1996; Näsland and Schneider 1996; Wagner et al. 1997; Barron 1998). In the study by Stuart and Coltheart (1988), a general measure of pre-school phonological awareness did not predict primary 1 reading progress until it was combined with letter knowledge. Wagner et al. (1997) suggest that kindergarten letter knowledge rather than word reading ability stimulates the development of grade 2 phonological awareness, although kindergarten phonological awareness is an independent predictor of grade 2 reading ability.

Study 2: Pre-School Predictors of Beginning Reading

The aim of our second study was to compare the predictive contributions of pre-school letter-sound knowledge, rhyme and alliteration awareness to later reading acquisition. To accomplish this, we monitored how 84 children made the transition between emergent literacy and beginning reading. Our first measures were taken at the beginning of the final nursery year when the children's mean chronological age (CA) was 4.22 years (Range: 3.71-4.75). Further assessments were administered at the end of nursery (Mean CA: 4.85 years; Range: 4.25-5.50), primary 1 (Mean CA: 5.83 years; Range: 5.25-6.50) and primary 2 (Mean CA: 6.87 years; Range: 6.25-7.42).

Nursery School Assessments. Two tests were administered in October: (a) BAS Recall of Digits—a test of immediate phonological memory; and (b) BAS Visual Recognition—a test of verbal encoding strategies as well as the ability to hold and recognize visual images. In May, we administered all of the tests described in study 1 and an additional test of emergent literacy: Recognition of Logos—12 common logos found on popular sweets, crisps, drinks, and breakfast cereals were presented for identification.

Primary School Assessments.   Reading progress was assessed at the end of primary 1 and 2 using the BAS Word Reading test (Elliott, Murray, and Pearson 1983). A test of arithmetic skill, the One Minute Number Test (Westwood et al.1974), was administered at the end of Primary 2.

Performance on the nursery and primary assessments can be seen in table III. The simple correlations between the nursery variables and primary school performance are summarized in table IV. Most of the nursery measures showed moderate correlations with primary school performance. Notable exceptions were Recognition of Logos, and also Early Reading Ability which correlated only with primary 1 reading. This confirms that pre-school experiences with environmental print do not have long-term effects on alphabetic reading (Masonheimer, Drum, and Ehri 1984). It was also apparent that most of the nursery variables were correlated not only with later reading but also with later arithmetic skill. This was true for letter knowledge and phonological awareness as well as the general abilities of vocabulary and phonological memory. Only Rhyme Production, however, appeared to show a stronger correlation with arithmetic skill than reading.

Table III.   Mean Task Performance (Standard Deviations in Parentheses)

Nursery Assessments			
October		May	
BAS Recall of Digits	49	BPVS	101
(t-score)	(9)	(standardized score)	(14)
BAS Visual Recognition	51	Logo Recognition	44.94
(t-score)	(10)	(%)	(15.42)
		Early Reading Ability	(1.06)
		(%)	(4.76)
		Letter-Sound Knowledge	9.43
		(%)	(17.39)
		Rhyme Production	38.45
		(%)	(42.24)
		Alliteration Production	15.71
		(%)	(25.76)

Primary Assessments			
Primary 1 (May)		Primary 2 (May)	
BAS Word Reading Age	6.00	BAS Word Reading Age	7.43
(years)	(0.61)	(years)	(1.24)
		One Minute Number Test	17.17
		(raw score)	(6.76)

Table IV. Correlations Between Nursery Predictor Variables and Primary
Reading and Arithmetic Scores

	Primary 1	Primary 2	
	BAS Word Reading	BAS Word Reading	Arithmetic
Chronological Age	−0.08	−0.05	0.09
BAS Recall of Digits (t-score)	0.32**	0.46***	0.44***
BAS Visual Recognition (t-score)	0.40***	0.47***	0.22*
BPVS (standardized score)	0.38***	0.25*	0.30**
Logo Recognition	0.10	0.11	0.07
Early Reading Ability	0.29**	0.15	0.06
Letter-Sound Knowledge	0.59***	0.49***	0.26*
Rhyme Production	0.33**	0.44***	0.56***
Alliteration Production	0.29**	0.27*	0.27*

$^*p < .05, ^{**}p < .01, ^{***}p < .001$

A series of hierarchical multiple regression analyses were conducted in order to identify independent predictors of primary school reading (table V). As a control, BAS Recall of Digits (phonological memory), BAS Visual Recognition, and BPVS (Vocabulary) were entered as the first step in the analysis. Together, they predicted significant variance in both primary 1 and 2 reading. Four separate continuations were conducted by altering the variables entered at the second and third steps. Neither Rhyme nor Alliteration Production made any significant contribution to the prediction of primary 1 or 2 reading when entered as the second or third step in any analysis. Letter Knowledge, on the other hand, was significantly related to reading when entered as the second or final step, indicating that the influence of early Letter Knowledge on reading was independent of Rhyme and Alliteration Production skills as well as vocabulary and phonological memory.

Table V also contains the results for a hierarchical multiple regression analysis with primary 2 arithmetic skill as the dependent variable. The results contrast with the outcome of the analyses predicting reading ability. This time Letter Knowledge was not a significant predictor after controlling for vocabulary and memory. Alliteration Production also failed to make any significant independent contribution to the regression. In the end, Rhyme Production emerged as the only significant independent predictor of primary 2 arithmetic skill. This suggests that pre-school letter knowledge has a selective beneficial effect on reading acquisition.

To produce a more comprehensive account of the interrelationships between the pre-school and primary variables, a path diagram was constructed using EQS (figure 2). Variables from four assessment points were included in the analysis: October and May of the final nursery year, and May of the primary 1 and 2 years.

Table V. Hierarchical Multiple Regression Analyses of the Preschool Predictors of Reading and Arithmetic in Primary 1 and 2

Step	Preschool Variables	Dependent Variable: BAS Word Reading						Dependent Variable: Arithmetic		
		Primary 1			Primary 2			Primary 2		
		ΔR^2	F	p	ΔR^2	F	p	ΔR^2	F	p
1	BAS Recall of Digits BAS Visual Recognition BPVS	0.28	10.27	***	0.37	15.41	***	0.24	8.64	***
2	Alliteration Production	0.01	1.30	n.s.	0.00	0.54	n.s.	0.02	2.32	n.s.
3	Letter-Sound Knowledge	0.17	24.83	***	0.08	11.91	***	0.00	0.25	n.s.
2	Rhyme Production	0.00	0.10	n.s.	0.01	1.10	n.s.	0.12	17.58	***
3	Letter-Sound Knowledge	0.18	26.39	***	0.09	12.33	***	0.00	0.51	n.s.
2	Letter-Sound Knowledge	0.18	26.84	***	0.09	12.68	***	0.01	0.69	n.s.
3	Alliteration Production	0.00	0.02	n.s.	0.00	0.00	n.s.	0.02	1.86	n.s.
3	Rhyme Production	0.00	0.02	n.s.	0.01	0.92	n.s.	0.12	14.85	***

*** $p < .001$

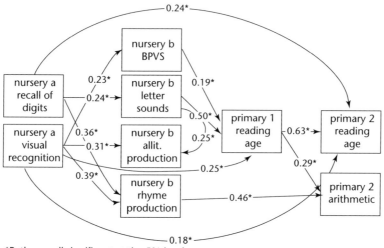

Figure 2.   Structural Equation Model Showing Preschool Predictors of Early Reading Achievement

The sample was slightly small for path analysis but not prohibitively so, especially if the results are considered in conjunction with those of the regression analysis. In order to produce the final model, fully saturated models were run for each of the longitudinal time periods (i.e., October to May of Nursery, October of Nursery to May of primary 1, etc.). A model was created by using all significant paths from these six fully saturated models. Finally, all non-significant paths were removed to produce the model in figure 2. Note that, although all of the covariances were included in this model, the only one that was significant was the link between Letter-Sound Knowledge and Alliteration Production which appears in the final diagram. The model proved a good fit for the data (X^2 (18, $n = 84$) = 21.45, $p > .05$, NNFI = .97, CFI = .99).

One of the most striking features is the extent of the relationships between early memory skills and later reading. Both BAS Recall of Digits and BAS Visual Recognition have significant direct connections to primary 2 reading. BAS Visual Recognition is also directly related to primary 1 reading and BAS Recall of Digits has an indirect effect on primary 1 reading via Letter-sound Knowledge. Vocabulary skills (BPVS) predicted primary 1 reading but had no direct effect on primary 2 reading.

By far the largest pre-school contribution to primary 1 Reading Age comes from Letter-Sound Knowledge. The pre-school phonological awareness measures have little effect by comparison.

Alliteration Production is significantly associated with Letter-Sound Knowledge and could be said to have an indirect effect on primary 1 reading but Rhyme Production makes no significant contribution either directly or indirectly. None of the May nursery measures predict primary 2 reading directly. However, the strong predictive relationship between primary 1 and primary 2 reading suggests that pre-school variables such as Letter-Sound Knowledge are part of a cumulative acquisition process.

Thus, multiple regression and path analysis produced converging accounts of the influence of pre-school abilities on the first two years of literacy acquisition. Both analyses suggest that pre-school Rhyme Production is not a good predictor of reading progress. After controlling for memory and vocabulary, Letter-Sound Knowledge, possibly concurrently linked to Alliteration Production, emerged as the strongest predictor of later reading.

TRAINING STUDIES OF PHONEME AWARENESS

A recent meta-analysis by Bus and van IJzendoorn (1999) has evaluated the impact of phonological training on later phonological development and reading progress. The 32 articles on which this analysis is based describe training studies that vary considerably in terms of location, age-group, type of training, number of subjects, extent of follow-up, and in the nature of the control group. While Bus and van IJzendoorn attempted to test the effect of many of these differences, investigation of factors such as the effect of onset-rime versus phoneme training or the effect of IQ was not part of the study. Overall, they found that the effect of phonological training on subsequent phonological awareness was strong in the short term and moderate in the longer term. For reading, the training produced only moderate effects in the short term and there were no significant longer term effects.

When Bus and van IJzendoorn (1999) compared the effects of the type of training, it emerged that a purely phonological training, e.g., Lundberg, Frost, and Petersen's (1988) program, was less effective than a program that combined phonological training with reading practice or letter knowledge, e.g., Byrne and Fielding-Barnsley's (1991) Sound Foundations program. This is consistent with the findings of Cunningham (1990) that phoneme awareness training in grade 1 was more effective in improving end of year reading when linked explicitly to the activity of reading. Letter knowledge seems to be particularly important. Elkonin (1973) suggested that phonemic skills were easier to acquire when the phonemes were concretely represented. It appears that alphabetic letters can fulfil this function for children who are acquiring phonetic segmentation skills (Hohn and Ehri 1983). Individual training studies have shown that phonemic training effects on decoding and reading are even more pronounced when this training is combined with instruction in letter knowledge (Ball and Blachman 1988, 1991; Byrne and Fielding-Barnsley 1989, 1990, 1993). Hatcher, Hulme, and Ellis (1994) have incorporated such findings with their own results from a study of poor readers to produce what they term the "phonological linkage hypothesis." The essence of this hypothesis is that phonological training is more effective when combined with key components of reading instruction such as letter-sound knowledge and linking the sounds in words to spelling patterns.

Study 3: The Effect of Reading Instruction on Metaphonological Development

In the third part of the study, we carried out a detailed process analysis of reading acquisition and development of metaphonological awareness in the primary 1 and 2 school years. As previously noted, reading instruction in the Dundee schools followed a "mixed" regime, which emphasized sight vocabulary and letter-sounds in the first year and some more complex orthographic structures in the second year. This study was conducted with a subset of 60 children from the larger sample (study 2). Detailed reports are contained in the papers by Duncan, Seymour, and Hill (1997, in press).

Literacy Acquisition. Three procedures were used to monitor reading development: (a) Letter-sound knowledge was assessed in November, March, and May during the primary 1 year, and again in November and May in primary 2; (b) Sight Vocabulary acquisition was followed using word lists sampled from the school reading schemes in November, March, and May of Primary 1 and November of primary 2; (c) Decoding ability was measured using nonword lists of varying characteristics in November, March, and May of primary 1 and primary 2.

Metaphonology. A new procedure, referred to as the Common Unit Identification task, was devised (Duncan, Seymour, and Hill 1997, in press; Seymour, Duncan, and Bolik 1999). The children were presented with pairs of spoken words and were asked to report the segments of sound that the words held in common. For example, given the pair "waste-paste," the child should reply "aste." The advantage of this procedure is that it permits a systematic assessment of explicit (meta-phonological) awareness of units of differing size within the internal structure of the syllable (see table VI). The procedure was applied twice in the primary 1 year, in March and May, and once in the primary 2 year, in March.

Table VI.   Examples of Stimuli from the Common Unit Task (Study 3)

	Simple Structure	Complex Structure
Onset	face-food	bread-brush
Coda	week-bake	paint-count
Body	mat-man	cloth-clock
Rime	boat-goat	paste-waste

The aim of these investigations was to obtain information regarding the linguistic units that were used by children in the initial phase of reading development. In this respect, we make a distinction between small units, equated with the phonemes of the language and their links with the letters of the alphabet, and large units, particularly the spoken rime unit and its orthographic equivalent (Duncan, Seymour, and Hill 1997). We wished to know whether the main emphasis in beginning reading was on the small or the large linguistic units.

The study of letter-sound acquisition indicated that the letters were acquired during the primary 1 year (see figure 3).

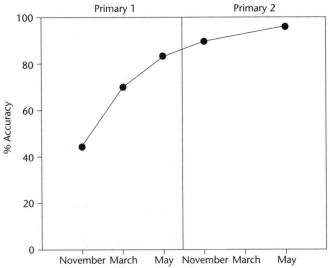

Figure 3.   Letter-Sound Knowledge on Successive Testings

The non-word naming experiments were specially constructed to test for an effect of large units (rimes) in reading development. Within each study, some non-words contained rime segments that occurred in familiar words. In the primary 1 study, these were based directly on the words in the children's reading schemes (experiment 1 from Duncan, Seymour, and Hill 1997). At primary 2, some non-words contained rimes that occurred frequently in the vocabulary of school children (experiment 1 from Duncan, Seymour, and Hill in press). In both cases, the experiment tested for an advantage in reading non-words containing high frequency rimes relative to non-words that contained unfamiliar rime structures. The results, summarized in table VII, indicated that there was no rime familiarity effect in primary 1 but that there was an emerging effect in primary 2. This outcome was interpreted, together with other data, as suggesting a small-to-large unit direction in orthographic development (Duncan, Seymour, and Hill in press).

The results obtained from application of the phonological Common Unit task in the primary 1 and 2 years are shown in figure 4. This gives accuracy scores for small units (onsets and codas) and large units (rimes and bodies) according to the complexity of the consonants contained in each word pair (see table VI). The simple onset and coda conditions correspond to a phonemic level of speech segmentation. In the primary 1 assessment, these small units were most accurately retrieved (95% and 73%) and were much easier to report than the larger rime units (20%). This pattern persisted in the primary 2 assessment. However, at this point, there was evidence of improvement in retrieval of rime units (49%).

The conclusion from these studies is that the direction of orthographic and metaphonological development in our sample was from small units (phonemes) toward large units (rimes). The implication is that the initial step in reading acquisition involved mastery of the letter-sounds and the achievement of metaphonological awareness of the phonemic constituents of speech. Rime structures appeared to become important only somewhat later in development.

Table VII. The Influence of Rime Familiarity on Nonword Reading (Percent correct) in Primary 1 and 2 (Standard Deviations in Parentheses)

	Rime Familiarity	
	High	Low
Primary 1	29.17	32.00
(N = 60)	(32.12)	(35.41)
Primary 2	69.30	60.02
(N = 57)	(31.91)	(32.62)

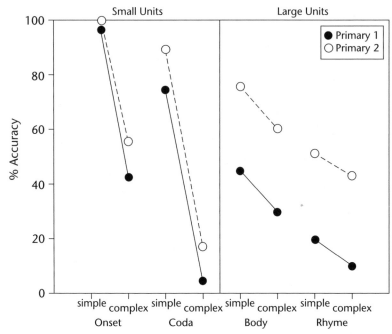

Figure 4.   Performance in the Common Unit Task in Primary 1 and 2

Study 4: Retrospective Case Studies

In the fourth study, we identified children who made poor progress in reading in the primary school. We then carried out a retrospective analysis that aimed to determine the earliest point at which their difficulty was detectable.

There were 21 individuals whose reading was delayed by more than 6 months at the end of the primary 1 year. A smaller group ($n = 6$) were delayed by more than one year at the end of primary 2. A first question is whether these instances of reading delay could have been identified at the pre-school nursery stage.

Rhyme Production.   The range of scores in the poor reader subgroup was 0% to 100% correct. This range completely overlapped the distribution observed in the main sample. Of the children who were delayed by over a year in reading at the end of primary 2, one child scored 100% on pre-school rhyme production. The other five children scored poorly in rhyming (< 10%) but shared this score with 54% of the main sample. It seems clear that there was no possibility of detecting the poor readers by considering pre-school Rhyme Production.

Alliteration Production.   As with Rhyme Production, accuracy ranged from 0% to 100% in the poor reader subgroup, making their performance indistinguishable from that of the main sample. Accuracy was lower (0-10%) among the six children whose reading was delayed by a year in primary 2, but 65% of the main sample also scored in this range.

Letter-Sound Knowledge.   Pre-school knowledge of letter-sounds emerged as the strongest predictor of later reading (study 2). The poor reader group recognized very few letters in nursery school (generally 0 or 1) but this was also true for 70% of the main sample.

The conclusion is that it would not have been possible to identify prospective cases of reading difficulty on the basis of performance on pre-school phonological and literacy tests.

The second possibility is that the beginnings of reading difficulty are detectable at an early point in the primary 1 year. Fourteen of the primary 1 poor readers and 4 of the primary 2 poor readers were tested in November and March of the primary 1 year. By November, the primary 1 poor readers had learned between 1 and 5 letter-sounds, but 62% of the main sample were already scoring above this range. The primary 2 poor readers knew far fewer letter-sounds (only 1 or 2) and scored below the level of 86% of the main sample. The process analysis (study 3) suggested that the initial stage in reading involves acquisition of the full set of letter-sounds and development of metaphonological awareness of small units (phonemes). Figure 5 shows a scatterplot of the relationship between Letter-Sound Knowledge and performance in the onset condition of the Common Unit task (both measured in March of primary 1). It can be seen that the primary 2 poor readers show delayed development on both measures. By this point, their range of Letter-Sound Knowledge (0-31%) overlaps with only 4% of the main sample. Their level of accuracy at Common Onset identification (17-63%) is comparable with only 11% of the main sample. Only 9% of the main sample and two primary 1 poor readers scored below this level.

In order to trace the higher levels of reading development, two further scatter graphs were plotted for data collected in May of primary 1, one to show the relationship between common onset performance and reading simple CVC non-words, and the other to relate common rime performance to non-word reading. It was apparent that children did not read more than 20% of the non-words until their performance was at ceiling in the Common Onset task. Only 1 of the primary 1 poor readers scored above 10%

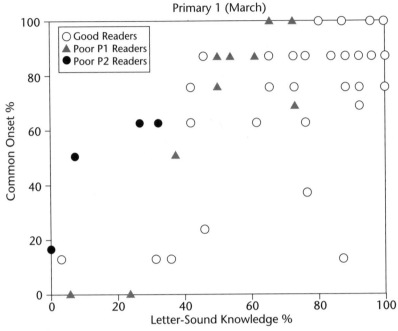

Figure 5.   Scatterplot of Letter-Sound Knowledge and Common Onset Identification in March of Primary 1

in the non-word naming task and all of the primary 2 poor readers performed at floor. Ability to identify common rimes tended to develop after decoding skills were in place and none of the primary 2 poor readers was able to score.

These data suggest that the origin of the reading difficulty can be traced back to the delay in acquisition of letter-sound knowledge and meta-awareness of phonemes early in the period of formal instruction in reading.

IMPLICATIONS FOR THE PREDICTION AND PREVENTION OF READING FAILURE

The results of this longitudinal study suggest that letter-sound knowledge and awareness of phonemes are more closely related to early reading than awareness of rhyme. In study 1, pre-school training in rhyming skill produced no detectable long-term benefits for reading in primary 1 or 2. In study 2, a pre-school test of rhyming was not a significant predictor of primary 1 or 2 reading, whereas pre-school letter-sound knowledge did predict primary 1 reading with a resultant effect on primary 2 reading. Study 3 established that the early stage of reading focused on letter sounds and meta-awareness of phonemes and not on rime structures. We were also unable to find any evidence of a link between pre-school rhyming and later reading difficulty (study 4).

The results present something of a puzzle. In the pre-school period, rhyming is an important phonological skill for children and one that can be assessed and encouraged readily by appropriate activities. But, when children start formal literacy instruction in primary school, the pre-existing rhyming ability appears not to have an immediate influence on the way reading is acquired. Further, these same children have great difficulty in performing a test of explicit awareness of rime units (the Common Unit task, see figure 4).

In the previous reports (Duncan, Seymour, and Hill 1997, in press), we suggested that these puzzling outcomes might be understood by adopting a framework for discussion of metaphonological development set out by Gombert (1992). Gombert makes a distinction between implicit (epi-linguistic) and explicit (meta-linguistic) awareness of language organization. It is proposed that a range of linguistic units (syllables, rimes, phonemes) may be represented at both these levels. There are two important assumptions regarding the mechanism underlying metaphonological development: (1) for a linguistic structure to become an object of explicit (meta-) awareness, that structure must already be represented at the implicit (epi-) level; (2) formation of an explicit (meta-) representation is an optional rather than a necessary outcome that depends on the imposition of an "external demand," usually a demand imposed by the task of learning to read.

We can first of all explore the notion that an implicit sensitivity to a particular sound is necessary for explicit awareness to develop. This implies that the emergence of explicit phoneme awareness in our primary 1 sample should have been preceded by an implicit sensitivity to phonemes. Although we did not include a specific test of this proposal, the involvement of pre-school Alliteration Production ability in the EQS model from study 2 was suggestive of this possibility. What was clear from our results, however, was the support for Gombert's assertion that implicit sensitivity to a sound is not sufficient to drive explicit phonological development. Pre-school implicit sensitivity to rhyme (even at a high level) did not lead to the emergence of an explicit awareness of rime in primary 1. Instead, an explicit awareness of phonemes emerged together with decoding strategies based on phonemes but not rimes (study 3).

One implication of Gombert's work is that attempts to identify children with poor phonological skills at pre-school are somewhat problematic. Pre-school implicit awareness of rhyme, although probably the most accessible skill to test (Goswami and Bryant 1990), may not be the most directly relevant to reading development in teaching regimes that emphasize the importance of letter-sound instruction. As we have seen, pre-school implicit awareness of rhyme does not determine reading strategy, and neither does it guarantee good progress in a "mixed" instructional regime. The implication is that it is not possible to identify potential cases of reading difficulty in advance by measuring implicit phonological skills in nursery school (study 4).

Gombert's (1992) second proposal was that there needs to be some external demand for explicit awareness to develop. He suggests that learning to read "plays a trigger role in the appearance of metalinguistic awareness" (p. 190). Moreover, different phases of development may make different demands of the child. In study 3, we observed a pattern of explicit phonological development from small to large units. During the first year of reading instruction, the children learned about letters and sounds and engaged in phonics activities. This type of instruction appeared to create an external demand for the development of an explicit awareness of phonemes (Duncan, Seymour, and Hill 1997). In the second year of instruction, the children, especially the more advanced readers, developed an explicit awareness of rime. As rimes were not explicitly taught, it seemed likely that the demand was provided by the orthography, and that children developed an explicit awareness of rimes as a means to deal with the irregularity in the English orthography (Duncan, Seymour, and Hill in press).

Our two main findings are: (1) that pre-school letter-sound knowledge, concurrently linked to alliteration, was the best predictor of primary 1 reading; and (2) that primary 1 reading initially involved the achievement of full letter-sound knowledge and the emergence of explicit (meta-) awareness of small units (phonemes). These outcomes suggest that the "bridge" between the pre-school and primary school phases of literacy acquisition is constructed from letter knowledge and phonemic awareness.

The retrospective investigation (study 4) suggested that the earliest point at which reading difficulty could be detected was seen in primary school as a slowness in acquiring the full set of letter-sounds and in developing meta-awareness of phonemes. The suggestion that reading difficulty is initially traceable to a delay in acquiring full letter-sound knowledge is consistent with other findings from our laboratory. We (Duncan and Seymour 2000) studied delayed reading acquisition in children from low socio-economic status areas of Dundee, and found that the delay was traceable to a lack of pre-school letter knowledge and delayed acquisition of the letters in primary school. Seymour and Evans (1999) examined disturbed reading in a dyslexic sample. Some individuals, referred to as instances of literal dyslexia, had great difficulty in acquiring the letter-sounds in response to instruction and had a very poor prognosis for subsequent reading achievement. A mild weakness of letter knowledge was also found to be widespread in the dyslexic sample.

Preschool letter knowledge predicted later reading (study 2), but could not be used to detect potential reading difficulty (study 4). The predictive effect seems to occur because preschool letter knowledge is possessed by a minority of children who go on to make very good progress in reading. The implication for prevention of reading failure is that it would be sensible to focus attention on the letters within a context of alliteration. Schemes that associate the letters with alliterative names and objects might be especially helpful in this endeavour.

REFERENCES

Ball, E. W., and Blachman, B. A. 1988. Phoneme segmentation training: Effect on reading readiness. *Annals of Dyslexia* 38:208–25.

Ball, E. W., and Blachman, B. A. 1991. Does phoneme awareness training in kindergarten make a difference in early word recognition and developmental spelling? *Reading Research Quarterly* 26:49–66.

Barron, R. W. 1998. Proto-literate knowledge: Antecedents and influences on phonological awareness and literacy. In *Reading and Spelling: Development and Disorders*, eds. C. Hulme and R. M. Joshi. Hillsdale, NJ: Lawrence Erlbaum Associates.

Bradley, L., and Bryant, P. E. 1983. Categorising sounds and learning to read - A causal connection. *Nature* 301:419–521.

Bradley, L., and Bryant, P. E. 1985. *Rhyme and Reason in Reading and Spelling*. Ann Arbor: University of Michigan Press.

Bruce, D. J. 1964. The analysis of word sounds by young children. *British Journal of Educational Psychology* 34:158–70.

Bryant, P. 1998. Sensitivity to onset and rime does predict young children's reading: A comment on Muter, Hulme, Snowling, and Taylor (1997). *Journal of Experimental Child Psychology* 71:29–37.

Bryant, P., and Goswami, U. 1987. Phonological awareness and learning to read. In *Cognitive Approaches to Reading*, eds. J. R. Beech and A. M. Colley. Chichester: Wiley.

Bryant, P. E., MacLean, M., Bradley, L. L., and Crossland, J. 1990. Rhyme and alliteration, phoneme detection, and learning to read. *Developmental Psychology* 26:429–38.

Burgess, S. R., and Lonigan, C. J. 1998. Bidirectional relations of phonological sensitivity and prereading abilities: Evidence from a preschool
sample. *Journal of Experimental Child Psychology* 70:117–41.
Bus, A. G., and van IJzendoorn, M. H. 1999. Phonological awareness and
early reading: A meta-analysis of experimental training studies. *Journal
of Educational Psychology* 91:1–13.
Byrne, B., and Fielding-Barnsley, R. 1989. Phonemic awareness and letter
knowledge in the child's acquisition of the alphabetic principle. *Journal
of Educational Psychology* 81:313–21.
Byrne, B., and Fielding-Barnsley, R. 1990. Acquiring the alphabetic princi-
ple: A case for teaching recognition of phoneme identity. *Journal of
Educational Psychology* 82:805–12.
Byrne, B., and Fielding-Barnsley, R. 1991. *Sound Foundations.* Sydney: Peter
Leyden Educational.
Byrne, B., and Fielding-Barnsley, R. 1993. Evaluation of a program to
teach phonemic awareness to young children: A 1-year follow-up.
Journal of Educational Psychology 85:104–11.
Cunningham, A. E. 1990. Explicit versus implicit instruction in phonemic
awareness. *Journal of Experimental Child Psychology* 50:429–44.
Duncan, L. G., Seymour, P. H. K., and Hill, S. 1997. How important are
rhyme and analogy in beginning reading? *Cognition* 63:171–208.
Duncan, L. G., Seymour, P. H. K., and Hill, S. in press. A small to large
unit progression in metaphonological awareness and reading? *The
Quarterly Journal of Experimental Psychology* (Section A).
Duncan, L. G., and Seymour, P. H. K. 2000. Socio-economic differences in
foundation-level literacy. *British Journal of Psychology* 91:145–66.
Dunn, L. M., Dunn, L. M., and Whetton, C. 1982. *The British Picture
Vocabulary Scale.* Windsor, England: NFER-Nelson.
Ehri, L. C. 1992. Reconceptualizing the development of sight word read-
ing and its relationship to recoding. In *Reading Acquisition*, eds.
P. Gough, L. C. Ehri, and R. Treiman. Hillsdale, NJ: Lawrence Erlbaum
Associates.
Elkonin, D. B. 1973. U.S.S.R.. In *Comparative Reading*, ed. J. Downing. New
York: Macmillan.
Elliott, C. D., Murray, D. J., and Pearson, L. S. 1983. *British Ability Scales.*
Windsor, England: NFER-Nelson.
Foorman, B. R., Francis, D. J., Novy, D. M., and Liberman, D. 1991. How
letter-sound instruction mediates progress in first-grade reading and
spelling. *Journal of Educational Psychology* 83:456–69.
Gombert, J. E. 1992. *Metalinguistic Development.* London: Harvester
Wheatsheaf.
Goswami, U., and Bryant, P. 1990. *Phonological Skills and Learning to Read.*
Hillsdale, NJ: Lawrence Erlbaum Associates.
Greaney, K. T., Tunmer, W. E., and Chapman, J. W. 1997. Effects of rime-
based orthographic analogy training on the word recognition skills of
children with reading disability. *Journal of Educational Psychology*
89:645–51.
Hatcher, P. J., Hulme, C., and Ellis, A. W. 1994. Ameliorating early reading
failure by integrating the teaching of reading and phonological skills:
The phonological linkage hypothesis. *Child Development* 65:41–57.
Hohn, W. E., and Ehri, L. C. 1983. Do alphabet letters help prereaders acquire phonemic segmentation skill? *Journal of Educational Psychology*
75:752–62.

Hulme, C., Muter, V., and Snowling, M. 1998. Segmentation does predict early progress in learning to read better than rhyme: A reply to Bryant. *Journal of Experimental Child Psychology* 71:39–44.

Johnston, R. S., Anderson, M., and Holligan, C. 1996. Knowledge of the alphabet and explicit awareness of phonemes in pre-readers: The nature of the relationship. *Reading and Writing* 8:217–34.

Kirtley, C., Bryant, P. E., MacLean, M., and Bradley, L. 1989. Rhyme, rime and the onset of reading. *Journal of Experimental Child Psychology* 48:224–45.

Lundberg, I., Frost, J., and Petersen, O.-P. 1988. Effects of an extensive program for stimulating phonological awareness in preschool children. *Reading Research Quarterly* 23:263–84.

Lundberg, I., Olofsson, Å., and Wall, S. 1980. Reading and spelling skills in the first school years predicted from phonemic awareness skills in kindergarten. *Scandinavian Journal of Psychology* 21:159–73.

Masonheimer, P. E., Drum, P. A., and Ehri, L. C. 1984. Does environmental print identification lead children into word reading? *Journal of Reading Behaviour* 16:257–71.

Morais, J., Alegria, J., and Content, A. 1987. The relationship between segmental analysis and alphabetic literacy: An interactive view. *European Bulletin of Cognitive Psychology* 7:415–38.

Muter, V., Hulme, C., Snowling, M., and Taylor, S. 1997. Segmentation, not rhyming, predicts early progress in learning to read. *Journal of Experimental Child Psychology* 65:370–96.

Näsland, J. C., and Schneider, W. 1996. Kindergarten letter knowledge, phonological skills, and memory processes: Relative effects on early literacy. *Journal of Experimental Child Psychology* 62:30–59.

Perfetti, C. A., Beck, I., Bell, L. C., and Hughes, C. 1987. Phonemic knowledge and learning to read are reciprocal: A longitudinal study of first grade children. *Merrill-Palmer Quarterly* 33:283–319.

Seymour, P. H. K., Duncan, L. G., and Bolik, F. M. 1999. Rhymes and phonemes in the common unit task: Replications and implications for beginning reading. *Journal of Research in Reading* 22:113–30.

Seymour, P. H. K., and Evans, H. M. 1999. Foundation level dyslexias: Assessment and treatment. *Journal of Learning Disabilities* 32:394–405.

Stuart, M., and Coltheart, M. 1988. Does reading develop in a sequence of stages? *Cognition* 30:139–81.

Wagner, R. K., Torgesen, J. K., Rashotte, C. A., Hecht, S. A., Barker, T. A., Burgess, S. R., Donahue, J., and Garon, T. 1997. Changing relations between phonological processing abilities and word-level reading as children develop from beginning to skilled readers: A 5-year longitudinal study. *Developmental Psychology* 33:468–79.

Westwood, P., Harris-Hughes, M., Lucas, G., Nolan, J., and Scrymgeour, K. 1974. One minute addition test - one minute subtraction test. *Remedial Education* 9:70–72.

Index

(Page numbers in italics indicate material in figures or tables.)

Alliteration, 183–84, 295
Alphabetic principle, training to comprehend, 226
Ambisyllabicity, 186
Anderson, M., 172
Arithmetic, probable cognitive skills and learning mechanisms underlying both readng and, 51
At-risk diagnoses, stigmatization and, 124–25
Auditory conceptualization, 35

Ball, E. W., 230–32
Behavior problems, 2, 120
Blachman, B., 230–32
Bloom, L., 121–23
Borstrøm, I., 26
Bradley, L, 110, 155, 249
Bryan, J. H., 121, 128
Bryan, T., 121, 128
Bryant, P. E., 5, 110, 155, 249, 275
Byrne, B., 163–64, 225–29, 233, 238, 239, 251

Cary, L, 250
Christensen, C. A., 159
Cognitive processes, deficits in, 14
Cognitive skills, predictive power of, 16
Computer-based intervention, 72–73
Concentration: language development and, 120; problems with, 114
Consistency, importance of (in phoneme awareness training), 250
Contextual information, use of, 10–11
Copenhagen Dyslexia Study, 252, 269–71; children of dyslexic parents and 267, 269–70; effects of training and, 265–67; hard core children in, 263–65; intervention in, 254–55; measures used in, 256–58, 258–60; methods in, 252–54; phonemic awareness training in kindergarten and, 252, 270; results of, 260–63; training program in, 255–56
Correlation coefficients, 32
Cramer, B. B., 159
Cunningham, A. E., 158, 166

Decoding: phoneme awareness and word, 111; poor, 96
Decoding strategies based on phonemes, 291
Delinquent and disruptive behavior, 2, 120
DEST. *See* Dyslexia Early Screening Test (DEST)
Developmental reading model, screening tasks in, 137–40
Dowker, A., 184–85
Dundee Longitudinal Study, 275
Dyslexia: core difficulty in, 247, 249; early screening for (in U. K.), 60–63; family occurrence and, 248; genetic research on, 15; prediction in children at risk for, 14–16; weaknesses at different ages and, 15–16. *See also* Copenhagen Dyslexia Study; Reading failure; Reading problems
Dyslexia Adult Screening Test (DAST), 68n
Dyslexia Early Screening Test (DEST), 62, 63–69, 69–71, 81; reading progress and, 75–76; using (for support), 71–75
Dyslexia screening: early, 58, 60–63; large scale (in U.K. and U. S.), 62; requirement of test for, 60–63
Dyslexic children: of dyslexic parents, 267, 269–71; linguistic characteristics of, 108; non-word reading skill of, 14; orthographic deficits in, 37
Dyslexic parents, 124; children of, 267, 269–71; need for training in phonemes for children of, 271

Early identification of reading failure, advantages of, 1–2

Early Literacy Development Profile, 77
Early readers, characteristics of, 121
Early reading skill: cognitive predictors of, 2–7, 7–12; letter knowledge and, 2–7; non-cognitive predictors of, 12–14; phonological awareness and, 2–7
Ehri, L., 88
Elbro, C., 22
Emotional control, language development and, 120
Emotions: language and (during early word learning), 121–23; written language problems and, 112
England. See United Kingdom (U. K.)

False negative and false positive predictions, 31, 124
Family environment, 12–14
Fielding-Barnsley, R., 163–64, 225–28, 233, 238, 239, 251
Fox, B., 203
Frith, U., 16, 88
Frost, J., 162–63, 223–24

Gallagher, A., 16
Genetic research on dyslexia, 15
Gombert, J. E., 293–94
Goswami, U., 5, 275

Hagtvet, B. E., 108–110
Hannon, P., 77
Head Start, 229
Heritability of phonetically based reading skills, 15
Herriman, M. L., 156
Holligan, C., 172
Home environment, 12–14
Homonyms, orthographic processing tests and, 37
Hulme, C., 5, 6, 7, 19, 173
Humor, language ability and verbal, 121

Initial consonants, discrimination of, 35
Initial phoneme deletion test, 35
Instructional activities for preschool and kindergarten children, 173, 175
Intelligence. See IQ

Intervention: advantage of early, 57; computer-based, 72–73; determining appropriate entry point for, 89–90, 96; effects of, 72–73; matching children with specific risk profiles to instructional, 148; multisensory, 78; prediction and educational, 123
IQ, reading success and, 153

Johnston, R. S., 172
Jolly Phonics program, 232–33
Jusczyk, P. W., 189–90

Kindergarten, children retained in, 135

Language: emotions and, 121–23; off-task (e.g., emotional) behaviors and, 112–18; stress and learning of, 113–19
Language ability, effect of training on, 261–63
Language play, spontaneous rhyming and alliteration in early, 180, 183–84
Late bloomers, 125
Layton, L., 164–65
Letter instruction, 229
Letter knowledge, 2–7, 10, 22–23, 35, 156, 172, 286; interaction between phonological awareness and, 160; lack of pre-school, 295; phoneme awareness and later reading and, 281; as powerful predictor of early literacy, 16, 160; prediction of reading and, 155, 248
Letter naming speed, 34, 35, 36
Letter naming tests, 35, 51; to predict later reading achievement, 99
Letter-sound correspondences, learning, 23
Letter sounds: knowledge of, 291–92; slowness in acquiring the full set of, 294; teaching of (in U. K.), 58
Letter sound task as predictor of reading achievement, 97, 157–58
Lexical organization, changes in children's, 185

Liberman, I. Y., 181
Literacy development: bridge between preschool and primary school phases of, 294; major difficulty with, 77
Literacy Screening Battery (LSB) (Flynn), 136–40
Literacy skills: behavioral description of emerging, 136; preschool phonological training and later, 164
Logo name recognition, 90, 100
Lonigan, C. J., 191
Lundberg, I., 223–24
Lundberg, L., 162–63

McGee, R., 120
Maclean, M., 155
Malapropisms, children's, 185
Metalinguistic awareness, 156
Metaphonological development: reading instruction and, 287–89; rhyme awareness as earliest stage of, 202
Motivation to read, 120
Multiple regression analysis, 32
Multisensory remediation, 78
Murray, B. A., 165–66
Muter, V., 5, 6, 7, 19, 154, 161–62

Naming of pictured objects, 33–34
Naming skill as predictor of early reading skill, 7–12
Naming speed, 11–12, 33–34. *See also* Serial naming speed
Naming tasks, 8–9, 11–12, 33–34
Nation, K., 11,173
Nesdale, A. R., 156
Non-word reading skill, dyslexic children's, 14
Non-word repitition, 8, 35
Nursery/infant screening and support system in U. K., 77–78
Nursery rhymes, 3, 156
Nutbrown, C., 77

Object naming speed, 34
Onset, defined, 218
Onset-rime hypothesis, 181, 182–83
Onset-rime sensitivity training, 225–30, 238–40
Onset sound, 170

Orthographic ability, preschool, 51. *See also* Spelling
Orthographic deficits in dyslexic children, 37
Orthographic-phonological connections, 38
Orthographic processing: measurement of, 38–39; as predictor of reading, 37–39; tests of, 37
Orthographic skills, 49; measurement of early, 39. *See also* Spelling
Orthographic tests, 37, 38

Parents' reading to preschoolers, 13–14
Petersen, D., 22
Petersen, O. P., 162–63, 223–24
Phase theory of reading acquisition, 88
Phoneme awareness, 34, 169, 171, 173; basis for development of, 249; defined, 248; difficulty in training at-risk children in, 251; early reading and, 292; explicit, 293; improved by training in kindergarten, 249; longitudinal studies of, 280–86; as predictor of reading, 248; successful approaches to instruction in, 210; training in, 249–51, 286–92
Phoneme awareness tasks, 280
Phoneme blending, 239
Phoneme deletion: to assess phonological awareness, 154; at ages 5 and 6 years, 7; tests of, 35
Phoneme-grapheme correspondences, 107; importance of understanding of, 175; phonological awareness and, 21
Phoneme identification tasks, training in, 165
Phoneme identification tests, 35
Phoneme-oriented training programs, 239
Phonemes, 220–21; decoding strategies based on, 293
Phoneme segmentation, 94; skills in, 173; tests of, 35, 36
Phoneme sensitivity training, 225, 237, 240; inõdividual differences in response to, 233–35; in kindergarten, 230–33

Phonemic awareness: 169, 171, 173, 248–49; prior to learning to read, 161; useful programs for training in, 166, 167
Phonemic patterns detected by young children, 208
Phonic reading skill, non-word reading skill and, 14–15
Phonological abilities, measurement of, 3
Phonological Abilities Test (PAT): rationale for, 18–19; record form for, *21*; subtests of, 19; use of, 19–20
Phonological awareness, 36, 156–58; activities to enhance preschool, 173–75; age of development of, 249; aspects most important for reading, 168–72; children's preschool, 154; as cluster of related skills, 169–71; conscious, 191; defined, 154, 248; early sources (precursors) of, 22; general, 179–80; heritability of, 15; impact of syllables and rhyme on, 193; importance of, 153; lack of, 63; letter knowledge and, 7; measures of, 154–62; phoneme-grapheme correspondences and 23; as predictor of reading, 2–7, 34–37, 110, 111; preschool, 161–62, 167, 172; preventing reading problems by daily play-oriented training in, 107; syllables in early, 188–92; world decoding and, 111. *See also* Phonological sensitivity
Phonological awareness development, 171–73, 202; evidence about syllable-based, 181–83, 185–92; evidence about word-based, 183–88; hypotheses about, 169–70, 181, 182–83; onset-rime theory and, 181, 182–83; rhyme awareness and, 203–204
Phonological awareness pretest, 194–95
Phonological awareness tests, 17–18, 196, 207
Phonological coding, 247

Phonological development, phonological sensitivity and, 235–38
Phonological distinctness, 22
Phonological information, phonemic representation and, 236
Phonological measures appropriate for preschool children, 36
Phonological processing, short-term memory and, 9–10
Phonological recoding, 221
Phonological representations, distinctiveness of, 35
Phonological segmentation, capacity for, 183
Phonological sensitivity: deep, 218, 223, 235, 238; development of, 191, 217–20; early, 3; learning to read and, 220–23; in pre-literate children, 223–24; shallow, 218; subsequent reading development and, 223, 224; the term, 218. *See also* Phonological awareness
Phonological sensitivity tasks: performance on deep, 219; shallow, 218, 219
Phonological skills, 4–7
Phonological tasks, prediction of reading skills and, 3, 158–59
Phonological training, 163–64; later reading skill and, 162
Phonological units, 192
Pig Latin games, 154
Poor readers, individual variations within groups of, 119
Pragmatic awareness, 156, 157
Predictions, 2–3, 146, 248; accuracy of, 17; in children at risk for dyslexia, 14–16; erroneous, 124; preschool, 51, 154, 159–62, 165, 167, 172, 173, 281–86; self-fulfilling erroneous, 125; use of single measures in, 18, 110
Predictive outcome presented in a 2 x 2 array, 32
Predictive validity, lack of, 32
Predictor of early reading skill, 7–12; most extensively studied, 2–3; preschool, 281–86
Predictors defined, 2
Preschool abilities of children with normal and dyslexic parents, 260–61

Preschool measures to predict reading, 51, 154, 159–62, 165, 167, 172, 281–86
Preschoolers, reading to, 13–14
Pre-School Early Screening Test (PEST) (in U. K.), 78–81
Preschool phonological awareness, activities to enhance, 173–75
Preschool rhyme training, effects on later reading, 277–80
Preschool screening for children with SEN (in U. K.), 76–81
Preschool test battery, studies of, 39–49
Preventive programs, 125, 126
Primary school, retrospective studies of children with poor reading progress in, 290–92
Pronunciation accuracy, 35
Pronunciation errors, 265
Pronunciation of final portion of words by very young children, 208

Rashotte, C. A., 251
Reading, preschool predictors of beginning, 281–86
Reading ability prediction, 33–34, 51, 154–55; letter sound tasks for, 97; oral language variables and, 108–111; phoneme vs. rime sensitivity and, 222; preschool, 281–86; single measures for, 18; visual perception and, 37
Reading comprehension: general language abilities and, 111; greatest barrier to, 96
Reading delay, overcoming early, 16
Reading development: competencies required in each phase of, 88, 89; phases and stages of, 88, 137; phoneme awareness and, 248–49; predictors of, 2–3, 7–12, 248, 281–86
Reading failure: appropriate delay in screening for risk of, 7; estimating possible, 95–97; improving prediction of, 146; screening for risk of, 7, 89, 90, 94, 95–97, 101; tests vs. teachers for predicting risk of, 134. *See also* Reading success and failure

Reading instruction, early (in U. K. and U. S.), 58
Reading precursors, identifying children's initial levels of, 136–42, 145–46
Reading problems: barriers to preventing, 111–12; challenges of predicting, 123–25; earliest point to detect, 294; early precursors of, 107–111; importance of preventing, 106–107; phonological processing and, 237; strategies to prevent, 105, 111; vulnerability of children at risk for, 117, 118
Reading skills: critical period for developing, 107; heritability of phonologically based, 15
Reading success and failure, documentation of factors that can explain, 153
Regression analyses, 32
Remediation. *See* Intervention
Research needed on predictive phonological tasks within the capabilities of preschoolers, 50
Rhyme with stressed vowel, 186
Rhyme awareness: as earliest stage of metaphonological development, 202; in phonological awareness development, 203–204; studies of, 276–80
Rhymes: early recognition and production of, 36, 99, 204–210; generation of, 207; phonological awareness and identification of, 209; word-level (and young children), 201–202
Rhyming, spontaneous, 183–84
Rhyming skill, 5–6, 35, 165; preschool training in, 292
Rhyming tasks, 3, 35, 99, 154, 155˝
Rime, 170; defined, 218
Routh, D. K., 203

Scanlon, D. M., 155
Scarborough, H., 15–16
Schneider, W., 167, 250
School failure, early intervention to reduce, 135
Screening that leads to intervention, 136. *See also* Preschool screening for children with SEN

Screening for risk of reading failure: appropriate delay for, 7; battery for, 89, 90, 94, 95–97, 101
Screening tests: for early reading failure, 16–22; future, 24
Second language learning, 113
Segmentation skills, 5–6, 94, 182
Segmentation tasks, 156; that predict reading skill, 3
Segmenting words into syllables and phonemes, 154
Self-fulfilling prophesy, erroneous predictions and, 125
Semantic/syntactic skills as predictors of early reading skill, 7–12
SEN. See Special education needs
Sentence memory as reading predictor, 51
Sentence segmenting, 94
Serial naming speed as a predictor and correlate of reading, 33–34
Serial naming tests most closely associated with reading, 33–34
Short term memory, phonological processing and, 9–10
Smith, L. B., 189–90
Snowling, M., 5, 6, 7, 11, 16, 19, 154, 161–62
Socioeconomic status (SES), 12–14, 220
Sound blending tasks, 3, 100
Sound Foundation Program, 226–30, 238–39
Sound structure of language, focusing attention on, 238
Special education needs (SEN): identifying and supporting children with (in U. K.), 59; literacy standards of children with, 57; preschool screening and support for children with, 76–81
Speech production, errors in, 187–88
Speech rate, 9–10
Spelling, prediction of, 97, 161, See also Orthographic entries
Stanovich, K. E., 158
Stigmatization of children predicted to be at risk, 125
Stress and anxiety, language learning and, 113–19
Students at risk of reading failure, assessing on basis of a screening test, 95–97

Successful and enjoyable learning experiences, 239; importnace of, 238
Syllable awareness, 182
Syllables: difficulties with English, 186; in early phonological awareness, 188–92; internal organization and structure of, 182, 187, 218; onset and rime in, 218; segmenting words into, 186
Syllable segmentation, 94, 182
Syllable training, 250
Symbol naming speed, 33–34
Syntactic awareness, 10, 11, 156, 157

Taylor, S., 5, 6, 7
Teacher judgement: in identifying at-risk students, 94–95, 134; importance of improving, 135–36
Teacher scale for rating kindergarten students, 140–42
Teacher training: importance of (for teaching phonological awareness), 167; to improve identification of children's reading precursors, 145–46
Torgeson, J. K., 251
Treatment. See Intervention
Treiman, R., 181, 182, 183, 187, 188, 189, 190–91, 202
Tunmer, W. E., 10, 156

U. K. See United Kingdom (U. K.)
Under-expectations for children, 135
United Kingdom (U. K.), special educíation laws and practices in, 58–60, 60–69, 69–71, 71–81

Vellutino, F. R., 155
Verbal memory as predictor of early reading skill, 7–12
Verhaeghe, A., 250
Visual images of letters and words, memory of (in reading development), 50
Visual perception as a predictor and correlate of reading, 37
Visual representations of words, memorization of, 38
Vocabulary: reading comprehension and, 96; technique for improving, 147

Wagner, R. K., 251
Walley, A. C., 189–90
Whole language programs, 233
Word awareness, 156
Word learning: interruption by
  emotions of early, 122; language
  and emotion during early,
  121–23
Word-level rhyme unit, 184
Words: drawing children's atten-
  tion to sound structure of, 210;
  with shared sounds, 189–90
Writing to Read Program, 147

Zukowski, A., 181, 182, 187, 189,
  190–91, 202